TWISTED JUSTICE

TWISTED JUSTICE

A Memoir of Conspiracy and Personal Politics

Oklahoma Governor
David Hall

TATE PUBLISHING
AND ENTERPRISES, LLC

The opinions expressed by the author are not necessarily those of Tate Publishing, LLC.

Published by Tate Publishing & Enterprises, LLC
127 E. Trade Center Terrace | Mustang, Oklahoma 73064 USA
1.888.361.9473 | www.tatepublishing.com

Tate Publishing is committed to excellence in the publishing industry. The company reflects the philosophy established by the founders, based on Psalm 68:11,
"The Lord gave the word and great was the company of those who published it."

Book design copyright © 2012 by Tate Publishing, LLC. All rights reserved.
Cover and Interior design by Blake Brasor

Published in the United States of America
ISBN: 978-1-61862-993-7
1. Biography & Autobiography
11.10.11

Dedication

This memoir is dedicated to

Jo, my wife

whose love and devotion
have sustained my spirit
for the past 56 years

Preface

My hope with this work is to inspire young men and women to consider a life in elective office; I want them to realize that those dreams can come true—but also to be aware of the dark side of a life in politics. I dream of the day when we will have citizen-officials who care more about what they can do for the people they serve than about re-election as career office-holders.

This memoir has been a wonderful adventure in writing and remembrance. This work is the story of my life, a reflection on the benefits of living in this free nation, of being allowed to accomplish my life's dream of becoming Governor of Oklahoma—before becoming a victim of vicious political persecution—and finally learning to overcome impossible odds to live a happy and productive life.

This is the true story from my vantage point. I have lived every moment of these days, and these accounts are my personal recollection of the events. There may be disagreements with my interpretation of history, but that's the blessing of writing these words myself.

None of the good things in my life could have come about without the love of my family and their everlasting support of my endeavors. It is especially true in the writing of my memoir; my wife, Jo, and our children, Nancy, Doug, and Julie, were inspirations for me.

The governorship could never have been won but for the dedicated support of thousands of Oklahomans who believed in a better way of life for the citizens of our state. The November 1970 election for Oklahoma's governor saw the narrowest margin of victory in the history of the state. County coordinators in 77 venues toiled endlessly to secure the victory. Nearly 200 lawyers volunteered their services during the recount to protect that hard-fought election. The names of these men and women names appear in the index, with my gratitude for their efforts.

My staff at the governor's office was unique in their dedication, youth, enthusiasm, diversity and belief in a fantastic future for Oklahoma. The key members were Geraldine Strain, my administrative assistant, Jim Hart, chief of staff, G. Dan Rambo, Legal counsel, Joe Carter, Press Secretary and Richard Wiseman, Chief of Security. Every other member deserves recognition and his or her names are in the index.

Special kudos go to Mim Eichler Rivas for her editing skills, for her inspiration, and for understanding my beliefs and dreams. Dan Eichler's contribution as the daily editor for the past year was the catalyst that enabled me to finish this work. Jim Hartz worked tirelessly on research, fact-checking, and the historical perspective of the memoir. Pam Prescott Paterson, Susan Moody, and Caren Harris provided exceptional secretarial and research assistance. Dr. Robert Blackburn and this dedicated staff at the Oklahoma History Center, the archivists of the Jack Anderson Collection of the Library of Congress, and numerous libraries and research sources aided me as well.

Others whose work and support have made this book possible include my son, Doug Hall, along with Milt Laird, Doug Hart-man, Dick Taylor, Robert L. Sexton, Charles Lampkin, Pat Dunn, Bobbie Kaye Ferguson, Pat Hazel, Sean Delalat, John Mugg, and Stratton Taylor.

Now settle back and enjoy the ride with me. I want each of you who read my memoir to know why I believe every day is going to be a good one.

Table of Contents

Prologue: Dark Days

The decision to break decades of silence began subconsciously; like a hunk of old tumbleweed, it gathered force, tossed by the winds of changing fortune that blew down from the east, billowing westward over the grassy Oklahoma plains of my beloved home state, and entered my being with the disruption of twisters sent down from the north, flooding my awareness as if from torrential rains driven from the south below. Eventually all of that busted down the dam I'd built to protect myself, the wall of positive motion and forward focus that had helped me move past broken dreams on to other frontiers and other adventures.

Here in sunny southern California, where I've worked and resided for over three decades with Jo, my wife and lifelong soulmate—and, in my humble opinion, the finest Oklahoma first lady to ever grace the governor's mansion—I finally accepted the obvious: I had unfinished business.

The truth had to be told.

Setting the record straight was necessary not only for my family and all the dear, good people who never stopped believing in me, but it mattered greatly to the history of Oklahoma and the future of America: It was time.

The choice to return in my mind to the dark days of March 1975 might not have been made, if not for the events of February 1999, when our nation lived through one of its uglier chapters: the Senate trial of President Bill Clinton, following his impeachment by the House of Representatives. Watching how a web of conspiracies had enmeshed themselves around the President—not to mention the palpable personal hatred from his political enemies that radiated off the TV screen—I found myself remembering what it felt like to stare down the barrel aimed at me by the same lynch mob. Though the eras were different, the dirty tricks and the ruthless tactics hadn't changed at all; indeed, I saw only parallels between the machinations employed to derail Bill Clinton and the same obstacles I had faced as a progressive Democrat, as governor of Oklahoma, and as the favored candidate once headed in all likelihood to the White House.

Aside from my own experiences, there is no question that as the prosecution-turned-persecution against Clinton neared its conclusion in the Senate, I was among the majority of Americans who resented the forces behind the impeachment effort in a deeply personal way—rightfully so, I might add. From my early days at Harvard Law School and the University of Tulsa Law School to my years as Tulsa County District Attorney—where I earned a spotless reputation as a hard-driving, fair-minded prosecutor, ultimately attaining a 94% conviction record of prosecuting over four hundred cases—I knew a little something about case law. And I knew that the legal merits of the case against the President were nil.

No serious legal scholar would have disagreed. Incredulous though a lot of Democrats were—as well as what was left of the moderate Republicans—a vendetta buoyed by a media circus dominated all public discourse. There were even bipartisan calls for an end to what was seen as a new scourge of personal politics. I was struck by the irony of that phrase; the truth is that politics are always personal, for better and for worse.

It's been true since the sandbox, since the lessons we learned growing up on the playground, since the days of junior-high-school social hierarchies. Asinine and juvenile as it seems, the main reason the president was so personally hated was old-fashioned jealousy—envy of his popularity and his brilliance; and more than that, it was bigotry and hatred because of the company he kept: the minorities, women, and other groups historically oppressed—especially the black community—who supported and loved him.

This kind of politicization of our legal system was exactly what the framers of our Constitution had warned against—and sought to prevent—in their separation of powers; we therefore grant rights of due process to every defendant that stands in front of the court. This meant that, as a DA, I never took a case to trial when there wasn't enough evidence to convict, no matter what I felt personally about the alleged crime, or how well a conviction might have benefited me politically. And yet the same basic rights of due process had been denied a President of the United States, as they had been denied a certain governor of Oklahoma: me.

Why? In the case of President Clinton, it was a question worth asking. What had he done that merited the non-stop assault on him, his wife, and his administration? He had, after all, never attempted to subvert the Constitution. Nor had he sponsored or abetted crimes against the nation (as in the Nixon years), nor had he attempted to unlawfully expand the power of the executive branch (as would be the case under George W. Bush and Dick Cheney). So why did they do it to him? As he himself later answered the question: "They did it because they could."

There is no other answer that I can better offer to the question much on my mind a little over three-and-a-half decades ago: Why had I been put on trial for a crime I didn't commit?

Of course, by the time I sat down to breakfast with Jo and our three teenagers on that overcast morning of March 14, 1975, a day destined to conclude the matter of The United States vs. David Hall, W.W. Taylor And Kevin Mooney, we had all ceased to ask why.

In the heady days of November 1970 that followed my come-from-behind victory over the Republican incumbent, Dewey Bartlett, by the narrowest margin in Oklahoma's history, I'd been caught off guard by how swiftly the effort at political retribution began. Bartlett, an oil man through and through, was fully backed by Big Oil, and he refused to accept that my grass-roots coalition of minorities, women, and labor- and working-class independents had actually unseated him. My campaign slogan, "Dump Dewey!" had been effective, but he probably lost because I'd been able to expose the polluting oil wells he owned and hadn't bothered to fix; no one really bought his claim that the oil runoff destroying creeks and waterways in the area was the fault of vandals.

Princeton-educated, from a wealthy Ohio family, with all the bearing of the blue-blood Republican that he was, Bartlett charged that the Democrats had stolen the election—and immediately called out the National Guard to secure the ballot boxes, But the statewide recount only confirmed my victory. Hell may have no fury like a woman scorned, but a thrown-outta-office Oklahoma Republican governor with power, money, and questionable friends in high places runs a close second.

And so in the spring of 1971, my first year in office, as I went to work on an ambitious agenda to enact twenty-one programs—including reforming education; rebuilding our infrastructure of roads, highways, and waterways; promoting industry and jobs; and reforming taxes—Dewey Bartlett went to work plotting my payback. In Washington, DC, Bartlett met secretly with Attorney General John Mitchell and Deputy General Richard Kleindienst. By no mere coincidence, these two men were later involved in the Watergate scandal, Mitchell being convicted of obstruction of justice and Kleindeist resigning after refusing Nixon's demand to fire Watergate Special Prosecutor Archibald Cox.

Based on records I obtained much later, it was clear from phone calls and calendar logs subsequent to that meeting that it set in motion an IRS investigation. As a model for the prosecution of Clinton in later years, it ballooned weekly into a multi-tiered, multi-phased process that was pursued with unbridled vigor—and by federal grand juries—throughout my term as governor and into the early 1980s.

Enter William Burkett, US Attorney and former head of the Oklahoma Republican party, personally antagonized by my victory over the candidate it had been his job to re-elect; he was now at the helm of these investigations that had yet to—and would never—reveal any financial wrongdoings by me. In 1974—because he could—he requested and manipulated the expansion of the investigations to state grand juries in Oklahoma and Tulsa Counties, operating simultaneously with the federal grand juries. It was bad enough that Burkett hated me, my policies, and everything I stood for; worse, Bill Burkett was the nervous type, and—most dangerous of all—a short man, said to have a complex the size of Texas to go with his stature.

To thicken the stew, Dewey Bartlett —not an unattractive man: thin, of medium height, with a sharp nose that suggested his high breeding and a crooked smile he used to his advantage on the campaign trail—had come back and won the office of US Senator from Oklahoma. In Washington and on Capitol Hill, Bartlett became the spokesman for the oil industry— an entity I had enraged, first by refusing to take money from them and then by enacting a long-overdue 2% tax hike on gross production that was funding the overhaul of Oklahoma's educational system—and making me a hero to the voters. To make me more of a threat to the national Republican hierarchy, and more of a thorn in old Dewey's side, there was the increasingly important role I'd been playing in the National Governors Conference, talk of the winning image I was projecting, and growing interest in my taking a run for the White House in 1976.

With all of that, you might say that I didn't need to ask why. Instead, I determined to keep my skin thick and my heart open, so I would never forget the reasons and the people that inspired me to seek public office in the first place.

The assault from the media complicated everything. It was no secret that the folks who ran The Daily Oklahoman—owned by archconservative Gaylord Enterprises—didn't like me, politically or personally. Dewey Bartlett had been their dog in the 1970 governor's fight, and the paper had predicted me to lose by a landslide. So, though I didn't much enjoy it, I wasn't surprised by the scathing remarks about me that filled the paper's editorial columns. But I was spitting mad when front-page stories began running with baseless rumors and distortions that paraded as facts. They hit me politically, for example, after my tax-relief bill passed that first year, giving 87% of Oklahoma citizens reduced taxes; but the almost-daily articles so subverted and misrepresented its actual effect that the perception was that I'd raised taxes. The Daily Oklahoman hit me personally, too, publishing illegal grand-jury leaks, allegedly handed to their offices by US Attorney Burkett —never any of the exculpatory testimony, just leaks that fired up insinuation and innuendo, day after day.

The worst of these allegations had come from testimony of Sunny Jenkins, my campaign finance chairman, who had systematically looted the campaign funds he'd raised in my name and secreted them in a Mexican bank account. Then, when caught by the Federal agents, he made a deal that allowed him to keep the money as reward for testifying against me in two state grand-jury actions and in the federal grand juries as well! What a deal! If you didn't know Sunny—a good ol' boy who hunted, fished, and womanized in grand fashion, an expert pilot, and a master manipulator—it was hard to understand how he'd gotten away with it.

───────────────

We'd stopped asking why Sunny had done it—temptation, greed, opportunity, all that—but the question of why we'd trusted him in such a responsible position lingered on. As a prosecutor, I'd learned to trust no one; as a political leader, in my effort to be less cynical, I'd forgotten some of those lessons.

    This awareness hung in the air that morning at breakfast. I was on trial for bribery. It was impossible, ludicrous, outrageous—a last-ditch effort by US Attorney Burkett to have something to show for his failed $3,000,000 fishing expedition. No sooner had I left office than the suit had been brought on the thinnest of grounds: the testimony of a soon-to-be impeached Secretary of State, John Rogers, a man I'd once considered a supporter, if not a friend.

    As we gathered around the breakfast table at our new home in Oklahoma City, much as we had done whenever possible at the governor's mansion, Jo and I shared our mood of guarded optimism with seventeen-year-old Nancy, sixteen-year-old Douglas, and thirteen-year-old Julie. We had never excluded our children from all the facts revealed from the tangled web of maneuvers against me. It was no secret that this show version of a trial had been condensed and rushed along at breakneck speed.

    We'd lived through the roller coaster of having our hopes raised, only to watch all of our requests for delays and change of venue denied. By this point, with the trial running just into its third week, the jury was already into a third day of deliberations. That boded well, I believed, even though the last few weeks had been accompanied by ominous weather: intermittent snow flurries, overcast skies, early spring winds. Reports of near-tornado gusts in parts of the state had given a somber aura to our daily trips to and from the courthouse.

While it occurred to me upon rising that morning that we were fast approaching the Ides of March, the first thing I said to Jo was, "It's going to be a great day today!" Of course, she laughed; Jo had heard that from me before—in fact, every day and every morning, even during the toughest stages of our journey together. She also knew that it's really a reflection of who I am, and how I feel about what's to come next.

No matter how tough our problems had been or might continue to be, I truly believed—and still believe— that each day is a gift from the good Lord. It's twenty-four hours of opportunity—a who-knows-what of possibilities, a turn coming up in the bend that might reveal a solution to those problems, a chance to meet someone new, to learn something different, to help someone else in need, to feel proud of your accomplishments and your service, to reveal truth in the midst of lies, to shine light where there is dark, to laugh, cry, remember, dream, love—to live. Some days aren't as great as others, but you sure can hedge your bets by expecting the best and by remembering, no matter what, that God moves in mysterious ways His wonders to perform.

With that in mind, at the breakfast table I reassured my family by letting them know that a verdict might be announced at any time, perhaps as early as a little later that day. Reiterating what Jo and I had believed from the start, I said, "This'll all be behind us soon. Finally, I'll be found innocent—or, at worst, it'll be a hung jury."

If Bill Burkett had been cast in the Snidely Whiplash role as my main antagonist in the movie version of this drama, critics might have called his portrayal over the top. Short, middling weight, soon to be bald, he came across as someone who'd never recovered from being disliked as a teenager. In and out of the courtroom, he behaved as though his position entitled him to always be right and to be in charge, any denial of which made his intensity and frequent nervousness all the more apparent. With a reputation as a Republican party hack toady, he played that role to a T—a flag-waving, right-wing conservative fanatic, subservient and cloying to anybody who could let him into the In crowd or who could give him a leg up.

Included in that group, as it turned out, were a couple of my friends. They'd told me that Burkett had been bragging that he wasn't going to be happy until he'd brought David Hall to his knees crying.

In a flash I was transported from the comfort of my home and family to the stark reality of the courtroom. Although separated in that chamber by a wooden railing, Jo and I communicated without words. We would later recall how we visualized holding fast to each other's hands, our souls locked in a silent embrace that gave strength to each of us as the minutes ticked by. Finally, the wait intolerable, the side door of the courtroom opened, and the bailiff led the jury in. A hush fell on the courtroom. Judge Daugherty asked, "Has the jury reached a verdict?"

The foreman stood and answered, "Yes, we have, your honor."

The clerk raised her hand, looked at the verdict she held, and began to read.

Before I recount the specifics of what happened next, it's important for me—and, I believe, for justice to truly prevail—to also include a few other whys. These have been put to me on more than a few occasions during the process of writing this book. Many have asked why I would want to dig up the past, as painful as it must be to reopen chapters that, for some, would be better left closed. The answer is simple: because of the lessons that accompany every experience. From the early days of my dysfunctional family life to my time in the statehouse and national halls of power, and all the way to the adventures that took me to the glittering chambers of the Kremlin and to negotiations in business in far-flung London, Paris, Geneva, and Riyadh, I consider myself to be inordinately blessed to have been taught extraordinary lessons. As governor, they helped guide my ability to stop one of the bloodiest prison riots in America's history, just as they inspired my actions toward prison reform on a broader basis.

I learned from winning, and I learned more from losing and then winning again—what I hope has been the result of the struggle to maintain my faith and determination, to retain my spirit and zest for life, to see and believe in the sunshine of the future. I wear my survival as a badge of courage with neither shame nor bitterness, only pride that I have been able to overcome all the obstacles and still have a bursting desire to share the path with others.

Beyond my own story, there are other whys that I think are worth exploring. Why, for instance, do the conspiracies behind the doors of the past—whether in Oklahoma, Washington, DC, or elsewhere—matter to us now? Why should we examine what the prerequisites are today for those in pursuit of prominence in leadership? At a point in history when respect for politicians is at an all-time low, why is it necessary to look at how the perception of political leaders has changed from previous generations to today's—especially with the developments in technology and constant shifting of the political terrain? Why is it vital that we address how the influence of money in the political process is jeopardizing our democracy and making it near impossible for anyone except those with vast personal wealth to run a winning campaign?

Another question that I find relevant, given the kind of public scrutiny the private lives of politicians must endure, is why any candidate would subject himself or herself and their family to the viciousness of the political game. On the other hand, why is it also incumbent upon the press to make sure that shadow candidates and their backers be accountable not to the money that put them into office but to the voters?

I hope you'll find the answers to those questions in the footnotes of my journey. For all the blows dealt me by the sword of personal politics, I can attest that its blade is most definitely double-edged—that touching people's lives in personal, positive, meaningful ways makes public service an unsurpassed honor. In revisiting how my personal and political dreams were formed, I recognize that some of the lessons came too late for me, but I sincerely hope that they aren't too late for the next young person who seeks the path of leadership.

Politics—past, present, and future—should matter to us personally. We are one people living on this small planet with decreasing resources; we will live or die as a civilization depending on whether we can figure out ways to live together. That's politics. Politics matter to me.

That's why I'm writing this book. I do so as both a former politician and public servant and as a private citizen; as both a former prosecutor and a former prisoner; as a businessman, husband, father, brother, son; as a lawyer and counselor; as a scholar and educator; as an author and public speaker;, as a human-rights activist; as a senior citizen who thinks that all of us who have lived and learned in our time have much to contribute to our contemporary debate; as an unabashed optimist who wants to help recapture some of our national innocence, and stem the tide of cynicism that bombards our lives from every media source; as a new-fashioned guy trying to stay in touch with the youth who will shape our future; as an old-fashioned guy hoping to revive the lessons of trust and responsibility that shaped the early years of this nation's history.

I write as a man who loves his country, one who believes passionately in our Constitution; I write as an American who believes that while there are people who can pervert the system, we have a glorious system that does work—and I believe that ultimately, if we don't give up, justice will eventually prevail.

Why am I writing? Because, thank God, I can!

Part One:

A Personal Journey into Politics

1930-1966

Dysfunctional Childhood

I am told that on the night before my birth, a full Oklahoma hunter's moon shone in the darkened sky. Mother hummed as Dad drove her to the hospital. The next morning, October 20, 1930, following a glorious Indian summer daybreak, I was born at St. Anthony's hospital in Oklahoma City. My birth certificate listed, "Unnamed Hall child," which I didn't discover until I received my Air Force commission twenty-one years later.

It seems that my mother wanted to name me John David, but my father insisted on just David. Apparently his refusal to bend had to do with his dislike of my mother's uncle, John Sexton. And so, as a compromise couldn't be reached, St. Anthony's had no recourse but to list me as unnamed on my birth certificate.

The disagreement over my name was a harbinger of much greater conflicts to come between the two branches of my family tree—the French family lineage of Sherman, Texas, and the Halls of Oklahoma City, Oklahoma. Learning the family history was a lesson in vantage points; as a child and through my teens, I was told the story of my naming from different family members. My first memory is Grandmother French's account, and she blamed my father for the dispute over my name. Grandmother Hall's version gave Dad a little more slack—just lack of communication, she said.

The best and most positive story came from my mother, who played down the argument—but she stuck to her guns on what my name should be.

Early on, I learned to take family stories with a grain of salt, considering the source and what might influence each version—great training for future dealing with legislators, lobbyists, and government agencies.

My mother, Aubrey Nell French, was the eldest of four daughters, born in 1905 to Benham (Ben) Audley French and Estella (Essie) Gertrude Sexton French of Sherman, Texas. Of English and German heritage, the Frenches were tall and fair; Grandfather Ben was 6'4" with strong, handsome features, and his daughters ranged from 5'5" to 5'10". Gregarious and fun-loving, everyone in the family shared an exceptional work ethic. Raised in the Church of Christ, the French girls were taught that family came first, followed by the church—and last, but not least, the pursuit of knowledge.

Mother: Aubrey Nell French, 17, Sherman, Texas, 1920

Those values could certainly be traced to Ben's father, my great-grandfather, George French, who had moved from upstate New York to Sherman in 1875, as well as to the newly arrived Iowa lass Alice Hendershott, whom he married three years later. George and Alice brought with them the political sympathies of the North and Midwest, but they had religious convictions very different from each other's. My great-grandfather was a devout member of the Church of Christ, but my great-grandmother and most of her people were Presbyterians. Even though both were as stubborn as they were committed to their faiths—both remained loyal members of their respective churches until they died—they always found common ground. In the process, the seeds of individuality, together with religious and political tolerance, were sown into the heritage that my mother's family would pass on to me.

Contrary to what one might assume, the political and social fabric of this area of North Texas and Grayson County spawned one of America's most remarkable Democrats, Speaker of the United States House of Representatives Sam Rayburn. From the nearby town of Bonham, he served for a record seventeen years.

Whether or not any kind of aspirations for elected office had occurred to any of my Texas relatives, I can't say. But I do know that the French family's quest for excellence was inter-generational. My great-grandfather George, a painter and decorator by trade, spent 47 years becoming the best at what he did, and ultimately bequeathed the intricacies of his training to his son Ben. With my grandfather's consummate skills of painting, graphic design, and lettering, he went on to make a name for himself in Sherman. One of his signature accomplishments was the logo he painted for Mrs. Tucker's Shortening Company, a prominent local business that boasted a caravan of trucks and railroad boxcars adorned by Ben French's work. In addition to the training, George instilled in Ben an intention to continually strive for perfection, to exude integrity, and to always lend a helping hand to the less fortunate. Such were the priorities passed on to my mother and her sisters.

From my maternal grandmother's side came the value of education. Before Estella arrived in Sherman, she had been sent to live for two years with her grandparents in Kentucky while her mother, Mary Yates Sexton, went ahead on her own and found work that put her in charge of housekeeping at North Texas Female College, which became Kidd Key College in 1919. Once she saved up enough money, Mary sent for her daughter; she was able to arrange for Estella, then in her third year of schooling, to become a boarding student there. My grandmother soon developed a love of art and music as well as a strong sense of individuality that translated in later years to a very progressive support of women's rights, particularly with respect to women's equality in the work force.

After completing her undergraduate education, Estella attended business school and worked as a clerk and secretary. As the story goes, it was her fastidious sense of style, plus her long, dark brown hair—worn elegantly pinned up in a bun—and her quick wit that captured Ben's heart.

My grandparents married in 1904. A short time later, Grandmother French stopped working outside of the home and devoted herself to being a full-time housewife. Estella and Ben had five children: four daughters and, tragically, a stillborn son. Though they never spoke of that loss, I do know that one of the brightest spots in Grandfather Ben's life was the birth of my brother, Wendell, the first grandchild—and the first boy in the French lineage. The two were great friends from the start.

My mother and her sisters were never pushed by my grandparents to start families. On the contrary, Grandfather French's desire for his daughters to be educated was practically as intense as his aspiration for perfection in his trade. His attitude, coupled with Grandmother Essie's belief in women's rights, inspired and influenced their daughters' dreams. The same value of education would be passed on to me.

Even though I was only three years old when Grandfather French died suddenly at 52, he loomed large in my memories as a proud, strong-willed man of uncommon good manners who was adored by his four daughters. What else I know of him I learned from my mother, from Grandmother Essie, and from my brother. My grandfather suffered from diabetes at a time when medicine provided some longevity with the disease, but his lack of discipline in using the medication contributed to his early death.

Without speaking to the subject directly, Grandmother Essie taught me how to live with loss. Never one to give in to self-pity, she stated that although it was a hardship to lose her husband after 29 years of marriage, she needed to stay strong for her family. Faith sustained her; to this day, I don't really know how Grandmother Essie, with her Presbyterian background (including a grandfather who was a Presbyterian minister), became such a devoted member of the Church of Christ. She never felt it necessary to explain her political beliefs, either.

When I was ten years old, during a visit to Sherman, an elderly African-American woman who had helped care for me as a toddler stopped by the house and told me stories about my grandmother's commitment to civil rights, and about her belief in racial equality. Our visitor also described what a generous human being my mother was, and recalled my grandmother's many kindnesses to her. At the time I thought first with pride that the women who mattered most to me were seen as people to be admired. Later, I realized that by their example, they were informing my attitude toward equality, diversity, and color-blindness.

In the quest to know more about the world that raised me, I suspect that my search has also been to get to know the safer, more innocent place in which my mother grew up. With a future destined for academic achievement, my mother was considered the most ambitious of the four French girls. At 5'9", Aubrey Nell French was a slim brunette with lovely hazel eyes that sparkled; she was nick-named Frenchie in high school. She was outgoing and a joy to be with. As a senior at Sherman High School, she met a dashing red-haired man who was a freshman at Austin College in Sherman.

That young man, William A. Hall, Jr., was my father. His nick-name, of course, was Red. His dad, William A. Hall, Sr., was of Welsh and English heritage, one of four brothers who were all trained in the art of farming by their father, a Presbyterian minister who lived the Lord's commandments with discipline and compassion for his sons and for his flock. Son Will, as my Grandfather Hall was affectionately called, dreamed of a life beyond farming or the ministry; at an early age, he joined the Hardwick Etter Company in North Texas, becoming a very successful salesman of cotton-ginning equipment.

Will descended from the pioneer farmers who came west for a better life. They came from the Carolinas in covered wagons in the 1800s and settled on farms in the rich, dark earth of North Texas. At the age of nineteen, Will met and married my grandmother, Theodosia Yeager —Dodie—a striking eighteen-year-old girl from a farming community near his home of Copeville, Texas. My grandmother Dodie was of stern German descent, with a family history of hard work, frugality, and a belief in the Lord, but Will charmed her away from her family.

Dodie Hall was 5'1", and slender with a figure that drew admiring glances from everyone she met. She learned the rules of life from the Old Testament: Hard work and obedience were rewarded; idleness and sloth were punished. Even with that heritage, she was fun-loving and sometimes "very naughty" for a strict Southern Baptist. Her delight in occasional sexual innuendos was apparent, but she would not tolerate a dirty joke. For example, she was fond of saying, "All you had to do was wave a pair of men's pants over me, and I'd get pregnant." In our teen years, she would never allow my date to sit on my lap while riding in her car; in that respect she considered herself our moral guardian.

Her family were farmers and employees of the Southern Pacific Railway. She and Will had two bright and energetic sons: my father, Will, and his younger brother, Earl Wayne Hall. As ambitious and thirsting for knowledge as my mother's family was, the Halls were equally as diligent, and held the importance of education in high regard. Grandmother Dodie had a rudimentary education through the eighth grade, but was a strong advocate of learning. Grandfather Will finished high school plus one year of business college.

A major change in Will's life occurred with his marriage to Dodie and his conversion to the Southern Baptist denomination. Their boys were reared in the Baptist church in the old-school manner, with revivals and a fire-and-brimstone message that served them both well over their lifetimes—although the boys would later confess that their moral compasses sometimes went askew. Dad's religious beliefs carried over into my life; I was raised in the Southern Baptist church and remained a member until my marriage. My father was a devout Baptist throughout his lifetime.

My grandfather Hall believed in saving 25¢ of every dollar he earned, and with my grandmother's devotion to frugality, they were a perfect couple. The result was a progression of savings that lead to the ownership of an ice plant in Farmersville, Texas, and, ultimately, a bottling business in Oklahoma City, Oklahoma. My dad, the older boy, was inquisitive and assertive, and wanted to know the how and why of everything. I am told that as a teenager he thought that he knew it all, and discipline was a real challenge.

Dad was certainly a rebellious teen according to Grandmother Hall. She delighted in telling me of his days delivering blocks of ice to the customers of my grandfather's ice company, and the complaints of his raiding their iceboxes from time to time. Dad did not argue with that, but his version was that he most always had permission for what he appropriated.

Growing up in the small, close-knit Southern Baptist community of Farmersville, Texas, Dad's inquisitive nature, high energy level, and quick temper didn't always sit well with some folks. Dad's habit of riding his motorcycle down the dusty farm roads at top speed and scaring the cows generated many complaints from the farmers. Grandfather Hall, on the road most of the time, left the discipline to my grandmother Hall. A petite woman, Mama Hall, as we all called her, was quick to punish and slow to forgive. She told me that enforcement of discipline on Dad was always a work in progress.

Instead of entering the local high school, Dad was packed off to Wentworth Military Academy. As it turned out, the move had the desired effect, as Dad prospered in that environment. It shaped his love of discipline, his patriotism, and fierce pride in military service. In 1921, at the age of twenty, he graduated from the academy with a second-lieutenant's commission in the Army just as World War I ended. Dad never forgave President Wilson and the Allies for signing the armistice before he got his chance to serve.

My dad and uncle Earl were good students and excellent athletes. Dad excelled in track and field; the 100-meter and 1500-meter races were his specialties, and he loved football and basketball. Earl played football with grit and ability; as an adult, Uncle Earl championed all sports, and was a major founder of the noted All-College Basketball Tournament in Oklahoma City held during the Christmas holidays each year.

Dad's political philosophy and his attitudes toward race were formed early in his life. He lived in Farmersville, Texas, as a boy and was surrounded by Democrats, and he became a dedicated party member for the rest of his life. The attitude of those in North Texas communities, with their Green River Ordinances and prejudiced views toward African-Americans—or anyone else who was different from them—angered my father. By his teen years, he held the conviction that all men are created equal; this resolution was so firm that the rule in our household was that if you ever used the N-word or spoke disparagingly of another race, it was off to the woodshed for a lickin' you would long remember.

I was taught to treat all people equally and to cherish diversity. Dad did this not only by fiat but also by practice. His best tennis-playing friend in Ada, Oklahoma, was Sid Gluckman, a Jewish department-store owner. As a seven- and eight-year-old, I spent many Saturday and Sunday afternoons working as a ball boy for their matches. Example is by far the best teacher.

After his freshman year at college in Sherman, Dad went to Baylor University for his sophomore year, majored in chemistry, competed in track, and graduated with a bachelor of science degree. He courted Frenchie, the Sherman senior he had met as a freshman, throughout college, and they were married immediately after his graduation in 1925. My brother, Wendell, was born in 1926 in Sherman, Texas. Mother wanted to advance her education, as she loved the excitement of learning. She began her college work at the College of Industrial Arts, in Denton, Texas, which in 1934 became the Texas State College for Women.

Soon after Wendell's birth, my father was hired in Stephenville, Texas, to coach football and teach chemistry at John Tarleton Junior College. Mother and Dad balanced the burden of school, caring for my brother, and Dad's work with a large amount of babysitting help from Grandmother French. In 1928 Dad accepted another job at the high school in Schulenberg, Texas, to coach football and teach chemistry. The same hectic schedule continued for my mother.

From left: Dad, William A. Hall, Jr., 28; Brother Wendell, 3;
Mother, Aubrey Hall, 25; Sherman, Texas, 1929

Mother commuted from Sherman until her senior year. That last year she lived at the college in Denton five days a week, and returned to Sherman on the weekends where my grandmother French and my Aunt Essie were taking care of my brother. Mother became pregnant with me during her senior year of college. I can only imagine the strain of that period leading up to my birth, as Mother drove those narrow two-lane asphalt roads through all kinds of spring weather, worrying about my brother's separation—and now with a second child on the way. Aunt Essie told me that on some weekends

Mother seemed disengaged, distant, and depressed. When Aunt Essie asked her about school, Mother's answers were vague, not in the manner of the fun-loving and witty sister that Aubrey Nell had been. But these instances of unusual behavior were intermittent, and the family took no special notice.

Grandfather Ben French, Brother Wendell, Sherman, Texas 1930

In the spring of 1930, the strain of the pregnancy, the weekend trips to Sherman, and the completion of her degree were taking a toll on my mother's mental health. This would later become a major problem.

Upon her graduation in 1930, she moved to Schulenberg, where Dad was enjoying his work. Mother's mental health problems became apparent there with depression, and she was prescribed the drug Belladonna. These doses were later believed to have exacerbated a schizophrenic condition that was silently developing; the drug, synthesized from a plant called deadly nightshade, sometimes produced hallucinations and delirium.

During this period my Hall grandparents had moved to Oklahoma City after my grandfather left the Hardwick Etter Company to start a new business venture. Grandfather Hall opened the Aunt Ida and Uncle Joe Bottling Company near downtown Oklahoma City in 1929 with the aim of bringing his two sons into a family business. This goal was accomplished in 1930, when Uncle Earl and my father both moved to Oklahoma City to become part of the bottling business.

The move to the family business involved a new role for my father. Uncle Earl became the inside man at the bottling business, and my father, Red, was the sales and outside man. My grandfather took an overseeing position, letting the two sons take the lead in developing the business. In the second year after the sons arrived, the name of the company was changed to the Hall Beverage Company, and a new plant was built on Linwood Avenue near downtown Oklahoma City.

My mother was apprehensive about the move, as my dad's new coaching job was very successful in Schulenberg. My mother cherished the independence she and my father enjoyed in South Texas, and while she was still frequently depressed, she felt secure there, and was very anxious about the move to Oklahoma. However, it looked at first as if the move to Oklahoma City was just what the doctor ordered for Mom; Dad later told me how happy she was in the new environment. Mother was active socially, and loved to have people around her. She liked to plan and host events that involved a number of people. She was fondly remembered for this talent by those who knew her in college and her early years in Oklahoma City.

She was initially pleased with the new home in Oklahoma City, her new friends, and the business opportunity. My birth in the fall of 1930 added to her burdens, but she was happy with her home and her friends, and she seemed to prosper in spirit and frame of mind.

The next two years were frenetic. My father was learning a new business and developing contacts in Oklahoma City. Dad was popular in his work with the Chamber of Commerce, active in his church, successful at the bottling company, and very self-assured. In 1932 he combined all this with a run for the Oklahoma State Legislature. He ran as a Democrat, confident of his chances, but he lost in the primary and was demoralized. The damage to his ego and his feelings of failure seemed to feed my mother's deteriorating mental health; her earlier euphoria over the move to Oklahoma City all but evaporated.

Storm clouds were gathering in the Halls' marriage, accelerated by my birth and the dispute over my name. By 1933, the differences had become extreme, and my parents separated. My mother moved to Sherman, Texas, taking Wendell and me with her. The change was devastating to my brother and me; although I was too young to appreciate the change in financial circumstances, it was very difficult for my mother to work, because she was then having periods of depression and lapses in judgment.

My father recognized that my mother's mental state was fragile, and that her capacity for making sound decisions was impaired; he and my Hall grandparents had discussed getting psychological help for my mother when the two separated. Dad always believed that this marriage could work, and that the early disagreements—such as my name and Dad's career move—were not the cause of her mental illness. Dad believed that with proper treatment, he and mother could have had a successful life together.

Mother must have had a plan to support Wendell and me when she moved to Sherman, but I never learned the details of her thinking. Instead, her advancing mental illness necessitated my grandfather Hall to contribute and aid with our support. Still, from the time I was two until I was four, she worked every day on my education. Mother's love of education and her teaching experience motivated her to home-school me, while she helped Wendell with the beginning of his formal education in the Sherman Elementary School near our apartment, where he was in the third grade.

David, 4; Wendell, 9; Sherman, Texas 1935

By the age of four, I knew my alphabet, could read at a first- or second-grade level, and was interested in Texas history. Instilling in me a love of education, my mother's work with me on my vocabulary and reading skills gave me tremendous confidence when I later started public school.

In 1933, two years after Mother, Wendell, and I moved to Sherman, my grandfather, Ben French, died. Grandmother French, now a widow with three daughters still living at home, was struggling financially in the heart of the Great Depression, and there were no funds to assist in the treatment of my mother. Grandfather Hall offered to send my mother to the Menninger Clinic in Topeka, Kansas, but my mother adamantly refused—as did my Grandmother French, who didn't believe the illness was far enough advanced.

Along with the separation and the 1933 divorce of my parents, a similar split was in the works for my father, his brother, and my grandfather in their bottling business. The problems were of a great enough magnitude that Dad decided to leave the business and strike out for California.

Since the breakup of his marriage, Dad had met and married Dorothy Draper, a woman thirteen years his junior. In contemplating his move to California, my father decided to take my brother with him—but Dad did not do it through the courts. Instead, on a sunny spring morning, as my brother walked to school, my father pulled up beside him, put him in the car, and drove off to California—without telling my mother.

It was the defining event of my mother's life.

To Dad's credit, as he left Sherman, he stopped and called the Grayson County sheriff to tell him what he had done. Inexplicably, the sheriff did not call my mother—or any of her family—until the next morning to let them know that my father had taken Wendell from Sherman. How it might have changed my mother's destiny if she had received that phone call the night before, I will never know. But I will also never forget the evening at home after my brother Wendell disappeared: My mother was frantic, and Grandmother French was crying. We all imagined the worst. Only four years old, I was bewildered and afraid.

At around eight o'clock that night, my mother, standing at the kitchen sink in our upstairs apartment in Sherman, broke into tears. As she was wringing dry a dishtowel, she screamed so loudly that it hurt my ears, and then she collapsed in a heap on the kitchen floor. In a panic, I went to her. She was unconscious, and I ran to the downstairs neighbor for help.

The rest of that night is a blur. My mother was taken away, and I saw her only once that week before she was declared mentally ill by the court and sent to the state mental health facility in Wichita Falls, Texas. After my mother was committed, I went to live with my eighteen-year-old unmarried Aunt Essie, her older sisters, Mary and Ruth, and my Grandmother French—whom I affectionately called Bamboo, a nickname given to her by my brother.

In 1934 the country was still mired in a deep depression, and Sherman was no exception. My Aunt Essie, Aunt Mary, and Aunt Ruth, bless them, were the sole support of my grandmother and me. Times were very hard, money was short, and many of the normal health standards, such as medical and dental care, suffered. For the next two years, it was a constant battle for my aunts to provide for us—and at the same time, with no experience at all with boys, to rear a four-year-old. But they persevered; my aunt Ruth and aunt Mary continued to help until they married in 1935 and 1937.

All four women continued my mother's educational practices for me in word development and reading, but my contacts with playmates and male role models were very limited. During this period I developed an ability to shut out the rest of the world, play alone, and create imaginary friends in scenarios that came spinning from the imagination that my mother had helped stimulate. Clothespins became my erector sets, and I built everything from airplanes to sailing vessels. I remember playing with those pins on the cool, smooth linoleum floor of my grandmother's kitchen. This enterprise provided me hours of enjoyment.

Though I was happy and able to feel relatively secure, thanks to the love and caring that I received from Bamboo, Essie, Ruth, and Mary, the separation from my mother took a toll. Inside, I battled feelings of bewilderment and fear—but I also learned how to immerse myself in the activities of the day, and how to maintain an optimistic attitude. Compounding the struggle and the stress on the four women who devoted themselves to my well-being was a sickly physical condition I developed, stemming from an undiagnosed appendix problem and from the lack of dental care.

These were the facts, as I now know them to be, of the first six years of my life.

Adaptation

While I was living with my aunts and grandmother, we received little news of my father and brother. At six, I was still grappling with the trauma of my mother's absence, and rarely asked what became of Wendell and Dad. On one occasion when I did ask, my Aunt Essie said simply, "Wendell's doing fine, or we would hear from him. Don't worry."

"But why doesn't he write?" I asked.

Aunt Essie would hug me and say, "You know he misses you, but he is just so busy with school that he doesn't have time."

My father and my brother settled in Montebello, a northern suburb of Los Angeles, where Dad had tried various sales jobs with only moderate success. What I eventually learned was that my brother and stepmother were at odds at every turn, and often the conflict was intolerable. She was only nine years older than Wendell, so her attempts at mothering were not successful. Moreover the presence of an infant half-sister, Ann, only added to the tension. The result was that Wendell was exiled to military school in Los Angeles County; his tuition and board for the school year 1936/37 were paid by Grandfather Hall.

Dad was motivated to leave the West Coast and return to Oklahoma by the hope of a better business opportunity back home. In the winter of 1936, he left my brother in military school in California; later that year, my father, Grandfather Hall, and Uncle Earl agreed to join together again in the Hall Beverage Company. The main office was at the plant in Oklahoma City, and a satellite plant was planned for Ada, Oklahoma. My grandfather's dream of being in business with his two sons was alive again.

But Dad returned to an uncertain family business relationship, which he had left only two years earlier. How would that work out now? Were there old wounds not yet healed? With these pressures, Dad made an unwise decision to leave ten-year-old Wendell alone in a distant military school with little communication and hardly any word about our mother—probably the worst thing Dad could have done for Wendell at that age. This compounded the instability caused first by the traumatic exit from Sherman, followed by Wendell's life with a disagreeable stepmother. Images of what Wendell must have felt when he was left behind still haunt me.

In the years before World War II, the Hall Beverage Company of Oklahoma City prospered, and expanded its product line to 37 different flavors of drinks; the firm made everything from strawberry and orange drinks to chocolate milk and root beer. The one missing element at Hall Beverage was a brand-name drink. In 1936, Pepsi-Cola started an aggressive program to unite franchise bottlers across the United States. Coca Cola was the market leader, but Pepsi-Cola saw a way to compete—and my family saw an opportunity to grow with Pepsi-Cola. The first nationwide radio commercial jingle was inaugurated by Pepsi-Cola:

> *Pepsi-Cola hits the spot,*
> *Twelve full ounces, that's a lot,*
> *Twice as much for a nickel too,*
> *Pepsi-Cola is the drink for you.*

The jingle was an instant hit, and Pepsi-Cola began to gain popularity. The main selling point for Pepsi-Cola in the middle of the Great Depression was its value of twelve ounces in a bigger bottle for a nickel whereas Coca Cola offered only six-ounce bottles for a nickel.

The Hall Beverage Company began negotiations with Pepsi-Cola, and in early 1937, the company won the Pepsi-Cola franchise for Oklahoma City and a major part of southern Oklahoma. This cemented the plans to expand and build the plant in Ada, and the Hall Beverage Company became the Pepsi-Cola Bottling Company. This was to be the family enterprise for the next seventeen years.

My father bought a home in Ada, and it was then that his conversations with Grandmother French led to changes for me. Finally Dad drove to Sherman at the start of the summer of 1937 and took me to live with him. Parting from my aunt and grandmother French was tearful and traumatic. The love and security I had with them was vanishing, and I was headed to a new environment.

Dad did his best to comfort me, but at the age of six and a half, the fear of an unknown future clouded my mind. That three-hour drive with my Dad was torture. My agonizing mood swings must have been as hard on him as they were on me. Dark thoughts crowded my mind. Dad must have sensed my insecurity because he started to describe life in Ada, our home there, and the school I would attend. It had some positive effect, but I was a long way from understanding what lay ahead. One thing I did learn was that in a few short weeks, I would be reunited with my big brother Wendell, and the happiness that brought me helped put my fears to rest.

It had been two years since my mother had been committed, and I saw her only one time and with very limited contact. It was terribly depressing to go to the state hospital and see her in that controlled atmosphere. I had a difficult time assimilating what had happened to my mother and what the future would bring.

I arrived in Ada at the new home and was greeted by two strangers, my tiny half-sister Ann, and my stepmother, Dorothy. I didn't want to be there, and I am sure it was no easier for them. I had decided to try to do the right thing in this new place and with this new family, but I was really not sure how to do it. My brother was still in California, and those first few weeks were difficult.

As soon as we arrived, Dad took me to the doctor who discovered my appendix required immediate removal. The surgery went forward with Dad at my side. I vividly remember the cone that was placed over my nose and mouth, the drip of the ether and its over-powering sweet smell, my counting backward from one hundred and falling into oblivion as I reached ninety-seven. The operation was successful, and the next day the whole family, except for me, left for Dallas.

During my first week in Ada, Dad had arranged for my brother to come by train to Dallas where the family would meet him. Wendell came the week after my operation. Five days passed while I recuperated in the hospital. The family met Wendell at the train, attended the Texas State Fair, and then returned to Ada.

Two vivid memories remain from those days alone in the Ada Hospital. First was the recurring smell of the ether, even in my dreams. Second was my deep disappointment in missing the trip to Dallas to meet Wendell and see the Texas State Fair. It hurt even more when the family returned and brought all the pictures of the good times that I had missed.

The surgery changed my life. With the poison of the appen-dix gone, I became more vital and energetic, and my overall health improved fast. Next on the list were my dental problems, which took nearly a year to fix.

There were other difficulties as well. I was fighting at school, and I was increasingly at odds with my stepmother. The one saving grace was the arrival of my brother, Wendell. We quickly renewed our bond. Although four years apart in age, the next few years were the happiest times of our lives for both Wendell and me. We shared a bedroom, rode our bikes to school each day, and did our chores together.

When I started school in the fall of 1937, I was scheduled to be in the first grade, but because of my home-taught reading skills, the principal of Willard Grade School promoted me to the second grade. Skipping the first grade was a great source of pride, and it helped me make the transition to my new life. There was another big change. Dad enrolled me at school as David Hall—no middle name or middle initial. This now became my lifelong name. My mother, however, never stopped calling me John David in all her letters and our times together. We never discussed my name, and I never corrected her.

In addition to his duties managing the Pepsi-Cola plant, Dad wrote a sports column for the local newspaper. He took Wendell and me to every high school and college sport that he covered—basketball, baseball, and football. This began an intense love of sports. When Dad played tennis on the weekends, I was the ball boy for the matches.

Dad was aware of my anguish in missing my mother and my Texas family. In the summer of 1938, on a scorching July day, he drove Wendell and me to see our mother at the state hospital at Wichita Falls, Texas. We were only allowed to visit for a few hours, which included a lunch together in town and a visit to a local park.

My mother had been given shock treatment that I thought had turned her hair white. She was gaunt, her face lined, and there was a small scar on her cheek just below her left eye. Her grey eyes bored into me as we talked. When she looked at me, her eyes captured mine and made me feel secure. But it was hard for me to express how much I missed her because it brought tears to my eyes. It was difficult to remember her soft, dark hair that smelled so sweet in earlier days.

The visit was Wendell's first since my father abducted him. No mention of that was made, but I could sense the fierce emotion when she hugged him tightly and kept his hand in hers much of our time together. Wendell said nothing about our troubles with our stepmother. He was bearing that cross alone. I know now that he was doing his best as my big brother to shield me from his own trauma. He was always that way. Not just my brother but my champion, my mentor, and my role model.

The lack of rain, the dry, straw-like grass, and dusty playground gave the park a surreal look—barren and lonely. It was sad and poignant to feel my mother's urgency to reconnect with us in that short visit.

Her affection and determination to show her love for me made that visit a happy event but tinged with a feeling of deep regret. I imagined her as a beautiful loving bird trapped in a cage with no hope for freedom. It was a vision that stayed with me for years.

As Dad drove out the gates of the state institution, I saw my mother waving from the door of her building. I was aware of a feeling of turbulence deep inside like an angry, unpredictable twister growing. Not surprisingly my bad dreams continued.

Dad did his best to preserve my links to the Texas family in Sherman. That same summer, at seven and a half, I was allowed to ride the bus alone from Ada to Sherman. Wendell would be coming to Sherman later with a relative. Dad took me to the bus, introduced me to the driver, put a note in my pocket with all pertinent data, and sent me off on the seven-hour trip. The driver sat me in the row behind him and monitored me the entire trip.

I was feeling pretty daring on that trip, traveling all that distance alone. I remember the green pastures of waving grass, the sleepy small towns at each bus stop, the fat, well-fed cows grazing beyond barbed wire fences, the beautiful horses galloping over meadows on the ranches I passed, and, most interesting to my young eyes, the diversity of people along the way. I wondered at these new sights and wondered about their relation to my life.

At journey's end I was met by my aunt Essie and grandmother French at the Sherman station. I was so proud that I had done this alone; my self-reliance and determination to cope, no matter what, was being formed and nurtured. Such a trip would never be considered as of this writing in 2011 with the fear of child abductions.

That summer and the two summers to follow were all wonderful opportunities to reunite with my aunts—Aunt Essie, the youngest and later sole support for Bamboo; Aunt Mary Cook, now a teacher; Aunt Ruth, a budding legal secretary; and Grandmother French, all of whom I had missed desperately the first year or two I was with my father. It gave me an opportunity to compare the relative advantages that I had living with my father: the financial security, the medical and dental care, and a stable, middle-class environment. It would have been extremely difficult for Grandmother French and my aunts to have continued to support themselves and me in a way that would have been beneficial to all of us. My Aunt Essie deserves enormous gratitude for having forgone many of life's good things from 1937 to 1944 to take care of her mother, all the while managing to fashion a career of her own with the National Life Insurance Company. She had become the sole support for my grandmother in 1937 after her sisters had married.

The summers in Sherman were typical of small-town America with all of the fairs, the picnics, and events that meant so much to youngsters in their lives. An important discovery came one languid summer afternoon at a wide meadow on the southeast side of Sherman where I watched a barnstorming biplane land and bounce to a stop among wild daisies.

Enthralled with the idea of flight, I had visions and dreams of being a pilot. To ride in the biplane was too expensive, so I could only look and wish. However, the pilot lifted me into the cockpit, and my imagination ran wild when I touched the controls; it was an unbelievable thrill!

My uncle Lowell Cook, husband of Aunt Mary—my mother's next younger sister—was a flying enthusiast himself. He had a tandem-seat, Piper Cub airplane, and I got many rides with him when I was nine, ten, and eleven.

Another highlight of Sherman was the large municipal swimming pool. I had learned to swim when I was eight at Loy Lake just north of Sherman. I was eager to show off my swimming prowess. Going to that pool with its clear, cool expanse of water was the most enjoyable part of any summer day. I could ride the bus from my grandmother's home on the east side of town down through Sherman to the west side where the pool was located.

My grandmother and my aunt Essie were not too strict, but at the same time they made rules and held me to a discipline that was very good for me. On these visits I was not, as some people would say, the star boarder, but instead, I had chores to do each day before I could meet up with friends, go to the swimming pool, or see a movie. As a young boy, I was learning to dress although I had no idea at this point in my life what correct color coordination should be, and so I had some very interesting experiences because of this. One occurred at a five and dime store in Ada when I was ten years old and saw a pair of bright-yellow socks that fascinated me. I bought two pair and began wearing them for special occasions until my Dad told me that they sorta clashed with nearly everything else I owned. So I put them away and saved them for my annual trip to Sherman where my father would not be supervising my wardrobe. I remember getting on the bus, taking my yellow socks out of my suitcase, and changing into them so I would be prepared for Sherman. I wore them many times until one of my female cousins made an off-handed comment about their blazing color and their lack of color coordination with my clothes. I was deflated. With that I packed them back in the suitcase and never wore them again. My urge to stand out in a crowd yet not be too different was growing.

The three summers Wendell and I spent in Sherman brought us even closer. He and my aunt Essie were the only family members who ever called me Dave or Davey. I loved my name, David, and even as a child, I would let people know that was how I should be called; Wendell and Essie were the only exceptions The other members of the French family always called me David.

Our camaraderie blossomed. Wendell was inquisitive and well read for a teenager. Although he was introverted to the point of extreme shyness and withdrawn in many social situations, he was a delight to me. The thing we loved most was to go to two double-feature shows on a Saturday instead of just one, as was the custom. It cost us a nickel or a dime for each of the shows, four movies in all. From noon until six, we could escape into that wonderful, cool world of motion pictures. Gone were the thoughts of family issues and the travails that we had experienced in our daily lives.

Like it was yesterday, I can remember wearing shorts, a short-sleeved shirt, and my high-top tennis shoes with laces floppy as

Wendell and I entered the theater. From the hot summer air outside to the first cool blast of the air conditioning inside, every visit was a treat to body and spirit. It was always crowded on Saturday afternoons, and we arrived early to jockey for good seats. Wendell and I first saw Howard Hughes's *Hell's Angels* and were captivated by the aerial dogfights and skill of the pilots. We traveled in our minds to darkest Africa while viewing *Trader Horn*, the first movie ever shot on location there.

I first gained great curiosity about films and began my lifelong love of movies in those afternoons. I remember as a child in Sherman going into that darkened theater and entering a fantasyland that had no relationship to my humdrum existence, and it gave me a feeling of power and escape.

As I look back, many of the movies of the late '30s fed a need for all Americans to begin to feel better about ourselves during what had been hard times for all. The stories lifted us out of our own troubles while providing hope for brighter days ahead—or at least those were my feelings. Wendell was a different story.

Things were improving in 1938 and 1939 with my stepmother and my new family. My anger and bad dreams were subsiding. I think now a large part of this change was the result of my stepmother and me trying harder. We developed a mutual respect and had the beginnings of a strong friendship. I never felt that she was my substitute mother; instead, I felt that she was more like a caring older sister.

With the improvements at home, my overall attitude turned more positive. Let me hasten to add that this didn't translate to the classroom, where the strict rules brought out the rebel in me. That said, I learned a lot about discipline in our household. The result was that with school, our church activities, and with the presence of my brother, my desire to please my parents strengthened.

Chores were a major part of the daily routine, before school and afterward. We lived on a three-acre tract a few miles east of Ada in a white-frame, two-story home to which Dad had added a den that he and a hired hand built. One acre was devoted to the house and a large lawn with a circular gravel driveway in the front that was lined on either side with rocks the size of basketballs, which my brother and I kept whitewashed.

Behind the house was a two-acre garden, which Wendell and I tended during the growing season. It was during those hot 100° summer days in July and August while hoeing and weeding the corn that I decided against farming as a career. Looking back, I can now see that my subconscious mind was forming the basis of my life-long support of farm subsidies; the hard work of that type of farming was probably the reason. Our other chores, such as lawn care, dish-washing, and "totin' 'n' fetchin'," were not nearly as repellent as that #^%@!! garden! The country's hard-working, tireless, and durable men and women who tend the nation's farms have my everlasting admiration and gratitude.

Our family had one radio in the living room and a two-party telephone line, which was invariably busy when we needed to make a call. The house had one bath until my second half-sister, Nancy, was born in 1938. Dad then divided the den and made another bathroom. Just a few steps out the back door was a storm cellar for the tornados that plagued the area during the spring and summer. The cellar had a dirt floor—often a few inches deep in water—a few shelves on one wall, and two benches facing each other. It was seven feet deep, five feet wide, and eight feet long. The wooden door at the entrance was covered with tin to preserve it. The storm cellar, or "fraidy hole," as some people called it, had to be cleaned regularly. Needless to say, we tried to avoid that chore, because snakes had a habit of curling up down there.

The First Baptist Church in Ada was an imposing buff brick building that covered nearly a city block. It was one focal point of our family life, and we regularly attended three sessions on Sunday: the morning Sunday school, the preaching service, and the Baptist Young People's Union (BYPU) in the evening. Sometimes we even stayed for a Sunday-night prayer service. Every Wednesday we attended the church supper and services afterward.

The pastor, Dr. C.C. Morris, owned the only radio station in Ada, and that gave him a wide audience in Pontotoc County, which produced an overflowing crowd at most services. This church was far and away the dominant religious force in Ada, and it mirrored the Southern Baptist influence in most small towns in Oklahoma during that era. Revivals were a major part of the summer programs, and most were held in the open-air tabernacle directly adjacent to the church. I have vivid memories of a traveling evangelist, Hymen Appleman, a converted Jew who preached passionate fire-and-brimstone sermons.

In June of each year, Wendell and I visited Sherman. Then in August we attended the Baptist encampment at Falls Creek in the Arbuckle Mountains of Oklahoma for sessions that usually ran a week to ten days. These trips are some of my fondest memories; the cool, clear, gently flowing creeks to swim in, the varied hiking trails, and the evening services were the highlights. The night services were held in an open-air wooden, thatched-roof brush arbor without sidewalls, built in a circular fashion, and it seated several hundred. The trees and foliage that encircled the tabernacle complemented its prominence in the camp area and gave the impression that God had given it a divine mission.

No visual aids were available as we know them today, but the preachers had an artistic assistant who used a giant blackboard and colored chalk to present pictures of the speaker's teachings. I marveled at the skill of the chalk artists, and their images remain in my mind today. The drawings had the same effect on me as sitting in a darkened movie theater and viewing a film.

The cabins, with men and women segregated, were simple frame constructions very similar to Army barracks, with double-decker, metal beds arranged in the military fashion. We were required to read one book of the Bible during the week, in addition to our other activities, and discuss its meaning. My first summer, at age eight, I chose the Book of Mark. I must have read it six times, and still could not grasp all that I was reading, but I slogged through, thanks to my brother's encouragement.

The middle of the week after my third time through Mark, Wendell saw my dejected look, moved closer, put his hand on my shoulder and said, "Davey, some of this won't make sense for years, but if you keep at it, I bet you'll start to see the meaning underneath the Scripture."

How right he was! The Book of Mark in fact became a personal primer for me of the teachings of Jesus and importance of knowing that even the most horrendous hardships can be overcome—and that the choices we make have consequences. Through Mark and the apostle Peter, who conveyed these teachings, I recognized that the call to leadership was actually a path to service.

———

In that era, the Ada Pepsi Cola Plant was sold, and in the fall of 1939, we moved to Oklahoma City, where my life took other positive turns. As the last semester of grade school in Ada had been the most successful for me academically up to that time, I was excited about having the opportunity to learn more at a big city school—Linwood Grade School on Northwest 16th Street. Another truly great bonus of the move was that we were now living within a few blocks of my Hall grandparents, plus Aunt Charlotte and Uncle Earl Hall. With love and support from my family members, I adjusted quite well to Oklahoma City. My demeanor at Linwood Grade School was 180 degrees from what it been in Ada.

Getting to know family members better and making new friends made life more joyful. The day we moved into our Oklahoma City home, I met a boy who lived just across the street, and we became instant friends. He was four inches taller than I, with a shock of dark brown hair and brown eyes. He made friends easily, and was the best storyteller I can remember. James H. (Jimmy) Webster would become my lifelong best friend.

We were inseparable, eating and sleeping at each other's homes and eagerly looking forward to each day of play. We walked to

Linwood Grade School together and shared every secret. Since the standard Monday-night meal at our home was liver and onions, Jimmy's favorite, he had a permanent seat at our Monday-night suppers. I loved hot baked potatoes, and his mother, "Mom" Webster, provided those spuds as a pick-me-up when we came home from school.

In those days, Jimmy won every wresting match we had. During the hot summer nights, we camped out in his backyard and sometimes created great mischief in the neighborhood. I was honored in later years to be the best man at his wedding, and he remains my dearest friend and advisor to this day.

Then there was Jane Hall Rodkin, another very dear friend my same age, who happened to be a cousin. A petite and beautiful child, Jane became an even lovelier adult. In addition to becoming the mother of three, she went on to attain great success as a dancer, singer, actress, and as entertainment figure. As the lead singer for our high-school dance band, Jane first stepped into the limelight by landing her own local TV show on WKY in Oklahoma City. In spite of a brief hiatus when her children were young, Jane never stopped pursuing her passion, and made us all proud by going on to make a national name for herself.

Besides being an inspiration, Jane was also a beloved and trusted confidant in all phases of my life. The two of us completed grade school, junior high school, and high school in the same class. In our teen years, she would skillfully break the ice with any girl in school that I wanted to meet.

Another close family member who came into stronger focus in these years was Jane's older brother, my cousin, Wayne Hall. All male family members worked at the Oklahoma City Pepsi Cola Company, which provided a shared work experience, family closeness, and respect for each other.

In the family bottling business, each of us had our assignments. At age ten, I was the plant janitor and maintained the inventory of the advertising signs. In the summer, I would get up at 5:30 a.m., eat breakfast, and then ride my bike seven miles to the plant to arrive at work at 7:00. This was the most pleasant time of the day, as the temperatures after 10:00 would be near the 100° mark most of the time. To offset the potential for heat exhaustion, we all took salt pills. Our day ran to five o'clock with an hour for lunch.

I loved the lunches, because I got to share a meal with my brother and cousin Wayne. Spending time with the older boys was a treat. We ate at the Nuway Diner near the intersection of Pennsylvania Avenue and Linwood Boulevard, a five-block walk from the plant. The scene of the three of us sitting at a small booth with imitation-leather padded cushions in the crowded diner could have been taken from the classic coming-of-age movie *Diner*. Wendell, normally shy, was really gregarious at these lunches. He'd start the conversations by saying, "Man, I'm hungry enough to eat two hamburgers."

Wayne chimed in, "Be sure to order Pepsi, or we'll catch hell back at the plant."

Four years younger and just being happy to be included, my comments were limited to, "I'll have just one burger."

Wayne or Wendell chose the topic for the day, with my cousin talking more about girls and our work, while my brother talked athletics and his latest poem. In those years, Wendell wrote many poems of action similar to Alfred Lord Tennyson's "Charge Of The Light Brigade." In later years, his poems became dark, brooding, and often associated with death.

It was a learning experience for me to listen to fourteen- and fifteen-year-olds candidly discuss their lives and their opinions of people we knew. I soaked up every story, and imagined every girl Wayne said was beautiful. Wayne and Wendell were very close, and their camaraderie was comforting to me.

─────────────────

My work ethic was developing with excellent positive encouragement from my dad and all the relatives working there. I was so proud when one of them complimented me on the job I was doing! This feeling carried over as I earned my own spending money and learned how to save. The value of time and the motivation to accomplish a goal was being practiced every day; more importantly, the discipline to complete a task and to appreciate the satisfaction of achievement were all becoming a habit.

The move to Oklahoma City brought a new church experience, as our family transferred our membership to the First Baptist Church at 9th and Robinson. My grandmother Hall and grandfather Hall had been members since moving to "the City," as our capital was known to all Oklahomans. This church was enormous in my mind; the sanctuary was dignified and imposing, with dark wood paneling, stained-glass windows, an imposing choir loft, and a massive organ whose tones reached your soul. I loved being a member, and was secure in my faith since my baptism in Ada.

The Sunday routine was a duplicate of the Ada experience. Attendance was not optional. The teachers that I had in Sunday school had a strong impact on my life. My grandmother Hall had been a pillar in the church since she and my grandfather had moved to Oklahoma City. Her years of faithful attendance had earned her great respect and the nickname of Miss Pepsi in recognition of the family business. My brother and I still delighted in putting our own words to some of the hymns to lighten the atmosphere of some of the more boring sermons.

While church life helped to cultivate an awareness of our inner, religious lives, I became increasingly aware of events happening outside of us around the world. I witnessed the drumbeats of war in Europe through the newsreels that went along with the Saturday movie matinees. I saw Adolph Hitler aggressively asserting his power and his horrifying dreams of conquest. Soon the events in Europe and the attack at Pearl Harbor would signal another dramatic change in my life.

The news of what had happened in the pre-dawn hours or December 7, 1941, was announced over the airwaves carried by our car radio as we drove home from church. A mix of shock, fear, and anger gripped all of us. For Dad, this was the call to action he had been waiting to answer since he was a student at Kemper Military School in 1918. As he had missed out on serving in World War I—

having received his commission as a second lieutenant just as the war came to an end—Dad had long been obsessed with the idea of serving his country. Now he had his opportunity, and the very day after Pearl Harbor, Red Hall began his quest to join the military.

But in the view of my grandfather and uncle, the timing couldn't have been worse. In the summer of that year, the Pepsi Cola business had been doing very well; my father was needed to sustain the growth. But Dad was determined; although he was forty years old, he was in excellent physical shape and refused to change his mind. Before long, he was accepted into the Army officer's training corps with the rank of 1st Lieutenant and was told to report to Florida in the spring of 1942.

In the period leading up to Dad's departure for duty, Wendell and our stepmother, Dorothy, had a number of intense contests of will and serious arguments; Wendell resented that Dorothy had taken our mother's place. Finally, Wendell left our house and went to live with our Hall grandparents in their home at the corner of 20th and Drexel, some six blocks away. So when Dad left for three months of training in Florida, Wendell stayed with our grandparents while I remained with my stepmother and my two half-sisters at the Oklahoma City house on 18th and May Avenue.

We continued with these arrangements after my father was assigned to begin active duty in Santa Monica, California. Later that year, however, in the summer of 1942, when he was ordered to Hamilton Air Force Base just north of San Francisco, Dad decided to bring the family there to live with him—everyone, that is, except Wendell.

In September of 1942, my stepmother, my sisters—Ann and Nancy—and I boarded the train in Oklahoma City, bound for Oakland, California. This was at the height of the frenzy in the year following the attack on Pearl Harbor. The war with Japan and the declaration of war against Germany and Italy created chaotic travel conditions. The trains were extremely crowded; it was very difficult to get seating, and we spent most of this trip in a chair car. The many servicemen traveling made it almost impossible to get a seat.

From Oklahoma City to San Diego, we traveled chair car, with me sitting in the aisle much of the time on a suitcase, and we slept in shifts as best we could. My stepmother did a valiant job of keeping us fed and in good spirits. The train trip to Oakland took about four and a half days, with a number of stops where we were sidetracked while troop and supply trains passed on their way to the various bases in the western United States.

We arrived bone-tired at the Oakland train terminal, where we were immediately met by my father. We boarded a ferry that took us from the Oakland train terminal to the dock at San Francisco, where my father had parked his car. Crossing the bay on the ferry and seeing San Francisco looming up ahead was an awesome thrill. My father, always a very practical man, gathered us at the rail and said, "Don't look up, or you are likely to get a splat of sea gull droppings on your face!" We all laughed—and tried our best not to look up. Ann and I were given the task of making sure three-year-old Nancy did as Dad said.

Sure enough, an elderly lady next to us suffered the first direct hit on a soft, wide-brimmed felt hat. I had never heard an older woman cuss like that as she admonished the birds! Ann and I covered our mouths to hide our snickering at that eruption.

As we plied the gray waters of San Francisco Bay, the cool salt air blowing in our faces, we looked to the north and saw the expanse of the Oakland Bay Bridge stretched on each side of Mare Island, the anchor and midpoint of the bridge. I could see Alcatraz Island as it appeared dimly and ominously in the fog-shrouded distance.

By the time we arrived, it was mid-afternoon and still overcast. We piled into Dad's four-door 1940 Lincoln and proceeded to drive through downtown San Francisco. We then drove to the fog-covered Golden Gate Bridge and across it into the gorgeous scenery that introduced me to Marin County. It was a spectacular view!

The home that my father had rented for us was in the town of Fairfax. We drove eight miles north and west through San Rafael and San Anselmo. Fairfax was located on the north slope of Mount Tamalpais in a beautiful green valley, which was originally settled by

Italian immigrants. Our rental was a four-story, shingle-sided building that originally had been part of a complex of dormitories for a religious order that had closed for the duration of the war.

I never knew what the religious order was. What I did know was that everything about this new life of ours was unfamiliar, almost exotic, and it provided me with a chance to spread my wings in new ways.

It was now September of 1942, and I was enrolled at Fairfax School. This facility was for seventh and eighth grade, what we now call middle school. The school did not have a student council; remembering my interest in student council at Taft Junior High School in Oklahoma City, and how it energized the student body, I approached our principal, Mr. Homer Sisk, suggesting that we create a student council for Fairfax school. With Mr. Sisk's approval, we formed a class committee, created bylaws and a constitution, and set up the structure of a student council. I proceeded to recruit candidates for class representatives, and we elected eight. The students elected me president. I took office and remained student-council president until my graduation in the spring of 1944. This was my first concrete work of government organization, and I was hooked.

After moving to California, I had the unique experience of being able to go to Hamilton Air Force Base with my father and spend the day on base while he carried out his duties as the mess officer. There were many firsts that occurred at that military base for me; one was that I had never been on a military base, and now I had a chance to see the aircraft, all of the machinery, and the material that went into making an air base.

Hamilton Air Force Base was designed for fighter planes to protect the harbor of San Francisco. The principal aircraft assigned was a fighter plane, the Bell Airocobra, a very fast interceptor that was built specifically for short-range defense. The compact cockpit made it difficult for a man over six feet tall to sit in it.

Now eleven, I could swim and enjoy the facilities at the officers' club. One of the young pilots tapped me on shoulder one day and said, "What's your name?"

"David," I answered with a quizzical look.

"I'm Tim," he said, "and I want to show you something fun in the pool."

Tim climbed to the high diving board with a mattress cover from his bed at the bachelor officers' quarters in hand. "Watch this!" he yelled. With that he jumped off the board, inflating the cover on the way down, and it became a flotation device just like our plastic air mattresses of today.

He paddled to the side of the pool as the air escaped and handed me the cover and said, "Now it's your turn."

The high board was a bit scary, but I was game and scrambled up the ladder. Cover in hand, I jumped off; the cover inflated, and I hit the water. I came up laughing and exhilarated. "Thanks, Tim. Is it okay if I do it again?" He gave me a thumbs up.

Another first was to run the officers'-training obstacle course on the base. With the war going on and the patriotic feeling in your heart, you felt like you were training your body so that you could be a part of the military when you got old enough to volunteer to fight the Germans and Japanese.

Soon after we had moved to Northern California, my father received orders to report to the Eighth Air Force in England for an assignment. He left in the late fall of 1942 and spent a year in Great Britain, again serving as a mess officer on various air bases and as a supply officer. He was 42 years old by this time, a captain—but too old to get into the flying program and too old to be in combat.

During my father's stay in England from December 1942 through the fall of 1943, his communication with us was by V-mail. This was a system in which each of his letters first went to the censors; next it was photographed, and the film was sent back to the United States, then printed out in a small size and then sent to the addressee; the reduction in size saved an enormous amount of money in weight and the cost of transport. V-mail was a constant joy, because Dad was very devoted to making sure that we got at least one or two letters a week describing what he was doing—within the confines of military censorship. He was restricted in what he could say, but events after the fact were okay.

He always started each message by describing his surroundings, new customs of the British he had learned, and his take on battles recently fought. Then he would share his thoughts of family and his advice to each of us. I never knew whether he was writing to Wendell as often as he did to us, but I hoped he was; Wendell and I exchanged letters, but he never mentioned getting mail from Dad.

To those of us at home, the most interesting and educational thing that my father did while he was in Great Britain was to send us all of the military maps that were not classified, showing the areas of the current battles. Each month we put these recent maps on our wall and tracked the actions. I can remember, in particular, the campaign to liberate North Africa from the great German general Erwin Rommel, as well as the campaign in Italy led by General Mark Clark.

We closely followed the activities of the armies of the United States and Great Britain as they secured northern Africa and Italy. For someone who had not been a motivated geography student, this was an exciting and personal way to learn about the rest of the world. What I learned from reading and studying these maps would later prove to be immensely beneficial as I taught navigation in the US Air Force at the San Marcos Air Force base, Texas, during the Korean War.

On the home front, the war effort was in full swing. Rallies all across the nation were held to sell war bonds. In school we bought US saving stamps until we had enough to buy a $25 war bond. My stepmother, Dorothy, took a job in the shipbuilding yards at nearby Sausalito to contribute to the war effort. She worked hard and was so proud of her contribution. My young sisters, Ann and Nancy, helped with household chores and tried in every way to do their part.

As a seventh- and eighth-grader, I was involved in gathering newspapers on the weekend, looking for scrap iron, saving foil from gum wrappers, and even balling string, all for the war effort. The entire student body at Fairfax School saved the aluminum foil from our chewing gum, rolled it all into one giant ball, and presented it to the proper authorities.

Our local war-effort committee created yellow felt badges the size of a silver dollar with a dark green E in the middle; these were awarded to the students who worked on those patriotic drives. The E stood for effort and efficiency, and we proudly pinned these to our clothing. I still have mine.

Rationing was in full swing. Gasoline, tires, and other essentials including sugar, meat, and butter were in short supply, and were needed for the troops; rationing was designed to get as much food, ammunition, and supplies as possible to the front line while keeping output at full throttle here at home. This meant that there were no luxuries, and often only the bare necessities in our everyday lives. This sense of sacrifice and patriotism affected everyone; it was common for millions of families to invite servicemen to their homes on weekends. Drivers never passed up a hitchhiking serviceman on the highway. It seemed that everyone was involved in some part of patriotic activity, and this common bond permeated our thinking.

During this time in California, communication with our family back in Oklahoma and Texas was mainly by mail; it was nearly impossible to make long-distance telephone calls. In emergencies, the usual method of communication was by telegram, which was delivered to your home by a Western Union messenger on a bicycle. Needless to say, families dreaded telegrams, because so many came from the War Department and began "We regret to inform you...." These were the notices of the deaths of servicemen and women, or reports of their having gone missing in action.

When a knock came at our door late in the day of October 24, 1943, and we saw a Western Union man, we expected the worst, but it was not about Dad. However, an equally devastating telegram informed us that my brother, Wendell, had died the day before. Further, the telegram stated that his funeral would be held the next week in Oklahoma City. My father was in England and could not return; my stepmother, my two half-sisters, and I were in Fairfax, and it was not possible to find transportation to Oklahoma, nor could we have afforded to travel there for the funeral. We were in shock, frustrated and bewildered. It was impossible to get a phone call through to Oklahoma, so we were left without the details of his death.

It was not until my father returned from England that I learned that my brother had committed suicide—a horrible ending for a life of great promise. At seventeen, Wendell was set to graduate from Classen High School in Oklahoma City and attend the University of Oklahoma in pre-med, with the goal of becoming a doctor. He was deferred from the draft because of his educational plans, and his future looked bright. But that was only one side of the story; Wendell had also internalized far too much pain to see the positive possibilities. The years of family strife, my mother's mental illness, the absence of my father and me, and his feelings of loneliness and isolation were too much for him to bear.

On that Sunday morning when my grandparents realized that Wendell wasn't home, they first thought he might have spent the night with a friend and then gone on to church. At church, my grandmother encountered a classmate of Wendell's, Louis Trost, and she asked him if he had seen Wendell. Louis said he had seen Wendell the night before, just as he left the dance.

Louis was probably the last person to see him alive. After leaving the dance that Saturday night, Wendell went home, took out his .22 rifle, went to a vacant lot across the street from Grandmother Hall's house, and shot himself. His body was discovered Sunday afternoon.

My brother's death took its toll on all of the family, but most heavily on me and my cousin Wayne. Wendell and Wayne were the same age and had experienced the same closeness that my cousin Jane and I had shared. I imagined that Wayne—like me—would forever wonder what he could have done to prevent the tragedy. I knew that he was haunted by the memories of Wendell's depression and apparent hopelessness—thoughts that were also to remain with me every day of my life.

As much as I missed my brother, the loss instilled in me an even greater drive to make something meaningful of myself, and to apply those lessons from the book of Mark and from life—which

Karl Olson, 14; David, 13; Olson home, Fairfax, California, Spring 1944

The bus ride took more than twenty-four hours. The poorly paved, switch-back-laced asphalt roadway over the mountainous terrain from northern California to the Oregon border took its toll on me: motion sickness. The bus ride seemed to last forever as we twisted our way through the Redwood Forest, rolled past the coastal bluffs leading to Portland, crossed the Washington State line, and made our way east to Walla Walla.

Now the immediate family was together. We remained in Walla Walla for two weeks before Dad was discharged. We left Walla Walla in August, with Dad driving my stepmother, sisters—Ann and Nancy —and me on a circuitous route to Oklahoma City. We wound our way through Wyoming, the Rocky Mountains of Colorado, and the wheat lands of western Kansas, emerging into the open spaces of Oklahoma. The conversations in our car were memorable, with Dad's recollections of his time in England. He told us that the British referred to their dear ones as "George," as a loving recognition of the monarchy. George became the new nickname for my stepmother; she kept it for the rest of her life.

The ten days of bumpy asphalt two-lane highways without air conditioning ended in the humid, hundred-degree heat that bore down on Oklahoma City. Dad was home from the war, and a new family era began.

Golden Times

In 1944, the Allies in World War II were gaining the upper hand worldwide. The Japanese were being defeated in the South Pacific. The island-hopping forces of the United States, Australia, New Zealand, and the other Allies moved steadily toward the ultimate target of Japan. In the European theatre of operations, General Dwight Eisenhower and his staff were directing the Allied forces as they moved steadily into Europe after the successful landing at Normandy on D-Day, June 6, 1944. The Lend-Lease Operation enabling Russia to receive the war materials necessary to thwart the Germans on the eastern front was in full swing, and although some-what unpopular in the congress during this period, it was depleting the German's will to fight.

On my return to Oklahoma, I was startled by the number of homes we passed where the flags with a single star were displayed in the windows, indicating that that family had lost a relative in the war. I was so proud to be an Oklahoman and see the same shared sacrifice I had also witnessed in California; in my 80 years, I have never seen the country more united—and the divisions more blurred—than at this time. The daily dispatches through the summer of 1944 and into the fall were indicative of the victory that lay ahead in 1945. A kindred spirit of determination felt throughout the Allied nations was a part of the daily prayers.

The public fears from that dark day of December 1941, through the disaster at Corregidor, the culmination of the Japanese conquest of the Philippines, were now memories—replaced by the victorious accomplishments at Midway, Wake Island, and Guadalcanal in the Pacific, and the unprecedented heroism of the Allied forces on the D-Day invasion of Europe. This patriotism swept the nation, and Oklahoma did its part. The Naval Training Station of Norman, Oklahoma, was a beehive of activity, with aviators training for duty, along with the artillery school at Fort Sill, the advanced Air Corps facility at Enid, and many other installations across the state.

All of these facilities gave the (normal) commerce of Oklahoma a tremendous economic shot in the arm, but the granddaddy of all installations, which eventually would employ nearly 40% of the work force in Oklahoma, was Tinker Air Force Base, a giant maintenance facility in Oklahoma City. The congressional influence of Senators Robert S. Kerr and Mike Monroney, Representatives Tom Steed and Carl Albert, and the other members of the Oklahoma delegation guaranteed Oklahomans a new lease on life after the terrible deprivation of the 1930's dust bowl and the Great Depression.

Our family in Oklahoma did its part. My cousin Wayne joined the Naval Pre-Flight Program in the fall of 1944, and the family went to the Oklahoma City Union train station to see him off. We all felt great pride and admiration as Wayne headed east to his first duty station. My father looked every bit the warrior home from service as he stood tall and straight, as if at attention, and waved as Wayne boarded the train. In my mind's eye, I could see Dad in his dress uniform—olive jacket, pink trousers, his captain's bars gleaming in the sun. How I wished he had worn his uniform that day! The pride on Dad's face radiating his love of family and country was so inspiring that my heart welled up; it was a moment I will never forget.

I spent the remaining summer days of 1944 getting reacquainted with friends, particularly with my dearest friend, Jim Webster, who still lived just four doors from our home. The work at the Pepsi plant made the time pass quickly, and before I realized it, fall had arrived. I re-enrolled at Taft Junior High as a ninth-grader. That fall semester was another transition in the molding process for my interest in and excitement about government.

Jim Webster, one of the most popular students at Taft Junior High, was elected president of the student council in the fall semester of 1944. Jim was good-looking, affable, and fun-loving, and he had the most sound reasoning for a fourteen-year-old that you could imagine. His friends at Linwood Grade School—friends who now came from Cleveland Grade School and the other surrounding grade schools—rallied to support him. For me, it was a chance to work for his election, get better acquainted with his friends, and outline a plan to run for that post myself in the spring. The rules limited Jim to just one term; as a result, I ran for the second-semester student-council president with Jim as my manager, and I was easily elected. Another helpful factor was the support of my cousin Jane Hall; she was very popular and widely acquainted with our classmates.

Taft Junior High, to us graduates, has treasured memories of first dances, first dates, first serious crushes, corsages purchased from Bill and Irene's Flower Shop on 23rd Street, fountain drinks and school supplies from the adjacent Veazey's Drug Store, and dreams of high school to come. Our teachers introduced us to such activities as woodworking, typing, advanced math, mandatory PE for both sexes, and other intellectual and physical stimuli that helped us through the difficult and awkward mid-teen years.

My cousin Jane and I were fortunate, because her brother Wayne and my brother, Wendell, had both gone through Taft four years before; many of the teachers remembered them, and were very glad to see other members of the Hall family in the student body. And when I got elected student council president in the spring of 1945, my second significant experience with student government, I gained key understandings in leadership: At the top of the list was the importance of setting clear goals. Next came the need to build coalitions for achieving those goals. And last, but certainly not least, was an early appreciation for the art of compromise.

The contributions that Jim Webster had made to my future dreams in reacquainting me with the students at Taft and managing the campaign for student-council president were more than just an act of friendship; it was an educational process. Thanks to his teaching attributes, patience, and people skills, my training flourished. I now had more confidence that my ultimate dream of the Oklahoma governorship might actually be possible. I never shared that dream in those days with anyone other than my most intimate family members and friends, but having made that decision in the days at Fairfax School in California, I was almost daily aware of what I wanted to do with my life.

The 1945 school year ended on a high note with good grades, a summer job coming up at the Pepsi-Cola plant, and the excitement of entering Classen High School as a sophomore in the fall. But entering high school in September brought many challenges. First up was competitive football. I was 6'2" and weighed 155 pounds, considerably underweight by today's standards. Coach Leo Higby gave me a tryout as left tackle in scrimmages against the upperclassmen. It was a physical disaster.

At the end of the first week of practice, I attempted to bring down a senior fullback, and the result was a torn cartilage in my left knee. As I limped off the field, I felt sorely disappointed and unhappy that I would have to tell my father that this injury might well end my football ambitions. God moves in mysterious ways, however, and that cartilage damage proved to be the door-opener for later athletic achievements that were really beyond my dreams at that time.

I rode the bus to Classen throughout September; in October, I purchased a Cushman, a two-wheeled motor scooter, with assistance from my father—on one condition. Dad put the proposition to me late one night when I was studying my Latin lesson at the kitchen table. Sitting across from me, he said, "I've decided to help you with the money for the scooter—with the condition that you put a Pepsi logo sign on each side."

"Wow," I said. "I'll do it."

Dad reached across the table and said, "Let's shake on it."

I eagerly grabbed his hand and shook it firmly. "Thanks, Dad," I said. "It's really going to help me with work on the weekends and basketball practice."

Smiling, Dad rose and said goodnight, and I returned to my studies. But within a few minutes, I found that I was so excited that I couldn't concentrate with all the thoughts of my new freedom and mobility. It was hard to go to sleep that night!

Other challenges in the fall of 1945 included the more rigorous academics of high school compared to junior high and grade school. I was determined to be as strong a student as possible, so I enrolled in a series of college preparatory classes, including the start of three years of Latin.

On the social scene, high school was very exciting, with a student body of 1,800. On my radar was another election, coming my way in the fall of 1945: sophomore class president. I used the skills that I had learned at Taft Junior High and Fairfax and won the race. I was riding high—for the time being.

As the sophomore year continued, I joined DeMolay, a Mason-sponsored young men's organization that provided a ready-made group of new friends and mentors. I continued working part-time at the Pepsi-Cola plant to earn my spending money, pay the cost of the Cushman motor scooter, and save money for what I hoped would be an automobile in future months. All of these activities made that high school year the fastest of any of my school years that I could remember up to that time.

But the cartilage damage to my left knee became so painful that an operation was necessary during the Christmas holiday. I was disabled for almost six weeks, and lost three full weeks of school. Nevertheless, despite being out of school for three weeks, by spring I was back on my feet and competing in basketball practice for a spot on the starting five of the following year's team.

However, those three weeks away from school, even though I kept up with my lessons, made a big problem worse for me. This problem was geometry; for some reason, I just could not get it. I went to my geometry teacher, Mrs. Grace Deupree, to ask for special help. She kept me many sessions after school and gave me an opportunity to take the exams and do the work that I had missed; the result was that with her careful and thoughtful teaching, I finally got an A in geometry for the semester. I will be indebted to her forever for taking her time after school to bring me through the weeks that I had missed, and for putting me on an even footing with the rest of the class. Her caring example taught me a life lesson in patience that I later used in my Air Force teaching, and in my service as an adjunct professor of law at the University of Tulsa.

The summer of 1946, going into my junior year, Dad taught me to drive a stick-shift automobile in preparation for my sixteenth birthday in October. I was absolutely addicted to the automobile, and to the thoughts of the freedom that it would bring me. I worked full-time that summer and part-time in the fall, saving all of my money. While I may have been learning about patience, I was a very normal teenager in other respects, and had zero patience when it came to wanting to drive my own car.

That desire overpowered my good judgment one evening when Wally Sorrels, a friend, was spending the night with me; we decided to secretly borrow my father's car and take a little joy ride. Of course, we planned to return it to the garage before anyone knew that we had taken it. At about half-past midnight, with the family in deep sleep, I took my father's car keys. Wally and I sneaked from my bedroom out to the garage, quietly opened the garage door, and silently rolled my father's car down the driveway onto May Avenue. We pointed it south, with one steering and the other pushing, rolled it a half block, started it up, and took off—with me at the wheel.

What we did not know was that the Sinclair gas station on the corner diagonally southwest of our house had been the subject of a recent burglary. Within two blocks, a police car that had been in the shadows watching the gas station gave chase, turned on his siren, and pulled us to the curb. We were arrested and taken to the Oklahoma City Municipal Jail. I told the officers we had taken my father's car.

The police officer called my father. My father, in a wisdom I would only later understand, told the police officer just to leave us in the holding cell until the next morning. He said he'd come down on his way to work to see about getting me out.

Wally's dad, Dr. Harry Sorrels, did the same, so we sat in that cold holding cell, with its concrete walls and its conspicuous graffiti, for six hours, contemplating the fate that we would suffer the next day.

We were lucky. Our fathers arrived at about the same time the next morning, and the police released us into their custody with the admonition that if this happened again, criminal charges would be brought.

My father and I had one of the most frank and disturbing discussions that we had ever had up to this time. My father's anger in explaining the gravity of my actions—for nothing more than a joy ride—certainly got my attention; I felt my teenage bravado disappearing with every word that he said. It was an experience I would never forget, and one I would never repeat. On the spot, I swore to my father, "You don't have to worry. I'll never try a shenanigan like that again."

Wally suffered a similar dressing-down, and we formed a pact never to be involved in anything like that again. In fact, the seeds of my passion for law and order began their germination that morning; I resolved that from then on, riding the Cushman scooter was the only option for me—until I was legally allowed to drive.

Dad was a tough, stern disciplinarian, but he did not hold grudges. Six weeks later, he resumed my driving lessons.

The summer of work at the Pepsi plant, the hot days, assisting at home with the yard chores, and the preparation and anticipation of competing in basketball in the fall of 1946, all hyped my enthusiasm for a return to school. I had such a marvelous year as a sophomore that my hopes were high for pursuing the election to junior-class president. School started, and the election was set; I began to campaign, but I had the attitude that because I had been so successful as a sophomore, perhaps I had earned the right to be the junior-class president without putting in the kind of work and effort that the election demanded. That mindset led to a crushing defeat; my sophomore-class victory had given me such a political high that it expanded my ego to a point that I should have recognized a danger sign. To put it another way, I just got too big for my britches. As tough a blow to my ego as it was, I deserved it; it was a real-life lesson that I would never forget.

The election winner, Robert Wood, ran an excellent campaign of just being himself, with no exaggerated idea of his importance. That election smack-down, combined with my experience in the joy-riding incident that summer, had sobered me to the fact that nothing good in my life was going to come without hard work, following the rules, and proper preparation.

Knowing this, I decided my junior year at Classen High School would be my year of redemption of spirit and attitude. The plan had three parts: a concentration on academics, a focus on improving my basketball skills, and a commitment to becoming a better person, with more interest in others. I set a series of goals to complete this transformation; the first was to try to learn the names of everyone in my high school, if possible during the fall of 1946 and the spring of 1947. I knew then, as I know now, that there is nothing that demonstrates that you care about people more than learning and using their names. I set about this task religiously each day. I told no one, and worked on this goal as if it were a classroom project.

By the end of the fall of 1946, I had mastered over 800 of the 1,800 names. The second semester, with the pattern formed, the work became much easier, and by April of 1947 I knew the first names of approximately 1,500 students in Classen High School.

My second goal was to prepare in the spring of 1947 for a run at the student council presidency for the '47–'48 school year. Academically, I continued pressing hard for the grade-point average I needed for college acceptance, working hard in math and Latin. History and English were my favorite subjects, and the dedicated teachers gave me inspiration. Lucille Willoughby, my Latin teacher, was middle-aged, with short, swept-back red hair, a slender nose, and a fair complexion lightly sprinkled with freckles. Armed with a very sharp mind that occasionally turned sarcastic, she demanded the best—and rewarded hard work. Her courses helped me more than any others in my later law-school studies. Her vocabulary-building mirrored my mother's early teaching.

Clara Meyer, a black-haired, graying woman, was another favorite. She taught civics with gusto; she made you understand the subject's importance. My clearest memory is her admonition that one of the great moments in life is when you discover that you have had "an original thought." She said that few people achieve this dream, but it will provide one of life's greatest moments.

Ms. Meyer bolstered my desire to enter politics.

Mrs. Elaine Tucker was the most exciting teacher I can remember in my high-school years. She was effervescent, full of enthusiasm, and attractive. Her manner was more in tune with students, and she drew out the best in nearly everyone. She taught speech and inspired so many of us. Later in the 1990s, I saw Mrs. Tucker several times while she was living in Casa Ma'ana, a retirement facility on the shores of the Pacific in La Jolla, California. My last meeting with her, when she was 92, was at lunch at Casa Ma ana. She had invited Bob Witty, a classmate living in San Diego; Carolyn Rexroat Warner, another classmate living in Phoenix, Arizona; and me as her guests.

Carolyn was a special favorite of Mrs. Tucker's, since she had won the national extemporaneous-speech competition during her senior year at Classen. Carolyn achieved fame in Arizona as State Superintendent of Schools and as a two-time Democratic nominee for governor. The author of many books, she is a national leader in education and a sought-after speaker.

Bob had a distinguished career in journalism as a writer, a newspaper editor, and a key executive at *The San Diego Union Tribune* and the Copley News Service before his retirement. He later headed the San Diego Historical Society.

In preparation for the 1946 fall basketball season, I tried out for the varsity, but didn't make it. I did earn a spot on the junior-varsity team. I was still skinny, the same weight and height, with a fierce determination eventually to make the varsity team. I dedicated my junior year to hours of practice and scrimmage against the varsity team. Coach Carroll Smelser gave us the opportunity to develop experience, agility, and smoothness; his basketball acumen was sound and simple: tough defense first. Most of us were tall, skinny, clumsy young men. Coach Smelser's rigorous calisthenics, rope-jumping, and defense drills helped overcome our inelegance.

Oddly, those basketball exercises and scrimmages helped us learn something none of us ever dreamed of: ballroom dancing. With many positive influences and resources for winning in the end, I rebounded quickly from my earlier election disappointment. The future again shone with possibilities.

In the spring of 1946, President Truman was in the throes of planning the post-war recovery for Europe and Japan. The Marshall Plan was set to revitalize a major part of the European economy. The realignment of industry in the United States from wartime to peacetime production was in full swing. The United Nations charter was signed on June 26, 1946, at the conclusion of the UN Conference on International Organization, and first implemented in the following October. Life was moving fast in America; President Truman seized the railroads, avoiding a national strike, and desegregated the US Armed Forces. The year ended with the premiere of Frank Capra's classic Christmas movie, *It's A Wonderful Life*.

In October of 1946, I turned sixteen, and my dream of owning a car was about to come true. My father was retiring his 1937 two-door Ford coupe with an 85-horsepower flat-head, V8 engine, with a stick shift. I used my savings and sold my Cushman motor scooter to buy it. My dad would not contribute to the maintenance or the insurance of the car, but because of my work with the family Pepsi-Cola Bottling Company, he agreed that I could visit the fuel pump at the plant and get gasoline free of charge. He allowed me to insert my car into the line of trucks when they were repainted in the spring of 1947, and my car became the same blue color as the Pepsi-Cola trucks.

The freedom the car gave to me in that winter of 1946 and the spring of 1947 was unbounded. Because of my joy-riding incident in the summer of 1946, I was more careful behind the wheel, with one exception: my propensity to tailgate. A few smashed grilles soon stopped that practice.

I never had a serious accident in that car, and I tried to use it for as many good activities as possible. I volunteered to the front office at the high school to use my car for student emergencies. Many times during the year, I was called from class to drive an ailing student home. I also volunteered my car for junior-varsity basketball trips to help Coach Smeller meet his budget. I was proud of his confidence in having four team players ride with me to those games while the JV coach transported the others. I took home other players who didn't have transportation after practice each day. This developed a great camaraderie among all of us on the JV team. It was a good omen of things to come.

The basketball, academics, and working at the Pepsi plant on the weekends cut into my social life, but I was still able to go to most of the dances and date several girls during that school year. I don't recall any strong romances, although many of the girls I dated became lifelong friends. Maybe it was the effort of remembering names or the fact that we've stayed in touch, but these many years later, I can summon their full maiden names: Pat Harper, Charlene Elliott, Joanne Denman, Sally Lou Wallis, Mary James, Pat Oller, and Patsy Bartlett.

Every one of these girls contributed in a special way to my store of knowledge about women, my social behavior, and, most importantly, how to treat others going through the same teenage experience.

In January 1947, with the academics always Number One and basketball Number Two, I began preparation in earnest for Target Number Three: the election for student council president in April. It was then that I learned much more about coalitions, about campaign preparation, and even the rudimentary parts of campaign finance. In designing the strategy for that election, I tried to get as many interest groups in high school involved in my campaign as possible. The number-one prize in this quest was the Classen High School band.

I had an advantage, because my cousin Jane was the singer in our high-school dance band—The Sooners—that played at all of our school functions. With Jane's influence, and the members of her band helping me, we got the support of the Classen High School band. In fact, at the assembly preceding the vote for student-council president, many band members appeared on stage and played as a part of my skit and speech before the student body.

I had enlisted the help of our sign-painter at the Pepsi Company to help me make campaign posters, using the blank side of discarded old Pepsi cardboard signs that we could later put in the hallways of the school. We painted "David Hall For Student Council President" in red, white, and blue on the blank side. After school, during January, February, and March, when I didn't have basketball practice, I would go to the plant and work with Lonnie Crawford, a talented African-American graphic artist and our sign-painter, and prepare the stockpile of signs that I was going to need for the election.

At the same time, I continued to hone my project of learning names; by this time, in March 1947, I was at the threshold of 1,500. By voting day in April, I told myself I would complete memorizing 1,600 first names of fellow students. Between classes, I practiced naming the students in the hallway as I met them; I did this every hour, five days a week. I devoted at least a couple of hours a week to reviewing the names, checking pictures in previous yearbooks to be sure I had them right. In less than thirty days, I finally reached my 1,600 goal.

My opponent for the student-council president, Arthur Swanson, was a student I had known since grade school. Arthur was a very good student, and I did not take him lightly as an opponent. The assembly before the election was the major test and pinnacle for both of our campaigns.

The popularity on the radio of the song "Open The Door, Richard" gave us a theme for my skit and speech during the assembly. We constructed a movable doorframe and door that we placed on stage, leading to the podium. In the opening segment of our campaign skit, Pat Williams opened the door to the strains of the song.

I followed him and took my place at the podium. Behind me there were more than 100 students in support. They wore jerseys, sweaters, letterman jackets, and coats denoting their various organizations—the Honor Society, the Courtesy Club, the Classettes, the Blue Jackets, and the athletes' Big O club. These individual students had endorsed me, although there were no formal endorsements from their organizations.

I had asked my friend John Brett's father, Judge John A. Brett, to help me write my speech. Judge Brett, a seasoned politician, gave some wonderful suggestions. The speech was not remarkable, except for one line that drew the greatest laugh, and the most applause of any line in any of the speeches given that day: *Classen has produced students—who have produced.* The sexual awareness of all of us at that age made that the laugh of the assembly.

After the assembly, we voted, and it was a victory day for me. I received a solid majority of all votes cast, thanks to the efforts of so many friends. After the vote, we had to turn in our campaign expenditures, as we had a two-hundred-dollar limit on campaign spending. Jack Merritt, who later became a four-star general and the United States representative to NATO, was my campaign finance chairman. Jack had done an excellent job preparing the reports correctly, and he kept the campaign within our budget. I would later learn, however, that there was quite a bit of uncertainty as to whether we should include the cost of all those signs I had made at the Pepsi plant, since we didn't actually put out any money for them.

It was my first encounter with "soft" corporate campaign contributions.

The other offices were filled with excellent students: Thornton Wright, the vice-president; Dorothy Darrough Logan, secretary; Jim Harbert, treasurer; and Robert Keller, parliamentarian. That election also taught me to be gracious to the losers, and involve them in the future. My first appointment was to name my number-one opponent, Arthur Swanson, to be chief justice of our Classen High School Court.

The spring of 1947 ended on that high note of the student-council election—plus we had a successful junior varsity basketball season. My grade-point average went up in my junior year, thanks to hard work, dedication, and the discipline to doing things the right way.

The academic year of 1946–47 was also a revelation to me on the issue of labor unions. I decided in my civics course to write a research paper on jurisdictional strikes, and chose the New York Stage Hands Union as the subject of my paper. I got an education on the ins and outs of the union activities, both good and bad.

This was on my mind the following summer because I was about to become a truck driver. I read extensively on the Teamsters Union in preparation for my work. Although we were not unionized at the Pepsi-Cola plant, in years past there had been attempt to organize our drivers. My grandfather was opposed to unions, and developed a plan to avoid them. My father, my uncle, and my grandfather sold the trucks and the routes to individual drivers, who then became independent contractors instead of direct employees. My inclination was in a different direction, but at that time I never voiced my feelings—even though from the start of my research on unions, I believed collective bargaining was good for all concerned.

The independent-driver plan applied to all routes except for the 500-some-odd stops of the African-American district of Oklahoma City. The company retained that district because of lagging sales and fierce competition over the years. My father asked me if I wanted to accept the challenge of this route. I said yes, so in the summer of 1947, I became the route salesman and truck driver for that district. Segregation still existed in the schools, and *de facto* segregation was still extant in many other parts of the city's daily life. I had never worked closely with African-Americans; the extent of my experience was with our sign-painter, Lonnie Crawford.

After learning the route, I decided that I was going to do my best to sell to each and every one of the more than 500 retailers. When I began, we were selling to less than 80% of these prospects; during that summer I used every bit of salesmanship and business acumen that I could muster to close the gap on that remaining 20%. I never got them all sold, although I came within five of my target number. By summer's end, I was servicing 531 of the 536 diners, convenience stores, groceries, and filling stations on that route.

The last five holdouts were all diners, and I made it a practice to eat in one of those last five prospects at least once every two weeks, but I just couldn't turn them around. That summer's experience was a valuable test of discipline and tenacity to reach a goal.

Driving these routes in the summers of 1947 and 1948, I made many fast friends in the black community. Years later, when I ran for governor, I carried many of those African-American districts by ten-to-one margins.

I banked the extra money I made as a route salesman in preparation for my senior year in high school, budgeting for clothing, maintenance of the automobile, and insurance. The extra money gave me a very good social life, too, for movies and dates in the summer of 1947. I was looking forward a much more active social life in the fall and spring.

As the company painted the Pepsi trucks late that year, I put my '37 Ford in line for another paint job. The result was that the car looked almost brand-new; it had white plastic wheel rims about four inches wide that looked like whitewall tires, a pretty spiffy look for a ten-year-old two-door coupe.

The fall of 1947 brought the student-council activities and the start of basketball practice. My social life was nil in September, but by late October, I had made the varsity basketball team. Our schedule began in early December 1947 and would lead to distinction for our team. Coach Smeller knew his talent; he had developed a team that could win the state championship, and by late January of 1948, we were in hot pursuit of that goal. By February, our hopes were even higher for advancing to the state playoffs. Victories over rivals like Northeast High, Capitol Hill, and Central High gave us confidence and courage to persevere.

Coach Smelser's discipline was paying off. We knew if we followed the plays, tightened our defense, and played with passion, our dreams might be fulfilled. It was not by chance that we were upbeat; our starting five of Pete Darcey, John Reddell, Guy Fuller, Bob Moser, and Pat Williams were an imposing force. The remaining seniors, Nate Graham, Jim Gonders, and I, contributed in every game. Our juniors, Tom Brett, Dale Jones, and Cal Stewart, were a significant presence.

Those were the days of underhand free throws. Coach Smelser would tolerate no other method; if you tried anything else, he'd jerk you out of the game. The same was true of most one-handed shots, unless you were within a prescribed distance from the basket. The three-point play did not exist, and the shots from the perimeter were normally two-handed set shots.

Pat Williams was our best two-handed shot-maker. Peter Darcy, our six-five center, provided the pivot and dominated most of the rebounding against other centers in our games. The intense high-school rivalry between Classen and Central High School near downtown Oklahoma City was legendary. To ease tensions before games, delegations were exchanged for assemblies. This worked most times, but one of my visits to Central High School was quite dicey when a rabid fan tossed an egg at our delegation. Bad aim saved an ugly incident. Later that week, we beat Central in a close game.

In March, our basketball team had advanced to play in the State Finals at the Civic Center auditorium in Oklahoma City, on a wooden stage erected especially for basketball. We were thrilled to play at this venue; the All College Men's Tournament was played there over the Christmas holidays. That was the good news. The bad news was that the floor had a tendency to buckle in spots, and gave you a sense of riding the waves. We had a big asset in our senior center, Pete Darcey, who was a very good shot-maker and one of the tallest high-school players in Oklahoma.

Our path to the title game was not easy. In the regional playoffs, we beat a tough Edmond team by only one point, then clobbered Oklahoma City North East by fourteen—but we only squeaked past El Reno by a point. In the state playoffs, we faced Muskogee and Ada to get to the finals, and we beat both by substantial margins.

Our opponent in the state championship game was Tulsa Central High School, one of the largest schools in the state, with a student body of about 2,200. The coach for the Tulsa team was Grady Skillern; he had some definite ideas about the way in which the championship should be handled, and he refused to allow his starting five to be photographed before the championship game. He thought that it was bad luck. Coach Smeller was just the opposite; he allowed the photographs.

We developed a ritual of our own on the path to the playoffs, hoping it might bring us some good luck. We wanted to offset our big-city-school image and show people that we were just ordinary guys who could well have been from Catoosa or Pawhuska, instead of Tulsa or Oklahoma City. All members of our team agreed to wear bib overalls during the playoffs; moreover, we would not wash them until we had won the championship. We wore these four to five weeks, and they became so stiff you could stand them in a corner. We wore them to school every day for four weeks. We did change shirts, but those blue-denim, patch-pocket, drop-leaf overalls were our trademark.

That glorious night arrived: We were playing for the Class-A championship of the state of Oklahoma. (Schools were divided on basis of student population into three classes, A, B, and C.) It was a great honor just to be on a Class-A team.

We were hungry for victory! The game seesawed back and forth. In the last seconds, a runaway lay-up by Tulsa Central made the score 31–30. Pete Darcey was slow coming back up the court, and was still near the Tulsa Central basket when John Rendell took the ball out with just seconds to play. He passed the ball full-court to Pete, who deftly caught the pass, turned, dribbled once, and made a clean lay-up. The buzzer sounded, and the game ended; we had won 32 to 31, thanks to Rendell's dramatic heads-up pass. The current NCAA finals were no more thrilling than that early spring night in the capital city where a young player's daring gave each of us a lifetime of memories. Our team stormed the court, congratulating Pete and John and all the starters. The night was ours.

Back: **Nate Graham, Bob Moser, Pete Darcey, Pat Williams, Guy Fuller, Coach Smelser.** Middle row:
David Hall, Jim Gonders, John Reddell, Dale Jones. Front row: **Cal Stewart, Tom Brett**

Photo courtesy of **Jim Smelser**

Oklahoma City Classen High School State Championship
basketball team, "Comets," March 1948

Our plans after the championship game included gathering at the
home of cheerleader Verna Lou Frye, whose mother had prepared
hors d'oeuvres and a large cake commemorating our championship.
Mrs. Frye, being a realist, had formed the words *State Champions* on
a set of lift-off wires so that she could make the cake fit the occasion,
win or lose. We chided her for such little faith.

The camaraderie of that team was unbelievable; for years afterward, many of us not only stayed close friends, but in some cases
became business associates. Pat Williams, one of the stars of our
team, became a law associate in Tulsa from 1968 to 1970.

A poignant story from that team involved Bill Pitts, a starting
forward until the middle of our senior year. Bill had to leave the
team and take a job to help with his family's finances. He shouldered
that responsibility with enthusiasm and passion, just as he played.
He worked full-time and helped care for his sister and his parents
while completing his high-school studies. This was the greatest sacrifice by anyone on our team. We all respected Bill's true grit.

In my political career, many of the team members made appearances at rallies, helped in canvassing the state, made speeches for me, and were very effective in helping me to get known across Oklahoma.

After the basketball championship, the next major event in my senior year was the awards ceremony at graduation. I received the history award and the best citizen award. In looking back now on those three years at Classen, I felt more like I was in a preparatory school for college than I ever could have imagined in a public-school setting. I think all of us who graduated in the '30s, the '40s, and the early '50s from Classen High School felt the same way.

My summer work was pure joy: I had my Pepsi route back for three months, and I focused like a laser to try to sell those last five customers who had eluded me the prior summer. I wound up signing four of them.

The social part of summer was punctuated with fraternity rush parties for the University of Oklahoma in Norman. I was concerned about how I could afford to join, but I felt that my savings would make it possible, if I could find a job as well. I talked it over with Dad, and although money was extremely tight, he agreed to contribute the fifty dollars per month in rent he was receiving from a studio apartment he and I had built adjacent to the south side of our garage. But he said he would do this only for my freshman year.

In September 1948, I joined Phi Gamma Delta, with a pledge class of twenty other freshmen. What tipped the scales for me was the fraternity's emphasis on academics; the other freshman pledges were serious students with outstanding high school records. It was a prophetic move; just ahead of me, in August 1948, a brash, dynamic alumnus of this chapter graduated from law school, beginning a spectacular career—J. Howard Edmondson. Later, as Tulsa County Attorney, his excellent record of achievement opened the way for him to be elected the youngest governor in the history of Oklahoma at age 33. What a role model he was for my ambitions!

Classes began in September; my path was pre-law, with a major in political science and a minor in history. My budget was tight, so I immediately began to look for part-time work. I landed a job collecting cleaning bills in my fraternity house, and I waited tables in our fraternity house for board. But it would take a third job to cover all my college expenses.

Walking into the memorial student-union building one morning, I looked up at its big, striking clock to see the time. Right then the idea came to me like the proverbial light bulb in my head: How much more studying could students do if they didn't have to go out for food while hitting the books late at night? *That's it,* I thought to myself. *I'll sell hamburgers after hours to the students on campus!*

I found a small, one-man diner on the east side of Norman, where I talked the owner into selling me the burgers for fifteen cents apiece; then I resold them for twenty-five cents. I made a good profit, selling as many as fifty burgers a night. Baskets lowered from dormitory and sorority-house windows gave me access to my customers. I was lucky that McDonald's was not a national chain in those days!

However, the owner of the diner had a bit of a drinking problem, and on some nights I found him in no condition to flip the burgers. On those occasions, I became chef and salesman!

To achieve my goal of making a name for myself on campus, there were certain important requirements. First, there was my attire: I had very few clothes for school and dress occasions, but with careful planning and drawing from my savings, I managed with seven dress shirts and slacks to fill the week. I had one dress suit for special events, and the hamburger profits enabled me to buy a sport coat.

Blind dates each weekend gave me a chance to meet girls from across the campus, as well as those in my classes. I had precious little money for dates, but two things helped this endeavor; the fraternity allowed our dates to share the Sunday-evening meal at no cost, and the lounge of the fraternity house had a terrazzo floor for dancing.

Then there was the prestige that came from having wheels. Freshman were not allowed to have cars on campus, so my '37 Ford had to go; however, I was permitted to replace it with a panel truck for my business. For those girls who had the courage to ride in a very old Plymouth panel truck, I had the use of those wheels.

Third—and what I wanted most of all—was to distinguish myself on the basketball court. I still had dreams of playing college basketball. I had no scholarship offers, so in October 1948 I tried out as a walk-on for the Oklahoma University team. Coach Bruce Drake was swift and direct in acknowledging my potential. "Hall," he said, "you have a lot of spirit. You're fast, and you might be able to red-shirt and practice for four years—but you are never going to get to play in a game."

My dreams were dashed—but there was a benefit beneath my disappointment. The truth is that I could not have maintained the kinds of grades important to me if I had made the team. During those first months, I developed a disciplined approach to classes, study, work, and social life. I outlined every hour of every day, including Sunday, with an annotated list of activities. I was amazed that with all that I was doing, I still had time to compete in intramural sports—that was the advantage of discipline. I kept this same plan during all four years of my undergraduate work; I did not even go to a movie on weeknights until my last semester.

Under the pressure of my schedule, I had to give up the hamburger business. The diner owner almost cried, as we had become good friends. I also had to give up the old Plymouth panel truck with the end of my delivery business.

To replace that income, I got a job selling clothes for McCall's Men's Store, the best campus men's-clothing establishment. McCall's had two locations in Norman: one downtown and one next to campus. It was a great job that paid seventy-five cents an hour, and I had a great boss. Quinton Hampton, a prince of a man in his late forties and an expert on college clothing, ran the place. Fair-minded, decisive, and honest, he made working there a joy. I learned the clothing sales business—and perhaps more important, how to dress: no more yellow socks! In addition, I learned how to run a steam press to earn extra money. Dean Rinehart, the son of Oklahoma State Senator Jim Rinehart, worked alongside me, operating the steam press. I will always be grateful to Quinton for hiring me for those three-and-a-half years.

In November of 1948, I witnessed the greatest upset victory in the history of presidential races in the United States. President Harry S. Truman, counted out by every poll, by all the metropolitan papers, and by the national news commentators, won a stunning upset victory over Thomas Dewey, the Republican nominee who was thought to be a shoo-in. *The Chicago Tribune* even printed their early edition with a banner headline proclaiming Dewey the victor. The Republicans were crestfallen, and the Democrats were jubilant!

In my freshman year, I didn't have a serious girlfriend, but that changed in the fall of 1949 when I met Peggy Marshall, a campus lovely from Norman. By the start of November, we had become an item; we would date that year and all through the 1950 school year. The first time I took Peggy to meet my fraternity house mother was noteworthy. Mrs. Jewel Hale questioned me closely afterward about how luminous Peggy's eyes seemed. Mrs. Hale's inquiry was a discreet yet direct question about whether Peggy took amphetamines, which had begun to be popular in some circles. Taken aback, I assured her that was not the case.

Peggy's eyes were so shiny that they captured your attention. I never took offense at the inquiry, nor did I ever tell Peggy about it. "Aunt Jewel," as we affectionately called her, was concerned with the well-being of all "her boys," helping wherever she could.

But my relationship with Peggy revealed a prejudice I had never before seen in Grandmother Hall. When she learned that Peggy was a Roman Catholic, she told me in no uncertain terms that I was making a mistake in dating her. It was one of the few times I ignored my grandmother—but I had long before decided that religious prejudice would have no place in my life.

I felt that Grandmother Hall's prejudice had developed early in her life, when she lived in a small farming community in North Texas. There, she was exposed to the rumors and misstatements made about the Catholic Church. These included the suspicion that the Catholic Knights of Columbus, one of the largest and most generous of Christian charities, kept firearms in church basements ready to overthrow the US government someday. Among other myths was that the pope in Rome controlled not only the religious rituals and practices, but all facets of Catholics' lives around the world. Bias against Catholics was common throughout the Bible Belt in the South, and persisted through World War II. After the war, the bias against Catholics flared again with the candidacy of John F. Kennedy, when he first appeared on the national scene in 1956. This issue, for the most part, was laid to rest with his election as President in 1960.

My father had no such religious prejudice, but was concerned about Peggy for another reason: He thought that we might marry before we finished our education. I assured him that this would not happen, but I'm not sure he ever believed it.

By the end of my sophomore year, I had raised my grade average considerably, and was in contention for a Phi Beta Kappa Key. I had also begun volunteering for the student-union activities board that coordinated almost all events on campus. During this time I was still active in intramural basketball; whenever I could find the time on a weekend, I played in various small-town basketball tournaments across the state.

There had been a lot of activism on the campus of the University. Of paramount concern was the civil rights issue. During my four years at the University of Oklahoma, 1948 through 1952, I witnessed the beginnings of the national civil-rights movement, and a focus on the rights of minorities in the state of Oklahoma. We were also developing a national awareness that foreign military interventions were not necessarily in the best interests of our country.

Black students were not yet allowed to attend the University of Oklahoma School of Law. After extended litigation through state and federal courts, and segregation-minded shenanigans, the Oklahoma State Legislature created a sham law school at the state's segregated Langston University, the only institution of higher education for African-Americans. The sham law school consisted of one student—with no faculty, no law library, and a bare classroom.

However, the rule of law eventually prevailed, and a female black student was admitted to the OU law school in 1949. Ada Lois Sipuel

Fisher welcomed by most of her classmates—but she was required to sit in a segregated section labeled COLORED. This may seem ludicrous today, but it was a regrettable fact of life then. And when Ada Lois Sipuel Fisher broke the barrier for black admission to the University of Oklahoma School of Law, it led to the complete integration of the university. While it was a significant civil-rights victory, this event, too long delayed, was a source of acute embarrassment for those of us who believed in equal rights at the University of Oklahoma.

The Korean War broke out in June 1950, and a large number of my friends and classmates at the University of Oklahoma were called up for service. Some signed up for the Marine Platoon Leaders School, and others were in the active Army Reserve. Many of these young men were sent to Korea without adequate training and died there in 1951 and 1952.

One of the most memorable days in the spring of 1951 was the address to the joint session of Congress by General Douglas MacArthur, after he had been recalled from the Korean War by President Truman. I can remember as if it were yesterday, sitting in the living room of the fraternity house with the radio turned on, listening to General MacArthur as he painted the picture of the war, spoke about his career, and ended his speech with that most famous quote of his from an old barracks ballad: "Old soldiers never die; they just fade away." This speech moved the hearts and minds of many of us who were enrolled in ROTC, because we knew that if the Korean War continued, we would be called to active duty when we graduated.

In fact, that's exactly what happened to me.

I had been active in support of some Democratic Party candidates growing up as a teenager, although I had never participated in a governor's race. Then, in the spring of 1950, my father became involved in a major way with the Johnston Murray campaign for governor. Murray was the son of Depression-era governor William H. "Alfalfa Bill" Murray. Alfalfa Bill was hands-down our most eccentric and interesting governor; his grazing sheep on the mansion lawn, growing vegetable-garden produce, and such innovations in the governor's private office of chaining visitors' chairs to the floor so that they could not push to the edge of his desk all illustrate his unusual tenure.

Alfalfa Bill was a strong contrast with his more passive and traditional son, whose administration was bland, except for the spirited plans of his wife, Willie. She dreamed of running and winning as the first woman governor of the state—and planned for it. However, it was not to be; it took until November of 2010, and the victory of Mary Fallin, a Republican, for Oklahoma to elect its first female chief executive.

Thanks to Dad's connections in the campaign, I got a summer job working for Murray. I was based in Nowata County, at the Green Funeral Home, the power center for politics in that northeast Oklahoma area. The funeral home also was the Green family residence, and I lived with them. My job was assisting and traveling with an old-time politician who was the classic example of a ward-heeler: Jack Foose. Jack was a 5'7" trim, energetic, mustachioed man in his late forties who loved campaigning—second only to his love of chasing women. I was never sure how many campaigns Jack had worked on, but he gave me valuable insights into many ways of campaigning—some good, some not so good. Jack was constantly telling me "war stories" of his exploits in politics and in his social life. He had one favorite saying about his own physical appearance; he had a rather large backside, and was continually kidded by some of his contemporaries about that ample rear. Jack's answer was always, "You can't drive a spike with a tack hammer." This invariably brought a great laugh from the men, although I never heard him try it out in front of the ladies.

The fall of 1950 came in a hurry. I was unable to campaign after the last week in August, when classes resumed, so I bade farewell to the Green family, to the caskets, and to Jack Foose, who had given me my first lessons in grassroots campaigning in Northeastern Oklahoma. My dad was pleased that the campaign progressed well, and that Johnston Murray was elected Oklahoma's fourteenth governor.

With the election of Murray, my father thought that he would be given a major state job, but as often happens in political affairs, he was relegated to a relatively minor position on the state corporation commission. Johnston Murray infuriated many Oklahomans after his term ended when he authored a scathing account of the problems in Oklahoma in an article published by *The Saturday Evening Post* entitled, "Oklahoma's In A Mess." I wondered why in the dickens he didn't fix those problems while he was governor.

With start of classes in September 1950, I was struck by the reality that in less than two years, the nation would have another presidential race. The hero of the European campaign, the architect of the invasion of Normandy, and the Supreme Allied Commander, Dwight David Eisenhower, had retired from the Army. The Republicans had snared him and were grooming him for the presidency. His likely opponent was Adlai Stevenson, the former governor of Illinois. The race was the highlight of our political-science class discussions.

Those who favored General Eisenhower touted his victory in Europe and his shining military record. Detractors noted his lack of domestic political experience and his authoritative manner.

Proponents of Governor Stevenson praised his record in Illinois, noting the economic and political complexities that he had successfully mastered, and compared his views with FDR's. His opponents characterized him as too far removed from middle-class America, and the problems of the common man. They said even his public speaking voice sounded "snooty." Those criticisms were offset somewhat when an enterprising Flint Michigan newspaper photographer, Bill Gallagher, sneaked a picture of Stevenson showing him sitting in a chair, legs crossed, with the sole of his shoe displaying a large hole—a classic picture. Stevenson lost the election, but Gallagher won a Pulitzer Prize for his photo.

At this point, politics were somewhat on my twenty-year-old mind, but romantic interests dominated my thoughts. The Christmas of 1950 had been a good one, except for a personal calamity, when a department-store mistake produced the worst embarrassment of all time for me and Peggy. I went shopping at a fine women's store in Norman, looking for a gift for Peggy, and bought a beautiful black angora sweater—all the rage at that time. I had it expensively wrapped, took it to her house, and put it under her family's tree. All went well until Christmas day, when she opened her packages with her family gathered around; instead of that black angora sweater, she pulled out an oversized bra and pink panties, probably five sizes too big for her.

Her sister told me later that she just laid them down and started to cry. Of course, I took them back to the clerk and complained loudly about the mistake, but the damage was done—and I'm sure that was the beginning of the end for us. I heard that story played back to me over and over, not only by my friends at college but at my fiftieth class reunion at Classen High School, when one of my classmates, Sed Kennedy, told the story to a group as we met at Frank Robinson's house for a get-together in June 1988!

Meanwhile, in January 1951, I was selected chairman of the Union Activities Board. This board would guide the major campus activities for the year of 1951–'52. I had chaired several committees in past years, and worked hard in leadership positions as a precursor to this promotion. Mary Lou Stubbeman, our director, played a major part in this triumph for me. Besides being a confidence-builder, the new post gave me a chance to learn more about governance. If I was really going to turn my dream of becoming Oklahoma governor one day into a reality, those organizational skills were going to be essential.

Dad's job frustration was compounded by marital difficulties with Dorothy, which led to a divorce in the first weeks of 1951. It was a split that helped neither one at the time, and in my communications with Dad, he seemed as like a rudderless boat adrift on an angry sea.

But my school work progressed well, and as the end of the spring semester of 1951 approached, I now had the leading grade-point average in the Air Force ROTC, and I was named Outstanding Junior Air Force ROTC Cadet for the 1950–'51 school year. That same month the annual Phi Beta Kappa dinner was held, and a Phi Beta Kappa key was awarded to me for the 1950–'51 school year. I was so thrilled to achieve that honor, marking my most well-rounded and best academic year to date.

The Phi Beta Kappa awards dinner was held at the Memorial Student Union at the University of Oklahoma on a Thursday night, and I had asked my father to attend the banquet with me. That night, Dad was seated next to me at the honoree's table. As my name was called, I stood up and looked at Dad; h is eyes were bright, his pride in me beaming from his face. It was a perfect night, except for the absence of my mother and Wendell. Dad hugged me, and we shared the triumph.

1951 and 1952 marked a difficult time for the family. After the divorce from Dorothy, my father married a prominent Democratic party official, Bertrude Fields, of Lawton, Oklahoma. That marriage was doomed, as Ms. Fields had failed to disclose a serious medical condition; they were married only a short time before divorcing. However, somehow the wounds between my father and stepmother, Dorothy, had healed, and they remarried.

An added burden to the Hall family in the years 1951 and 1952 was that the parent Pepsi Cola Bottling Company was putting great pressure on us to invest more money in the bottling business to expand our franchise—or to sell it. These negotiations and demands by the parent company eventually resulted in the sale of the franchise. It was a bitter pill, because the company had been in our family since 1937.

Meanwhile, my relationship with my father was as complicated as ever, particularly toward the end of my junior year. In the spring of 1951, he was still concerned that I was going to marry Peggy Marshall; he did not know that Peggy planned to go leave for the East in the fall to attend Randolph Macon Woman's College. Because of her decision, our relationship was already cooling; we corresponded briefly, but our romance was effectively over.

Nevertheless, in an effort to try to divert me from spending the summer dating her, Dad arranged an out-of-town job for me with

United Transports, a vehicle-transportation company that delivered cars for General Motors across the Midwest. My cousin Jane's father-in-law, Roy Woods, owned the company, and found a job for me in Kansas City, Missouri, at the Buick, Oldsmobile, and Pontiac assembly plant for the summer. I would be a yardman there; a yardman drove the cars as they came off the assembly line to the transports for loading. This new experience would give me a background in the Teamsters Union—which was my Dad's selling point for me to leave Oklahoma for the summer. I was required to join the Teamster's Union and obtain my union card. I was eager for the assignment because of my paper in high-school on jurisdictional strikes among the stagehands in the theaters on Broadway.

The work was intermittent; in a normal eight-hour shift, I might work for five hours and have three hours of somewhat idle time. I hated having nothing to do, so I started gathering up gravel and filling in the holes in the parking ramp for the cars as they came off the assembly line. I got my first personal lesson in jurisdictional conflicts within the union when I did that little extra work; the union steward stopped me halfway through the first day that I took on this task, and told me that this was not my job; my job was to assist in loading the trucks. There was another person assigned to patch the holes in the parking ramp.

I got the message very clearly: I should stick strictly to my job, and not attempt to do anything else—or help anyone else in their job—without the foreman's direction. After writing my paper in high school and meeting the problem head-on, I began to understand the intricacies of the union, and the difficulties inherent in its operations.

Another eye-opener was an attempt to attend a meeting of our local. I read the posted notice of the July 1951 monthly meeting, and I went to the union hall at the appointed time. When I got to the hall, I found a notice on the door that said the meeting had been postponed to a later date, approximately one week later. The next week I went to the union hall and found that the union meeting had been held earlier in the day. I had the same experience in the August meeting; I never actually got to attend a local meeting during my summer as a teamster member!

Despite these negative experiences, however, I never lost faith in the importance of unions for creating a voice for workers, and for providing them with fair wages and safe working conditions.

An unplanned challenge occurred that summer. The terrible flood of 1951, at the confluence of the Kaw and Missouri Rivers, inundated all of the industrial district in the area between Kansas City, Kansas, and Kansas City, Missouri. Water rose around the General Motors plant. During the early part of the flooding, there were calls for volunteers to help in the sand-bagging operations, but very few people showed up. The Civil Defense authorities were stymied.

Then an announcement was played on every radio station. It said that two hundred women had reported for duty, but more volunteers were needed. Though this report was a gross exaggeration, over the next two hours, hundreds of men appeared to lend a hand. The authorities must have laughed long and hard about their innovative approach to solving their manpower problem! Another frailty of human nature appeared when the flooding reached the stockyards, and managers released pigs, calves, and cattle to keep them from drowning. There were reports all over the Kansas City area of people stopping their cars to pick up a pig or a calf and put it in their car.

Men were recruited by the auto-plant managers to drive nearly 2,000 new vehicles that were parked in the lot to higher ground. The managers apparently passed out the keys to the cars indiscriminately, hoping to get them out of the way of the floodwaters and keep safe from ruin. A great number of keys, however, were given to people whose intent was not to help the company, but to steal a car; the exact count of stolen cars and how many cars were lost in the flood was never known, but there were over 100 cars unaccounted for by the end of the disaster.

The flood ended my job in Kansas City, since the repair and rehabilitation of the plant, the yard, and all the equipment took months. After only six weeks there, I went back home for the rest of the summer. Back in Oklahoma City, I needed another job, because my former Pepsi route had been given to another man for the summer. I found a job as a night guard at *The Daily Oklahoman* newspaper; my shift was four to midnight. I made the rounds of part of the Oklahoma Publishing Building on Third and Broadway, turning a time lock at each station to show that I was on duty. This meant that out of each hour, I had about twenty minutes of actual work and forty minutes of down time in which I could read, study, or do most any other thing I wanted. It was actually a lot like my Teamsters job, except that there were no potholes to fill.

I could not leave the premises, of course, and I could not go to sleep and miss the next time-clock appointment. So I used that extra time to outline in great detail my senior-year aims at the University of Oklahoma. My primary objective was to continue keeping my grade-point average high, making sure that I did well in Air Force ROTC, because I knew that I would be going into the United States Air Force in the summer of 1952. My term as chairman of the Union Activities Board would begin in September of 1951, and I got a running start on those plans and activities during these August evenings at The Daily Oklahoman.

My senior year seemed to fly by, but despite the excitement and the flurry of activity attending the approaching end of my four years of college, I found time for reflection. The fall of 1951 had started well, with my selection for Pe-Et Society, an honor society for the ten outstanding male students completing their junior year. I felt so blessed to be a part of this group!

But all of my campus activities had made it impossible for me to continue supervising study hall at the fraternity house. When I gave that up, I lost my free room and board. However, with an ROTC stipend, and what I made at the clothing store, I was able to get through the year with a fairly fat wallet. I had gone two years without financial support from any of my family; I had no debts, and I had met all my monthly expenses.

The University of Oklahoma during the four years that I was a student grew from approximately 8,600 students in 1948 to more than 12,000 by the end of 1952. The university's basketball and football programs had gained national attention, and football was king. The dynasty that was to become part of American football lore was beginning with coach Bud Wilkinson's innovate style and daring plays. He would later set a national record for major universities with 47 victories in a row—a record that stands to this day.

The rivalries with the University of Texas and with the University of Nebraska were the great football legends of those four years. The competition with Nebraska gave me the opportunity to see Cornhusker great, All-American Bobby Reynolds, and our own Heisman Trophy winner, Billy Vessels, in their prime.

Vessels was the story of the small-town boy from a dysfunctional family who made football history—and then went on to an exemplary and success-filled life. He helped put the University of Oklahoma on the map as a national football power. Coach Wilkinson was the toast of Oklahoma, and the famous red tie that he wore at each game became a symbol of victory during those four years. His platoon system was exciting to watch, and there were many heroes on those squads.

One inspirational player the students loved to cheer for was a reserve who didn't play much, except when we had a substantial lead in a game. Then a chant would start up in the stands for Boyd McGuggan. That chant was a wonderful thing to hear—and it was even better to see the coach put McGuggan in and let him play. It reminds me of the present-day story that was made into the movie *Rudy*, the true story of a young man who wanted to play so badly for Notre Dame.

Beyond the campus, the news was not encouraging. Through the fall and spring semesters, the Korean War waged on after a terrible winter of cold and suffering for our troops. Casualties were on the minds of everyone in ROTC as we prepared for our service. Each month there was more bad news, with former classmates on the lists of dead, wounded, or missing in action. The euphoria of our approaching graduation was tempered by the news.

Eisenhower and Stevenson where in full pursuit of their presidential goals, with secondary roles being played out by Republicans

Senator Robert Taft of, Ohio, California's Governor Earl Warren, and Harold Stassen, Governor of Minnesota. Democrats chasing Stevenson were Truman's Vice President, Alben Barkley of, Kentucky, along with Senator Estes Kefauver of, Tennessee, Oklahoma Senator Robert S. Kerr, and Senator Richard Russell of, Georgia. These political events were flashing through my mind, but my primary focus was on campus and all the activities there.

During my senior year there had been no steady girlfriend. I was dating several girls and having a wonderful social life, enhanced by my work on the Union Activities Board; this went very well, and gave me a great year of experience in administering a comparatively large organization with multiple activities.

One of my fraternity brothers, William G. "Willie" Paul, was named as the outstanding student in the senior graduating class of 1952. He was also courting the daughter of the president of the university, and finally won her hand and heart. The wedding was set immediately after graduation in the spring of 1952, and for the university, it was the event of the decade. The university symphony orchestra played for the affair, and there were twelve or thirteen groomsmen and twelve or thirteen bridesmaids. The wedding was held at the McFarlin Methodist Church, the largest sanctuary in Norman. It was absolutely the top occasion of the social season.

Of course, the bridegroom and most of the groomsmen in the wedding—me included—were slated to report to the armed services after the big event. Even at times of celebration, anxiety about the future was competing for our attention.

Willie Paul's being named the outstanding senior earned him a coveted gold medal, the Leitzer Award. There were ten candidates nominated for the award; each was designated a Leitzer honoree. This group of ten students was selected each year from the graduating senior class as the outstanding members of the class, not only for academic achievement, but also for student activity participation, leadership, and other qualities that showed promise for the future. Paul and two other members of our fraternity were named Leitzer honorees: Sam A. Wilson and me.

To have three out of ten Leitzer Award honorees was a phenomenal accomplishment for any organization. Our fellow fraternity members were extremely proud—and the Leitzer Awards proved to be very prophetic. William G. Paul went on to have a distinguished legal career in Oklahoma City, later becoming the general counsel for Phillips Petroleum Company and culminating his legal career as president of the American Bar Association. Sam A. Wilson went to the Harvard Business School and worked for a number of companies before deciding to go out on his own in the oil-field-supply business in Austin, Texas. He made a tremendous success of that business, building it into a financial powerhouse before retiring in Austin to devote his life to charitable pursuits.

Graduation came in June 1952, ending my four joyous years as a student. The graduation ceremony was held at Owen Field, the scene of so many University of Oklahoma football victories. There were 2,500 students in my graduating class, about 300 of those from the College of Arts and Sciences. I received a Bachelor of Arts degree with a major in political science and a minor in history.

As I sat among my classmates, waiting for my trip to stage for my diploma, I reflected on my favorite professors of those past four years. My mentor in American History, Dr. John Ezell, had broadened my knowledge and inspired me to learn all I could about the early years of our Republic; he became a close friend, and was later the custodian of my papers at the university.

My freshman English professor, Dr. Stanley Coffman, opened vistas through literature that have piqued my imagination all these years. His requirement of numerous essays tested my discipline and perseverance, but it was worth it. Later, in my practice of law, I would often think of those lessons and the rules he preached to me.

The most thought-provoking of all my professors, however, was Dr. M. L. Wardell. He taught a survey course on the causes and effects of World War II, a conflict which had barely ended when I started college in 1948. Dr. Wardell stirred my passion for learning and oral expression to a point that I had never before experienced; his free-wheeling classes required maximum student participation, and they were pure joy. He demanded daily newspaper readings of current events and editorials; then he expected every student to participate in the ensuing classroom discussions. The assortment of theories and arguments—some well-reasoned, lucid, and coherent, some not—gave the course a unique vitality.

A few days prior to graduation, our Air Force ROTC commissioning ceremony was held. Weeks before, in preparation for the occasion, I had been required to produce my birth certificate. I went to the Oklahoma County Birth Records office, where I ordered my certificate and waited while it was prepared. That's when I learned for the first time that I was listed as "unnamed Hall child" on the document. Panicked, I asked the clerk how to have my name corrected; Oklahoma statute required an affidavit from a close family member to verify a person's name.

Grandmother Hall provided the affidavit. I prepared it with the name "David Hall," with no middle initial, because that had been my name ever since I had lived with my father. Grandmother Hall signed it before a notary, I returned the document to the clerk, and a week later I received the completed birth certificate—with my grandmother's affidavit attached as a permanent part of the document.

During my Air Force commissioning ceremony, my mind wandered, musing on the events of my birth and my entry into this world without a name, the dispute between my parents, the sequence of events leading to their failed marriage, and the eventual evolution of my name by assumption. All of these snapshots of my life flashed through my mind as I waited to receive the gold bars of a second lieutenant.

These scenes were tinged with bittersweet memories of my mother—of our separation, of her wasted intellect, trapped in the downward spiral of mental illness. As the commander in charge of the ceremony read my name, I made a promise to myself that I would visit my mother, to somehow let her know how much I treasured her love, and all she had done for me. I also vowed to visit my

French family in Texas and tell them again how much I appreciated their love and support through all these years.

These were promises that I would keep.

After the many ceremonies were completed, awards presented and commissions accepted, it was now the middle of June 1952. I had received my orders to report to Lackland Air Force Base in San Antonio, Texas, on August 2, 1952.

As a graduation present, my father had given me the deed to a small piece of property near Lake Arrowhead in California. On it was a one-room, rustic cabin without plumbing, electricity, or even a stove. It was located in a division called Smiley Park near the present town of Running Springs. It was several miles from Lake Arrowhead, but at the same elevation, and there was a beautiful vista looking out to the southwest on the San Bernardino Mountains. These were small properties, and each of the lots with a cabin was worth about $600; so, with six weeks before I reported to the Air Force, I decided to go to California and sell the property. Because I had no idea that my path would ever take me all the way to the West Coast, selling the property made the most sense at the time. With my,studies ended and my commission as an officer and a gentleman not set to begin for several weeks, the timing also worked out.

But I was extremely nervous about making the trip on my own. I wasn't really sure this was even a good idea. Little did I know what a wonderful summer lay ahead in Southern California.

Maturity

To get to California in the least expensive way, a classmate of mine, Harry Clarkson, and I made a deal with car dealer Oklahoma City to drive a nearly-new 1952 Cadillac to California and deliver it to another dealer in Bakersfield. We had four days to make the trip. However, by driving night and day, we planned to reach LA in a day and a half; this would leave us two-and-a-half days to use the Cadillac to see as much of southern California as possible.

Harry Clarkson was TV-handsome, tall with brown eyes and brown hair. He was very outgoing, and was on the fast track to becoming a television personality and an anchorman in Washington, DC; he had made a strong impression the prior summer interning at one of the stations there. The incentive for Harry to make the trip was his strong desire to see a live TV production of a show originating in Los Angeles at 5:00 a.m. each weekday. We were both eager as we drove off with high spirits and dreams of adventures to come.

Our first adventure occurred on Day One, just past noon, west of Amarillo, Texas, in the heat of the panhandle summer. Our four-door Cadillac DeVille, although "near new"—or, as it would be called today, "previously owned"—developed an overheated radiator. We pulled into a country gas station to cool off and refill the radiator.

The locals at this rural gas station were obviously scrutinizing these two college boys driving a Cadillac. The proprietor of the station was a buxom, redheaded woman in her forties, who looked like she had some experience in dirt farming or some other line of hard work. She had the biceps of a seasoned arm-wrestler. When we went in to pay the bill, her manner was curt, her eyes unfriendly, and her body language combative. What had we done? Harry and I exchanged quizzical looks. Then it hit us at the same time—Harry and I knew what she was thinking. From her demeanor and the way she thrust the change back at me, it was apparent that she thought we were two "rah-rah" college boys out on a lark, driving an expensive car.

We had to change her mind. I spoke first. "Whoa, ma'am, you've got us all wrong."

She snapped back, "Whaddya mean?"

"For starters," I replied, "we're just trying to get to the West Coast the cheapest way we can by driving this car out for the transport company."

She eyed us curiously. Harry chimed in, "It's a heck of lot better than hitchhiking."

The woman broke into broad grin. "Well, why didn't you tell me that in the first place?" she said. With that, we related our circumstances: graduation, me going to the Air Force, and Harry heading to work after this trip. She laughed heartily and gave a whoop. And before we left, she and I ended up arm-wrestling.

She won.

Harry and I chuckled all the way to Los Angeles. We took three-hour turns driving while the other slept. We hit LA in less than thirty-six hours, so we had more than two days to explore. We bought a map and began to master the freeway system. We went to Lake Arrowhead and visited the property that my dad had given me; what a mess it was! To sell it, I would have to dig a trench for a water line and make some repairs. I had to think about whether this would be worth the effort.

In the interim, we returned to Los Angeles for a couple of days of sightseeing. For two young Sooners, we had the hoot of our lives driving that big Cadillac around LA, cruising along Hollywood Boulevard past Grauman's Chinese Theater, and down to the La Brea Tar Pits, our heads on a constant swivel as we tried to spot movie stars while putting on a VIP show ourselves.

In the end, we arrived in Bakersfield on time, bushed but happy. We delivered the car nearly empty, but with no dents or damage. Then we took an even more expensive vehicle back to LA—a Greyhound bus.

Earlier we had made contact with the local Phi Gamma Delta chapter house at Occidental College in Pasadena and found that we could stay there at no charge, as long as we helped with the chores. There was no food service in the summer. The house was across the street from "Oxy," and we could use the college pool. This locale was in the Eagle Rock district at the northeast terminus of an LA streetcar line. The streetcar meandered through the city for two hours to Inglewood, with stops near many LA attractions, such as the USC campus and the farmers' market. On our budget, the cheap ticket on the trolley and the sights we saw on the line were a bonus.

The men at the Phi Gam house were great sources for helping us learn about the LA area and the least expensive way to do it. The most helpful was Jim Goss, who also invited me for the first time to play California-style volleyball in outdoor sand pits. It was a blast— I loved it! Harry regretted having to leave, but after a few days, he caught the train and headed for Washington, DC—I don't remember whether he ever got to see his 5:00 a.m. TV show—and I stayed to complete the sale of the cabin near Lake Arrowhead.

I knew I needed a car for my Air Force duty, which convinced me to sell the cabin. But there was a big hitch: How would I get to and from the cabin, and who would help me with the digging? There hadn't been enough time for Harry and me to do it while we had the Cadillac, so I had to come up with a better plan.

Joe Bob Harrison provided the answer. Before we left Oklahoma City, Joe Bob, a lifelong friend, had said that he would fly out to spend some time with me before I went into the Air Force. Fortunately, we were able to continue staying at the fraternity house. Joe Bob rented a brand-new 1952 Oldsmobile convertible, which was our means of transportation around LA and Southern California for the next three weeks. He also volunteered to help me repair the cabin, dig the water-line trench, and use his car to go back and forth to Smiley Park. What a break for me!

A college classmate, Harlan Hobgood, had a sister who was a talent agent in Los Angeles. She arranged dates for us with two up-and-coming starlets. The young women were delightful, but we only had funds for about a week of such activity. This was heady stuff for us! The week ended on a high note with the girls. Joe Bob and I always wondered later how their careers turned out.

Job Bob and I took in all the sights of Los Angeles: the Huntington Art Museum, Griffith Planetarium, and Forest Lawn Cemetery, where we saw da Vinci's "The Last Supper" done in stained glass. And a new fad was just the thing for two college grads on a tight budget: all-you-can-eat buffets.

Late one evening we went into a small, intimate bar in the Santa Monica area west of downtown. As we were walking in the door, a beautiful blonde rose from the back of the bar, ran up, threw her arms around Joe Bob, and hugged him. It turned out that, in the muted light, handsome, 6'2" Joe Bob was a dead ringer for movie star Rock Hudson. The blonde woman was actress Marilyn Maxwell; s he had dated Hudson and thought that Joe Bob was he! We had a great laugh and sat down for a brief conversation with her. It was a terrific story to tell in later years in Oklahoma.

Anytime we were touring Los Angeles and southern California, we had occasion to use the freeways, which were brand-new to us, since we had none in Oklahoma. One of the thrills of our first or second evening in the convertible was going down Arroyo Seco Freeway from Pasadena into LA doing about ninety miles an hour; luckily, we didn't get a ticket.

Thanks to Joe Bob's help, I completed digging the water line, repaired the cabin, and sold the property near Lake Arrowhead.

Bless him! I banked the $600 from the sale of the cabin for a later purchase of a car. Joe Bob stayed until the second week in July and then flew back to Oklahoma City, leaving me at Occidental College. To save money, I decided to take the train to Santa Fe, New Mexico, visit with friends, and then hitchhike to Oklahoma City.

The train ride was very, very long—and boring. I was 21 years old, and I had spent my entire life with most of my time scheduled into activities; I was always looking for ways to make better use of my time. I felt it was important to have a real vacation, or at least a working vacation with glamorous excitement. Now here I was, with nothing to do but stare out the window at the high-desert landscape and let my mind wander. With the clack of the rails in my ears, those long hours provided time for deep reflection of where I was on life's journey. I played back the triumphs and trials of my life. Just dreaming of future possibilities—and my ultimate political goals—made the time pass quickly. Sooner than I imagined, I was at the Santa Fe station.

Waiting to meet me was Mary Jean Straw, a bright, lovely close friend from college. Her parents, Johnny and Irene Straw, had graciously invited me to stay in their home. I spent a week with the family, exploring Santa Fe and having a wonderful visit with Mary Jean. She had been one of the most outstanding female graduates in that class of '52. I had an immensely enjoyable week with Mary Jean, talking about her future plans, my military service, and the state of the world at the time. Her mother, Irene, and I competed in designing a crossword puzzle for the other to solve. Irene finished mine five minutes faster than I did hers. Bummer!

On my last day, Mary Jean and Irene took me to the edge of Santa Fe to start my hitchhike back to Oklahoma City on Route 66. We hugged good-bye, and I waved as they drove away. With a bag at my feet, I stuck out my thumb.

I hitchhiked without incident back to Oklahoma City. On the way home, I reflected on conversations during which Mary Jean and I had discussed our opportunities for the future. She shared my optimism for America's continued leadership in the world, for a successful conclusion to the Korean War, and for the growing sentiment toward racial equality. It was exciting to be stepping into adulthood; there would be no turning back, and the promise of the future stretched brightly before me.

I had three or four days before reporting to Lackland Air Force Base in San Antonio. Packing all my clothing and schoolbooks, I stored them in my father's garage in Oklahoma City. My plans were to bus to Dallas, then take the train to San Antonio—but Joe Bob Harrison came through again. A licensed pilot, he offered to fly me to Dallas, and I eagerly accepted.

The appointed date arrived, and we climbed aboard a Cessna 182 that Joe Bob had rented at Downtown Airport in Oklahoma City. It was a bright August morning; we warmed up the aircraft at the end of runway and started the take-off roll. We came off the runway a bit slowly, however, and nipped a tree at the south end of the runway, snaring a very small branch in our landing gear. Joe Bob looked at the leaves and said it was not worth it to return to land. We flew on with the leaves blowing off the branch.

On the flight to Dallas, we replayed our California adventure before we arrived at Love Field and were directed into the traffic pattern. As we prepared to land, we were a bit close to a passenger jet landing ahead of us, and the turbulence bounced us like a rowboat on giant wave. I held my breath but exhaled with a "Thank you, Lord," when Joe Bob righted the plane. We landed safely—with the tree branch still lodged in our landing gear.

Joe Bob and I had lunch, and then he had a surprise for me. He gave me his own first lieutenant bars that he had earned after graduating from Oklahoma Military Academy. I treasured these bars, and put them on the day I was promoted to first lieutenant. It was a fine memento of our many good times together.

I thanked Joe Bob, we shook hands, and I headed for the Dallas train station where I climbed aboard for the 275-mile trip to San Antonio. On board were half-a-dozen ROTC graduates just like me, preparing to report to Lackland Air Force Base. One of the young lieutenants was a bright, funny, slightly balding Harvard graduate from Boston, with a perfect accent. His manner, sense of humor, and Boston-Irish bearing matched perfectly with his name, Eddie Ryan. He turned out to be the best pal I would have in the Air Force, and he became a close lifelong friend.

On the train ride to San Antonio, Ed and I hit it off from the start, talking most of the way. He was out of money, so I loaned him a hundred dollars to tide him over until we got to San Antonio, where he could arrange to have money sent from Boston. Ironically, of all of the people I served with in the Air Force, Ed was probably from the richest family, and here I was, loaning him money!

We arrived at Lackland Air Force Base for a week of orientation before we were sent to the various bases to fulfill our two-year commitment to the United States Air Force. None of us were flight-rated; it was a bit of a problem for the Air Force to decide where to put all of its ROTC grads. Some of us had backgrounds or degrees in political science, liberal arts, and business; the result was that the assignments to the various bases were based more on the need for training officers than any other factor.

Ed and I were assigned to San Marcos Air Force Base halfway between Austin and San Antonio. This was a helicopter and light-plane training base with two major missions. One goal was to train Army liaison pilots to fly a tandem-seat artillery-spotter aircraft, the L-19 Bird Dog, in Korea. This plane was a spin-off of a Cessna 170 with a more powerful engine, adapted for short-field landings. The second mission was to train United States Air Force and Army pilots to fly helicopters.

We were assigned as academic instructors in the flight school. Ed was assigned to teach a basic weather course to the Army student pilots, and I was assigned to teach basic navigation. The assignments fit each of us to a T; with Ed's Irish wit and open manner, he was very popular with the students, and he was able to draw from everything he had been taught by his mentor in the weather section—career Warrant Officer Orien Benton, so named because his father had always wanted to visit the Orient.

The course I taught gave me valuable experience in thinking on my feet and making simple examples of navigation issues such as drift. It was amazing how quickly some students grasped the concept of drift, and how other very-well-educated class members did not. I taught six one-hour classes each day, with a different group each session. My classroom held 32 students seated in desk chairs, with florescent lights above and windows on three sides. The flight students spent an hour a day with me for the six-week course. I taught from a raised platform at the front of the room with a twelve-foot blackboard stretching behind; a podium at one corner of the platform held my notes and class lessons.

In explaining wind drift, I diagrammed a rowboat crossing a river, and compared the concept to the flow of the river. Standing on the platform, pointer in my hand, it seemed simple—but formal education was not the only gauge of who understood these concepts and who didn't. Many of my college students had trouble, while the less-educated with work experience caught on quickly.

My mentor was an older first lieutenant, Antonio Bengalis. He had survived the Reduction In Force, or RIF, as it was termed after WW II, and was then just trying to get in his twenty years of service. Mustachioed, of medium height, and slender, the Italian-American was a joy as a teacher. His favorite statement to me when I would question him was, "I may not always be right, but I am never wrong."

Time now passed quickly. During those two years, I taught the course 22 times, with a different group of men attending each month and a half. It was challenging and invigorating. I felt great pride and patriotism to see the tangible results of these men learning to fly, graduating, and departing for the front lines in Korea. But it was somewhat overwhelming at first, because as a second lieutenant, I had many class members who outranked me by two or three grades. The rule is that the instructor is the ranking officer in the room, and that's the way it was done.

I will never forget my first class. I walked into the classroom with half the class sitting down already. As I walked up to the front, one of the class members said to me, "Lieutenant, you'd better sit down, because the instructor will be along in a few minutes." That was typical of how we "shave tail" lieutenants—wet behind the ears—looked to all the seasoned officers that we had on base. Many of the men in the program had come back from combat in Korea and were eager to gain their wings, to receive additional flight pay and future advancement.

One story touched my heart. A student in his late thirties, about 5'5", slightly built, and dark-haired, had been a pushcart vendor in New York City before the Korean War. He had volunteered, gone through basic Army training, and become a sergeant; he had a distinguished battle record in Korea, and had made lieutenant in a battlefield promotion. His K-12 education was rudimentary, but he was now eager to learn. It was a struggle for him to master weather and navigation; nevertheless, he made it through the class. He just needed someone to believe in him.

Another student I had, a colonel, needed someone to make sure that he didn't just coast to victory. A second tug at my heart and conscience came with that colonel, a West Point graduate, who was sent to the flying school to get his wings as an additional skill before he became head of the Army Signal Corps. This man was bright, very polished, eager to learn, and did his assignments weeks ahead. He was my best-prepared student.

However, when we got to the final exam, he nearly flunked the course.

I was going around the room, watching all the students get their flight-course lines drawn, when I came to the West Point colonel. He had inexplicably drawn his course line 180 degrees off; he mistook the starting and ending locations on his map.

I walked around the room and thought about it for a bit. I knew how embarrassing it would be—to him and to the Army and the Air Force—if he drew his course lines backward and flunked the course. I came by his desk, and quietly said, "You should examine your course direction." Immediately the light flashed, he corrected it, and went on to pass the course. That's the only time I ever remember in those two years giving any test help to a student. I still believe I did the right thing.

Another challenging issue of teaching that course had to do with my own youth and inexperience, and how to relate to the men. Many times the older and more experienced men in class would have questions that they wanted to ask that were not relevant to the course. I wanted to know these men, so I could better understand them—especially the combat veterans. For that reason, in the initial sessions of any new class, we took the first ten minutes to talk about any subject. During these discussions, I was just another student like the rest of them. Politics was the only issue off the table.

Many instances of accidents and unfortunate circumstances had caused some of these men to flunk out of flight school and face the embarrassment of having to return to their units. So I tried to make the classroom experience as meaningful and as non-threatening as I could. However, one standard remained: They had to master the material to be able to navigate a plane when they went onto Korea, or wherever they might be assigned. And I never varied in my deter-mination that when they left my classroom, each one of them would be prepared to do the job.

To help motivation in basic navigation, I distributed a *Saturday Evening Post* story of Charles Lindbergh's famous trans-Atlantic flight, "33 Hours To Paris." I compared his aircraft, the Spirit of St. Louis, to the L-19 to give my students an idea of the odds against Lindbergh. That article was mandatory reading—and it helped.

One of the perks of being in Texas instead of Korea was that we could easily go home for Christmas. That holiday in December 1953 produced one of the funniest episodes of our time at the base. Tom Flanagan, a Fordham graduate, had talked his way onto a mili-tary air transport from our area to the East Coast so that he could spend Christmas with his family in Brooklyn. However, Tom had not arranged for a return trip on military transport, and had to fly back on a commercial aircraft. Unfortunately, he had to board the airliner with a non-standard carry-on: a parachute that had been checked out to him for the military flight. It was his responsibility to return it to the base in Texas!

So here was Tom, getting ready to board his return flight on a commercial airliner, toting a military parachute. He said that the startled expression on the face of the stewardess as he came up the stairway to airplane was something for the ages. She was not only astonished, but insisted on introducing Tom to the captain so that he could explain his need for a parachute—this was years before DB Cooper bailed out of the back door of a Northwest Airlines 727 with $200,000 of Northwest's money strapped to his waist, handed over to keep him from blowing up the plane. Tom regaled us with his story that brought belly laughs from all.

Just about the time I celebrated my 22nd birthday in October of 1952, I tried out for the base basketball team. Another ROTC grad, Jim Holt from Maryville, Missouri, was the coach; he had arrived on base the same week as Ed and I. Jim was a basketball aficionado; he was a great fan of Oklahoma A&M and coach Hank Iba, who had once coached in Jim's hometown. We hit it off right away. I made the team, but I was never sure if it was my ability or my friendship with Jim.

This was the first time I had ever played on an integrated squad: 50% black, 50% white. We played against white opponents in southern Texas, and against all-black colleges in the South, but our favorite competition were Air Force bases and Naval Air Stations. Our team gelled, and our spirit was A-plus. Our star player was an African-American six-footer who could dunk the ball, an unusual feat in those days.

Near our small installation was the huge Bergstrom Air Force Base, a Strategic Air Command center. Their basketball team was the favorite of General Curtis LeMay, the commander of SAC. We beat them in a very close game—and the reports were that the general was not pleased. The victory gave us bragging rights for the rest of the year, and years later, when General LeMay was the vice-presidential candidate with George Wallace, I met with him—and could not resist reminding him of that loss.

All of us ROTC trainers felt terribly lucky to be in Texas and not Korea, and to have at hand the social life of nearby colleges and the recreational resources of the area. Two miles from the base was Southwest Texas State Teachers College in San Marcos. That school was a pet of then-Senator Lyndon Johnson, the US Senate Majority leader at the time. With his influence, the college prospered; it had a vibrant student body and very good academic standards. My half-sister Ann attended the school for one semester. It's now known as Texas State University-San Marcos.

Just thirty minutes to the north was the University of Texas campus at Austin, which was also a weekend target for us. Many of us had friends at UT from our college days.

The recreational area in the hills west of San Marcos, the river waters at nearby New Braunfels, and the access to Austin gave us a great diversity of activities. We had the best swimming and boating in the summer, and there were many outlets for sports in the winter.

It was during this first year at San Marcos that Ed Ryan and I had many talks about his experiences at Cambridge and Harvard and about my experiences at Oklahoma. Ed knew of my plans to return to Oklahoma for law school and a career in politics. One evening while having dinner at the officers' club, out of the blue, Ed said, "Have you ever thought about going to the Harvard Law School?"

I laughed and said, "Heck, I probably couldn't get in. Why, do you think it's a good idea?"

"It will broaden your view of the world and give you contacts for later in your career that would be valuable," he replied. "And you might be surprised about getting admitted, because the school wants diversity across the country."

"What about the tuition?" I asked.

"Well, it isn't cheap, but there are all kinds of scholarships available."

For the next hour, we discussed the pros and cons, and the idea began to germinate in my mind. I knew I could compete—but could I get in? The next day I called the Harvard Law School admissions office and asked for brochures. A week later I received them, and read that an entrance exam would be given in Austin in just a few weeks. That cinched it; I would take the exam and see how I would do. So in the spring of 1953 I went to the University of Texas in Austin to take a competitive exam for admission to Harvard Law. In a way, it was a wild shot in the dark, because my plans were to return to Oklahoma and enroll in the OU Law School when I had completed my Air Force commitment.

I did very well on the law-school placement test. In fact, when my results were submitted to Harvard, I was offered a scholarship for one year of free tuition. According to my figuring, that scholarship—along with my GI Bill and a part-time job—would do the trick. I wanted to see how I would do in that environment in preparation for the political life that I hoped to lead. Prior to leaving San Marcos, I had to post a $500 bond to secure a place for myself at a Harvard dorm. That was a first!

The $600 I had received from the sale of my dad's property in California was enough for me to buy a 1946 four-door Packard Clipper a few months before I left San Marcos. Perry Ward, a family friend and radio and TV personality in Tulsa, had located the car and prepped it for me. It was seven years old and was in excellent running condition. After finishing my Air Force commitment in San Marcos, I returned to Oklahoma City for two weeks, then left on the drive to Cambridge to begin the 1954 fall semester at Harvard Law School.

Meanwhile, a number of introductory instructions arrived from Harvard. One of the most important was a reading list of approximately 100 books that I should have read in college or before—and if not, I should try to do so over the summer. I had read most of the books on the list; I had seen the movie *The Oxbow Incident*, but had never read the book—which became one of the most influential in my understanding of justice. It was the story of how mob hysteria incited the lynching of an innocent man. The other book that captivated me was probably the most essential primer for law school that I ever read: *Common Law and Common Sense* by Oliver Wendell Holmes.

The trip to Boston was my first trip to the northeastern part of the United States. That September drive through Pennsylvania, New York, and Massachusetts was an education in the differences of the scenery—and in the various languages and dialects spoken.

Fall and I arrived in New England at the same time in 1954. The Harvard campus was ablaze with color in the third week of September. My first days were a flurry of activity, including class enrollment, assignment of living space in law-school housing, and getting to know the roommate who would be my companion for the next year. I was extremely lucky to be assigned to Hastings Hall, a nineteenth-century building that included two bedrooms and a sitting room—with a wood-burning fireplace in each of the suites.

David, 23, enters Harvard Law School, September
1954, Cambridge, Massachusetts

My assigned roommate was Edwin Wilkins, a 1951 Princeton graduate and a lieutenant in the Navy; he had completed Naval ROTC the same way that I had completed Air Force ROTC. Ed was six feet tall, a ruggedly handsome, slender man with a somewhat withdrawn personality—but an excellent sense of humor. We had a lot in common, but also many differences. That made for a fascinating period of getting acquainted, exchanging life stories, and learning how to best survive our first year at law school.

Our middle-class family backgrounds matched, but our regional cultures were worlds apart. I had never had minestrone soup, and Ed had never eaten fried okra. We had similar ROTC experiences, albeit Ed's was Navy and mine Air Force. The clothing we brought to school was so different; as an undergrad, Ed had worn a tweed sport coat and chinos to class, and carried a book bag. His dress suit was a lighter-weight but dark-colored tweed. My undergrad dress had been gabardine slacks, white shirt, and sweaters—and I had never heard of a book bag. My single-breasted dress suit was light gray; it seemed really out of place the first time I wore it.

Ed Wilkins, Princeton '51, and David, Oklahoma University '52,
roommates at Hastings 55, Harvard Law School, September 1954

Ed had a daily subscription to *The New York Times*, and I received copies of *The Daily Oklahoman* each week; we had two markedly different perspectives on the news. As classes began, we were so busy that neither of us had much time for newspaper reading, but every morning we took a look at the condensed information that appeared in *The NY Times*.

Our suite included basic furniture in each of the bedrooms, but no furniture in the living room, although we had a circular window seat that looked out over the yard between Hemingway Gym and some classrooms. On each floor of Hastings Hall, there was one suite of two bedrooms with a single room across the hall for one person; three of us shared a common bath. (The third was John Lifland, one of the outstanding students at Harvard Law; he won the Moot Court competition in his freshman year—and went on to become a federal judge in Newark, New Jersey.) Our fire escape was a 1¼" hemp rope that we were instructed to pass out the window and then use to scramble down the side of the building—from the third floor.

Wilkins and I decided that we would furnish the living room from the local Salvation Army thrift store. We drove the four-door Packard to the Salvation Army headquarters and proceeded to investigate. The result of our shopping was a foldout sofa bed, a set of giant moose antlers to go over our fireplace, two very well used oriental rugs, and a wonderful framed picture of Abraham Lincoln. We lashed our purchases on top of the Packard and headed back to Cambridge from downtown Boston, looking like a scene out of *The Grapes of Wrath*.

Grandmother Hall had furnished me with a hot plate to take to school, so we could heat coffee in the mornings. The principal dining area was at the Commons Cafeteria, which was an excellent place to eat and available to all of the law-school students. There were additionally two social eating clubs, the Lincoln's Inn and the Chancery Club. Ed and I joined Chancery Club; it gave us an opportunity to get acquainted with upperclassmen, to make new friends, and to have a social outlet for the limited amount of spare time that we had.

Classwork started, study routines began, and the school advised us to form study groups, which would make the transition back to academic life easier. Each of us was encouraged to join a debating club in preparation for the annual Moot Court Competition. Many of us were also athletically inclined; I played basketball three times a week at the Hemingway Gym adjacent to our dormitory. Through the fall, we organized touch football games on the weekends in the park just outside our window.

Our study groups were remarkable occasions to see the different ways in which individuals prepared for classwork. Some preferred the traditional way of taking notes in bound volumes, but others were diligent in taking notes, typing them, and then condensing them so that they would be easier to review for the exams. In each course, there was one exam for the entire school year, which was either pass or fail. The study groups proved very useful, although almost all of these groups had what we jokingly called guiding lights. These were the most confident lads, who were always convinced they had the right answer and the correct way to diagnose each legal issue—no amount of factual information or logic could change their minds.

The year progressed with more speed than I would have thought possible; the blur of lectures, study, social activities, athletics, and concerns about the future consumed us. Near Boston, there were several of women's colleges—Radcliffe, Wellesley, and a little farther west was Smith and Bennington—that provided ready dating opportunities. Although I resolved not to date during the school week, the weekends were a different matter.

One of my classmates, Jack Driscoll, was going with a beautiful student nurse in the Boston area, and asked me if I would like to go on a blind date with one of her classmates. I did, and met a lovely, brown-eyed, dark-haired girl who was bright and engaging. We went out again, and on that second date I asked her if she would like to visit a friend of mine, a paraplegic who had been injured in a swimming accident in Oklahoma. He was being treated at the nearby Mass General Hospital in hopes of rehabilitating his spinal cord.

Hilton Gallion had been a student a few years behind me at Classen High in Oklahoma City. He had been on a college preparatory track and had a bright future, until he dove into a hidden tree stump just below the surface of Lake Murray near Ardmore and severed his spinal cord. As a paraplegic, he only had the use of a few of his fingers, but his mind was clear as a bell. He had come to Mass General hoping that some new techniques and procedures would help his condition.

I took that lovely student nurse with me to meet Hilton, and immediately a connection sparked between the two of them. I felt like a third wheel, and within a few minutes, I realized that the chemistry between them did not include me. It was the end of my dating that young lady, as she had become tremendously enamored with Hilton. In many ways, I felt very good about it, because it was a treat for him to be sought out by such a lovely girl.

During the school year at Harvard, I had an Air Force Reserve assignment as a teacher's aide in the ROTC program about a mile from Hastings Hall at another one of the world's premier universities, the Massachusetts Institute of Technology. I looked forward to being a full instructor the following year. If I had any misgivings about whether or not I was up to the task, they were soon overshadowed by the sheer enjoyment of rubbing elbows with students and faculty, men and women who were engaged in cutting-edge research in more than two dozen fields. Their discussions gave me an imaginative perspective in areas that I had never considered before.

I also had two part-time jobs: I was a basketball referee for the intramural program at the Harvard Business School. This gave me an athletic outlet, and it was more lucrative than most other available part-time jobs. My second job was delivering the mail during the Christmas holiday in Cambridge. Going door to door in the city was a revelation to me; the people, the weather, and the different traditions were all a new experience. My delivery route was concentrated in an area of many black families, and as a semi-Southerner raised in an area where *de facto* segregation still existed, it was enlightening to encounter so many well-educated African-Americans. This reinforced my Air Force experience with the black officers and enlisted men and affirmed the notion that there's no difference between whites and blacks except skin color.

On the morning of Christmas Eve, the post-office supervisor advised us that once we completed our mail run that morning, we were off the hook for the rest of the Christmas holiday. Prior to Christmas, I had been invited to Binghamton, New York, for the holiday, if I could find time for the trip. My hostess, Lieutenant Doris Kliment, was an Air Force nurse from our base in San Marcos, who was visiting her parents in Binghamton. We had dated for several months before I left the Air Force, and we looked forward to seeing how we would feel on seeing each other again.

Since I would not be working, I quickly called Doris and asked if the invitation was still open. It was. I prepped my old Packard and hightailed it off to Binghampton.

The late afternoon was snowy, driving from Boston through western Massachusetts and the beautiful Berkshire Mountains, three hundred miles to Binghamton. The quiet charm of the white slopes with the trees edging the road and the empty roads made the trip a breeze. I had met Doris's parents, John and Bertha, on a trip they'd made to Texas the year before. Being in their cozy home that Christmas, learning the customs they had brought from Europe, seeing Doris, and basking in the warm welcome her family gave me was a boost to my spirits after the past weeks of studying.

Early on the morning of New Year's Eve, Doris and I drove down to New York City to be a part of the Times Square scene at midnight. What a madhouse it was! It was terrific, but once was enough. It seemed twice as crowded as I had imagined after my years of seeing only pictures of the celebration.

Doris and I tried to give our romance a chance, but by the end of the visit, we knew that we would always be friends but nothing more. Still, as those memories flash by, I am thankful for her friendship, for that blessed Christmas, and for her family's inviting me to become a part of their lives. It broadened my store of wisdom for understanding people and decision-making in the years to come.

My experiences in Boston and at Harvard, such as mail delivery and the different cultures I encountered, reinforced my commitment to for public service, and enlarged my views about civil rights and the importance of racial equality—in life, as well as in the law books. During my time at Harvard, there was no Baptist church close to the campus, but there was a Methodist church just next door to Hastings Hall, and I attended many Sunday services there. The minister was very involved in integration activities in the South, and several of his sermons during that year were devoted entirely to those issues.

The world seemed my oyster as I looked to the future, and everything about that year at Harvard Law had unfolded magically—well, almost everything. When our final grades were posted, I received a cold dose of reality: My grades were good in two courses, average in the next two, and abysmal in the fifth. Wham! I had earned only a D in property law. My chances for my scholarship continuing the next year evaporated.

It was time for major soul-searching. First, I weighed what had happened: Property was the only course I had not religiously outlined and summarized—an obvious mistake. Was I too complacent? Did I just not get it? No—it was my lack of diligence in the course that did me in. I understood the material, but sure as the devil, I had overestimated my ability to retain and explain when it came to the exam questions. This had never happened to me before. I had to dig deep in my psyche to bring forward that reserve of strength that had always sustained me, and forced me to face up to the truth about my own failings; I shouldered the blame—and resolved to make the best of the situation.

At a conference with the school authorities, I was told that I could return next semester and repeat the property course—and if I maintained all my other courses, I could continue and graduate with the class of 1957. Would I go home with my tail between my legs, or would I find a silver lining, and not dwell on disappointment, or regret a lost opportunity? I had a life-changing decision to make.

After two days of thought and review, I knew what to do.

Without the scholarship, finances made it impossible to continue at Harvard Law. But I knew that this year would help in my ultimate goal of becoming Oklahoma governor. I decided to return home that summer and enroll in the OU Law School at Norman in the fall of 1955. At the time, I felt that my decision was merely a practical one. But as later events played out, it was more like God's hand directing me in a circuitous path toward fulfilling my ambitions.

Back in Oklahoma City, I sat down with my dad to talk about the summer, and what I would do until fall. He surprised me with an intriguing offer. Dad had planned to build a garage and shop complex behind his home that summer, and he asked me and my 87-year-old Grandfather Hall if we would consider doing the construction. We both agreed, and it became one of the most enjoyable summers of my life. My grandfather was an excellent carpenter, and now I would have the chance to work with him and get to know him better. "Bampy," as Wendell had named him, was my teacher, and I was his helper. What a refreshing break from law school, the trauma of my near-failure, and the rigors of the past year!

Bampy did not believe in power tools, so we sawed every board by hand, and drove every nail with a claw hammer. He taught me more carpentry in the sixty days it took to build the structures than I could have learned in a year of apprentice work as a building-trade union member. We bonded as men, not just relatives, and I was so proud to be at his side.

A special treat came at the end of those hot summer days when Dad, an accomplished carpenter himself, complimented us on the skill and excellent work we had done.

The summer ended, and when I interviewed with the dean of admissions at the University of Oklahoma Law School, I was advised that I would have to repeat the property course, which might delay my schooling by as much as a year. The dean, J.B. Fellows, was a wise and understanding man, and he suggested to me that I consider going to the University of Tulsa Law School. He thought that they might accept my property grade from Harvard instead of repeating the entire course. He called the dean of Tulsa Law, John Rogers —a graduate of the University of Oklahoma and one of Tulsa's outstanding lawyers—and asked him to interview me. I made the 88-mile trip up the Turner Turnpike to Tulsa, all the way hoping for the success of my coming meeting.

Dean Rogers and I had a lengthy discussion about my year at Harvard, and discussed what I hoped for the future. We hit it off well, and the meeting ended with the promise that he would admit me to the Tulsa Law School without the loss of any of the credits that I had earned at Harvard—and I wouldn't have to repeat the property course. I began the fall semester two weeks late because of the administrative red tape that I had to plow through, but it was a catch-up process.

The study habits that I had learned at Harvard served me well, and I was very successful in the course work at the University of Tulsa. The environment at TU Law was a marked contrast to what would have been the scene at OU; Tulsa University was a night school with smaller classes—twenty-plus students—and the majority were married and working full time. It was a no-nonsense classroom atmosphere. The OU law school was a full-time, all-day program, with larger classes and a more relaxed campus atmosphere.

For me, Tulsa was the best move. I was then certain of my goal: a career in politics and getting elected governor one day. The opportunity to meet new people and learn the ways of a new city and its nuances were invaluable. Tulsa was a contrast to Oklahoma City; city government in Tulsa was more conservative—choosing to annex new areas, for example, only when the residents could support city services. Oklahoma City annexed willy-nilly, without considering the cost of services—just eager to expand its square miles. Tulsa was more heavily Republican, and less influenced by events at the state capitol than Oklahoma City.

Ultimately, even though it was necessary to work full-time for the duration of my studies there, I managed to place in the top three or four students in the rest of my law-school career, and graduated with top honors. I was a member of the Law School Student Government, president of a local legal fraternity, and active in Law Day.

During the years of Tulsa Law School, some of the most dramatic changes in my life occurred. The first of these had to do with the necessity of finding a job that would sustain me during the time I was in law school. I was fortunate to find a position with State Farm Insurance Company as a claims adjuster in their Tulsa district office. This gave me an opportunity to get to know the city, to meet lawyers, and to learn who "the good guys and the bad guys" were among the Tulsa legal community. This gave me a chance to become very good friends with the lawyers of the Truman Rucker firm, who represented State Farm Insurance. Joe Best and Guerny Cox of that firm were wonderful mentors.

With a very full plate, I didn't really feel there was room in my life for a serious relationship—although I was entirely open to the possibility of dating. So in early December 1955, when Clyde Graeber, a classmate in law school, asked if I'd like to go on a blind date with the roommate of an American Airlines stewardess he was dating, my answer was, "I'd love to!" It turned out that the roommate, also a stewardess, was moving to Tulsa and didn't know anyone. No other recommendation or description was forthcoming—but on a cold winter night after class, Clyde and I drove to the Tulsa Municipal Airport to meet the incoming American flight from New York.

I'll never forget the sight of Jo Evans in her uniform walking off the airplane. I thought she was the most beautiful girl that I had ever seen. Her dark hair framed a lovely strong face, beautiful lips, and a figure to knock your eyes out. She was the friendliest, most open-mannered girl I had met in years, and I may not have realized it at the time, but I was smitten.

As we walked to my car, I opened the passenger door, made sure she was seated comfortably, and closed the door. When I walked around to my door, I found to my great surprise that she had leaned across the front seat and opened my door. *What a thoughtful girl*, I mused. This had never happened to me in all the years since I started dating—another indication of something very special about her.

We had a wonderful first evening of exchanging information, getting acquainted, and sharing some of our impressions of Tulsa, both being new there. That first date was a dream come true; here was a girl whose values matched mine. She was not afraid to speak her mind, and she had mustered the daring and flair to leave her small-town beginnings. From Rose Creek, Arkansas, on the southeast side of Petit Jean Mountain, she had struck out to find a more interesting and exciting life.

As I walked her to the door at the end of our date, I wondered, *Should I try to kiss her goodnight?* I didn't want to rush her, but lordy, I was entranced. We paused at the door, and she turned to me, her brown eyes shining.

"What time are you going to pick me up tomorrow night?" she smiled.

Awkwardly, I stammered, "Tomorrow night?" Gaining a little composure, I continued, "Maybe we got our dates mixed up, because we don't have one set for tomorrow night."

The look on her face told me she had really goofed. Blushing, she responded, "I am really sorry. I got your name confused with my date for tomorrow night. His last name is Hill. Will you accept my apology?"

I laughed as we shared a treasured moment that spoke volumes of what was to come of our relationship. "You bet I will," I replied with an enthusiastic grin.

Later I learned that Mr. Hill was David Hill, a professional golfer who was to be her date the next evening. That little bump quickly evaporated, and we started seeing each other whenever she was in Tulsa from that point on. The most difficult part of the relationship was her flight schedule and being in distant cities, which required long-distance phone calls and ran up a bill that was out of sight. So much for not being ready for a serious relationship!

I continued the courtship for the next six months. Each date brought us closer, and we learned so much about each other. Our Protestant beliefs meshed perfectly, although she was Presbyterian, and I was a Southern Baptist. Our dysfunctional family backgrounds—her father deserted the family soon after her birth—matched the pain I had suffered with my mother's illness. We shared a mutual desire to build a life of family security, devoid of divorce, rancor, and bickering.

I felt God's guidance as Jo and I moved closer to making a commitment. The glow that surrounded us was first mentioned by my best friend, Jim Webster, after he and his wife, Reba, had met Jo. Jim pulled me aside that evening and said, "David, you'd better not let her get away. She's a keeper."

In those weeks of making a decision, I am sure that Jo was wondering about where this path might lead. We edged nearer to a point of commitment, but each of us had misgivings. The specter of my father's failed marriages hovered in my mind, and I had told Jo the history of my mother's illness and shared with her the diagnosis of her doctors at the state hospital: She would remain institutionalized for the rest of her life. I wondered how Jo would feel about my mother's condition in years to come.

But we believed in a shared vision: to be of service to others, in whatever path we took. This commitment to a shared career expressed our love most clearly; no longer were they just *my* goals, now they were *our* goals. Jo and I had both overcome challenges in the past by perseverance, trust in the Lord, and supreme optimism. That, to me, was the firmest foundation on which our lives together could be built.

I knew she was the one, and I asked her to marry me. Thank goodness she said yes!

During these halcyon days of law school, starting a marriage, and working full-time, Jo stood by me and bolstered every effort to make studying easier at home, and to take as much of the burden off of me for the tasks of daily life as she could. We were both working full-time jobs, and I was attending law school full time at night, carrying fourteen to fifteen credit hours. Then, in the fall of 1956, we were blessed with the news that we would have a child in the spring of 1957. This cast a new light on our lives, as we had to prepare for something neither one of us had ever experienced! Since the beginning of our marriage, we had been living in a one bedroom, semi-basement apartment that was not conducive to rearing a child;

our landlord, on learning of the impending birth, said, "When the baby arrives, y'all won't be able to stay. Sorry, but the lease says no children." He did indicate he would allow us a month or so after the birth to find another place, however.

The State Farm job was a wonderful experience, but it took so much time that I began to look for other employment, and became a land analyst with the Shell Oil Company. The hours were more regular, and it provided additional study time for me, as well as an increased salary. The job gave me a textbook education of the oil industry in Oklahoma; the two years that I spent with Shell gave me not only new knowledge, but friendships that lasted a lifetime— including fellow Shell employees Carroll Ralls and Don Pearson, also a law-school classmate. Carroll and his wife, Nadine, would become entwined in our lives through all our political campaigns. Nadine became my personal bookkeeper during my days in the governorship. Another thing I discovered about Nadine Ralls early on was that she ranked as the best cook of fried catfish and hush-puppies that God ever put on this earth.

From the time that Jo and I were first married, we discussed our great interest in politics, as both of us had come from backgrounds where we had worked on campaigns, and we were both very conversant with Democratic Party politics. We helped in a number of local races in Tulsa, and worked on one Congressional race during the first year that we were married, well into the time that our first child was due.

While participating in the political activities, we met a wonderful couple, Elizabeth and Edsel Edson, who had returned from working with an American oil company in Libya. They had decided to make their permanent home in the Tulsa area. Edsel was a retired Marine, and Elizabeth was an extremely active Democratic Party member in Tulsa circles. At the time, we were searching for a place to live when the baby came. Elizabeth and Edsel had a small two-bedroom home that they were selling; we worked out a transaction whereby Jo and I moved from the sub-basement apartment after the baby was born into the two-bedroom house in the southeast part of Tulsa, just off of 45th Street and Peoria Avenue. It was a godsend to have a home for our new baby, and to have a stable situation as I completed law school.

In the spring of 1957, as the birth of our first child approached, we had the good fortune to have Dr. Walter Sanger as Jo's obstetrician. His care and advice helped through a tough period as Jo worked into her eighth month of pregnancy, while I worked for Shell and continued night law school. It had rained with a vengeance in Tulsa that spring; the week of April twelfth was no exception. We knew the baby was due. Then tragedy struck: Dr. Sanger suffered a heart attack and died.

The evening of April 18, we were playing bridge with Nancy and Bruce Clark in the Brookside area of Tulsa when Jo's time came, and the race was on to the hospital. We had come to the Clark home with a suitcase prepared for the hospital, but Jo refused to go to the hospital until she had a shower. We raced home, she showered, and we were off to St. John's Hospital, just four blocks from our apartment. Once there we were introduced to Dr. Sanger's associate, Dr. Robert Dillman, who would perform the delivery. Dr. Dillman greeted Jo with warmth and understanding, took her to the delivery room, and a few hours later in the morning of April 19, Nancy Leigh Hall was born.

Jo and I were ecstatic. We loved children, and this beautiful, dark-haired, brown-eyed infant was the answer to our dreams. Two blessings occurred that morning: The first was the beginning of a lifelong friendship with Dr. Dillman, who became a positive and supportive part of the fabric of our lives. The second blessing—truly a gift from God—was Nancy's birth—the first bright star of the three children who would array the heavens of our life.

The Dream Begins
(Salad Days)

In late summer of 1957, at the end of a hot August day, Jo had just put four-month-old Nancy to bed. I was in a four-week break before the fall semester at Tulsa University Law School would start, and we had time to talk. We sat facing each other on the sofa in the small living room of our 900-square-foot frame house on 45th Street in Southeast Tulsa. I had made two sofas from two hollow doors and some wrought-iron legs, cushioned with eight-inch foam-rubber pads half the size of a twin-bed mattress, with two comfortable bolsters as back supports. Jo had covered the sofas in what I called bright tennis-court green, and with our light-beige rug, the room was bright and had a Danish Modern look. Two lamps on end tables matching the sofas, reflected the light on the off-white walls that we had painted ourselves.

Jo spoke first. "Nancy's almost old enough for me to go back to work."

"Are you sure you're ready? And how are we going to work out baby-sitting while we're both at work?"

"Just like we've done each time we had a challenge," Jo responded. "Just look how we handled the finding of this house and the move from the apartment."

I chuckled. "That was a lot different than handling this little cutie of ours. How can you stand to leave her?"

Jo smiled at me and said, "Just like you've done with Shell work in the daytime and law school at night."

So that night it was decided; Jo went to work as a secretary for an engineering firm in Tulsa. We were a typical young couple struggling with childcare, school activities, and a limited social life. The past months had been difficult living on my salary alone.

Over the next months, we continued our activities in the Democratic party, helping a Democratic candidate, Herb Wright, in his Don Quixote-like quest against the entrenched incumbent Republican, Page Belcher, in Oklahoma's First Congressional District. We also helped as much as time would permit in the campaign J. Howard Edmondson, who was running for governor; t he dynamic, 33-year-old county attorney was lighting a prairie fire across the state in his upstart governor's race. Jo and I were making friends of party workers countywide. I had kept up my contacts from high school and college, and many of my friends now working and living in Tulsa showed a great interest in the Edmonson campaign. In the crystal ball of my mind's eye, I could see the nucleus of my own future campaign organization.

Jo and I discussed our desire to have a second child. Preparation for such an event required a reworked budget; we would focus on increasing our income, while never sacrificing our shared goals. Then, wham! Shell Oil put my political ambitions front and center. I was offered a promotion with a better salary, more chance for advancement, and the prospects of a life in the oil business.

Jo and I had a tough decision. Would we take the safe, conservative path that lay with Shell Oil? Or would we follow my dream to become governor of Oklahoma?

"You always told me you were going to be a corporate lawyer," Jo joked.

"Wait a minute," I said. "You stinker! You and I agreed a long time ago on our shared goals in politics."

"Don't be so sensitive," She laughed. "I'm just pulling your chain!"

That conversation ended with a passionate kiss to seal our choice. Politics it would be—and, as Sherlock Holmes would have said, the game was afoot.

In late fall of 1958, my senior year in law school, I sought a position with the county attorney in the hopes that this might be a path to my future. Jo and I talked it over; I think she was somewhat reluctant, but we decided that this would be our best direction, leading ultimately to the governor's office. J. Howard Edmondson's stunning victory in November played out before our eyes as he became the youngest governor, at 33, in Oklahoma history. I had just turned 28.

Newly elected Governor Edmondson was set to take office in January of 1959—taking many of his old colleagues with him. In so doing, he virtually stripped the county attorney's staff of some five or six lawyers, and the incoming county attorney, Robert D. Simms, was in desperate need of assistants to carry on the work after Christmas of 1958.

Now my acquaintanceship with the law firm of Truman Rucker, made when I worked for State Farm, proved valuable. The firm's lead trial attorney, Joe Best, was a good friend of mine, and he knew Robert Simms very well. When I approached Joe Best to ask for an introduction to Robert Simms, so that I might inquire about a job when I completed law school in the spring, he generously obliged. That opened the door for me with Simms, and the result was that he agreed to hire me—and to my surprise, County Attorney Simms wanted me to start work before I finished law school. I mentally shouted hallelujah, and accepted the offer. He also hired another assistant, John "Mickey" Imel, a senior law student at the University of Oklahoma and former star footballer for the Sooners.

Neither of us had completed our law degree, and neither had taken the bar exam, but County Attorney Simms needed assistants in January 1959. To our great surprise, he presented a request to the Supreme Court of the State of Oklahoma to allow Mickey and me to be given special permission to become assistant county attorneys to practice in the county attorney's office and to try cases. The Supreme Court reviewed our school records, took recommendations from various sources, and on January 28, 1959, by special order of the Supreme Court, Mickey and I were admitted to practice in the courts of the state of Oklahoma. We were immediately appointed assistant county attorneys, and became members of Simms's staff—at the beginning of the last semester of our senior year in law school!

This was a heady challenge. Knowing that we were very fortunate, we doubled our efforts to be of service in the job, as well as to complete our school duties and prepare for the state bar exam in June of 1959. Mickey and I were so eager that we took every opportunity to work on any case, although neither of us was lead attorney. The joke among our colleagues in law school was that we had participated in seven or eight trials each, and therefore we would probably be guaranteed to pass the bar exam, since failing us would cause all of those cases to be subject to reversal. Mickey and I studied hard, each making excellent grades the last semester of our respective law schools. Happily, we both passed the bar exam; in fact, when I saw the bar-exam results, I felt the same rush I'd felt at Classen High when we won the state championship in basketball. I felt like I had launched a long one-handed jump shot from the corner of the court—and it swished.

I pumped my fist with excitement and pride, yelling to myself, "Yessss—nothin' but net!"

Money was short, and Jo continued her work as a secretary for the engineering firm. Sweet Mother Nature answered our earlier prayers, and Baby Number Two was set to arrive in August 1958. This precipitated one of the great personal sacrifices made by any family member to help us achieve our goals; in the next few months, Jo and I were in quandary as to how we would manage two babies, just sixteen months apart. Jo's mother, Ruth Evans, came to our rescue. Ruthie, as I affectionately called her, took a five-month leave of absence from her job to be with us at that birth. Then, as Jo planned to return to work, Ruthie would stay on to care for our infant children.

Ruthie, a nurse's aide in the OB section of the Saint Anthony Hospital in her hometown of Morrilton, Arkansas, had persuaded her supervisors to give her the leave and keep her job for her until she returned. I will always be grateful to those Catholic nuns who administered the Morrilton Hospital for allowing Ruthie this time off. Ruthie's assistance enabled us to pay our debts from law school, maintain our small home, and care for our growing family

Doug's birth signaled a special moment in the Hall clan. My dad's pride and joy at having a grandson to carry on the Hall name was unbounded. He had loved Nancy when she was born, but I sensed a special bond approaching with Dad and Doug. Doug's birth also eased the unspoken sorrow that Dad and I still felt every day for our loss of my older brother Wendell.

Doug inherited Jo's sparkling brown eyes, dark hair, and perfect skin. We marveled at how fortunate we were to have a healthy, happy boy. I first saw Doug in the hospital nursery and noticed how wrinkled he was, and I said to Jo, "He looks like a little old man." I was only kidding, but she was ready to box my jaws. But she was all smiles when she came home and presented Nancy with her new brother. Thank goodness Ruthie was there to help, or I would have never made it.

Four months later, however, our euphoria gave way to worry as a scary virus infected Doug, requiring a return to the hospital for several days, and a substitution of goat's milk for a length of time. His recovery was quick, and we said our blessings as we brought him home from St. John's Hospital.

On reflection, the months before Doug's birth had sped like a flash of lightning across the sky in an Oklahoma thunderstorm. Becoming acclimated to the county attorney's office and trial duties, studying for the bar exam, learning from the older lawyers in the office, and making plans to help in Bob Simms' upcoming re-election campaign in 1960 filled my days.

Simms had been easily elected in 1958 after serving as chief prosecutor in the office. County prosecutors were elected for two-year terms at that point in Oklahoma history. I decided to throw myself full steam into the campaign to help re-elect Simms, just as most of the other assistants did. By working twice as hard as would have been expected, I naturally ascended to a leadership position—the best possible preparation for my own future.

Some assistants were reluctant to campaign as hard as I thought they should, so I took up the slack where I could. If an extra hand was needed at a rally to pass out bumper stickers, I was there. I helped silkscreen campaign signs on four-by-eight plywood sheets and erected them all over the county. I wasn't afraid to ask for contributions, which helped me learn the do's and don'ts of fund-raising. Most enjoyable for me was working the streets in the small towns of the county—Jenks, Sand Springs, Broken Arrow, Skiatook, Owasso, Bixby—meeting new people, listening to their concerns, and learning what they needed. I wasn't worried, because Simms's opponent was hardly on anyone's radar; still, I didn't want to leave any stone unturned.

Jo's mother returned to Arkansas at the end of 1958. She left Jo and me better organized and steady in our finances, more ready than ever to pursue our dreams. For our growing family, which now included baby Doug and toddler Nancy, prospects in the legal arena and in politics had become even brighter. This was especially true after I'd passed the bar exam and was working as lead attorney in minor cases.

By the start of 1960, Mickey Imel and I were both assisting in murder trials, and soon we were taking lead positions in other critical cases. This new responsibility, plus the prospects of a much more settled financial life, lifted our spirits. We also needed a larger home to accommodate our growing family; with Doug's birth and my advancement in the county attorney's office, we were fortunate to sell our small house and move to a more desirable area.

The house we purchased in January 1960 was a wonderful Tudor stucco two-story in the heart of the Maple Ridge addition in the older part of Tulsa, near downtown. This was a graceful, tree-lined, well-kept section of Tulsa built in the late '20s and early '30s. Any of the homes could have been a Norman Rockwell neighborhood painting.

Although the lot was not particularly large, we had tall, majestic oak trees in the yard. The neighborhood was home to a lot of professional people, and our children were lucky to attend Lee Elementary, one of the premier grade schools in Tulsa. Jo chose to be a full-time homemaker, although from then on she occasionally took part-time work to help with expenses.

Once we settled into our new neighborhood, the search was on for a church that could become our religious home. From early on in our life together, Jo and I had resolved that we would become one, not only within our marriage, but in our church affiliation; in our first discussions, I told her about my baptism at age seven—by immersion—as a member of the First Baptist Church of Ada, and how, after moving to Oklahoma City, our family transferred our membership to the First Baptist Church there. Though I'd attended services at the Baptist Church and other denominations when I was in college in Norman, for the most part, as a student I was not active in any church.

Jo's experience during her college years was similar. She was reared in a community dominated by Baptist churches, but her beliefs were more in line with Presbyterianism. Initially, we weren't in a hurry to affiliate with a specific denomination, but after our marriage and the birth of our children, we were determined to find a church to join and build our lives in harmony with our faith.

During the first four years of marriage, we visited more than twenty churches. We found that the Presbyterian denomination met each of our beliefs. Our favorite church was the First Presbyterian Church, pastored by Dr. Miller. His sermons seemed to speak most closely to our spirits and hearts. The size of that church, however, was so large that we thought our growing family would be better served in a smaller, neighborhood environment.

With the move to the Maple Ridge area, our family joined Southminster Presbyterian Church in the nearby Brookside neighborhood, some twelve blocks from our new home. It was a blessing—and obviously God's will for us. We became active, and our children, Doug and Nancy, attended Sunday school regularly, as would our later-arriving third child, Julie Beth—who was still, as they say, just a twinkle in our eyes. We loved the church, and for many years Jo volunteered in the nursery and I taught Sunday school classes for high-school seniors.

Teaching Sunday school to the high-school seniors was a perfect counterbalance to my weekday work in the criminal courts. It also nurtured my desire to be of service to others, give guidance to young people, and have the repartee of inquiring minds challenging me each Sunday. I always tried to surprise my class each week; once I asked a visiting young lady to give the closing prayer in Hebrew. She was the teenage daughter of a Jewish lawyer friend, Charles Whitebrook. The class loved it.

The religious compass that Southminster church gave to our lives guided each of us in years to come. All five of us became lifelong believers, but Jo and I felt that the children should decide their own church affiliation as adults. Nancy became a devout church worker. This was reflected in her adult life when she became an elder in the Torrey Pines Christian Church in La Jolla, California. Julie Beth, a lifelong Presbyterian, became the youth-and-family director for Westminster Presbyterian Church in Westlake, California, and Doug was a true believer.

Jo and I tried to be active in every organization that we could pack into our busy lives. Her passion was the Maple Ridge Association, the preservation group for our community. She worked as a volunteer with the Children's Medical Center in activities as varied as secretarial help to outings for both the physically and mentally disabled. She also volunteered as a secretary with Legal Aid.

The volunteer work was great fun for me, and an outlet to hone my skills at name-recognition and retention. I delighted in going to a first meeting of a new committee, learning all the first and last names, and then showing up next month and reeling them off.

I volunteered with bar-association committees, helped with Law Day activities, and raised funds for multiple sclerosis and the Boy Scouts of America. I tried helping in every fundraising endeavor that I could, and succeeded in earning a reputation as someone who, although extremely busy, could be depended upon to help in charitable causes. My dad had a maxim he followed, and it proved true for me: Find the busiest man you can to help on a project, and when he commits, success will follow. This proved so true with well-organized people!

The faith and teaching of doing good works had been imbedded in my heart and soul as early as I can remember. The Falls Creek days of reading the book of Mark, Wendell's inspired pushing me to be diligent, and the teachings of Christianity from the Halls and the Frenches all formed the mosaic of my desire to serve. The satisfaction of these pursuits always settled my mind as I closed my eyes each night to go to sleep.

During these years, my Dad's life settled down, as he and my stepmother found a common ground in their marriage and finally were very happy. They were both active in the First Baptist Church in Oklahoma City. They also prospered in shared interests in Masonic work, Dad in the activities of the Shrine and my stepmother in the Order of the Eastern Star.

Dad was proud of my accomplishments, albeit very critical of my being slightly overweight. He loved Jo and the children, and complimented her continually on the good job she was doing with our children.

On the national scene, the presidential election of 1960 was upon us. The Nixon -Kennedy battle was ongoing and exciting for all of us who participated. My next-door neighbor, Harry Crowe, was an avid Nixon supporter, and Jo and I were avid Kennedy supporters. We loved our neighbors so much that we mutually decided before the election that we would have a thirty-day no-political-talk period between our families until after the vote. We felt like this would guarantee our continued friendship, no matter who won. The Crowes had the largest Nixon sign in the neighborhood. We had the largest Kennedy sign.

Kennedy's directness, his style of campaigning, and his message of equality for all men was in contrast to what I thought about Nixon. I had followed Nixon's career somewhat, and was appalled at his tactics as early as his defeat of Helen Gahagan Douglas in the California Senate campaign of 1950. Then, and later in his Senate years, he seemed obsessed with Communism; he inferred that Gahagan-Douglas was a Communist, saying she was "pink all the way down to her underwear." She responded by tagging him with a nickname that stuck with him for the rest of his life: Tricky Dick. In the nationally televised Nixon -Kennedy debates I, like millions of other Americans, felt that Kennedy's performance and deportment were more presidential. Moreover, I identified with John F. Kennedy's beliefs as a model for my own future, and I could see Jo as Oklahoma's first lady with the same caring and empathy for all peoples as I saw in the Kennedy women.

The drama of the 1960 presidential election finished, of course, with Kennedy's narrow victory. At the same time, with no opposition in the primary, Robert Simms was easily re-elected to the county attorney's office. He was a low-key campaigner, very popular, and one of the state's most able prosecutors; he garnered the most votes of any county officer on the ticket. Simms was the third in a line of lawyers who had returned from World War II and had been elected county prosecutors, starting with Robert Wheeler, followed by Howard Edmondson, then Simms. This was a political dynasty of sorts that lasted nearly 25 years because of their spotless prosecution record, an extremely high conviction rate, and no scandals.

With the Kennedy -Johnson victory, many opportunities opened in the legal profession in Tulsa. The US attorney's office for the northern district was available, and a number of candidates applied, including my fellow assistant district attorney, John "Mickey" Imel, and me. All of us had our sponsors, all of us had our strategies to get the job, and all of us actively sought the appointment; I even went to President Kennedy's inauguration to seek support.

President Kennedy chose Mickey Imel, which turned out to be an excellent decision; Mickey made an outstanding US attorney. For me, it was one of those events where losing something I badly wanted turned out to be more helpful than if I had won; I re-doubled my efforts as an assistant county attorney, volunteering to try as many major cases as Bob Simms would allow, and started to develop a reputation as a very successful prosecutor.

Jo and I continued building our lives with our goal of advancing as far as I could in politics—but at the same time making sure that our family life was our main focus. In the spring 1961, right after the loss of the competition for US attorney, Jo became pregnant with our third child, and the due date was in August 1961. Meanwhile, to strengthen my knowledge of the law, I had received permission from Bob Simms to apply for a special two-week advanced prosecutor's school in the summer of 1961. This would require that I attend Northwestern University to study under Professor Fred Inbau, who was preparing aspiring district attorneys across the nation. He specialized in sophisticated interrogation techniques.

Jo and I thought that the school, which ran through the first week of August, would not interfere with the timing of the baby's birth, so I made the trip to Chicago, completed the course, and returned home just two weeks before our daughter Julie Beth was born early in the morning. What a glorious day that was! I got to see her in Jo's arms, our new baby girl, brown-eyed like Jo, waving her arms and flexing her fingers—full of life. We knew from those first days what a sparkplug of energy she would be.

A few days after we brought Julie Beth home, Jo and I were drinking tea at our breakfast room table, talking about our family financial burdens. By now those burdens were weighing heavily, and not getting the US attorney's job had left me with a decision: how long to continue in the county attorney's office. In 1961, it appeared that Simms would complete another two-year term.

It was after 9:00 p.m., and the children were all asleep. These talks at night had become almost a ritual during the months before Julie Beth was born. As the old German clock in the hallway chimed the half-hour, Jo said, "We can do whatever needs to be done."

"It's not just the financial pressure," I replied, "It's also deciding whether to stay in the county attorney's office, or think about private practice."

"But you're doing so well there—and even though you didn't get the US attorney's job, there will be plenty of opportunities in the future." She looked lovingly at me. "Don't be in such a hurry," she said. "Take some time, and let's see what happens."

A week later, with Jo's support, I decided to stay with the county attorney's office and work during the next year for Bob Simms's re-election. But Jo and I still held fast to our desire to pursue our own political goals.

Then another door opened. In January 1962, a district judgeship became available in Tulsa County, and Bob Simms was selected for the post—which meant he would have to resign as county attorney.

Simms's resignation laid the appointment of a new DA in the laps of the Tulsa County commissioners; the law gave them the power to appoint a new county attorney to fill out the remainder of Simms's term—and that appointee could then run for election in November of 1962 for a full two-year term. When the county commissioners asked Simms for his recommendation. he surprised everyone in the office by calling a meeting of all the assistants to tell us that he would leave the choice of his successor to us. He said he would abide by our decision. So the die was cast: We would somehow have to decide among ourselves who the next count attorney would be, and Simms would recommend our choice to the commissioners.

There were two candidates in our office vying for the post. Don Cameron, the civil assistant county attorney who had been with Simms for a number of years, was one; he was a trusted assistant, and an extremely good lawyer. However, Don was somewhat introverted, and his campaigning abilities were lacking—serious deficiencies for a job that required an outgoing personality and interpersonal constituent skills.

I was the other candidate, of course. In Bob Simms's last election, I had actively managed the campaign, and he was easily re-elected.

The assistants were divided; many were loyal to Cameron for his long service. Others were concerned that a formidable opponent might enter the race against him. The assistants called for a personal interview with Cameron and me.

The ten assistants had a week to think it over; then they gathered in Simms's office late on a Thursday night. Simms was not present. The oversized office was dominated by a massive desk on the east side of the room, with a black leather high-back judge's chair for the boss. The wall behind it was decorated with a beautifully detailed six-by-eight picture of downtown Tulsa. A long, dark-green leather couch stood against the south wall of the room, and there was space in front of the desk for nine or ten cushioned office chairs.

One chair was set up facing the desk, with room for all the assistants to place their chairs looking toward the "hot seat." Don and I would be brought in one at a time and quizzed, and then the other assistants would go into closed session and nominate the new county attorney.

Don went first, as I waited in my office for them to call me when it was my turn. It seemed like an eternity while I waited, but was really only about forty minutes. Then Bob Caldwell, one of the older assistants, stepped into my office and said, "Come on, David, it's your turn."

I followed Caldwell to the boss's office and took my seat in the proper chair. It was an unusual moment, to say the least; all of us in the room had worked closely in preparing and trying cases over the years. We knew each other very well. As I waited for the first question, I noted that their faces for the most part were friendly, but serious. I could understand their anxiety, because all our jobs could depend on their decision. I, too, was anxious, but I tried to control my emotions. The interrogation started, and I fielded every question with an honest and straightforward answer. The assistants went about their work very diligently, and their questions were well-thought-out and to the point.

All went smoothly until the final question: "If we don't choose you, what will you do—stay in the office or leave?"

Before answering that question, I took a full minute to think. Time seemed to stand still. Then I made one of the most daring statements that I ever made in my life, especially to group that had my future in their hands. I said firmly, "If you choose Cameron, then

I intend to go out and organize the groups that I worked with to elect Bob Simms— and try my best to defeat Cameron and become the county attorney."

As soon as I had said those words, I wondered if they had been too aggressive or too threatening, but they seemed to have the opposite effect. I think that my passion for the post—and the successful experience that they had with me as the campaign manager—was the tipping point. They chose me as their candidate, and Simms in turn recommended me to the county commissioners. They approved my appointment to serve out the remainder of Simms' term, and I immediately announced for election in 1962.

I was thirty-one.

Don Cameron was most gracious when it was over; he resigned and entered private law practice. Meanwhile, 1962 was marked with some great successes in the courtroom, along with support by both local papers, *The Tribune* and especially *The Tulsa World*. The press was mostly favorable, which discouraged many potential rivals, although the Republicans did field a candidate. With maximum effort from all of us in the office, we easily won the race.

Our first order of business was to make sure that we had an impeccable record in the county attorney's office. Our duty was to vigorously pursue convictions of those defendants we believed were guilty beyond a reasonable doubt. I instructed the assistants that if they felt the facts didn't meet that standard, then we should never put anyone through the indignities of being charged when we knew that they might not be convicted. This was our office policy; this attitude produced positive community support and improved law enforcement during my years as county attorney.

The power to charge people with crimes, and the power to manage grand juries, are the two strongest weapons of the county attorney. Business people, politicians, or private citizens can be smeared by simple innuendo, by being called to testify before the grand jury, or—at worst—by facing false charges. Reputations and lives can be ruined—and that's why my admonition was so crucial. This issue was the one that I emphasized most as the county prosecutor.

However, this did not diminish the vigor and passion with which I pursued criminals. This same passion earned me a nickname among the assistants, which never came to my ears until years later: Crime Wave Dave.

The most famous case I prosecuted was one that reverberated through school-maintenance departments across the nation. In the maintenance department of the Tulsa Independent School District, a group of employees had put together a scheme to have the school district acquire surplus property from the US government after the Korean War. The US War Surplus Property Office was authorized to sell at ridiculously low prices, and, in many cases, to donate to public-school districts such surplus property items as D4 Caterpillar tractors, road graders, precious metals, titanium, copper, stainless steel, and a variety of lumber, construction, electrical, and other supplies.

The conspirators had the US Surplus Property Office deliver the equipment, metals, and supplies to the loading dock of the school maintenance department. The load would sit on the dock, never to be put into inventory; then it would be appropriated by this group and shipped to a private lumber company in Tahlequah, Oklahoma, to be resold or used for their own benefit.

Our office was one of the first to break such a case, and the ripple effect was felt in school districts across the nation. A grand jury was called, and I proceeded to present the case while working with state and federal agencies. *The Tulsa World* was instrumental in breaking the story, and their courthouse reporter, Ken Neal, did an amazing job of investigative reporting, which was of tremendous benefit to the grand jury—and to our office.

The grand jury investigating these crimes did its work with competence and dispatch, returning indictments that resulted in the conviction and imprisonment of one of the key employees of the maintenance department. A byproduct of the investigation was the uncovering of false names on the payroll, and numerous embezzlements of school property. But in some cases, those crimes had been committed years before, and prosecution was blocked by the statute of limitations.

After the investigations began, and throughout the trials and convictions, a group of zealots opposed to the investigation of these crimes—and to the work of my office—circulated a petition to call a grand jury to investigate me and my office. Their claim was that I was a part of a Communist, Zionist conspiracy to subvert the Tulsa Independent School District. In furtherance of this conspiracy, I was alleged to have attended a World Zionist convention in Switzerland.

Oklahoma law at that time allowed a grand jury to be called if 200 citizens signed a petition making the demand. This group of right-wing extremists, headed by an elderly man named L.G. Burt, circulated the petition and got the 200 signatures, and a grand jury was called. The Oklahoma attorney general, Charles Nesbitt, was authorized by statute to conduct the grand jury, and I was to step aside. He came to Tulsa, I stepped down, and for two weeks the proceedings went through my public life, my private life, my business affairs, and every other facet of my life. At the end of the grand-jury session, I was completely exonerated; the claims were found to be false and ridiculous. The grand jury wrote a glowing report of the outstanding work I was doing as county attorney. It was a vindication beyond my wildest dreams.

This extraordinary exoneration report by the grand jury came in the late spring and early summer, several months before the 1962 general election. As a candidate, I told the voters to use the grand-jury report as their basis for judging my performance as the county prosecutor. I won the fall election in a near landslide, and enjoyed the best margin over my Republican opponents of any race in my public career.

Tulsa County Attorney family portrait: from left:
David, Julie, Nancy, Doug, Jo Hall

L.G. Burt, the man who accused me of conspiracy, was later declared mentally ill and committed to the state mental facility at Vinita, Oklahoma. He died there.

The sobering reality of politics is that a false scandal can easily take wing, even if it is later proved ridiculous and baseless. The first news story of such an event usually gets the most press; seldom does the exoneration gets the same prominent space, either in print or by the broadcast media. One of the first lessons I learned as a candidate or officeholder is that you need a rhino-thick skin; the best demeanor is to hold your head high, don't lose your cool, and keep a smile on your face while your opponents lurch about.

But it's tough to do with arrows sticking out of your back.

The grand jury completed its work more than a year ahead of the firestorm surrounding the assassination of President Kennedy in November 1963. The many theories, the rush to judgment by some—even the most outlandish scenarios were given coverage by the press. The lingering doubts for years afterward made me wonder if we would ever know the complete truth. For my money, I believe Lee Harvey Oswald was a delusional killer seeking a spotlight for the implausible causes he espoused—and I've never seen any compelling evidence that anyone else was involved. I believe that in his mental state, he saw himself as the avatar of the dark forces opposed to the President and our system of government.

Years later, I came to understand these forces, when I experienced a dose of such hatred. Little did I imagine the brutality and vilification that lay in my future.

In politics, timing is everything, a lesson taken as gospel by Jo and me as we contemplated our future. The recognition of our position was the subject of a heart-to-heart talk we had in early December of 1963. "Time to start thinking about our re-election campaign next year," I announced.

"How tough do you think it will be?"

"I feel really secure about 1964," I replied, "but it's the goal of the governorship that has me thinking."

"How so?"

"Because of the massive publicity we got on the Tulsa School District case, the conviction rate since then, and the decision by the grand jury last year, I think it may be time to think about the governor's race."

The '66 race was already being discussed in Tulsa, with Dewey Bartlett favored by a lot of Republicans. Dewey was an attractive state senator, a native of Ohio, a Princeton graduate, and a former Marine who had moved to Oklahoma and tried his hand at farming and ranching—while he just happened to inherit an independent oil company from his father.

On the Democrats' side, former governor Raymond Gary and Preston Moore, an attorney from Oklahoma City, were the names heard most often. "If I could win the county attorney race by a large margin, the way my name is spreading, I think I could surprise them in the '66 primary," I mused.

"Hold your horses," Jo quickly injected. "Raising all that money and putting a winning team together would be tough. Let's just sleep on this for a few weeks and then decide."

Over the seven years of our marriage, I had learned to listen to Jo's counsel about people and politics—and heed it. It sounded like good advice to me, so we waited. The extensive good press of the past year in Tulsa continued to spread across Oklahoma; it gave me the courage and confidence I needed to fulfill my life's dream to run for governor. But it was not until our near landslide victory in my second county attorney's race of 1964 that Jo and I agreed to make the run for that state office in 1966.

The preparation for the governor's race began in earnest in January 1965. There would no incumbent, as the sitting governor, Henry Bellmon, could not succeed himself; a new succession law was set to take effect in 1966. Whoever was elected governor in 1966 would be the first chief executive eligible to serve two consecutive terms.

My strategy was based on several factors. First was the desire to take the success I had as county attorney and convert it directly into a statewide office, rather than running for the state legislature, the US Congress, or some intermediate office before attempting to run for the governorship. The blueprint that J. Howard Edmondson had used when he ran his winning campaign from county prosecutor directly to the governorship was one that could be duplicated, if I pulled out all the stops—a powerful incentive.

Second, after four years of a Republican administration, the Democrats were eager to find a champion to bring the office back to them in 1966.

The third factor was a cultural phenomenon: Youthful candidates seemed to have the edge at this time in history. Kennedy's presidency on the national scene and Edmondson's victory in Oklahoma had increased the appeal for younger blood, and the notion of trusting younger people with more political opportunities was pervasive throughout the nation.

Fourth, the leading candidate for the Republicans was Dewey Bartlett, who had represented Tulsa in the State Senate for four years. Since I was in the process of building my own constituency in Tulsa, I would immediately be splitting his Tulsa-based vote. He was not unpopular; in fact, it was a given that a Republican would ordinarily carry Oklahoma City and Tulsa. But the reality was that if I got the nomination, and had a solid base in both cities, I only needed to cut his margins; that factor, added to the traditional large margins Democrats usually amassed outside the major cities, could deliver the victory to me.

Fifth, the people of Oklahoma would be learning of my deep roots in Oklahoma City, Tulsa, Ada, and the University of Oklahoma. Conversely, Bartlett could be portrayed as a carpetbagger, a transplant from Ohio, a fellow who hadn't grown up in the state. Moreover, we could portray him as an elitist, out of touch with the common people of Oklahoma, an Ivy Leaguer from Princeton, not a state school, and a rich oil-and-gas company owner.

All these factors were positive. I believed with a passion that I had a winning platform—a man of the people with the vision to strengthen and revitalize Oklahoma.

My biggest hurdle was financial; I had very little funding to run against a wealthy Republican. But that did not deter me, because I had spent so many years as a fund-raiser for multiple sclerosis and the Boy Scouts of America, and as a helper for other candidates; I felt that I knew most of the financial sources for Democratic candidates, at least in northern Oklahoma. And my friends from my earlier years in Oklahoma City and at the University of Oklahoma would know people who would be of help to me in all parts of the state.

However, I had not considered the size of the state of Oklahoma—and the importance of having a connection in every county. There are over 900 towns in Oklahoma, and in the twenty-two months that I ran, I visited every one. Still, I did not have the background or personal history in many of these areas that I needed. This was exemplified by an incident in Idabel, a deep southeastern town, when I went to a local social gathering to get acquainted with people on the same day I was there to make a speech at another event. As I went through the crowd, Jo heard someone say, "Well, I'm not sure whether he's a politician or the new minister at the Baptist Church."

Jo and I were anxious. Had we overestimated our chances? Was my recognition and publicity too centralized in Oklahoma and Tulsa counties, the major metro areas? Although I had received a lot of good publicity across the state, name recognition was still a problem. I tried to counter it with enthusiasm, excitement, and new and vigorous activities in campaigning that had never been used before.

The number-one campaign innovation was a 28-car train that we assembled at the Union Station in Tulsa on a Saturday in April 1966. We boarded nearly a thousand enthusiastic supporters, then traveled the rails to Oklahoma City to open our campaign with a parade downtown and a rally at the Skirvin Tower Hotel. It was the largest passenger train that had departed from the Tulsa Station since World War II. Gaining massive state publicity, we did a Harry Truman -type whistle-stop in each of the small towns along the way. The chair cars were filled with excited, motivated supporters, and we provided some type of entertainment for each car, using local bands, folk singers—all sorts of music to energize the crowds.

What we found, though, was that there was so little interest in each individual town that we decided to have everyone get off the train and crowd around the rear of the train. This created a huge photo op and gave us the appearance of great support at each of the whistle stops.

All of this worked well until we got to Oklahoma City. We had covered ninety miles of track and arrived at about eleven o'clock Saturday morning—to find the downtown streets nearly deserted.

We formed our parade group, using all of the people on the train, the bands, bright flags, and red, white, and blue banners, and marched to the hotel to open the campaign. Our publicity staff directed our camera crew to shoot pictures only of the parade participants.

In the months leading up to the election, not only did I have the statewide campaign to conduct, but we had a very busy county attorney's office that required all the attention I could give it. I was extremely fortunate to have S. M. "Buddy" Fallis as the chief pros-

ecutor; he was a veteran in the courthouse and an excellent administrator, a short man with a solid build, a result of his wrestling days.
Buddy's shock of brown hair was thick, and his eyes could make a
hostile witness feel very uncomfortable during cross-examination.
His serious demeanor disguised a sharp wit, and his determination
to succeed as a prosecutor nearly matched mine.

Buddy was the heir-apparent to the office, and ran it effectively
on the days that I was gone. The people who had helped me in the
campaigns for county attorney now looked toward helping Buddy.
In preparing for the governor's race, and in an effort to help prosecution across the state of Oklahoma, the staff and I had put together a
book called *An Oklahoma Criminal Form Book*. There was no central
legal reference book of that type that could be used for prosecutors across the state to prepare charging documents to fit proper
crimes. This publication proved to be invaluable in helping county
attorneys in the 77 counties to determine what charges to bring in
often-confusing situations.

The success of the form book solidified my reputation for legal
acumen among the county attorneys. As a result, I was endorsed by
the State County Attorneys' Association. It also helped to gain the
support of the State Bar Association in my quest to create a new
Oklahoma district-attorney system. This change would provide the
newly elected district attorneys with four-year terms—and much
larger jurisdictions. This was a radical departure, since each county
had been autonomous, having their own county attorney with assistants, and there was some resistance. But the progressive wing of
the legislature backed the bill, and it passed; there would now be 22
district attorneys in place of 77 county attorneys.

For those incumbents who were running for district attorney, this
was a tremendous blessing, and gave me much support and recognition from lawyers in those various towns across the state.

My campaign had very limited finances, so we used all sorts of
cost-cutting measures during those years. One covered my transportation from Tulsa to Oklahoma City and back on the Turner
Turnpike. This turnpike, 88 miles long, was Oklahoma's first and

most successful toll road; it connected six small communities as well the two major metro areas.

To cut costs, I had my campaign aides take me to the turnpike entrance and let me out. From there I would thumb a ride as cars with Oklahoma license plates entered the turnpike. I would start a conversation with the driver, then listen intently to learn what was important to that person. At the other end, another campaign aide would pick me up.

This was very effective during the good weather, but it didn't work so well in snow or rain. It was an innovation no one had ever tried before—and those rides came in handy when volunteer airplanes were not available. I met many interesting people who were astounded to see a candidate for governor thumbing a ride from one end of the turnpike to the other. It gained not only favorable publicity, but it gave me an opportunity to meet people who might not otherwise have an interest in politics. Many of them, after spending an hour or so with me, volunteered to help the campaign—and surely they told the story to every one of their friends and acquaintances.

We divided our fundraising activities into different strategies that would work in various counties. One strategy, effective in Oklahoma and Tulsa Counties, was an early-morning breakfast. We didn't have the resources to give away a car, like Oprah Winfrey, but we did tape two-dollar bills under selected chairs as a door prize. It was still a bit of an anomaly to find a two-dollar bill in circulation, and people were always excited if their chair happened to have the two-dollar bill. These breakfasts, and some individual fundraising activities, provided us with enough funds to carry on a creditable campaign, although we never could compete with the money spent by the established candidates: Preston Moore, who had been National Commander of the American Legion, and Raymond Gary, who had previously served as governor.

I placed third out of thirteen candidates, just 10,000 votes behind the winner. The runoff between Raymond Gary and Preston Moore ended with Moore winning the Democratic nomination—but he was defeated by Dewey Bartlett in the general election.

My showing was excellent for someone who had never run a statewide race, but it was a tough, bitter pill to be beaten, and it took me some time to get over the shock, as I had never lost a race since high school. Having missed the primary runoff, I decided to retrench and overcome my three biggest obstacles. The first goal was to build better recognition in the rural areas. The second was to target farm organizations in the less-populated counties. The third obstacle was financial; I needed a stronger "war chest."

Jo and I were determined that we would go forward.

I was most heartened in the primary by the minority vote. In the black districts of both Oklahoma City and Tulsa, I was dominant. The advantage in Tulsa was easy to explain; I had hired Caesar Latimer, the first black assistant county attorney in the history of Oklahoma. This popularity in the black community was also enhanced by my appointment of the first black legal secretary, Shirley Foster, a single mother rearing a child at home. Another factor was my support of the lawsuit to strike down the miscegenation statute in Oklahoma, which was declared unconstitutional.

In Oklahoma City, one of the little-known advantages that I had was the years that I had spent in the black community driving a Pepsi-Cola truck and getting acquainted with every one of the five hundred thirty-five Pepsi-Cola retailers. I knew the shop owners, barmen, and convenience store people on a first-name basis, and many of them were pleasantly surprised when they learned that I was running for governor, and almost all of them pledged their support.

This time I would not have the advantage of the county attorney's office for all the publicity it generated, as I had decided to finish my second term as prosecutor at the end of 1966 and enter private practice. However, my strong finish in the primary gave me confidence that I would be successful in four years, even against an incumbent.

The most important factor in my first governor's run was the lack of funds to carry on a proper campaign. In fact, things were so bad at one point during the campaign that *Time* magazine, whose correspondent was covering a portion of the primary in Oklahoma, featured an article about the "Credit Card Governor." The article referred to the many times I would be traveling across the state and run out of money. Someone in our party always came forward with a credit card and paid for what we needed to continue to the next stop.

It was clear that we had our work cut out for us—but the road to the governorship still lay before us, beckoning.

The Long Road

With Bartlett's victory in 1966, the conventional wisdom was that the Republicans would hold the governor's seat for eight years. Bartlett would serve his first term until 1970, and under the new law, he would be able to succeed himself.

I knew from our analysis of the 1966 race that Bartlett's strength was concentrated in the metropolitan areas and supported by the big-city press. So I set out to learn as much as I could about rural Oklahoma, and to court every small-town newspaper for its support. Small-town editors with state reputations were led by Jim Nance of Purcell, 40 miles south of the capital.

It was hard to believe, but even in the late 1960s, more than 52% of our gross state product came from agriculture. The constituency of the most powerful legislators lay in areas outside of Oklahoma City and Tulsa; the giants of the legislature in that era were State Senator Roy Boecher from Kingfisher—then a small town on the old Chisholm Trail, less than an hour's drive from the state capital—and Representative Ray Fine of Gore, a town about 130 miles east of Oklahoma City, on the banks of the Arkansas River.

At the state capital, the most powerful department heads were Lloyd Rader, director of welfare; Mike Conners, head of the tax commission; and Hayden Donahue, director of the state's mental facilities. My mission now was to get to know these men. All were

Democrats, and securing their support—either tacit or real—was a part of my strategy to win the primary in 1970. I knew that I had to cultivate these men and get to know them and other progressive rural legislators for what they really were, rather than what I may have read in the metropolitan press, such as *The Daily Oklahoman* and *The Tulsa Tribune*. These newspapers continually panned, deprecated, and slanted stories on the worth of these men and their value to Oklahoma; a prime example was the crusade that *The Tulsa Tribune* carried on against Ray Fine, vilifying him in every way that they could in his races, implying that his district in eastern Oklahoma was politically corrupt.

In almost every election in that district and similar rural Democrat strongholds, the Republican Party fanned out poll-watchers, not from the area but from Tulsa, trying to intimidate local voters. These poll-watchers' actions were preceded by metropolitan-press news stories of suspected voter fraud; the stories were bogus, but they sold papers on the streets of Tulsa.

I soon discovered that regardless of how much I had read and how much I thought I knew about the history of the trends and the idiosyncrasies of Oklahoma voters, I still had much to learn. The Native American influence and culture across the state in the 1960s had not developed into a powerful political force, nor had the 8% or 9% Hispanic population concentrated in the southwestern part of the state. However, the growing strength and political influence of the black communities in Tulsa, Muskogee, and Oklahoma City had already become a powerful force, counting in many instances 10% to 15% of the state vote. I had carried these areas in the '66 race, but I was determined that the margins were going to be greater in the race of 1970.

And finally, I learned why more individuals chose not to be involved in public service but pursued careers in law practice, business, and other private-sector paths: the cost of campaigns, the loss of reputation, the possible loss of earning power, and, most seriously, the potential of being smeared with lies and innuendo.

I also learned how hard it is to refute such allegations, even if there was no basis in fact.

Since my term as county attorney had ended in December 1966, it was necessary to make a living until the campaign of 1970. I was honored to become a partner in the Tulsa law firm of Kothe, Eagleton, and Hall. Charles Kothe was a brilliant legal mind and a first-class "rainmaker" in the profession. He had made his name as a labor-negotiations lawyer for the National Labor Relations Board, and was one of the very first in the nation to recognize the importance of the Equal Employment Opportunity Commission sector of the practice of law. He had represented the National Association of Manufacturers and was honored in many circles as one of the outstanding men in his field.

John Eagleton was the steady, solid influence in the office, and my addition was to help in the trial practice, as well as to develop new clients. From the beginning, I fully disclosed my intention to run again in 1970, and this was acceptable to both partners. Both men were Republicans, yet there was no acrimony in our political discussions. They were delighted to have someone as active, forward-looking, and dedicated to liberal causes as I was in the Democratic Party.

This association lasted for almost two years, until I realized that it was going to be impossible to carry on my duties in the law office and at the same time do the necessary work it would take to win the governor's race in 1970. Leaving Kothe and Eagleton was a sad parting, because I had enjoyed the work I had done with these men; I valued their advice, their integrity, and, most of all, their dedication to providing the clients with the best possible service.

After many discussions with Jo, with her support and blessing, I moved into my own office in the Petroleum Club Building in Tulsa, where I began a practice that was to last from 1968 through the race of 1970. One of the great benefits of that move was to give me an opportunity to form a partnership with David James, an outstanding young lawyer who had been one of my assistants in the county attorney's office. David had grown up next door to me, and I had watched him develop into a bright, steady, purposed attorney of integrity. His role was to handle his own cases and many of mine, to allow me the time to campaign.

Our practice dealt mostly with corporate activities, and I became adept at representing small non-public companies with fewer than 500 stockholders. In addition, we handled many other business and institutional cases, coupled with a limited personal-injury practice. David's specialty was transactional law and securities, and he was preparing for a much greater role in this field. In a few months' time, one of the great criminal-trial lawyers in Oklahoma, Pat Williams, joined us. Pat and I had played on the same high-school state-championship basketball team, and we were classmates at the University of Oklahoma. Pat had been the county attorney in Pawhuska, Oklahoma, then an assistant district attorney in Tulsa before turning to private practice. I was pleased to have him join the firm; he was noted for taking unusual fact situations in civil and criminal law and turning them to the advantage of his client.

One of the most dramatic cases he handled while in our office was the defense of a man accused of manslaughter. Not only was the criminal charge dismissed, but Pat was able to bring an action against the insurance carrier and collect a double-indemnity policy for his client—a marvelous piece of work, and one befitting a Gerry Spence, a Melvin Belli, or an F. Lee Bailey.

Then there was an important relationship that had been brewing with Ronald Goldfarb, a brilliant young lawyer based in Washington, DC. Ron was an honors graduate at Yale Law School, and served as a rackets prosecutor on Attorney General Robert Kennedy's staff. In years to come, Ron went on to develop a distinguished career as an author. He later formed his own law firm and literary agency, representing many successful authors.

Ron came to Tulsa for research on a book he was writing on bail-bond reform. He was investigating a program sponsored by the Tulsa County Bar Association for minor criminal cases in which defendants were often released into the custody of their attorneys rather than posting bail. This form of "own recognizance" release was very popular with the criminal bar and judiciary in our county, and other groups across the nation were considering similar programs. Ron was comparing bail-bond practices nationwide; in his book, *Ransom*, he carefully outlined our process and the good results for all concerned. The book sold well and served as a blueprint for bail reform.

Ollie Gresham, a Tulsa attorney, was a good friend of mine; he had originally supported my campaign for governor, and as an advocate of the bail-reform plan, he first introduced Ron to me. Ron and I became friends and began exchanging ideas after I told him of my plans to run for governor in 1966. This friendship blossomed, and after I left the Kothe Eagleton firm, Ron approached me about forming a Washington, DC partnership.

That partnership would consist of Stephen Kurzman —also a DC lawyer with outstanding credentials—Ron, and me. This was an adjunct to my legal work in Tulsa, and had great potential for connections for my political future. Kurzman, Goldfarb, and Hall had offices in the Grange Building at 1660 H Street in Washington. It was a match made in heaven politically, because Kurzman, a Republican, had been the legislative aide to Senator Jacob Javits of New York. Ron Goldfarb served in the cadre of Attorney General Robert Kennedy's prosecutors, and I was the outlander who would hopefully be sending business to Washington.

Although my agenda was set for a run for governor in 1970, in the summer of 1967, there was a lot of speculation that Democrat Mike Monroney, the senior US Senator from Oklahoma, was in for an extremely tough race in 1968. In August 1967, one of the state's most aggressive political figures, State Senator Gene Stipe from McAlester, approached me to ask if I would consider running for the nomination for United States Senate in the Democratic primary against Monroney. Stipe promised his support and pledged to raise a significant amount of money for me—but he cautioned me that it might be better for all concerned if his role would only be that of an advisor.

This idea of a Senate campaign was a complete departure from anything I had contemplated. Jo and I talked it over and decided that I should first go to Washington, meet with some high-level Democrats, and discuss the decision with my Washington law partner, Ron Goldfarb. On the trip, I visited several prominent Democrats; some thought it might be a good idea, others indicated that it was neither the time nor the right thing to do to try to challenge an incumbent Senator with Monroney's seniority.

The most telling advice came from Robert Kennedy. Ron had arranged a meeting with him to ask his opinion, and we met in Kennedy's busy office, with files spread his across his desk. I felt the political energy that radiated from him as we talked. He was shorter than I had imagined, more intense, with the sleeves of his white shirt rolled up, his hair rumpled, and a sparkle in his eyes that matched his incisive New England wit. I could fully understand why President Kennedy had relied so heavily on his advice. I thought about what a great team those brothers made, and the accomplishments that might have been possible had John Kennedy lived. And Robert's work as Attorney General in the civil rights era had made me a fan from the beginning. Kennedy was charismatic and unusually warm in his manner to someone he had never met before, a contrast to many of the New Englanders I had known at Harvard. I liked him.

The question was whether or not I would have the support of the Kennedy forces in Oklahoma.

Kennedy answered that Monroney was too strong and too well financed for anyone to beat him in the primary. Then, looking intently at me, he told me straight out that it was the wrong thing to do. He said that his people would not help me, although he hoped that I would continue in my pursuit of the governorship.

As blunt as his message was, I took it to heart. We shook hands. His was a solid, firm grip that conveyed sincerity, and our meeting ended on an up note. As Ron and I walked down the hall from Kennedy's office, we shared the same thought: He would be a friend in the future, and I should heed his advice.

I looked forward to my next meeting with Kennedy, b ut I would never see him again. In less than a year, in a crowded ballroom at the Ambassador Hotel in Los Angeles, at the end of the California primary, he would be killed by an assassin's bullet.

As for the question of a Senate bid, with information I received from other sources, it became apparent that Stipes's group had not asked me to run because they thought I was the best candidate to beat Monroney; it was an effort to split the potential vote for former Governor J. Howard Edmondson, who was considering the race for the Senate in 1968. With all these factors in mind, I discussed it with Jo, and we talked late into the night about what we should do. Our decision was to thank those who had urged me to run for the Senate—and continue with the governor's race.

Jo was the great leveling force in all of these decisions, and in building our agenda for the 1970 campaign. She encouraged grass-roots funding and the development of core supporters in every county, rather than depending upon the ten or eleven most populous counties, as we had done in the 1966 race. And now, because of our excellent showing in the 1966 race, it was not nearly as hard to open doors to be able to talk to potential campaign supporters and contributors. However, because we would be running against an incumbent governor, the chances of major campaign donations from any of these sources turned out to be slim.

A prime example was when the most successful black Oklahoma oilman, J.J. Simmons of Muskogee, Oklahoma, took me to meet the chairman of the board of Phillips Petroleum Company, William Keeler, to talk about supporting my campaign. The opportunity to meet Keeler in person was one not to miss, even though I was certain that his group was already committed to Governor Bartlett. Phillips Petroleum, being one of the major industrial employers of the state, had tremendous sway; they were the most powerful financial force in the northern part of the state, and whether they decided to assist in my campaign or not, it was part of the political ritual that I needed to meet Keeler.

I got a pleasant surprise when Simmons and I met privately with Keeler. In our discussion, Keeler said he would see that some funds were raised for me, although the company could not take any direct part in the campaign. As I learned later, this translated into a donation of $2,500, which was channeled through Simmons. I appreciated that very much, but upon seeing the amount, I was sorely disappointed, because money was an issue, even though we were doing better than we had in the first campaign. I later learned that the same group that helped put together the $2,500 for my campaign produced more than $100,000 for the campaign of Dewey Bartlett.

In fact, the greatest issue for Jo and me to stress in the matter of grassroots fundraising was the tremendous grip that the oil industry had maintained on previous governors throughout the history of the state. That history had only been broken by one other governor during those heydays of oil exploration leading up to the giant companies now operating in Oklahoma: the administration of William H. "Alfalfa Bill" Murray, from 1931 to 1935.

Jo and I decided on an important principle: No one segment, no one industry, and no one person would be solicited for the kind of support that would make us beholden to just that single interest. Our intention during those days was to be obligated only to the grassroots people from all over the state who helped in our campaign; it was our intention to "dance with them that brung you." This philosophy didn't sit well with some of the power-brokers, because they had expected us to prostrate ourselves before them and beg for funding.

Governor Bartlett's strength in the polls—and his unlimited campaign funds—discouraged many strong candidates from running. But the lessons I had learned in 1966 led me to believe that with my populist campaign, the right kind of platform, and most of all, the courage of my convictions, it didn't make any difference how much money the other side had; I believed that we could beat them when it got down to a one-on-one race. Visiting the 939 cities, towns, and villages of Oklahoma became the most important part of my campaign; we still ran into the obstacle of "David who?" in some areas.

And the general election was still a long way off—yet the truth was that going into the primary, I'd spent every cent getting ready to run. I needed to raise money—as quickly as possible. To almost everyone on the outside, this would not have boded well for any campaign. But mine wasn't just any campaign; for me, it was a mission.

Even with the money issues, I was determined to run an all-out sprint in the 1970 Democratic primary and secure the nomination for governor. Taking a page from the '66 primary playbook, I continued the practice of fund-raising breakfasts and soliciting small, grassroots contributions. Leaving no stone unturned, I was highly confident that we were going to win, and I would be the nominee for the Democratic Party. A hectic pace continued through to the end of the primary, and the night of the primary, I went to bed satisfied that I had done my best. The final pollsters' reports showed a commanding lead for me.

Waking up the next morning, I didn't want to jinx anything, but I couldn't help saying, "It's going to be a great day." Lo and behold, it was a phenomenal day—far beyond our best-case projections! I won in a walk—well, almost a walk. I amassed more than 48% of the vote and narrowly missed winning the Democrat nomination without a runoff. State Senator Bryce Baggett, my nearest opponent in vote totals, would be my run-off primary competitor for the next three weeks.

To heal the wounds of the primary and start the unification of the supporters of the defeated candidates, I called for a summit meeting for party unity at the Northwest Hilton Hotel in Oklahoma City. Every former primary candidate attended, including Baggett. One by one, all smiles, each speaker promised a united front once the run-off primary ended. While the TV cameras rolled and the press took notes, those assembled also pledged a clean campaign for the next three weeks.

So much for pledges! Within four hours of the end of the meeting, a desperate Baggett broke the truce and started slinging mud.

He challenged me to debate and ridiculed our campaign; I believe he would have tap-danced on the capitol steps if he thought it would get him any publicity.

My strategy was to ignore Baggett. Instead, I ran against the entrenched governor with every speech I made. Twenty-one days later, the run-off ended, and the nomination was mine; it was no contest—and now the real objective was Bartlett.

The warm and fuzzy feeling of a victory soon collided with reality. Doubts clouded my mind now, because I knew that better-funded candidates who might have run in the primary had begged off because they didn't believe they could beat Dewey Bartlett. Now I really had to take the measure of Bartlett, for now it was the one-on-one contest that I had asked for.

Just who was Governor Dewey Bartlett? Well, for starters, he was a popular Republican who had a lot of friends in high places in Oklahoma, including the oil industry, various segments of business, and the banks. It wasn't that people didn't like him—it was just that he had no familiarity with middle-class and low-income families. As a State Senator from Tulsa, his political proclivities had been passive, rather than progressive. During his tenure, the Democratic-Party-controlled legislature more or less ignored him.

He was a nice-looking man with a lean build and a somewhat forced but engaging smile, but he often came across as distant. Bartlett had a good reputation in the oil business, and since he had taken up politics, he was considered a comer in the Republican Party. His victory in the 1966 governor's race was remarkable not for the margin, but because he was the second straight Republican governor elected—and for the first time, under the new law, he could succeed himself.

Bartlett came from a wealthy family in Ohio. Schooled in the East at Lawrenceville prep and Princeton University, he was removed from the day-to-day ups-and-downs that are part of the fabric of the average Oklahoman's life. He was a quick study on business issues, well financed in his campaign, and somewhat aloof to those who met him for the first time. A Roman Catholic, he succeeded in a state predominately Protestant.

As the incumbent, he was unopposed in the Republican primary, giving me an opportunity to gain recognition and dominate the political news stories while he waited in the wings, confident of his position. He reveled in the support of the metro press; in the year preceding the 1970 election, I can't remember an unfavorable story on him appearing anywhere.

His strengths: incumbency, money, positive press, and a non-controversial record.

His weaknesses: lack of understanding the average Oklahoman's needs, indifference to education, ignorance of rural issues, and, most telling to me, his failure to provide the badly needed jobs for Oklahoma. Over the past 22 months of canvassing the state, I had seen first-hand the unemployment problems, the need for education reform, Bartlett's favoritism of the cities, and his meager track record on bringing new business to the state. As Bill Clinton in 1992 would hammer the slogan "It's the economy, stupid," my team and I in 1970 championed, "Jobs, education reform, and the rural voters."

The closer November 1970 came, the harder I worked—and the more I knew that this election would be a defining moment in Oklahoma history. It was the past versus the present. The eleven-year difference in our ages, plus my boundless energy, helped me. Bartlett's complacency angered schoolteachers, union members, college professors, small farmers, and low-income workers. His money, his metro press coverage, and his oil-industry support had lulled him into a belief that he was invincible.

Goliath was about to meet David—and the pebble in my political slingshot was the coalition for change in Oklahoma.

In the final months of the campaign, we divided the state into four major sectors and put a campaign coordinator in charge of each one. It was his job to call all of the county chairmen in his sector on a daily basis, get a report, and turn it into the state office so that we knew exactly what the temper of the public was in each of those four sectors. Sixty days out, the polls all seemed to favor a re-election of Governor Bartlett by a seven- to ten-point margin. These daily reports started to fluctuate between the 60th day and the 30th, but then, from that point on, the polls moved steadily toward our campaign.

This trend was not reflected, however, in the metropolitan press.

In deciding what was fair and what was unfair—in playing defense and offense against the Republican incumbent—we produced bumper stickers that seemed to be the most effective; they were red, white, and blue with a bold "David Hall For Oklahoma" emblazoned on them, and we distributed those in every precinct. Then, three or four weeks from the actual November vote, I learned that many of Bartlett's paid advertisements that were to run in rural newspapers had been withdrawn by his campaign; he appeared to be doing so well all over the state that they didn't think it was necessary to spend those dollars. In addition, we received information from such diverse groups as the Oklahoma Road Contractors, the Independent Oil Association, and other power-brokers backing Governor Bartlett that they, too, were taking it for granted that Bartlett would be re-elected.

On the national scene, this mirrored a false sense of security in Republican-held state houses all across the country, still basking in the glory of riding Richard Nixon's coattails in the 1968 Republican victory. For the Democrats, Jimmy Carter was on the move in the Georgia governor's race, Rueben Askew in Florida, Jim Exon in Nebraska, Dale Bumpers in Arkansas, John West in South Carolina, Wendell Anderson in Minnesota, Dick Kneipp in South Dakota— all of us young Turks in emerging movements at the state level.

My message of increased funding for schools and the need for statewide kindergarten and support for special education resonated with struggling young parents and minorities across Oklahoma. Our state ranked 46th of 48 in per-pupil expenditures; only Mississippi and Louisiana were below us—pitiful, to say the least. The president of Oklahoma Education Association, Betty Ward, put it best: "Bartlett has failed the needs of Oklahoma's school children, and it's time for a change."

Jack Patton, a banker and higher-education advocate from Norman, and a close advisor, asked, "David, with the lack of funding at the university level, how can Oklahoma attract the industry that we need to build the state? With 55% of our college graduates leaving the state, how can we expect to compete?"

My pledge to the middle-income families was that there would be no increase in taxes for them. Democrats and Independents warmed to this commitment.

With job creation as the campaign's main focus, we tried to devise means to call attention to the fact that Governor Bartlett had failed to provide new jobs for people, and we thought that the best way to get at this issue was to conduct interviews outside the unemployment offices in the major population areas of Oklahoma—Tulsa, Muskogee, and Oklahoma City. For publicity, we made TV "ambush" interviews; as an unemployed person left the office, I would greet them on the sidewalk with the cameras rolling. "Hello, my name is David Hall, and I'm running for governor." Most people would accept my handshake and pause, seeing the camera. "May I ask you a question?" I continued.

"Sure."

"Can you tell me what Governor Bartlett has done to help you get a job?"

"Not a thing!" was the standard reply—in many cases with a descriptive expletive.

We then took a release from the person, sent the film to our ad man, and a 30-second campaign spot for television was born. In the TV markets of Lawton and Ada, we submitted the interviews as news sound bites, and invariably got some of them aired.

Then, about eight days out from November 7, we suddenly saw a dramatic change in our day-to-day contacts with our county chairmen. The rural areas had suddenly become more energized by our campaign; it looked as through many of these rural counties that we had hoped to carry with simple majorities were now going to deliver us a much larger margin—though this trend was never reflected, during that last week, by any of the polls that we saw in the metropolitan newspapers or in the mass media.

But I still needed a lightning-bolt issue; with Bartlett's lead still 6% to 7% in the polls as we entered the final week before the election, I knew we needed a bombshell to give me momentum.

Nationally, environmental concerns were coming to the forefront—and it was true in Oklahoma, too. As county attorney, I had encountered air pollution in the refineries of West Tulsa. I knew environmental pollution could touch a raw nerve in voters, if presented the right way.

Researching pollution in Oklahoma, I found that the protection of clean, free-flowing streams was a concern of young and old. This issue became our secret weapon. Two young men on my team, Bob White and J. T. Weedman, found a Bartlett -owned well near Shawnee—a well whose containment pond was leaking black, scummy oil into just such a creek. To eliminate any question of the authenticity of this pollution, we had hired an independent, non-partisan newsman to shoot the film and to verify that the holding pond was leaking so that we would not be later accused of having sabotaged one of Bartlett's wells.

The film of the leaking oil-well pond was made into a one-minute commercial, showing a split screen with Bartlett's polluting well pond seeping into that free-flowing stream compared with a pristine, clean, environmentally correct well. This was a shocker. Five days before the vote, we ran the film on every TV outlet in Oklahoma, using our last ad dollars.

I had rolled the political dice.

For the first twenty-four hours, we sweated out the result. Would it sell the voter on "Dumping Dewey"? Did the majority of the state care that much? Incensed at being exposed, the Bartlett forces offered a thousand-dollar reward for information on who had caused their well pond to leak. I felt that we had wounded the mighty Goliath—but was it enough?

By noon the next day, I got my answer. The response was terrific; Sierra Club members and other environmentalists who had been on the sidelines in the campaign came to our aid. Anglers, Boy Scouts, and Girl Scouts rallied to support my efforts. These new environmental converts to the campaign joined elementary teachers, blue-collar workers, African-Americans, small soybean and wheat farmers, college student leaders, and various minority groups to help close the gap. It was a successful exposé.

But two days from the vote, I still wondered if our gamble would pay off at the polls. The clock was ticking. The day before the vote, last-minute polls still showed Bartlett ahead, but the margin had narrowed. Was it too close to call?

Jo on election day, November 1970, with campaign
mascot, "Governor," at home in Tulsa

Election Day was a flurry of activity—almost a blur. After Jo and I had voted in Tulsa, we went to Oklahoma City, making stops at campaign events in several shopping malls and bowling alleys until the end of the day. I felt confident, but cautious. Whatever the results were going to be, I could feel a level of support that buoyed my spirits like nothing else. However, it also was a reminder that if I won, I would bear the weight of living up to making the difference the voters counted on me to deliver.

With Doug, Nancy, and Julie in tow, Jo and I went to the Hilton Hotel at Northwest Expressway and May Avenue to await the results of the vote. The hotel had designated the ballroom as Sooner I, which had been the name of our original campaign-helicopter tour of eastern Oklahoma back in the 1966 campaign.

The early returns started coming in right after the polls closed, and they showed a significant lead for Governor Bartlett. Taking the numbers in stride, I reminded everyone that these were primarily the population-center reports coming in, and they did not reflect what was going on in rural Oklahoma. Still, as my four main coordinators finished up their day's work in their sectors, they all came to Oklahoma City, and I don't think I've seen longer faces on any campaign workers than I did on those men—they were very concerned.

Wait a minute, I said to myself. *Could they be right to be glum?* Mentally reaching down, I pulled up my socks and repeated to myself, "Get your head on straight. Remember, David, you didn't come all this way to lose!" I felt as I had all those years before, playing in close basketball games. I did a gut check—and I knew that I had given my all.

I could feel victory close at hand.

Sometimes I can be a cockeyed optimist, but truly, in my heart I had felt for the last twenty-two months that we would win the race, even though it might be close—perhaps much closer than any of us had imagined. At 9:30 on election night, we received the first bulletin across the wire service indicating that the trend was beginning to show a change in the vote totals in favor of the Hall campaign. Ron Goldfarb, who had come from Washington to assist us with writing speeches during the campaign, had written two speeches for election night; one was a concession speech, thanking everyone for their help if we lost, and the other was an acceptance speech. I never knew there were two versions until later.

To this day, I don't remember what Ron wrote in the concession speech. With everything running much too close to deliver either speech, it wasn't until midnight, as our campaign advisers, Jo, the children, and I waited in our hotel suite with our eyes glued to the TV, that the national networks decided to call the race. So many times I had waited for juries to deliver verdicts, both when I was a DA prosecuting a case and in private practice when I was representing a client; in all those instances, right before verdicts came in, I would always say a silent prayer that, regardless of my stake in the matter, justice would be served.

That's the same prayer I offered during the last second before the results were announced. Resolved to be triumphant even in defeat, I barely heard my name when the network called the race for David Hall as the governor-elect. After I finished hugging Jo and the children, we all made our way to the ballroom.

My victory speech started out with Jackie Gleason's famous line: "How sweet it is!" Those words at the beginning of the acceptance speech were meant to tell everyone that an average Oklahoman, without unlimited financial resources—unlike the opponent—had been able to accomplish a miracle in the face of unbelievable odds. And mounting the podium, I realized just how sweet it really was.

That speech was a hit, too—a resounding thank-you to all who had helped in this Herculean effort, an announcement to the state of Oklahoma that a new day had dawned, and a new populist philosophy was about to take over the State House. But in the midst of the balloons and confetti and the cheering and hugging that went on for what seemed like forever, I felt the weight of history upon me. The populist reign for another man of the common people was about to begin in Oklahoma, sending out tsunami-like political waves that amazed a complacent Republican Party: A political David had slain their Goliath.

We all went to bed that night happy in the thought that the race had been won, and looking forward to the transition period to get ready for the new administration. The next morning, however, we awoke to a completely new problem: Because of the close vote—fewer than 3,000 votes separated us—the Bartlett campaign had demanded a recount. To preserve the ballot boxes, Governor Bartlett was prepared to call out the National Guard in each of the 77 counties. As state procedure required, Governor Bartlett posted the necessary fee for the recount; in an effort to protect our hard-fought victory, the Hall campaign also posted the fee for a recount. Otherwise, the Bartlett campaign could be declared the winner any time they gained the lead.

At the time the recount started, no one knew how long it would take, but as it turned out, it was an eleven-day exercise in democracy. Again, we were handicapped by the fact that we did not have the funds to employ lawyers in every county to supervise the recount; but in the process of the campaign, we had received enough support from members of the state bar that we were able to attract 199 volunteer lawyers—enough for more than two lawyers in some of the counties—to supervise the recount in their areas, and to assist in other areas. This was a phenomenal outpouring of generosity by these men and women, who spent a large part of these eleven days helping to ensure that an accurate count for our side was given.

The final recount at the end of the eleventh day was touch-and-go up until the last three counties were counted. Finally, with the count ending in Nowata County, we won the race by a margin of 2,187 votes out of more than 700,000 cast. It was the closest governor's race in state history—and the beginning of the term of Oklahoma's twentieth governor.

On that celebratory evening in mid-November, when the final count was in and we knew that we had won the race, we gathered in our headquarters in the Founders Tower in Oklahoma City. For the first time I breathed a sigh of relief as the reality began to sink in—to me as well as Jo, our staff, our supporters, and our loyal friends across the state—that indeed the dream had come true.

Oklahoma's future was now in my hands.

Part Two:

Governor Hall

1970-1975

Dark Days, Revisited

During those excruciating minutes on that gloomy afternoon of March 14, 1975, just before the verdict was announced, as I stood in the courtroom in a surreal out-of-body state with every tiny detail of the trial passing in front of my eyes, I prayed—as I always did—for justice.

Even with evidence of the flagrant injustice in the hands of others, I refused to have my faith broken. After all, prosecutorial overreach and judicial misconduct are two of the main reasons that appeals are granted. This thought calmed me enough to realize that there would be a means of appealing an unfair verdict, if it came to that; without question, without exception, every ruling on this last day of deliberations by Judge Daugherty reeked of bias.

In my mind, I replayed everything that had happened from the moment of arriving at the courthouse. I recalled how just getting to judge's chambers meant my attorneys and I had to push our way through the dense group of trial-watchers. Unlike the passionate contingencies outside on the steps, the throng inside the building appeared less concerned with what was at stake; they were more ravenous for any kind of drama—a restless crowd turning resentful for being made to wait for some sort of spectator sport.

Here, too, Judge Daugherty had helped fan those flames with an earlier decision to move the trial to the largest courtroom available, where— besides those directly involved and our families—an additional 100 to

120 people could be seated. Considering the non-stop media barrage, it was still barely room enough to accommodate the crowds that had been gathering these past weeks.

Jo and I had weathered many political storms, and we believed our faith would see us through.

A Dream Fulfilled

The blustery winds of early November had added to the flurry of activity at our headquarters at Northwest Oklahoma City's most visible landmark, the 25-story, octagonal Founders Tower Office Building. Thanks to United Founders executives Gerald Barton, Horace Rhodes, and Bernie Illie, we were allowed to keep these offices until our team would move to the governor's quarters in the capitol building. The first frost of the coming winter had put an exciting chill in the air as my energized staff savored the victory and worked with hurried anticipation toward our assuming the reigns of power.

It was exhilarating for me to walk into that office the first morning after the recount victory, shake hands, exchange hugs, and feel the uplifting spirits of the workers and advisors already on the job to affect the transition. With the recount ending, the real transition work had begun for the new Hall administration: staff slots to be filled, times lines for appointments, decisions on which department heads to keep, which department heads to fire, inauguration planning, and, most important, the strategy for presenting our program for Oklahoma to the legislature.

Once I had been officially declared the winner of the gubernatorial race, it was amazing to me how quickly the landscape changed with the influential groups across the state. Those who had been reluctant to give our candidacy the credence that we thought it deserved suddenly wanted to do everything in this interim period to ingratiate themselves with the new incoming administration. The very best example of this was the Oklahoma Road Contractors Association, who, prior to the election, had been very leery of giving any direct support to our campaign. Some individuals of the association had helped us because they believed in our mission, but the great majority of the contractors had amassed a war chest for Governor Bartlett, and had gone marching to his tune for many months before the election.

Now Ernie Honnegar, an emissary from the road contractors, had contacted Sunny Jenkins as for a meeting with me. Sunny and I knew that Honnegar had been designated by that group to try repair relations between my team and the contractors due to their support of Bartlett. Late in the afternoon the day before we were to meet with Honnegar, Sunny and I discussed our strategy. "You know Ernie was favorable to us, and he personally donated," said Sunny.

"Yes, you told me that—but I knew from reports from our Tulsa supporter, Bill Rollins and others, that Ernie's donation was just a token."

Sunny continued, "Well don't be too hard on him. We can sure use any money that bunch gives us to pay off some of our debts. And it wouldn't hurt to have their support in the legislative session."

I mulled over what Sunny had said for a few moments. What he didn't know was that I had also talked over this issue with Jo; with my brain trust advisor, Ira Sanditen ; and with my incoming legislative advisor, G.M. Fuller— and each had the same opinion: Be very wary of Greeks bearing gifts. "Sunny, let's see what Ernie has to say at the meeting tomorrow before we accept anything from them," I said.

This didn't sit well with Sunny; I surmised he had already told Honnegar that I would accept any help.

We knew that immediately after my election, a number of the road contractors who represented the organization gathered together a substantial amount of money: more than $400,000 in contributions. That's when they asked for a meeting with me, to discuss how they might assist us in helping with any of our campaign debts, or any expenses that we had been unable to pay.

The next morning, the meeting took place in my temporary office in the Founders Tower. Sunny, Ernie Honnegar, and I were present. Ernie said how pleased he was at our victory, and assured me of his support throughout the campaign. As I listened, I thought of that wonderful political axiom: *Victory has many fathers, but defeat is an orphan.* I gave Ernie as much time as he wanted to make his offer, and then I surprised him—and Sunny—when I turned down the offered donations. I was candid but pleasant, and the meeting ended on a cordial note; but afterwards, in private, a red-faced Sunny asked me why I had turned down the money.

"Sunny," I said, "it's a new day. We will retire our debts with money from the people who believe I can change Oklahoma, not the same old crowd that has always held the power." Privately, I chuckled to myself that I was much like the fictional hero Yancy Cravat in Edna Ferber's classic historical novel *Cimarron.* As a candidate for governor in the story, Yancy turns down the political boss's money because he wants no strings.

Declining the offer from the road contractors was probably one of the best decisions I ever made, because it created a ripple effect, broadcasting the word to all that it was not business as usual at the governor's office—and that there might be some rather earthshaking changes coming.

The end to "business as usual" was both good news and bad news to the power-brokers who had opposed our candidacy. But it had to be wholly infuriating to the Republican hierarchy, because so many dreams and ambitions of various Republican operatives had been dashed upon the rocks of defeat. Such was to be expected; unbeknownst to me, however, plans to thwart our administration were well under way during this transition period—before I actually took the oath of office. Even if someone had warned me about these plans, they might have sounded too far-fetched to be believable.

Meanwhile, my focus was on delivering on the promises made to the citizens of Oklahoma. In an effort to help incoming new governors, the National Governor's Association set up a school for governors that took place in Pinehurst, North Carolina. It was a three-day workshop with experienced governors from both parties leading seminars for new governors starting off their administrations, offering much information and background of what others had experienced in the same new setting. These seminars were absolutely the most valuable preparation for governing, in addition to my review of Oklahoma history and the information that I had learned on the campaign trail.

The guiding light of all these seminars, in my opinion, was Governor Nelson Rockefeller of New York. He was a four-term governor and probably had more experience than anyone else on all of the issues that could arise for an incoming governor. Rockefeller, a liberal Republican, inspired me as a public servant; here was a man born to wealth, whose commitment to lift up those in poverty and to fund education and the arts counted for much with me. I was fascinated with his success in a state with predominant Democrat registration. His one blind spot, I felt, was lack of law-enforcement background. Listening to his experiences and hearing of his adroit handling of the reigns of his state for four terms was like a doctorate degree in political science.

Another important lesson from of an experience that immediately followed the trip to North Carolina. Since Jo and I had not had any time to ourselves for almost twenty-two months, we decided after completing the seminars to take four days off in Bermuda and enjoy each other's company before we stepped back into the firestorm of starting an administration. We took a bungalow at a resort in Treasure Key in the Bermudas, and proceeded to have four of the most wonderful days that we could remember in the last few years. Not only was it romantic and inspiring to be with each other in that atmosphere, but we decided we would do something we had never done. We were out boating one day at a far sandbar about a mile offshore. Neither one of us had ever been skinny-dipping, and we decided that this was as good a time as any to try; we both dropped our suits and jumped into the surf. Exhilarating! We laughed, splashed, and enjoyed it—and after we had finished, we lay on the beach, gathered ourselves together, then headed back to the resort, feeling that we didn't have a care in the world.

As usual, things were not necessarily as they seemed. As we walked in to dinner that night, we heard a few snickers around the room, and saw quite a few eyes directed toward us. It wasn't long before a kind soul came up to the table, leaned over to me, and whispered in my ear that people with binoculars had really enjoyed the swimming and sunbathing that they observed on a distant sandbar earlier in the day. Jo and I sat there, red-faced and embarrassed; the first thing that crossed our minds was, "Are we going to see a picture of that in the Oklahoma papers?" The Lord was with us on this trip, however, for no such photo ever appeared in Oklahoma—and to this day we laugh and joke about that experience.

But this interlude served as a warning: Be careful in your private life, because it could be translated to public eyes. It was a warning I took to heart, as did Jo.

While we were away attending the Governor's Training School and enjoying our very brief vacation, our political enemies were already starting to implement their payback agenda. What's worse, it was at this point that my own campaign finance chairman, Sunny Jenkins, concocted his scam to create a fundraising apparatus that he would then loot and stash in a Mexican bank account. Perhaps most insidious was how Sunny, manipulator that he was, managed to pull this off at the very moment when the campaign had exhausted itself of funds; it would be much easier, even with energetic fundraising, to explain empty coffers as the result of payments on long-due bills. Suspicion wouldn't be raised until it was too late.

Some of the political machinations weren't new. The same forces within the Republican Party that had harassed Leo Winters, the Oklahoma treasurer, four years before—to the point of precipitating a criminal charge against him, which later resulted in his exoneration— were hard at work, making plans to continue their endeavors against Winters. N ow they added me as a target. Perhaps the most irate of all the Republican hierarchy was the Republican Party campaign chairman: William Burkett, a man who would later swear public vengeance against me. Burkett, who had taken it as a given that Governor Bartlett would be re-elected, had hoped that this might well result in a federal district judgeship for him sometime in the future.

Though the result of my election altered those plans, it gave him an opportunity to become the United States attorney for the western district of Oklahoma. And from that elevated station, Burkett would have all kinds of ammunition to finds ways to ensnare me and those close to me.

The main reason that I didn't sense any of these dark maneuvers was that I was focused on an entirely opposite and more powerful reaction coming from many quarters. During the transition, before I was sworn into office, it was a time of great euphoria; friends from all over the country had followed the campaign, and now they called to give me words of encouragement and talk about what could be done in the future—not only in Oklahoma but across the country. One was a friend I met at Harvard, John Loeb, Jr. John was the son of the principal partner in the famous Loeb Rhodes Investment Firm of New York City.

I hadn't seen or heard from John in several years, but immediately after the recount ended, I received a call from New York. Gerry Strain, my newly selected administrative assistant and trusted confidante, took the call, put the caller on hold, hurried to my desk, and said, "It's an old friend from Harvard, John Loeb. Do you want to take the call?"

I was flattered, because I had not heard from him in a long time. "You bet, Gerry! Put him on!"

John's deep, aristocratic voice came over the phone: "David, I am so proud of you. I just wanted to add my congratulations"

"Thanks, John. It's great to hear from you." We talked for a few minutes, recounting our friendship, and then ended with plans to talk in a few weeks. I told Gerry after the call that this was a valuable contact to use in evaluating the many New York investment firms that I knew would be soliciting Oklahoma's bond and other financial business. But I had to remember that John spoke from a rock-ribbed Republican point of view.

Later, it was his encouragement, combined with the counsel of a man I was to meet in 1972, attorney Gene Wyman of Los Angeles, that would light the spark and inspire Jo and me to consider national office, assuming we succeeded in the governorship. The target year was 1976.

The hectic activity of the transition period included the awesome task of recruiting a staff, reviewing the protocols for an incoming governor, and starting the very difficult process of appointing some 3,500 people to various boards, commissions, and administrative posts within state government. I faced the daunting challenge of supervising 37,000 Oklahoma state employees, and some 27 agencies, commissions, and various committees. Many of these were governed by statute, many required the Senate approval for appointment, and every one of them required a thorough vetting to determine who would be the best person for that particular job. The most cherished appointments in the administration were highway commissions and boards of regents at the universities; they would be the hardest to fill. All of these issues came into play during the transition period.

My inauguration day arrived with all the traditional pomp and ceremony that for so many years had only existed for me in dreams and far-fetched aspirations. I soaked in every ounce of it, overjoyed to be sharing it with Jo and our three children, Nancy, Doug, and Julie Beth—now twelve, eleven, and eight—and with everyone who had helped make this day possible, including the forward-thinking people of Oklahoma. The day began with a wonderful prayer breakfast highlighting two exceptional speakers and religious figures, Oral Roberts, the television evangelist who had influenced so many people around the world, and the Reverend Ben Hill of the AME Methodist Church of North Tulsa.

These two great men had taken entirely different paths for spreading the Word; Reverend Roberts had touched millions of men, women, and children around the world, and the Reverend Ben Hill had ministered to his flock in a relatively small geographical area, but he had had an unbelievable impact not only on his parishioners' belief in God but on the civil rights movement throughout his church group.

The beginning prayer and statement was given by Reverend Hill, and it mesmerized the audience—so much so that it made Oral Roberts' closing oration rather difficult—perhaps the only time anyone had ever seen him upstaged by a fellow speaker in the religious community. The text of Reverend Hill's message has hung on my wall ever since.

The prayer breakfast morphed into a reception in the Blue Room of the capitol building prior to the actual swearing-in ceremony, at which all the living former governors attended as we prepared to transition into the new administration. Major General Laverne Webber of the Oklahoma National Guard, one of our finest soldiers, had made all of the arrangements for the platform and the accommodations for actually taking the oath. A 21-gun salute was carried out by the Oklahoma National Guard, and the ceremony began with prayer and reverence.

Inaugural platform, swearing-in ceremony, January 14, 1971. From left: Jo Hall, Governor Elect David Hall; Speaker of the U.S. House of Representatives Carl Albert; Mrs. Albert; Lt. Governor Elect George Nigh; South steps of the Capitol Building, Oklahoma City, Oklahoma

The day was sunny, the air crisp, the crowd was excited and somewhat boisterous in their reaction to each of the events, and the culmination of a life's dream gave birth to a spiritual recognition about what can be accomplished when people join together, believing in something greater than themselves. Legendary Democratic speaker of the House of Representatives Carl Albert introduced me at the swearing-in ceremony, and Supreme Court Justice William A. Berry administered the oath, with Jo standing at my side. I took the oath on the small, worn, leather-covered King James Bible given to me by Grandmother Hall. After I took the oath, Jo and I turned to the lectern to address the audience, and the first words I spoke were, "Thank you." I had never felt so humbled and so privileged as I did at that moment. In the flicker of an eye, all of the toil, the disappointments, the small victories before, and the giant victory in the end came together in a blinding light of warmth that spread over the assembled crowd.

Inauguration reception in the Blue Room, Oklahoma State Capitol, all living Oklahoma Governors, From left: Governor Elect David Hall, Governor Dewey Bartlett, Governor Henry Bellmon, Governor George Nigh, Governor J. Howard Edmondson, Governor Raymond Gary, Governor Johnston Murray, January 14, 1971

Following the ceremony, we again moved to the Blue Room and spent the rest of the afternoon in a reception line, greeting the friends, supporters, and officials who had gathered to witness the ceremony. It was a joyous and tiring time. We then proceeded to the governor's mansion for the transition to the new family home.

Coming from our modest Tulsa house, it must have seemed like a fairy tale to the children to move into the mansion. It was a joy to watch our children choose their bedrooms. Nancy, the eldest, had first choice, but she deferred to Doug for what I thought was the best bedroom. It was located near the back stairs and had its own bath, and the other two available bedrooms shared a bath. Nancy figured that Doug and Julie Beth would never get along sharing the bath, and thus her decision. With Doug appropriately assigned, Nancy chose the bedroom just to the right of the circular staircase leading up from the first floor. Julie Beth took the remaining bedroom on the northwest corner of the second floor. Years later, she told us that the bed in that room frightened her; it had a massive, dark sculptured wooden headboard that loomed above her head, and it seemed to have an ominous life of its own.

We all rested, ate a light supper, and then dressed for the evening ceremony when "the people's party" would come together and celebrate the beginning of a new era in Oklahoma history. Jo's inaugural gown was a true work of design genius: fabric of heavy, white silk; flowing lines that accentuated her figure; and a regal, white silk coat that complemented her silhouette, drawing admiring glances. This ensemble had the overall effect of dramatizing her long, dark hair, flashing brown eyes, and tan skin. The press reports described her as one of Oklahoma's most beautiful first ladies.

In anticipation of this event, the giant shopping mall of some 200,000 square feet on 23rd Street in Oklahoma City, known as Shepard's Mall, had been reserved for the evening with the anticipation of a large crowd. The huge turnout was beyond expectations, however, with some 35,000 Oklahomans attending the inaugural ball in this covered shopping area. It was so inspiring to be with all of the men, women, and children who had done so much to make this dream come true! There were tears in my eyes when Jim Webster, the lifelong friend who had given me my first real political boost in junior high school, joined us at the podium. With his wife, Reba, by his side, he watched as Jo and I danced to the strains of "Moon River," our favorite melody at the time.

Less than three weeks after these festivities ended, I had the opportunity to have the Reverend Ben Hill be my guest at the mansion and a chance to thank him for his appearance at the prayer breakfast. He was accompanied by my good friend and former law school classmate, Ed Goodwin.

Breakfast in the Governor's Mansion dining room: from left: Reverend Ben Hill, AME Methodist Church, Tulsa, Oklahoma; Governor Hall; Ed Goodwin, publisher, Oklahoma Eagle; Tulsa, Oklahoma, January 1971

Leadership, I had learned early in my life, is more than motivating and empowering others to follow; it's also about surround yourself with the right people—those who will push you even further than you believe possible. Without a minute to waste, a grinding agenda of those first few weeks began bright and early on the morning after inauguration. To fashion our strategy and serve as my closest advisors, I had recruited a three-man "brain trust." These three, Ira Sanditen, Gerald Barton, and G.M. Fuller, had really come together as a team in the trenches with me during the last six months of the campaign.

Sanditen, a brilliant real-estate investor and business guru, was a member of the famous Sanditen family of Oklahoma, founders of the extremely successful Oklahoma Tire and Supply Co. (OTASCO). Fifty years old, and also an Oklahoma University graduate, Ira had been my friend and loyal supporter during my days as a county prosecutor. During the campaign, he had been the point man and bridge to the Tulsa Jewish community, assisting in introductions and fundraising, and was my mentor in understanding the emerging strength of Israel. Disabled and confined to a wheelchair since a tragic auto accident while in college, he directed his energy—and a burning desire to succeed—into his business ventures, his marriage, and the pursuit of ambitious political goals. His political philosophy matched mine; he was liberal when it came to people, and conservative when it came to property.

One of his greatest traits was his sensitivity to other people—and respect for their time. "David, your boundless enthusiasm and energy must be disciplined," he said. "You need in-depth understanding of the value of time to all people and all issues. You are an important official, but remember how important everyone else's time is to them. Don't abuse it."

I nodded and felt chagrined for the number of times I made others wait.

"And prioritize the issues regarding time as well," he went on. "That's where your other advisors and I can help most. Don't be afraid to delegate to the right men and women."

I endeavored to take all his words to heart, as I knew he had my best interests in mind.

Gerald Barton, at forty, had been a classmate from college. Married to a very bright lawyer, he was a visionary in his field; a developer of resort hotels, he was active in the Young Presidents organization, and was the consummate time-allocation expert. He might well have been a Henry Ford or John D. Rockefeller in another era. His knowledge, keen sense of timing, and ability to seize opportunities were valuable assets in the overall planning for my political victory, as well as the implementation of our programs.

G.M. Fuller, forty-five, was a polished, highly successful Oklahoma City attorney, well-dressed and well-spoken, and was a much admired member of the bar who had distinguished himself as a member of the Oklahoma State Legislature. His integrity and honesty were without question. He brought to "brain trust" a vast knowledge of the working legislature, experience in shepherding and advancing bills through that body, and—most importantly—an ability to work with the speaker of the Oklahoma House of Representatives and the president pro tempore of the Senate. He would be the point man for the legislative program of my administration. I was blessed to have G.M. as a friend and counselor.

After the election, these men put the finishing touches on the plans for Oklahoma that I would present to the first legislative session. They had worked day and night with my staff to perfect the strategy for implementing my program as we constantly reviewed the resources available to me. These men were volunteer "one-dollar-a-year" men, who believed in my plans for Oklahoma—and who wanted to be a part of our mission to move Oklahoma forward. They helped formulate the cornerstone issues to implement my campaign promises:

Adequate education funding for pupils and teachers alike.

New business to bring the jobs I had promised.

Financing for these programs—while keeping my promise of no new taxes on the middle class.

Closing the loophole on Oklahoma corporations who had never paid a dividend tax because their headquarters were located in the state, a concession more than three decades old.

Repairing 525 deathtrap bridges and roads across the 77 counties.

These were the building blocks that would bring Oklahoma out of yesteryear and into the modern era—while we developed the tax reform that provided 95% of Oklahoma's tax relief.

It's hard to believe, but I had never been in the governor's office or the rooms that the staff would occupy until the day I was sworn in and Bartlett's crew vacated the premises—without a single offer to view the office, share information, or any other normal courtesy between the victor and the vanquished. Bartlett was bitter, and he did his best to make the transition difficult for me. As I walked the marble floor on the second level of the capitol building, headed for the southeast wing and the suite of offices occupied for the past four years by Bartlett, I envisioned a scene different from what I found. As I passed the two granite pillars on either side of the entrance, I glanced above and saw engraved the word *governor*, and my heart leapt. I was the man, and this was my office.

As I opened door, Gerry Strain, who had already been inside, came running to me and said, "You're not going to believe this! They've stripped everything—not one folder, not one paper clip, none of the appointment files, no paper, nothing! I'm surprised they didn't take the light bulbs!"

For a moment I hesitated, then with a laugh, I said to Gerry, "Well, I guess Dewey is still teed off about us exposing his polluting oil well." She laughed heartily, and we proceeded into the suite.

So the Hall administration's new headquarters would start from scratch. With the euphoria of victory still swirling around me, the insult of the bare drawers, empty shelves, and no pencils made no impression; I felt that Bartlett's sophomoric lack of civility was his problem, not mine. It would later be contrasted with the transition that occurred when I left office and Governor David Boren came in—after weeks of sharing information and documents. It was perhaps one of the most peaceful transitions in the history of the state.

As we restocked the governor's office with basic business staples and established a daily routine, I began to get wind of a troubling concern. It went back to a family vacation we had taken over the New Year's holiday, when Jo and I took the kids to Acapulco for three days in the sun and the surf. There I received a call from the chairman of the board of Phillips Petroleum, John Houchin, asking if he and his family might join us for dinner in Acapulco. I agreed, and the Houchin family came down on the Grumman II private jet of the Phillips Petroleum Company to be with us for one evening. This was a dramatic turn of events compared to the encounter I had had early in the campaign with Phillips executive William Keeler, when I sought a donation from him and members of his company.

I had already appointed a Phillips employee, James Hart, who was leaving the company, to become my chief of staff. He had been a college roommate of mine and was an international negotiator for Phillips Petroleum during his years of service with them. He was a highly respected employee and had been a brilliant student during our college years. The son of a widowed mother, Jim knew the value of hard work and thoughtful organization.

The one thing that I had failed to vet properly was that Jim was a registered Republican, and I received all kinds of panning in the newspapers for having made what was seen as a gaffe. Jim immediately changed his registration.

We had a lively and most enjoyable dinner hosted by the Houchin family at Carlos and Charlie's Restaurant in Acapulco. But it came as no surprise that Mr. Houchin had an agenda of his own—besides getting acquainted and meeting the new governor and his family. He wanted to discuss the future of the oil-and-gas gross-production wellhead tax in the state of Oklahoma. Of course, the topic was raised informally, as this dinner was more social than anything else. Then, when I mentioned our need to retire for the evening, as we were set to return to Oklahoma the next day, Mr. Houchin asked if our family would consider riding back in the Phillips Petroleum Company jet with his family, rather than flying back on an commercial airline. I hesitated, looking the kids, who were all three excitedly mouthing a silent yes. I turned to Jo, who nodded approval, and I said to Houchin, "Thanks, that would be great. We'll be glad to join you."

We had never been on an aircraft like that, and it was quite an experience. The ride was five or six hours long, and the first order of business was an excellent lunch prepared by an on-board chef and served by a charming female attendant. Then Mr. Houchin and I secluded ourselves, and he explained Phillips Petroleum's position on any future oil-and-gas taxes. I listened carefully for nearly two hours, asking some questions and making very few comments, and then Houchin looked at me intently and asked, "Well, what do you think, Governor?"

I paused, then carefully answered. "John, your points were very interesting, and I will carefully consider them." That was the bottom line of my whole conversation with Houchin. The rest of the trip was uneventful, and when we arrived at the Oklahoma City airport, we were given a special clearance through customs, and we proceeded to our rented home.

I was to learn some ten days after our return that Houchin had gone before his board and told them, in no uncertain terms, that he could assure them that there would be no change in the oil-and-gas gross-production tax because of his salesmanship on that trip back from Acapulco. He had heard what he took to be an acceptance of his position, instead of listening closely to my actual words—a big mistake on his part. His take on our conversation was 180 degrees from mine, and would later serve as a major source of embarrassment for him when I introduced a 2% increase in the gross-production wellhead tax—which was the cornerstone of our administration's financial reformation of the state of Oklahoma.

Mr. Houchin and I never spoke again after the plane ride from Acapulco. It was William Keeler who would later give me the details of Houchin's presentation to his board. There was no real reason for me to worry when this issue was raised, but I was not so idealistic as to ignore the power and wrath of an embarrassed oil-company executive.

After the inauguration, the workload accelerated at a furious pace, with appointments, meetings with the legislators, and meetings with the brain trust to discuss the implementation of the 21 campaign promises. Most of all, we focused on the three biggest hurdles that we faced. The first was the passage of a 2% increase in the gross-production tax on oil and gas to provide the funds that would bring solvency to the state. This legislation guaranteed teachers' retirement, special education, and statewide kindergarten.

The second hurdle was the reformation of the income-tax code to give reduced taxes to 95% of Oklahoma families, while increasing taxes for the wealthiest 5%. Thirty-eight years later, I would see this same strategy repeated in 2009, with a similar program introduced at the federal level by the newly elected President Barack Obama.

This tax reform included a change in the domestic corporation tax, which had been a special law for state corporations; they paid no state tax on dividends issued to their shareholders if they had their headquarters in the state of Oklahoma.

The third hurdle was making certain that the programs we implemented would bring about the jobs that had been lost during the Bartlett administration, and that were sorely needed for the future of Oklahoma. This was done by dramatically increasing the funds for the Industrial Development Department to attract new industry. In the four years of my administration, this investment—and our ongoing outreach to companies in the United States and around the world—produced more new industry for the state of Oklahoma than the previous Bartlett and Bellmon administrations combined. The next four years provided a multi-billion-dollar influx of businesses to the state.

Part of the credit for the development, passage, and implementation of our top programs should also go to a "kitchen cabinet" I assembled early on. We met weekly for breakfast at the mansion during the legislative session, and enjoyed a constant flow of pragmatic, collaborative ideas. This working group consisted of Senator Ray Fine of Gore, Oklahoma; Commissioner Mike Connors of the Oklahoma Tax Commission; Lloyd Rader, director of the State Welfare Department; Senator Roy Boecher, of Kingfisher, Oklahoma; and Hayden Donahue, director of the Mental Health Department.

In hindsight, I'm proud to say that the manner in which our speedy transformation of the status quo was made possible ought to be a beacon to all public servants on state and national levels today. Leadership and bi-partisan cooperation were crucial in the process, as were two seasoned and articulate legislators who guided their respective houses. Senator Finis Smith of Tulsa was the president pro tempore of the Oklahoma State Senate, and Representative Rex Privett, of Pawnee, was the speaker of the Oklahoma House of Representatives; these men were bright and savvy, and their leadership was invaluable in passing legislation. Both were progressives, both understood the needs of Oklahoma, and both showed unbelievable courage during this first session.

They might well have qualified as examples of what President John F. Kennedy described in his book, *Profiles of Courage*, prior to his successful victory in 1960. For these men to have led their respective houses against the onslaught of the Independent Oil Operators lobby, the Republican conservative hierarchy, and the well-heeled Republican party was a testament to their statesmanship, and their pragmatic approach to fulfilling the needs of the people of the state of Oklahoma.

All of this was the great news. Not so great was the fact that the payback agenda against my administration—and against me personally—was soon in full force, amplified exponentially through four of the five major metropolitan newspapers in the state. They had opposed me as a candidate, and cranked it up several notches, once my victory had been sealed, with an almost-daily "bad press" campaign. Each of these four metro papers seemed to take turns in attempting to derail the programs that we were working on to benefit the middle- and lower-income families of Oklahoma. Bill Atkinson's paper, *The Oklahoma Journal*, was the only major metropolitan paper that supported the administration.

The great advantage I had over many previous governors was the legislative liaison I had chosen, G.M. Fuller. He was one of the most respected of Oklahoma's former legislators, and was credited with having the most evenhanded, intelligent, and pragmatic approach to legislation of any person who had ever held that post. The credit for passing nineteen out of twenty-one campaign platform promises that I had made was due to his efforts in working with Speaker Privett and President Pro Tempore Smith. Without G.M, it would have been impossible to accomplish what we did for education, job creation, and tax reform.

G.M.'s ability to help stave off the negative press was paramount to passage of these reforms. *The Oklahoma Journal* gave him a voice in the metropolitan areas, and the great majority of rural newspapers were able to coattail their coverage from the accurate accounts of the *Journal.* This didn't solve the problem, but it surely blunted the effect of the other four metro papers.

But the deliberate bad press campaign carried out by those four newspapers was more of an effect than a cause of the real danger lurking in the political shadows. Though there had been murmurings that powerful forces on the national scene had decided I was a threat, I thought there was no reason to take them seriously. It was only later—in 1972, when Oklahoma State Treasurer Leo Winters came to me to say, "Governor, watch your back," or words to that effect—that I understood just how much I had rocked the Establishment boat.

Winters had learned that a meeting had taken place in Washington, DC, in April 1971 between the defeated former Governor Dewey Bartlett and two Washington political heavyweights, Attorney General John Mitchell, and Deputy Attorney General Richard Kleindienst. This meeting represented only one exchange among the three prominent Republicans, but it was part of an ongoing secret conspiracy. It resulted in John Mitchell's launching an IRS and FBI strike-force investigation of me and my administration under the false designation of an "organized crime probe."

As time would eventually tell, each conspirator had his own agenda. The blue-blooded, Princeton-educated Dewey Bartlett, humiliated by our successful campaign to "Dump Dewey," wanted to avenge his upset defeat. Mitchell and Kleindienst had a different motive: to neutralize a potential threat to the Republican national agenda by targeting selected Democratic governors for investigation. Washington columnist Jack Anderson later exposed this specious political hatchet job by naming more than half a dozen of the Democratic governors, including me, who had been victimized by this plot. But Anderson's columns were written in 1975; during those first months of my administration in 1970, all of this scheming was being put into play without any knowledge on the part of me or my advisers.

Nor did we initially suspect how neatly the dots connected to the local level, and how part of this multi-pronged offensive against me was the appointment of William Burkett, as United States district attorney for the western district of Oklahoma. Bill Burkett could use that office to deliver payback at the same time Attorney General Mitchell could benefit by having a prosecutor in place malleable enough to look the other way when it came to improprieties on the part of Mitchell's firm. Such were interwoven agendas that Leo Winters brought to light for me later on.

And then there was Sunny Jenkins. Aside from the fact that I was too swept up in the euphoria of those first few months in office to suspect that he could possibly have concocted a criminal scheme—the reelection-campaign funds he was diverting to his private Mexican bank account—even when the truth came out, it was hard for me to believe. His motivation, other than greed and the temptation of access, remains mysterious to me even to this day. Why did he do it? Was he acting alone? There were no answers; all I know is that when I was confronted with proof of his activities, the shock came as a real blow. Sunny had been a trusted member of my team, our chief fundraiser, not to mention that he had been a prime and loyal supporter throughout the twenty-two months leading up to my election in 1970—even using his own private aircraft to transport me for campaign events.

Just as shocking—and even more sinister—was the manner in which the IRS and FBI investigations were being conducted. Here, too, because I had no reason to even imagine a motive, I remained ignorant of the directives coming down from the highest levels of government targeting me. I did not know that investigators had recruited my former private secretary, Dorothy Pike, to become an informant. Pike's subsequent theft of two years of my personal financial records, and the delivery of those to the IRS, was not to be discovered for some time. During this period, moreover, unexplained burglaries of the offices of many of my campaign personnel in Tulsa, and of the records that I maintained in an office adjacent to the mansion, had not yet come to light.

A harbinger of the Nixon administration's activities in the Watergate scandal was unfolding in Oklahoma.

But those intrigues remained in the future. In the meantime, our progressive mandate bore fruit; incredibly, the first session of the Oklahoma Legislature yielded the realization of all but two of the campaign promises I had made. Regrettably, the way one of these victories was implemented—an oversight on the practical level—would later damage my reputation with the thousands of wage earners in Oklahoma who had been my strongest supporters. By the time I caught the oversight and sought to fix it, the political heat made it tougher than ever to do so.

Vision Expanded

The seeds of Watergate had begun to germinate on June 13, 1971, when The New York Times published "The Pentagon Papers," the Department of Defense's secret history of the Vietnam conflict. Later in the week, The Washington Post also published the papers. During 1971, an organization dubbed the Plumbers was formed by the Nixon White House to stop leaks in the administration. On September 9, 1971, these plumbers burglarized the offices of Daniel Ellsberg, the former defense analyst who leaked the Pentagon Papers.

Midway through 1971, I was suspicious that a routine IRS audit was in fact the beginning of a targeted campaign directed by higher-ups in the Nixon administration. That was confirmed in 1972 when I learned of the Mitchell-Kleindienst-Bartlett meeting of April 1971. From that meeting, the initial steps of the conspiracy had moved swiftly through September 1971; this burgeoning investigation required that I hire counsel and investigators of my own to rebut any attempts to falsely paint me as corrupt, or to damage my reputation in order to prevent any future political advancement.

At about this time, I was rapidly gaining national attention for my work on education and my position in the National Governor's Conference. The dramatic change in the financing of Oklahoma's education system had vaulted me to a position of prominence in the Education Commission of the States, and the teachers' organizations that backed me began to support a move to have me become chairman of the Education Commission of the States.

At this time, Oklahoma was being recognized nationally for the completion of the Kerr McClellan Arkansas River Navigation Project. The formal dedication of the project was held at the Port of Catoosa on June 5, 1971. Senator John McClellan of, Arkansas, and Senator Robert S. Kerr of Oklahoma had championed the Arkansas River Project and secured the appropriations with the help and guidance of Speaker Carl Albert and the Oklahoma and Arkansas Congressional delegations over the years. It was the largest project ever undertaken by the US Army Corps of Engineers up to that time, with nineteen locks and dams stretching from the Port of Catoosa, near Tulsa, along the Arkansas River through Arkansas to the Mississippi River. This project, coupled with the prestige and power of Speaker Albert, put Oklahoma in the brightest national spotlight that it had ever received in governmental or business circles.

Carl Albert, known as the "little giant of little Dixie," was the highest-ranking federal official in the history of Oklahoma. As speaker of the US House of Representatives, he was third in line for the presidency in the event of a national disaster. His nickname came from his slight stature, his Rhodes Scholar intellect, and his roots in the southeast village of Bug Tussle, Oklahoma. A magnificent orator and a life-long Democrat, Albert had been a political idol of mine since my high-school days; we first became acquainted in my senior year at college when he visited the campus. Through his enormous influence in Washington, Oklahoma had unlimited access to the elite of the capital. This provided an unprecedented opportunity for me as a first-term governor; if I needed an appointment with a federal agency head, a call to Speaker Albert's office made it happen.

President Richard Nixon was the featured speaker at the dedication of the Kerr McClellan Arkansas River Navigation Project, and, as governor, it was my honor to introduce him. In preparation for the event, the First National Bank of Tulsa had arranged for the VIP guests, who would be seated on the stage, to be transported the last few miles to the dedication site by rail. The train was made up of several luxurious club cars, which were pulled by a diesel engine to a ramp just a few feet from the stage. The stage faced a large audience; forming a backdrop to the stage was a view of the navigation waterway and the terminus docks at the Port of Catoosa. The day was sunny, the temperature was mild in the low eighties, and the crowd was bubbling with anticipation.

The makeup of the notables on stage that day was a Who's Who of the coming Watergate scandal. President Nixon was seated in the front row, directly behind the lectern. I was seated on the president's left, with Jo next to me. United States Attorney General John Mitchell and his wife, Martha, were behind us. Just across the row was Secretary of Commerce Maurice Stans, soon to be tagged as the Watergate "bag man."

Just as I had no idea that any of these individuals might see me as a threat, I had no inkling at the time that the President's paranoia would lead him to create an enemy's list, or perform any of the other lawless acts later revealed. I actually found him to be congenial, particularly on that day when I was his host.

Speaker Albert, Senator Harris, and Senator Bellmon were prominent on the stage. Secret Service agents were sprinkled in the platform seats with their dark glasses gleaming. From Arkansas, Governor Dale Bumpers, Senator John McClellan, and Mrs. McClellan were up front. Also present were congressman from Arkansas, officials of the US Army Corp of Engineers, leaders of groups supporting the navigation project, and local officials.

McClellan-Kerr Arkansas River Navigation System dedication, June 4, 1971, Port of Catoosa, Oklahoma: Governor Hall introduces President Richard M. Nixon

The sides and back of the open stage were ringed with security officers, Secret Service agents, Oklahoma Highway Patrolmen, and my personal security officers. Before the proceedings started, a small turf war developed at the front corners of the stage between the Secret Service and my personal security officers as to who had priority of position. It was quickly reconciled, and they stood side-by-side. Then, while the dignitaries were taking their seats, I noticed Mrs. McClellan and the senator standing before his designated seat with puzzled expressions on their faces. I quickly went to their side and asked him, "Senator, may I help you?"

"There is no seat marked for my wife," he replied.

"I'll take care of that."

After hurrying over to the third row, I asked a Secret Service agent to give me his padded chair and carried it back to the first row. Doing what was logical, I made a space between the senator and the congressman next to him, and inserted the padded chair for

Mrs. McClellan. She beamed, and in her soft, Arkansas accent, said, "Thank you, Governor."

I laughed and said, "Anything for the man and his wife who made this project possible!"

Chuckling to myself, I returned to my seat and wondered who the bonehead was who had failed to provide a chair for her. I could laugh about it and feel good that all had worked out—even though in the political world, as I was learning, little things always had the potential of blowing up inter bigger things.

A footnote to the day, at least for those in the know, was the presence of Republican Congressman Page Belcher, whose persuasion of President Dwight Eisenhower in 1952 to keep this project in his first budget had been an important step in supporting the efforts of Senators Kerr and McClellan. Belcher's opposition to almost every other Democratic initiative in his career in Congress was almost forgiven, but not quite.

The celebratory atmosphere was further enhanced just before the start of proceedings when a local radio personality, Vic Bastion, parachuted into an open space near the stage. The crowd roared.

Due to the national press coverage of this event, I was asked to appear in New York City on The Today Show with Barbara Walters at NBC studios for a segment on the navigation project. Jo and I arrived in New York the day before the interview, checked into our hotel, ate an early dinner, and went to bed at 9:00 p.m. because we had to be at the NBC studios the next morning at 4:00 a.m. We arrived on time, and Jo and I were graciously greeted by the staff. Jo was seated in the studio so that she could watch the interview, and I went to makeup to be made ready for the camera. I was then led to the interview desk, seated next to Ms. Walters, and wired with a microphone.

I was given a few instructions as to the length of the segment and where to look during the interview. Before the television camera's red light came on, Ms. Walters leaned over and whispered in my ear, "Governor, when we have twenty seconds left in the interview, I am going to put my hand on your right leg." Thank goodness she warned me! The appearance on national television was exciting enough, but it was Barbara Walters's manners, warmth, and terrific sense of humor that made it most memorable.

These events were a boon to me, as was my continuing friendship with Jim Hartz, a young television reporter from Tulsa whom I had met during my county-attorney days. His career path led from a cub reporter for Channel Six in Tulsa to being the co-host of The Today Show for a number of years. He remains today one of the great voices and television hosts in that network's history. His work over the years with Barbara Walters, Frank McGee, Chet Huntley, David Brinkley, and John Chancellor gave him the respect and equal footing with these icons of television news. In his later years, he would head the Will Rogers Commission in Oklahoma during the very successful tenure of Joe Carter's directorship of the Will Rogers museum. Jim Hartz was, and still is, a great sounding board for me on many, many issues. One of my treasured memories is of his joining me for several days in my southeastern Oklahoma stump-speech tour in the 1974 governor's primary campaign.

At first, I was careful not to interpret such moments in the sun as the Barbara Walters interview as anything more than part of the job description of being an effective governor. But it was evident, as the months passed, that the dramatic victory over Dewey Bartlett had given me a great deal of positive attention by the Democratic Caucus of the National Governor's Conference. This became apparent when I was chosen as one of four Democratic governors to be a part of an eight-governor special delegation to the Soviet Union in advance of President Richard Nixon's planned visit in 1972.

This honor took me completely by surprise. The trip, arranged by the National Governor's Conference, working with the Nixon White House, was set to begin in October 1971. The four Democratic governors chosen were Warren Hearns of Missouri, who led the delegation; Dale Bumpers, Arkansas; Marvin Mandel, Maryland; and me. The Republican governors were John Love, Colorado; Stan Hathaway, Wyoming; William Milliken, Michigan; and Luis Ferre, Puerto Rico.

The choice of Dale Bumpers was fortuitous. We were closely aligned with our states' adjoining interests, and both had been a part of the navigation-project celebration. We also shared a personal relation, as we had both married Arkansas girls; Jo was from Morrilton, and Betty was from Charleston. In the next four years, the friendship blossomed through tennis matches, speaking engagements, shared political philosophies, and many joint projects to benefit our states. On the trip to the Soviet Union, Dale would be my closest friend.

The trip was deemed a cultural exchange mission, and the delegation spent two weeks in the Soviet Union and three additional days in Romania. As the day approached and I prepared, there were numerous things about Oklahoma that I wanted to spotlight for this historic occasion. To showcase the most important aspects of life in Oklahoma, I put together mementos that I hoped would resonate with the Soviets and the rest of the world at the time. These items symbolized our state's contributions to agriculture—including the development of a hybrid of winter wheat that was used worldwide—along with our Native American heritage, leadership in the oil industry, and the importance of faith and belief in a higher power that was a staple of life in Oklahoma. It was also my honor to carry gifts for dignitaries we would be meeting, and to bring several dozen simple Indian headbands with one feather for schoolchildren, along with a supply of Kennedy half-dollars, which were coveted at that time all over Europe.

In language preparation, one of my aides, Rex Sparger, endeavored to teach me twenty common Russian phrases. We practiced over several sessions, and I asked Rex, "How'd I do on these?"

He paused way too long, then answered, "Well, Governor, I will say this: The Soviets have never heard these phrases with an Oklahoma accent." And he was right.

Because of my civil-rights stance, the work I had done in advancing the goals of minorities, and my work in fighting the anti-Semitic forces in our state, the National Jewish Conference had asked me to be one of two governors on this trip to present a petition to Premier Kosygin of the Soviet Union, asking him to allow Soviet Jews to immigrate to Israel. Governor Marvin Mandel, a passionate Democrat and the only Jewish governor in the nation at that time, and I carried this petition with us on the trip.

The USSR and the United States were still experiencing the chilly relationship of the Cold War. Anti-Semitism was rampant in the Soviet Union, and many Jewish citizens wished to immigrate to Israel. But fearful of losing some of its brightest minds, the USSR was making it almost impossible for Soviet Jews to leave. All religious groups were suffering discrimination; churches were turned into museums with no services, and it was a dangerous time for evangelicals from the United States to travel there.

President Nixon's forthcoming trip in early 1972 was taking on greater significance as the two superpowers jockeyed for dominance on the world stage. The war in Vietnam dominated the front pages of US newspapers, and President Nixon pledged in April 1971 to bring 100,000 troops home by December. The USSR conducted a nuclear test in eastern Kazakhstan in May. In the United States, on June 20, 1971, the Twenty-Sixth Amendment to the US Constitution, granting eighteen-year-old citizens the right to vote, became law with the ratification by the Ohio legislature as the 38th state. Oklahoma missed being the deciding state by mere hours.

Two days before leaving on the trip, we flew to Washington, DC, as all of the eight governors were asked to meet with President Nixon at the White House prior to our departure. On the surface, the trip was to be an educational and cultural exchange; but, in fact, it was to give President Nixon the opinions of eight different governors about what they were to see, hear, and discern on this visit. The second night in the capital, we were invited to an evening session—no dinner—at the Soviet Embassy to be briefed before we started the trip.

No mention had been made whether wives were to be invited to the Soviet Embassy, but since Jo had accompanied me to Washington, I asked her to go with me to the embassy. It turned out that she was the only first lady in the group; she was admitted to our tour at the embassy, even though I think there was some jealously on the part of some of the other wives. Foreign Minister Anatoly Dobrynin of the Soviet Union was our host, and he was gracious in spending a couple of hours going over what we would see and do on the trip. His English was perfect, with only the faintest accent. He showed us a 30-minute film made by his government on the recent innovations in the Soviet Union; one of the highlights of the film was coverage of a giant canal that was being dug, and we saw in that film that there were no spectacular, large earth-moving machines doing the work, but literally hundreds of pick-and-shovel workers excavating parts of the canal. The total impression that was left with most of us was that their methods were not nearly as advanced as they claimed.

Stan Hathaway, of Wyoming, who of all the governors on the trip probably said the least, had a terrific sense of humor. Built like a fullback, just under six feet tall, with brown eyes and thinning hair, he had a presence that put you at ease. When he did talk, it was always worth a chuckle. As the film finished, he turned and whispered to me, "If they wanted to impress anybody, you would've thought they would have at least one modern earth-mover machine in the film, whether it was running or not."

I laughed and nodded in agreement. We finished the tour and headed to our hotel.

The next day the trip began with a Pan American flight to Moscow. The National Governor's Conference had designated Governor Warren Hearns as the head of our delegation, and he was an excellent choice. On our late-evening arrival at Moscow's international airport, our pilots taxied to the gate, stopping short, and a mobile staircase was set against the plane for us to deplane. As I stepped out the door, the cold October wind brushed me, and I could see the twinkling lights of the city piercing the night. I wondered why such a facility had no covered access to the aircraft. I was to learn that many things we take for granted in the United States were not yet the same in the USSR.

Down the steps, we were whisked through customs with VIP treatment. At the curb to meet us were three black limos for transport to our hotel. Each governor was given a private room, and a concierge was available on every floor.

In our briefings before the trip, we learned that our rooms at the hotel were certain to be bugged. The proof came when we scripted our discussions among ourselves in our rooms on that first night. Sure enough, the next morning Governor Ferre was the first to discern that the tourist guides had been briefed on our conversations, giving proof of the eavesdropping.

Governor Ferre, a handsome, slightly built Puerto Rican, with flashing dark eyes and a well-trimmed mustache tinged in gray, took on the duty of keeping a journal of every day of the trip, which he dutifully recorded. Later, true to his word, he furnished each of us with a copy when we returned home.

We were provided with excellent tour guides, and in addition to all of the governmental and manufacturing visits we made, we saw the very deep underground subways. We marveled at the depth of the subways, as they were 600 under the ground in some cases; they had been designed as bomb shelters in the event of an atomic war, and were lavishly adorned with marble floors and wall coverings. In place of the advertising we see in the United States, there were Communist slogans and patriotic photos displayed. The subways were some of the cleanest public facilities that I had ever seen anywhere. High-speed escalators delivered the passengers to all levels. The swift acceleration of the subways from station to station was faster than I had experienced in New York City.

The visit to Moscow continued with trips to manufacturing production areas, Jewish synagogues, and to administrative offices where we were briefed on the five-year plan currently in progress in the Soviet Union. That night there was a dinner with dignitaries, with much toasting and vodka consumption. These toasts were difficult for me, because I was a non-drinker, so I had to fake the toasting; otherwise, I would have been an embarrassment to the rest of the delegation.

One startling fact was that we saw very little automobile traffic on any of the streets of Moscow. We learned later that there were approximately one or two cars per family in the United States, whereas the ratio in the Soviet Union at that time was one car to 35 families.

On the fourth day in Moscow, we were scheduled for a formal conference between Premier Alexei Kosygin and our delegation. The night before this meeting was to take place, Governor Mandel and I sat down to strategize the best way to present the petition to Kosygin and what we reasonably could expect as a consequence; neither one of us suspected that we would be under the fierce scrutiny not just by the Soviet authorities, but by Nixon and his close circle. Only time would reveal to what extent.

In my room that night, Mandel, tapping the tobacco in his pipe and lighting it, lead off: "At this meeting tomorrow, when do you think is the best point at which to give the Premier the petition?"

"My guess is to make it at a time that will not disrupt any other discussion."

He nodded, taking his pipe from his lips, and said, "If Warren Hearns agrees, let's make it the last thing on the agenda."

"Okay," I responded, "but let's let Warren decide if we put it on the agenda or just do it when it's our time to speak at the end."

"Good thinking," Marvin said. "We'll talk to Warren."

Governor Hearns decided to forgo a possible incident during the conference if Marvin and I presented the petition without any prior notice. Instead, he said he would present the petition on our behalf to Kosygin's aide, and then allow Marvin and me to speak to the issue during our responses at the conference. Good diplomacy, I guess, but Marvin and I would have preferred to just spring the petition as a surprise.

Governor Hearns was a no-nonsense administrator with strong Midwestern flavor to his speech. His political logic and persona were a perfect example of what is meant by Missouri being the "Show Me" state. Of medium height, average build, graying hair, strong features, a commanding voice, and incisive wit, his sixty-plus years also gave him gravitas among us younger governors. I looked up to Warren and felt that our mission was in good hands.

His job, on this day, was to lead us in the five-hour discussion that our group had with Kosygin in a formal conference area of the Kremlin. The governors were arranged on one side of a long, dark, polished-wood conference table, and Premier Alexei Kosygin, his staff, the interpreters, and other dignitaries from the Soviet Union were arranged on the opposite side. Premier Kosygin set the agenda and touched on every part of Soviet life, Soviet political aims, and Soviet-American relations—in more detail than any of us could have wished to hear. To me, the most interesting part of this apparent propaganda indoctrination by Kosygin and his staff was to see the different facets of the leader of the second-most powerful nation in the world. Although Kosygin was trained as a technical bureaucrat in administration, he had been a Communist party operative for most of his adult life.

We saw at least six or seven faces of Kosygin during those five hours, ranging from the warm, ingratiating diplomat, to the professorial repository of Russian history, to an eye-twinkling grandfather, and ending with the stern, cold, Stalin -like technical countenance of the most important man in his country—and the biggest impediment to freedom in the world.

At the end of that session, Premier Kosygin delivered what I thought was a threatening message to let us know that the Soviet Union stood ready to do whatever was necessary to preserve their way of life. It was a revealing episode in world politics that I felt privileged to witness. In participating in the discussion, we were allowed to ask questions, we were allowed to make a statement on issues, and Governor Hearns conducted the exchanges in a strong and professional manner. We presented our thoughts on the virtues of democracy and our way of life as strongly and forcibly as Kosygin and his staff had presented the Soviet worldview.

National Governor's Conference delegation meeting in the Kremlin,
Moscow, USSR. From left: Governor Hall; Russian aide; Governor
William Milliken, Michigan; Premier Alexi Kosygin, USSR;
Russian interpreter, delegation leader Governor Warren Hearns,
Missouri; Governor Luis Ferre, Puerto Rico; October 1971

As the conference was ending, Governor Hearns gave Mandel and me our chance to comment on the petition to allow Soviet Jews to immigrate to Israel. Marvin and I stated our positions briefly, beseeched Kosygin to give it favorable consideration, and then sat down. There was a long pause. With hard eyes, Kosygin fixed a cold stare first on Mandel and then on me, but made no comment. I was left with that poker-faced image, accompanied by his obvious agitation. Mandel later confirmed he had the same reaction. We both hoped it had given the old Communist some real heartburn. Governor Mandel and I had done our job, but we had no idea what effect it would have on the policy.

When that day's session ended, we were treated to a lavish reception in one of the main ballrooms of the Kremlin, with celebrities of the Soviet Union in attendance. One of the most interesting was the first woman cosmonaut, Valentina Tereshkova. She was an attractive, articulate woman dressed in the uniform of the cosmonauts, and she provided one of the most unusual interviews and encounters that we had. Dale Bumpers and I compared impressions and agreed that she was typecast for the part.

The next day our travels continued, with an overnight train ride from Moscow to St. Petersburg on the Red Arrow express. Since the distance was not long enough for an overnight trip, the train was slowed down so that you went to bed as you boarded in Moscow and awoke the next morning to the strains of the Soviet national anthem when you arrived at the St. Petersburg station. My recollections of that ride include seeing the female sleeping-car attendant dressed in a military-like uniforms, weighing in at about 180 pounds and looking more like a college linebacker than a railroad employee. A first for me were the cotton covers on the wool blankets furnished in the sleeper bunks, which could be taken off and laundered: big saving on dry-cleaning.

We visited cemeteries for the millions of people who were killed in the terrible siege of Leningrad, as the city was called during WWII. Hundreds of the dead were interred in huge mass graves, which stretched for blocks in the cemetery; I could only guess at how many thousands were buried there. The reports I had read during WWII of the millions killed at Leningrad by the Germans was now stamped indelibly on my mind. During our remaining two days in the city, we made the normal tourist stops, visiting the Hermitage and seeing the site of the beginning of the Russian Revolution.

National Governor's Conference Delegation in Leningrad (now Saint
Petersburg), Russia. From left: Intourist guide; Governor Dale Bumpers,
Arkansas; Governor Hall; Governor Ferre; Governor Hearns; Governor
Milliken; Russian aide; Governor Marvin Mandel, Maryland; Governor John
Love, Colorado (partially obscured); Governor Stan Hathaway, Wyoming;
National Governor's Conference official; Russian officer; October 1971

Our next stop was Tiblisi, the capital city of Soviet Georgia. This
republic was the birthplace of Joseph Stalin, as he was born in the
small town of Gori. We enjoyed this visit very much, as the climate
was similar to southern California, and the people were warm and
friendly. The presence of churches—and their apparent use—was
more pronounced in this area than any in any other that we toured—
a sharp contrast to Moscow. Giant statutes of Joseph Stalin seemed
to be present throughout the city.

This visit completed, we embarked on an Aeroflot plane to
Romania, where we spent the last three days of the trip. This was
one of the most delightful times of our trip because of the open and
cordial ways of the Romanian people in general—but it was a stark
contrast to our encounter with Premier Nickolas Ceausescu, the dictator of Romania. A tyrannical, self-absorbed despot, he would later
be overthrown and his atrocities and greed exposed. I had brought
an ornate Native American headdress of the Pawnee tribe of Oklahoma to give as a special gift to the premier. When I presented it

to him in session with his aides and our delegation, he adamantly refused to try it on for the cameras. He gave no explanation and was very rude in his refusal. I thought that perhaps the reason was that he had a wig on, and felt it might come off while wearing the head-dress! A more pleasant highlight of that first day was our attendance at a folk opera in the evening. I had never been an opera fan, but I was quite taken with the performance.

On our last evening, at a restaurant in the city of Cluj in the Transylvania district—most famous in our country for being the home of the legends of Count Dracula—I celebrated my 41st birthday by doing a traditional Romanian "handkerchief dance." This was where I first discovered what a good dancer John Love was, and also how adept Dale Bumpers was at learning dance steps. These two governors took the honors for learning the dances and performing well. The next day, we completed our tour in Romania and flew back to Moscow to catch a Pan American flight to the United States.

On our arrival at Dulles Airport, late in the afternoon, we were whisked by limo directly to the White House to meet with President Nixon in order to be debriefed about our trip. We sat in the Oval Office, prepared to give our impressions to President Nixon. All of us had met the President several times before, at the briefings held before we left for the Soviet Union and at our National Governor's Conference meetings the previous February of 1971. However, on the Democratic side, none of us knew Nixon as well as some of the Republicans did, nor did we know of some of his idiosyncrasies. In the debriefing, he was incisive and very focused, a very quick study on each of the issues and reactions that we had to Premier Kosygin.

I remember that Nixon listened intently to Warren Hearns as he gave a summary of our visit with Kosygin. But he wanted more, and asked each of us in turn to give our impressions of the Soviet Premier. He bestowed the same concentration and intense interest on the four Democratic governors as he did to the Republicans, showing no partiality for party but giving equal time for each of us to respond. Although somewhat aloof and a bit stiff in manner, he seemed to soak up each impression, evaluate it, and mentally cata-logue what we said. I had no idea he would be such a good listener.

After approximately two hours, the debriefing ended, and we prepared to leave. President Nixon asked one of his aides to bring some mementos to give us in remembrance of our visit to the White House that night. We were each given a small white cardboard box adorned with the presidential seal. I was pleased to receive the gift, but its delivery was a bit surprising: President Nixon took the indi-vidual boxes and tossed them across the room to each of us as we sat facing each other on the two couches. Luckily, all of us caught our boxes as they were pitched, and there was no embarrassing groping on the floor to pick them up.

Dale Bumpers and I exchanged surprised looks, and we could hardly wait to see what was inside. Good manners prevailed, how-ever, and I did not see one governor open his box until we were in the limos headed to our hotel. I was sitting in the limo next to a gov-ernor who will remain nameless; with a twinkle in his eye, he turned to me and said, "I had always heard Dick Nixon was no athlete, but his pitching arm worked pretty well tonight."

I laughed and responded with a smile, "Could he pitch for Yankees?"

My friend guffawed. "No," he said, "he'd more likely pitch for a little-league team." It was good-natured banter after a most excit-ing trip. All eight governors were compatible, and no one tried to upstage the others. Oh, yes—if you are wondering what was inside the little boxes, each held a beautiful set of gold cufflinks with the presidential seal, which I greatly appreciated.

My return trip to Oklahoma was marked by a feeling of intense pride at having been a part of the delegation. Even though it was clear that my political star was rising on the national level, I still felt truly humbled to have been one of the eight selected governors, and to have been given the rare opportunity to get to know firsthand the foremost challenge to America's future.

But there was something I was missing about the final meeting with President Nixon. Over the years, I have reflected many times about what that was. As future events would bear out, two of us in that room were already major targets for investigations by his administration, and I now think that not only was he debriefing the eight of us for information on his pending trip to Russia, but he was also taking a very personal look up close at Governor Marvin Mandel and me.

It was now late October of the first year of my administration, and credentials for a run for national office were beginning to manifest themselves. The turnaround of the state economy, with the pursuit of new industry, was going at a faster pace than any of us realized, and by the end of that first year, it was evident that we were going to be able to set records for new industry brought into the state during my administration.

On the state and national political scenes, I was perceived to be a moderate conservative on property issues, and liberal on social issues—those affecting people and protecting individual freedoms. My long history of civil-rights support gave me liberal creditability. As county prosecutor, I had employed the first black assistant county attorney in Oklahoma history, and he had been the first black assistant to prosecute a white person in the history of the state. In addition, I supported the appeal of the case that broke Oklahoma's miscegenation statute. In the governor's office, our staff was 15% minority, and in 1971, I appointed the first African-American woman, Hannah Atkins, to the Board of Higher Regents for the state of Oklahoma's education system.

On a personal note, my alarming weight gain during this first year, which accelerated on the trip to the Soviet Union, was a worrisome issue for Jo and me. A photograph with Jo and Vice President Hubert Humphrey shocked me.

Oklahoma First Lady Jo Hall, Vice President Hubert Humphrey,
Governor Hall at a reception in Oklahoma City, Fall 1971

On November 15, 1971, I weighed 256 pounds and was very concerned about my health. Returning from a speaking engagement just before Thanksgiving, I decided it was time to talk to Jo about my health and what it meant to the family, as well as to my job as governor. We were sitting in the upstairs den in the Southwest corner of the second floor. Jo was on the small couch, and I sat in the lounge chair facing the TV. This intimate sitting room was separated from our bedroom by the master bath at the mansion. The children were all in bed. I leaned forward, turned off the TV, and said to Jo, "I've got to lose some weight."

"David," she responded, "you've already told me you were working on a plan. Anything new?"

"Yesiree," I continued. "When I looked at the scale this morning, I knew I had to speed up my efforts. I don't want to have a heart attack and leave a 35-year-old first lady to raise three children by herself. I have an idea I want to bounce off you."

"Okay," she said, laughing.

"What would you think about the us going to a spa for a week to get a jump start?"

She smiled broadly and looked so happy that I was glad I had made the suggestion. "That's great," she said. "What's your thought about the right spa?"

"Remember when Gerald Barton touted the La Costa Spa and Resort in Carlsbad, California, as a great spot for the family? What do you think?"

"Let's do it," she said quickly.

That night we agreed to try it. Later, as I leaned over in bed to kiss her good night, she said, "It's going to be nice not to worry about losing my man." Laughing, I kissed her, snapped off the light, and went to sleep.

The next morning I set in motion a plan for a week at La Costa over the New Year's holiday. It also occurred to me that this was a favorite destination of one my strongest union support groups, the Teamsters.

National Promise

The definitive act of the Watergate scandal took place at 2:30 a.m., June 17, 1972. Howard Hunt, who said he formerly worked for the CIA, and four other men were arrested while trying to bug the offices of the Democratic National Committee at the Watergate Hotel and office building in Washington, DC. Two days later it was learned that among the Watergate burglars was a GOP security aide. The Washington Post *ran a story that US Attorney General John Mitchell, head of the Committee to Re-Elect the President, (CREEP), denied any link to the operation.*

Christmas of 1971 was the first chance for the family to reflect upon our first year in the governor's mansion and to evaluate the changes that had occurred in our lives. We had one of the most enjoyable Christmas vacations that we could remember, with a trip to Park City, Utah. We spent the time outside riding snowmobiles with the whole family, and we were able to share more one-on-one time together than we had for most of the previous year.

The children had been living in the mansion for a full year and were acclimating to the Oklahoma City life in better fashion than Jo and I could have hoped for. They became involved in church activities, made many new friends, and participated in the activities of their schools. Living in the mansion was a fish-bowl existence, and it was moving to realize how this made the three children a tight unit and most helpful to each other.

By now Doug had developed an interest in the Taft Junior High Band and learned to play the trumpet. Later, entering Northwest Classen High School, he excelled in football as well as his academics. Pursuit of excellence in academics and athletics wasn't surprising for Doug, but some years later I had to ask him, "Doug, why did you choose the trumpet?"

"Dad, do you remember your Herb Alpert records with the Tijuana Brass and 'A Taste of Honey?'"

"Yes, I do."

"Well, I got hooked on his trumpet playing, and thought it would be cool to play like him. But, to be honest, what sold me was the cover of his album."

"How's that?"

"Well, er, ah, there was this good-looking model with whipped cream for a bikini on the cover of the album, and that clinched it!"

His explanation said a lot about a fourteen-year-old boy's thinking! It was a reminder that over the course of the first year in the governor's mansion, Doug had come of age. By that first Christmas, Jo and I were already realizing that the boy was all man.

Nancy completed junior high at Taft, then enrolled in Northwest Classen, where she was active in student government and made friends easily. She was our most empathic child, and continually helped other young people with problems. Nancy's warmth and magnetism earned her a place on the Northwest Classen student council. She was also engaged in her church work, as well as helping when Julie or Doug needed a big sister's advice or assistance.

Julie attended Cleveland Grade School and would later attend Taft Junior High. When we moved into the mansion, she displayed such chutzpah (as the Jewish members of our extended family got me in the habit of saying) that one would not believe she was just ten years old. For example, there was the adult-like behavior she showed toward the daughter of one of Jo's closest friends, Janet Young. Janet and her little girl, Teresa, had stayed with us for a time when she first moved to

Tulsa; Janet and Jo were American Airlines stewardesses before their marriages, and lived together in New York City for two years. Janet and Teresa became a part of our family, and to this day we treat Teresa as our fourth child. Teresa was four years younger than Julie, but they were constant companions on Janet's frequent visits to the mansion.

Late in 1971, Julie, pushing the envelope, had learned to drive on the helipad, using our 1968 Chevrolet navy-blue station wagon, affectionately named Lurch. Jo and I never knew who taught her, but in our absence, she motored around the helipad—at age eleven. When Teresa visited, they played "hitch-hike," with Julie driving and Teresa thumbing a ride at the edge of the helipad. It was a blessing that no accidents ever occurred, nor was Teresa hit.

This practice ended one warm spring day when Jo and Janet returned to the mansion early from a trip, stepped out on the south porch, and observed our Chevy wagon slowly moving across the helipad—with no apparent driver. Julie was so short that she couldn't be seen at the wheel from a distance. Teresa, age seven, was sitting in the front passenger seat, but she wasn't visible, either. Jo called the guard to check on the car, and Julie was found out. So ended her driving days until she turned sixteen and it was legal!

On the first day at their new schools, Jo took Julie to her grade school, and Nancy and Doug were delivered to school by one of my security guards from the Oklahoma Highway Patrol. The guard drove Nancy and Doug in the limousine, and they thought this was the pits. Both asked the guard to stop a block from their school so that they could walk in without the commotion that the limo's presence would cause. The ride home was accomplished the same way.

That night Nancy and Doug asked if they could be driven in Jo's car and deep-six the limo. For the next several days, Jo delivered all three to school in her car. After that, the guard drove Jo's car to take them all, and this was the pattern until Nancy and Doug were old enough to have their own cars. This ended the first lady's carpooling.

Jo's poise and aplomb provided a model for future first ladies; she carried out her duties with grace and charm that made all of us so proud. Jo's mother, Ruth Evans, had come from Arkansas many times to be with our children during the campaign when we were on trips, to assist us in any way that she could. She gave our children the security and guidance that they needed when we were not available. I will always be thankful for the unselfish sacrifice of her time to make our lives better.

Jo had begun work in transforming the mansion into a warm and friendly environment. She succeeded in providing not only an official home for our family, but a gathering place for our children's friends and classmates. She achieved that delicate balance, so important in public life, of sufficient privacy for our children to grow and mature but to still feel a part of this once-in-a-lifetime experience. We taught the children that this mansion life was only temporary—a privilege, not a right.

The opening of the legislative session brought my second "State of the State" address to that assembled body. We continued my bold agenda of the two issues not passed in the first session and outlined aggressive plans for roads, education, new building construction, attention to veterans' affairs, and the upgrade of the Oklahoma Historical Society.

On a personal note, I had returned from a week at a health spa and was on my way to a dramatic weight reduction in the next five months. By early May, I lost 63 pounds and ended the dangerous eating practices of my past. My discipline and success were relayed to Jean Nidetch, the founder of Weight Watchers, and she invited me to be a speaker with her at a Weight Watchers event in Oklahoma's Civic Auditorium that summer. I was much smaller at that point, and tried to give inspiration to a spirited crowd of women. Mrs. Nidetch was the perfect host, and it was a banner day for me.

The federal grand jury called by US Attorney William Burkett in Oklahoma City had been in session many months. I was aware of this fishing expedition by Burkett as he tried desperately to find something on Leo Winters. I was satisfied that in my case the grand jury had nothing to go on, but my experience as a prosecutor gave me a wariness as the proceedings dragged on. I had still not learned from Leo Winters of the mandate to target us, a scheme originating from the April 1971 meeting of Attorney General John Mitchell, Richard

Kleindienst, and Dewey Bartlett. But I knew that if they could find something about Winters, they could paint me as guilty by association, or vice-versa. I was still receiving rumors about Sunny Jenkins' clandestine activities, but as yet I had no concrete proof.

Later I discovered that the IRS had been secretly investigating my financial records since the Mitchell mandate. This was another step in the strategy to destroy State Treasurer Leo Winters and me.

Meanwhile, as the legislative session ended in the summer of 1972, I embarked on a bold plan to bring 4,000 jobs to one of the most depressed areas of the state, near McAlester. The legislature had appropriated $600,000 to aid a study on the feasibility of gasifying high-sulfur coal in that area, using an HGTR atomic reactor to complete the process. Gulf Atomic, a division of Gulf Oil, had developed the reactor in their La Jolla, California, facility, and were eager to assist in making this venture a reality. In conjunction with our industrial-development team, I secured the services of Stone Webster Engineering to design the bench plant. With the power of House Speaker Carl Albert solidly behind the project, as it was in his district, I obtained a $300,000 grant from the federal office for coal research.

The plan was to eventually build two coal-gasification plants in Speaker Albert's district, which would employ 2,000 workers in each plant. The economics would depend on two factors: a market for the synthetic gas and the production cost being less than the prevailing rate for natural gas. The issue of the market became a given when a consortium of utilities anchored by San Diego Gas and Electric gave their endorsement to the plan. Step One was to build the bench plant on a very small scale to prove the process. The feasibility study was in gear, and the dialogue among all parties began.

Then two stumbling blocks arose in the road to success. The first was the price of natural gas; it lingered at a low level that made the potential synthetic gas too expensive. The second was more immediate and pragmatic: I would need another appropriation in the 1973 legislative session of a million dollars to complete the bench plant and prove the process. But I optimistically continued through the summer and fall to work toward that goal.

In the summer of 1972, the Democrats were in an uproar over which candidate should win the nomination to run against the incumbent, Richard Nixon. The trauma of the Vietnam war and its devastating toll on the American political psyche was the dominant issue; every opinion poll confirmed the voters' disgust with the length and muddled conduct of the war. This attitude had earlier doomed President Johnson's thoughts of running in 1968, and dashed the spirit of the Democratic party in the ensuing presidential defeat.

Now, with President Nixon still grappling with some sort of end to the war, the peace-movement advocates within the Democratic party had their champion in Senator George McGovern of, South Dakota. He had been slowly gaining ground, and it appeared that he might well be the party's nominee. An additional list of candidates, all impressive, were vying for the honor, including Senator Fred Harris of Oklahoma.

The convention was held in Miami in August; it was a rousing and boisterous event culminating in the selection of George McGovern to head the ticket and Thomas Eagleton as the vice-presidential nominee. To most observers, that had been a foregone conclusion; Senator Fred Harris made a valiant attempt to gain the nomination, but was unsuccessful. His earlier Senate campaign victory over Bud Wilkinson in the 1964 Oklahoma race had vaulted him to national prominence, and for years it had looked as if he could be a serious contender in 1972.

The Democratic National Convention was a singular thrill for me, because I had been a political-science major in college and had spent most of my adult life either in politics as an active candidate, or working to help someone else; to head our delegation to the convention and be in the position of helping to select the nominee was a dream fulfilled. Jo and our children were enthralled at being a part of it.

Actually, only two of our children accompanied us to Miami, Doug and Julie. Nancy was working at Six Flags over Texas, the amusement park in Dallas. In her place, however, Doug had invited Ron Walker, a close buddy of his from Temple Baptist Church and a high-school football teammate. The additions to our party were wonderful, as we enjoyed opinions from them on their assessment of the candidates. Allowing our children to bring a friend on these major trips was a pattern we maintained our years in office; we loved including the younger generation of Oklahomans on our official working trips, because we heard their mostly unbiased reactions. On this trip, for example, the kids thought McGovern would be an excellent President, but weren't sure that he had the toughness to take on Nixon in the campaign.

At the convention, I was looking ahead to 1976 in my quest for a wider network of contacts across the nation. Excellent advice and consideration came from our soon-to-be party chairman, Robert Strauss. I would find out months later that he was already interacting with three other Democratic governors with national aspirations who had been elected in 1970: Jimmy Carter, Ruben Askew, and Dale Bumpers from Georgia, Florida, and Arkansas respectively. When you added these names to the front-runner for 1976, Senator Ted Kennedy, it was a young and dynamic group for the future.

Robert Strauss was one of the most affable, skilled political figures I had ever encountered. His acumen on keeping many balls in the air, his storytelling ability, and his charismatic personality made him a force across the nation. Once I asked him how he returned all the important phone calls that came to him each week. He smiled wryly as he said, "I always return my calls." Then he explained his strategy: He prioritized each call, and those he considered most important, he tried to return immediately. For those of lower priority, he would wait until lunchtime in their time zone, call them back, and leave a message expressing his disappointment in having missed them!

Earlier in the year, I had been fortunate to make the acquaintance of Senator Henry "Scoop" Jackson, another potential candidate in 1976. I had admired him for many years. We became friends, and he did me the great honor of attending my 42nd birthday celebration in October 1972. He and his wife, Helen, became good friends of ours; one of the wonderful things that Jo did to show her appreciation of their friendship was find a toy poodle as a present for Mrs. Jackson. Jo took the beautiful white poodle in her tote bag on a flight to Washington and presented the dog to the Jacksons. Helen Jackson was thrilled with the new fluffy friend that joined their family. We would see the puppy in her arms in pictures of their family during the next few months.

The teachers and educators had been successful in having me selected as chairman of the Education Commission of the States. This added workload was welcome, as it gave me speaking opportunities across the nation. Meanwhile, I had taken on another leadership role to become chairman of the Interstate Oil Compact. Further, I now played an active role in the Interstate Mining Compact, due to our groundbreaking work in coal gasification. These positions—and the expertise that they allowed me to accumulate—were part of the momentum that seemed to be giving me a lift as a potential national figure—something that was being recognized in the press with articles by such publications as *The New Republic* and Jack Anderson's syndicated columns.

Since early in the spring 1972, I had been peppered with rumors about Sunny Jenkins ' questionable fundraising activities, to the point that I confronted him with that information. Jenkins again denied any improprieties. What none of the rumors had yet suggested was that in addition to mismanagement, he had been socking a great deal of money away in the Mexican bank account that he had created for himself. Even with his denial, and my ignorance of the extent of his wrongdoing, I felt that it was in the best interest of the administration, and of my own personal situation, to remove him from the staff and secure a new fundraising chairman. Sunny had been such a good friend over the years that I wanted concrete proof before I made any accusations against him—but that proof would not come until much later.

Christmas 1972 provided a respite from the rigors of governance and an opportunity for the family to reconnect and review our lives for the past year. The joy of anticipation of this uninterrupted time together was reflected in our official Christmas card picture.

Official Christmas picture. From left: standing, Jo, Nancy; sitting, Doug, Governor Hall, Julie; front and center, Hilda the Saint Bernard

Challenges

Former Nixon aides G. Gordon Liddy and James W. McCord, Jr., are convicted January 30, 1973, of conspiracy, burglary, and wiretapping in the Watergate break-in. Like dominoes falling, White House key staff members H.R. Haldeman, John Ehrlichman, and Attorney General Richard Kleindienst resign.

The pace of the administration in Oklahoma, and the peripatetic development of events on the national scene, were both good news and bad news. The good news was that the state was booming, thanks to the initiatives that my administration had put forth. New business coming into the state was at an all-time high, and we could already project that our administration would produce more new business than all of the administrations in the last twelve years combined.

State Of The State message to a joint session of the Oklahoma
Legislature. From left: Lt. Governor George Nigh; Oklahoma Speaker
of the House of Representatives Bill Willis; President Pro Tempore
Jim Hamilton; Governor Hall at the podium, January 1973

The bad news was that contemplating a run for national office in the
coming years was demanding more time and putting more stress on
me and my family. Several times during the first six months of 1973,
I crossed paths with Jimmy Carter in different parts of the country,
never guessing that he was preparing for a run for the Presidency at
the same time.

During the February meeting of the National Governors Conference in Washington in 1973, I had occasion to meet at the White
House with John Ehrlichman, President Nixon's confidant, his
number-two man in the White House and a trusted strategist. Next
to H.R. Haldeman, Nixon's chief of staff, Ehrlichman was the most
powerful executive staff member. It is ironic that three years and
ten months after this initial meeting, John Ehrlichman and I would
each face dramatic reversals in fortune; we would have an encounter
of a much different kind—inside the gates of a federal penitentiary.

Governor and Mrs. Hall, National Governor's Conference
meeting, Washington, DC, February 1973

In Oklahoma, the1973 legislative session moved along at a slower pace compared to the previous sessions. As was traditional in our state and in others, and as it played it out in my own administration, the power of the governor lessened after the first two sessions; it was going to be very difficult to gain passage of the bill to remove the sales tax on prescription drugs. This was the last plank in my original plan for Oklahoma, however, and I stubbornly refused to give up on it. I suspected that the bill was in trouble early in the session, when G.M. Fuller, my legislative point man, asked for a private conference with me on the issue.

Gerry Strain set the appointment for G.M. When he arrived, she buzzed me on the intercom and then ushered him in. I was glad to get this one-on-one time with G.M. to tell him again what a magnificent job he had done in the last two sessions, and give him kudos for his efforts in this one. Then I paused and said, "What can I do to help you?"

"Governor, you've got a tough problem with Lloyd Rader and the Welfare Department," he replied.

"How so?"

"Well, this bill to remove the sales tax on a prescription is taking money from tax funds earmarked for welfare; it's been a sacred cow since the 1930s, and the welfare lobby is adamant about defeating any bill that would affect their source of revenue."

"I knew that when we started. But how do you suggest I overcome it?"

"Somehow, you've got to get Rader to do a one-eighty and support you."

"Thanks a lot," I laughed. "I'd find it easier to convince OU fans that we ought to let Texas win next year's football game in Dallas!"

"I don't know how to tell you to do it, but I do know that Rader helped us with the bills we passed in '71, and you know him as well as anyone on our team."

I paused, leaned back in my chair, and looked at G.M. intently for several minutes before I spoke. "What would you think if I took him fishing?"

G.M. sat up straight and gave me a broad grin. "Whatever it takes, Governor," he said. Our meeting ended with my assurance to G.M. that I had absolute faith in my vision for Oklahoma, and wouldn't stop until the last stone was turned over. I told G.M. to defer debate on the bill, and I would get back to him.

As busy as I was with the legislative session, I continued my momentum in testing the waters on the national scene. Across the nation opportunities arose for multiple speaking engagements to different groups everywhere, from Seattle, Washington to Phoenix, Arizona, Boston, Massachusetts, and numerous such appearances in California.

Several interest groups invited me to these cities, including education advocates, teachers' associations, the National Education Association, meetings of the Education Commission of the States, and City Clubs such as one in Phoenix. An enthusiastic support group in these areas that developed for me were members of various

Jewish fundraising organizations and politically active people who favored the integrity of Israel.

One of these speaking engagements brought me to Los Angeles at the insistence of Robert Keefe, a Democratic operative and insider in Hubert Humphrey's presidential campaign. Bob Keefe had arranged an introduction for me with Roz and Gene Wyman, one of Los Angeles's most high-profile power couples. Gene, an outstanding corporate lawyer heading one of the west coast's most prominent firms, was of medium height, a handsome, bespectacled man, with bright twinkling eyes, a shock of brown hair, and the most charming manner of any person in politics that I had ever met. He was a political force in Hollywood circles, moving on the A List with such dominant personalities as Lew Wasserman, and was the treasurer for Hubert Humphrey in California.

Roz was a celebrity in her own right, having been elected to the Los Angeles City Council when she was only 21; she was instrumental in bringing the Dodgers to the West Coast. She was a lovely, gracious, dark-eyed brunette, the consummate hostess, with three energetic and extroverted children. When we met the Wymans, Jo and I formed an immediate friendship with them, which blossomed quickly, as we shared a common philosophy of life, of family, and our dreams for the future of this nation.

So began a mentoring process by Gene that gave me confidence, inspiration, and great hopes for the future—but most importantly, he was an honest sounding board and close friend who believed in me. At the same time, I was developing a better understanding of East Coast politics through the auspices of John Loeb, Jr. His congratulations call just after my inauguration had been a first step in renewing our friendship.

John was a tall, slender, aristocratically handsome man, with dark, intense eyes, dark-brown hair, and a cordial yet somewhat aloof first impression. He was the son of one of the founders of the famous Loeb Rhodes investment firm in New York, and was a friend from my days at Harvard. With my election as governor, that friendship resumed for several reasons: First, the Loeb Rhodes investment firm was very interested in doing business in Oklahoma, with the possibility of our expanded road program, new turnpikes, and other projects. Second, with Carl Albert's great prestige and power as Speaker of the House, his influence was enormous across the spectrum of American life. The Loeb family was intensely interested in maintaining the status quo of the present tax regulations as they existed in 1973; I was certain, after getting to know of their interest in Oklahoma, that one of the reasons I was being courted was that they hoped that they might have influence with Speaker Albert.

As our friendship reignited over the last two years, John began to encourage my national ambitions; he endeavored to help me in the New York City area. He arranged two luncheons for me in New York that were of primary value in introducing me to new groups of people. One luncheon included some of the power-players and businessmen in the city at the 21 Club, including the editor of *The New York Times*. A second luncheon was a fundraiser for Israel; the featured speaker at that luncheon was a general destined to be the prime minister of Israel, Yitzhak Rabin. This man in later years would have more to do with the attempt to gain peace in the Middle East than perhaps any other Israeli official of his decade. John Loeb took me as a special guest to that luncheon and seated me next to General Rabin to give us a chance to become acquainted, and for Rabin to give me his thoughts and predictions of the future of Israel.

At the luncheon, John made a donation to the Israeli Forest Development Fund in my name, as a token to show my support for Israel's continued existence as a state and their freedom to be a world power. The was a gracious act, and I think it came about as a result of my having taken the petition for the immigration of Soviet Jews to Israel on my trip to the Soviet Union in 1971.

On one of the trips to the East Coast, Loeb asked me to meet in New York with him and his father, along with a family advisor, Marvin Millard. When I arrived at the meeting, there was a fourth man I had never met, but I had read many of his opinions: former Supreme Court Justice Abe Fortas. I learned that he was a close family friend and counselor to the Loeb family. I was so pleased, because I had great respect for Mr. Fortas. He had weathered his own traumatic times from political enemies, and I admired his grit.

The purpose of this meeting quickly evolved into two parts. Part One was to form friendships and a personal relation with John's father, Mr. Millard, and Mr. Fortas. Part Two was to let me know that they would serve as advisors, to give me some ideas of the bumps and pitfalls that I might encounter in trying to put together a national coalition of financial supporters.

A touching moment for me came when former Justice Fortas gave me his card with his private telephone number, and told me that if I ever encountered any legal questions of any kind, not to hesitate to call him directly to seek his advice.

In preparation for this meeting, John and I had discussed his father's support of Richard Nixon in 1972, and his unfortunate misdemeanor conviction for violating the federal campaign-expenditure statutes in his donations to that campaign. John gave me a full explanation of his father's role, and I was satisfied that he was more a victim than a miscreant. I told John that I wanted to comply fully and strictly with all the rules regarding fundraising, and he pledged to do so. An interesting side note was that neither John nor his family or friends ever contributed a cent to my campaigns for governor in 1966, 1970, or 1974. I had never asked them.

On the West Coast, Gene Wyman had arranged for me to meet some of the Democratic activists and financial powers in San Francisco at that time. He introduced me to Walter Shorenstein, one of California's wealthiest real-estate investors, as well as a major donor to the Democratic party. Gene arranged the introduction to coincide with a speaking engagement I had in San Francisco; Gene could not be in San Francisco with me, so I went alone to Mr. Shorenstein's office. I was pleasantly surprised at the very cordial greeting I received, and surmised that Gene had given him a complete rundown on me.

As I entered his office, Mr. Shorenstein walked around his desk and shook hands with me. He motioned to two comfortable chairs, and we were seated facing each other. "Glad to have you in San Francisco," he said.

"Thanks for seeing me. I know how busy you are."

I liked his manner, and as we talked, he warmed to our conversation. It was obvious he was a power player in politics and business as he spoke with firm conviction, and his questions were succinct. "Tell me about your philosophy of politics," he said.

"I like people," I began. "I have been a champion of minority rights all my life. I believe everyone deserves a chance, regardless of color, race, or religion. In my state, that was sometimes plowing new ground with many entrenched interests."

I recounted my work in the black community, my firsts in black hiring in the county attorney's office, my trip to the USSR and the petition for Soviet Jews to immigrate to Israel. I didn't realize that Gene had already briefed him on this trip, and even told him of my forcing a State Securities Board member in Oklahoma to resign for making anti-Semitic statements. He responded, "I am pleased to hear your stand on social issues—but what's your stand on fiscal responsibility?"

This was meat-and-potatoes to me, and I quickly said, "I govern a state that demands a balanced budget each year, with no debt. I have met that challenge the past two years, and I've improved on the system by closing loopholes, giving 95% of the people lower income-tax rates and bringing in jobs and creating new industries at an unprecedented rate. I think of myself as a conservative on property."

"You seem pretty proud of your record," he said, smiling.

"You bet, sir. As Dizzy Dean always said, 'If you done it, it ain't braggin'!'"

He liked that, and we both laughed heartily. We talked for another half hour, and I felt that we had created a bond of shared philosophy. He seemed to react favorably, but I could tell that though he was warm and affable, he was very careful in his alliances. When we finished, he surprised me by saying, "Governor, I would like to help you become better known in northern California."

Gene Wyman had laid the groundwork well for me, and when I left Mr. Shorenstein's office, I felt very encouraged and looked forward to our next meeting.

Shorenstein didn't waste any time. He arranged for a talented publicist, Madeleine Day, to work with me so I could learn the political ropes in Northern California. She counseled me on each appearance I made in the Bay Area. From that time on, I began to be mentioned in Herb Caen's column in *The San Francisco Chronicle* as a potential up-and-coming national candidate.

In addition to Gene Wyman's efforts to help me in San Francisco, a trucking-company owner in Oklahoma and one of my early financial supporters in the 1970 victory, Howard McCormick, had introduced me to a wealthy Republican businessman in San Francisco named Al Wilsey. On my second trip to San Francisco, Wilsey took me to meet a dear friend of his, Joseph Alioto, the mayor of San Francisco. Little did I know how indebted I would be to Al for the introduction!

It was my first encounter with the famous Joe Alioto, one of the most colorful mayors in the history of the city. He was a gifted lawyer, and a political strategist to rival Tip O'Neil of Boston. Alioto became a friend almost from the first time we met; later, when the federal investigations of me reached a fever pitch in 1974, he became a trusted advisor and strategist for me. He had faced his own false accusations over the years, and was battle-tested in the amorphous world of slanted stories, innuendo, and outright lies by the opposition. On my trips to San Francisco, Mayor Alioto furnished me a car and security driver at each appearance.

Al Wilsey and I also developed a close relationship that continued through the tough years and beyond the terrible aftermath of my trial. But before those chapters had unfolded, our friendship grew out of a real mutual-admiration society. The very successful Wilsey was highly regarded in the business world, as was his flagship company, Wilsey Bennett. Jo and I became friends with his former wife, Pat, and enjoyed her company no end. Prior to their marriage, Pat was a popular TV personality in San Francisco; her roots were shared with a famous Oklahoman, the legendary coach of the Texas University Longhorns, Daryl Royal. Pat and Coach Royal were both natives of Hollis in the deep southwestern part of our state.

These activities were heady stuff for a small-town boy from Willard Grade School in Ada, Oklahoma; I marveled at the unbelievable trail that had led me to this point in my life. I continually felt humble. At the same time, I felt lucky to be in this position, and to be surrounded by people of great integrity who knew how to build a national operation. The possibilities for the future came rushing at me—game on!

I suppose you're wondering whether I ever took Lloyd Rader fishing in hopes of changing his mind about supporting my bill to remove the sales tax from prescription drugs. You bet I took that 65-year-old Oklahoma political legend fishing! We journeyed to a remote trout farm in the Ozark mountains of southeast Missouri for a two-day trip. Lloyd's apparel for getting in the water was the same for the two days: He took off his suit coat—still dressed in white shirt, tie, black trousers, belt, suspenders, and his ever-present snap-brim hat—pulled on his waders over his clothing, and followed me into the stream. What a humorous political cartoon that would have made for *The Daily Oklahoman!*

Rader told me that this was his first fishing experience in over forty years. He was pretty good with the fly rod, and caught more than a dozen good-sized trout. We ate fried trout and hush-puppies and swapped stories for two days. I pitched my prescription bill as hard as I could. Did I change his mind? No way! I struck out, and my bill was shelved by the legislature.

Welfare Earmarks 1, Governor 0.

The industrial development of Oklahoma and the upbeat mood of increased job opportunities created across the state were at an all-time high in my administration. As of 1973, economic improvements were proving to be politically advantageous, too. This was a subject that came up one day over lunch with a friend who, as it happened, had almost single-handedly put the fan in fanatic when it came to Oklahoma University football. "Well, David," he said, "what do you think is your most important accomplishment as governor so far?"

I gave him a laundry list of the things that I had done, and told him how proud I was.

"No you've got it all wrong," he said. "The most important thing that has happened in these first two years is that the OU football team has beaten Texas two years in a row!"

Hey, if he wanted to give me credit, I couldn't argue!

On a much more serious note, part of the agenda that I had presented to the Legislature in the '71 and '72 sessions was the reformation of the prison system in Oklahoma, with a priority of meeting the federal standards required for housing of prisoners. Before these bills were put into place, the crowded conditions and the lack of state funds had caused frustration and discontent among the prisoners, especially at the main penitentiary at McAlester. Although I had decreased the population at the McAlester by more than 30%, it was still in an overcrowded condition, and this began to bubble into a full-blown disaster in the summer of 1973.

Richard Wiseman was my most trusted security aide, and our friendship began during my years as county attorney, while he was a state trooper assigned to our district. A handsome 6'4" broad-shouldered man with a lean, Gary Cooper-type build, he made a significant impression either in uniform or civilian clothes. We had been close personal friends ever since he was unavoidably late to court as a state's witness before Judge James Geoppinger in Tulsa. The judge was unfairly berating him, and I stepped in and defended him aggressively. I told Judge Geoppinger that Richard was on duty; he had made sure the bailiff knew of his delay, and he didn't deserve that dressing down in open court. Geoppinger backed down, but I don't think he ever forgave me for interceding. During my campaign, I decided that if I won, I would name Richard to head the security detail for my governorship.

While in Denver making a speech, I was handed a note containing an urgent request to call my chief of staff, Jim Hart—ASAP. My security officer, Richard Wiseman, guided me to a telephone in a side room just off the ballroom and put the call through to Jim. Wiseman handed me the telephone.

"Governor," Jim said, "you've got a riot at Big Mac. The prisoners have taken more than twenty guards hostage, and it's the damndest mess you could imagine."

"What's George [Lieutenant Governor Nigh] done?" I asked.

"He's got state troopers and local law enforcement already at the prison, but he needs to talk to you now."

"Okay, Jim. Get the operator to put me through to him, and I'll call you right back." While waiting for Lieutenant Governor Nigh's call, I told Richard to contact our pilot and have the plane ready to leave Denver by the time I got to the airport. Nigh came on the line, quickly briefed me, and I thanked him for handling things so far. I said I would be in the air and headed home within the hour. Under state law, Nigh would be in charge until I crossed the state line and assumed the duties of governor. I asked him to keep me informed of developments as I flew to Oklahoma.

As I dialed Jim Hart back, I planned my action and was ready when he answered. "Jim, I will be there in less than five hours," I said. "Alert Derryberry [my attorney general], General Webber [the National Guard commander], and Bill Mayberry [the highway patrol chief] to be ready for a meeting in my office as soon as I arrive at the capitol. Call Warden Page and tell him what I am doing; then make arrangements for a telephone hook-up with all appropriate parties for a conference call from my office"

The riot was now in its seventh hour. Upon arriving at the capitol building, I immediately assembled a team, including the attorney general, the commander of the National Guard, and officials directly related to the administration of the prison, and we sat down in an emergency session in my office to determine the best path to follow to quell the riot and create stability at the prison. It was nearly 7:00 p.m., and darkness would soon shroud the prison. I had already ordered the National Guard called out, and they were in the process of surrounding the prison to prevent any prisoners from escaping. I had reviewed the demands of the prisoners, and I had formulated my own battle plan.

In my office, the team members were seated on either side at the long conference table that stretched in front of my desk. I had used this table countless times for meetings, but in my thirty months in office, I had never faced a crisis that involved the lives of 23 hostages. Jim Hart informed me that the telephone hook-up was ready, and Warden Page was on the line. My administrative assistant, Gerry Strain, sat at my side with her steno pad to record notes of this session for me.

I spoke first: "Our first order of business is to save the lives of those guards held hostage, and to contain the prisoners inside the walls. This is no time for pointing fingers or playing the blame game. I want you to focus on solutions, and we have little time. Right now, I want a succinct status report from Warden Page. "

The warden's deep voice came crackling over the telephone speaker as we all listened intently. He said that the situation was still dire, the inmates controlled a number of cellblocks, fires were burning in buildings all over the prison grounds, but no hostages had been killed, and the inmate leader was waiting for our response to their demands.

"Thanks, Warden, I appreciate your being brief," I said. Turning to the table, I continued, "I want each of you to give me your assessment and tell me what you think we should do."

Each of the men took his turn, and to their credit, they kept their suggestions short. Still, it took nearly forty minutes for each to be heard. When they finished, I thanked each one and said, "I think I should tell the inmates I will negotiate with them—and leave for the prison immediately. Let me hear how you feel about that."

The warden spoke first. "I think it's dangerous, and might give an impression of weakness to the prisoners."

Another official chimed in, "I think it's too dangerous also."

The support for negotiation was about evenly divided. I was assessing each response and weighing it with my own experience. "I know it's dangerous," I said. "I know it's risky. But to save those lives, it's a risk I am willing to take. I believe if the inmates know they will be heard, I can save the lives of our men. I think the riot leader will jump at the chance to be heard."

The meeting ended with my decision to go to Big Mac.

In preparation for going to the prison, I reviewed the history of the key members of the prisoner leadership of the riot, and particularly its leader. From my experience as county attorney, and with the number of felons I had prosecuted over my career, I felt that I had a very good idea of the personality of this man. It appeared to me that this was the most important event of his life, and it may well be that he craved the spotlight much more than he was interested in obtaining the demands that the prisoners had set forth. An idea flashed in my mind: What about putting him on TV?

By now the National Guard had surrounded the prison and were reinforced by as many state troopers and law-enforcement people as we could muster. Armed with the additional knowledge that enough of the demands were already in progress to be implemented, I was hopeful that reason would prevail. But on this sort hot summer night, there was no rational thinking by any of the prisoners involved; that that was the reality of where things stood as I flew to McAlester with attorney general Larry Derryberry, my key staff members, and my adjutant general.

Landing at the airport, I completed preparation for a television crew to proceed with me into the prison. As I walked up the front steps to Big Mac, I glanced to my left and took a salute from a bright, intelligent-looking young captain named David Boren, who had been one of the leaders of the Appropriations Committee in helping to pass my agenda while he served in the legislature. I returned the salute, walked through the doors to the prison, never knowing at that time that same young captain would be my chief opponent in the 1974 governor's race.

With steel-eyed focus, I strode down the long prison corridors to the prisoner-controlled cell block. To say that I had no fear wouldn't be accurate; but I knew that any *display* of fear would be disastrous. At last I stopped and stood some twenty feet away from the leader of the prison riot. In the shadows behind him, I could make out some of the 23 hostages held as his bargaining chips for negotiations. With cameras ready, I told him that I was offering him an opportunity to appear on statewide television to outline his demands. I thought at the time that he was somewhat taken aback with the ease in which I agreed to have him speak, and we began with that.

The television camera crew that accompanied me was nervous, but I thought they were brave in the face of this unknown situation—and they were eager for the story. I knew I was taking a huge gamble, but lives were at stake, and it was no time for the faint of heart.

The riot leader drew a scrawled list from his prison jeans, unfolded it, and began to read. "First, we want better meals, and no more crowded cells." His words tumbled out at first, and then he gained composure, speaking more slowly. He didn't swagger, but he tried to convey a confident air to let the world know that this was his fifteen minutes of fame. He finally finished and appeared quite satisfied with himself. He had been bolstered by yells of encouragement from the other inmates.

The result of his TV appearance—and the ensuing negotiations—brought about the end of the riot and the release of every one of the guards. My gamble had paid off.

My reward was the joy and relief that I saw etched in the faces of the 23 men whose lives we had saved, something I would carry in my thoughts for the rest of my life. There had been one prisoner killed in the riot, and more than $22,000,000 dollars in damage done to the buildings at the prison. But the 23 hostages had been saved, Oklahoma was on the road to implementing the prison reforms that had previously been voted by the Legislature, and compliance with federal court guidelines was falling into place.

There are lots of tough decisions to make when you're governor, but this next one was a doozy. Let me jump ahead to late fall of the year: It was a chilly Friday night, the last day in November 1973. After dinner at the mansion, Jo and I were planning to get to bed early. The next morning we were headed to the annual Oklahoma

State University–Oklahoma University football game at Lewis Field in Stillwater. Ted Bonham, a dedicated OSU fan, and his wife were to be our hosts. Jo and I were watching the news on TV in the second-floor sitting room when the phone rang, and the Oklahoma Highway Patrol cadet on duty said, "Governor, Coach Switzer is on the line, and he says it's urgent."

Thanking the cadet, I took the phone. "What's up, Coach?"

"Governor, sorry to bother you tonight, but it's those damn groundskeepers up at Lewis Field in Stillwater."

"How's that? Is something wrong?"

"They are out watering down the grass to slow our boys down tomorrow. I want you to do something about it."

Earlier in the year, when Barry Switzer had been named head coach at OU to replace Chuck Fairbanks, I had called to congratulate him and told him if I could ever help, call me. But I never thought he would ask this kind of a favor. Chuckling, I replied, "Barry, what can I possibly do?"

"You can have the National Guard helicopters fly up tomorrow morning and dry off that field before the game starts!"

Now I was really laughing, but I realized that Switzer was dead serous. So I paused a few moments, then said, "You've gotta be kidding. As much as I'd like to help, if I did something like that, those OSU fans would lynch me."

With a few more words, I tried to pacify him, and when the conversation ended, he reluctantly said he understood. Whether they actually watered the field or not that year didn't matter, as the score was OU 45, OSU 18. Coach Switzer sure didn't need any help from me!

The unrelenting campaign of *The Daily Oklahoman* with their venomous PR attacks was very distracting to the administration of the state government, and a fraud on the people of the state of Oklahoma about what was going on in the state. It had begun in the late summer and early fall of 1973, as the unfolding plans of the US attorney and the United States Justice Department began to take shape as a three-pronged offensive. Investigations had been generated in Tulsa and Oklahoma City, and the US attorney, with the district attorneys of both cities, began instigating grand juries to be called and investigating allegations against my administration.

It is my belief that those investigations called by those district attorneys, S.M. Fallis, Jr., in Tulsa and Curtis Harris, the district attorney in Oklahoma City, were begun for correct law-enforcement purposes to investigate certain allegations, however untrue they might later prove to be. On the other hand, the agenda of US Attorney William Burkett was entirely different; his agenda, apparently, was to manipulate state grand juries to keep as much heat on people who had been favorable to me as possible, to try to obtain some kind of testimony that would allow him to bring federal charges against me—without endangering his investigative sources, where his procedural abuses, Gestapo tactics, and justice run amok could be exposed to the light of day.

The manipulation of state grand juries was an old tactic, steeped in the yellow journalism of the past. For example, in connection to the federal grand jury that had been in session for over a year investigating alleged IRS income-tax abuses by me, investigators did more than merely put pressure on those close to me; in the case of my former secretary, Dorothy Pike, they secreted her in a Falls Church, Virginia, hideaway so that she could not be subpoenaed by my legal representatives to offer exculpatory testimony for me. In addition, I later learned that in the interviews held by the IRS all over the state with various associates, supporters, and donors of mine, whenever an exculpatory message was about to be delivered by one of these people, the interviews were stopped, and no records were made of any of the exculpatory statements given to the IRS agents.

It later became apparent that only evidence that might be indicative of some illegal activity was to be taken; any exculpatory evidence showing that there was no illegal activity was not to be written down or placed in any of the notes that could later be demanded by my defense team.

Evil Forces

Former Nixon aides G. Gordon Liddy and James W. McCord, Jr., are convicted on January 30, 1973, of conspiracy, burglary, and wiretapping in the Watergate break-in. Key White House staff members H.R. Haldeman, John Ehrlichman, and Attorney General Richard Kleindienst resign. Televised Senate hearings begin. In congressional testimony, Alexander Butterfield reveals taping of the conversations and telephone calls to the President's office. On October 20, 1973, the "Saturday Night Massacre" occurs; President Nixon fires special Watergate prosecutor Archibald Cox, and Attorney General Elliott Richardson and Deputy Attorney General William Ruckelshaus resign. The year ends with the White House unable to explain the 18½-minute gap in one of the tapes subpoenaed by the House Judiciary Committee.

In the midst of a multitude of crosscurrents working both against and for me, I was riveted by news of the unfolding Watergate drama. President Nixon's dictatorial attitude toward any move to make him accountable ran against the grain of everything I believe about a Constitutional democracy. As the year played out and the revelations of arrogance and manipulation at the presidential level mounted, I knew from my own investigative experience that these scandals take on a life of their own. Nixon was slowly being cornered by the discovery of his misdeeds, and those of his minions. It was no great surprise that he used his naked power to thwart every attempt to discover the truth. I knew then that the lingering suspicions that I had all through the months of 1973 as to whether I was on the radar of the Nixon Justice Department's "jack-booted" investigators might in fact be true.

President Nixon was getting high marks for his efforts to end the war in Vietnam, and this was offsetting some of the odor coming from the Watergate disclosures. Nixon still seemed to think that his resounding victory in 1972 had given him *carte blanche* to do as he pleased with presidential powers. The tragedy of his thinking was that many Republicans in Congress were becoming wary of their president, and Democrats were ready to pounce politically on the crisis of confidence that Nixon had created.

With much to think about and much to navigate, one of the real joys 1973 brought for me was a visit to the LBJ Ranch near Austin, Texas, to spend an exhilarating day with former President Lyndon B. Johnson and Mrs. Johnson. The Milk Producers Organization was a strong backer of my administration, and their local representatives—Preach Griffith, from Oklahoma and Milk Producers exec Dave Parr, of Little Rock, Arkansas—had arranged for the Milk Producers' jet to fly Governor Dale Bumpers and me down to the ranch—exciting times for two young governors.

When the jet landed at the ranch and rolled to a stop at the ranchhouse back door, LBJ and Lady Bird greeted us both as old friends, and, before we knew it, Dale and I, along with the Milk guys, Preach and Dave, had climbed into a four-door Lincoln convertible with the president at the wheel and headed out on a tour of the ranch. With LBJ driving, Dale in the right front seat, and Preach, Dave Parr, and me side-by-side in the back, top down, and the tires kicking up big clouds of dust, we headed out across the dirt roads that wound through the ranch.

President Johnson was intent upon eradicating a red-ant problem that had created large mounds some six feet in diameter across his pastures. As we drove across the ranch land, with Secret Service agents in a car some twenty yards behind, eating our dust, we came to one of these giant anthills and stopped. LBJ pulled up by the ant hill, leaned out of the car with his long arms holding a plastic push-button bottle of insecticide, began to shake it, and sprayed it on the ant hill, ending his work with this statement: "That will teach you bastards to come on my property, and you better not come back!"

Then we went onto the next anthill with the same admonishment to the ants as he sprayed them. All four of us roared with laughter at the passion of the President on such a mission.

On the tour, the president suddenly picked up the communications device on the dashboard, and said, loudly, "Bird?" He clicked it and said it again louder: "Bird?" Then Mrs. Johnson answered, and he said to her, "Please get one of those Secret Service men to bring us some jelly beans. We need some out here pronto."

Sure enough, in a few minutes we saw a speeding car approaching, and it pulled up next to us. A Secret Service agent stepped out and handed the president a large bag of jelly beans of every color. "Have some jelly beans," LBJ said, passing the bag first to Dale. "Be sure to take enough to hold you till we get back to eat," he continued.

I watched Dale, and he was careful not to take too many, but in the back seat, Preach, Dave, and I pigged out. The jelly beans were good.

We continued the tour through the wooded areas and saw in the meadows deer that roamed the 2,500 acres of the Johnson spread. These deer caused the ranch hands more trouble, because they were always leaping over the protective fences that encircled the ranch.

Dale and I had failed to wear hats, and I got a terrible sunburn. Dale was lucky and didn't suffer as much. As we returned to the ranchhouse and moved to the porch for lunch, Mrs. Johnson saw my sunburn and began to search for some lotion. She found it, came over to my chair, put some on her palms, and smoothed the lotion over my bright red checks and blistered forehead. I couldn't thank her enough. I looked up at her as she applied the cream, and I thought of my mother, Aubrey, while we lived in Sherman, Texas, doing the same thing when, as a four-year-old, I had suffered a similar bad sunburn. What a dear, personal moment with Mrs. Johnson!

She was such a warm, caring person, and I believe she was one of the most gracious and effective first ladies in the history of this country.

The day ended with the President walking us to the waiting jet, biding us an enthusiastic farewell, and inviting us to come back in the future. As the jet took off, the pilot circled the ranch, dipped his wings, and we were headed home.

Leaning back in my seat, I reflected on my feelings after the day that I had spent with that great man. I thought about his civil-rights legacy, his rise from humble beginnings, and his adroit handling of the presidency that first year after the assassination of John Kennedy. I felt then—as I do now—that the Lord gave LBJ the strength of conviction, the physical stamina, and the common sense to unite the country in those dark days.

On a note even closer to my heart, I thought how much LBJ reminded me of my father. Dad had never lost his Texas roots; like the President, he had the bursting energy and passion for living and being with people, always wearing an immaculate Stetson hat. And, most telling, he had a philosophy identical to LBJ's—that America was a big tent with room for every race, religion, and creed.

In studying LBJ's life before this visit, I had learned so much about his overcoming odds and fending off the political slings and arrows aimed at him, and how he had persevered and become President. Politically, the most important lesson I learned from him was that there was no dishonor or failure in the use of the art of compromise to secure a victory for the citizens of the country.

Looking to the future for Dale and me, I knew that the Milk Producers saw us as two of the new Young Turks of the Democratic governors, and could well expect us to move up the ladder. I have no doubt that they wanted LBJ's assessment of us personally, as well as a favorable attitude that we would have for them and their members for providing us such intimate access to the President.

The Daily Oklahoman's efforts to vilify me in news stories with slanted coverage intensified to a boiling point during mid-1973 and leading into the fall. US Attorney William Burkett, relentless as ever, had not only expanded his investigation from the federal grand jury into every aspect of my administration, but in the midst of that fishing expedition, he continued to pound the media manipulation with leaks claiming that I had diverted funds from the campaign for my own personal use, and never declared the money or paid taxes on it.

From the very start, I'd been so fortunate to have attorney Frank McDivitt in my corner. Robert White, an aide of mine, had recommended that I talk with McDivitt when I first learned that the IRS was conducting an investigation. The best legal strategist I've ever met, Frank had represented some of the major Oklahoma real-estate developers in tax matters and had a spotless reputation for expertise and integrity. Although limited in his criminal and trial experience, he was a detail-oriented person down to the most minute of details, and an astute tactician, on top of being a person of the highest quality. Frank McDivitt was my bedrock and the strongest single legal force in my whole encounter with the federal government. Like the greatest of athletes, he left nothing behind and brought the best of himself to the process—along with documentation of every conversation, every telephone call, and every inquiry to which he was privy, as well as creating a paper trail that not only protected me in the overall case, but absolutely thwarted the efforts of the IRS to bring an action. Mr. McDivitt became a lifelong friend to me and my family, and helped me weather the darkest days ahead.

Growing up in Texas and Oklahoma, I learned back when I was very young that rattlesnakes and other vermin don't handle defeat very well; when at first they don't get their prey, they'll look for any other way to prey, prey again. That was the case of the reptilian US Prosecutor William Burkett, who had called a second grand jury in 1973 after the first grand jury was unable to agree on any indictments relating to my tax situation. This was when, in addition to Mr. McDivitt, I hired a former IRS commissioner in Washington, DC, Sheldon Cohen, to also represent me in our efforts to defend any attempt by the IRS to bring an action. Mr. Cohen's advice and counsel, and the work that he did, were invaluable in making certain that no indictments for tax issues were ever returned.

While all of the investigations, tax matters, and very derogatory metropolitan press stories were swirling across the state, I was, of course, gearing up for the re-election campaign. And along with that preparation, I was continuing to pursue my national goals. During mid-1973, my California mentor Gene Wyman, and John Loeb, Jr., came together at a weekend visit to the mansion in Oklahoma City. Loeb was single at the time, so one of my staff arranged a blind date for him to have as his dinner companion, and we dined with Mr. and Mrs. Wyman, their children, and our children.

Ironically, the blind date was the sister of Jack Taylor, the investigative reporter at *The Daily Oklahoman*, who had made it his career to bring down my administration. At the time of the dinner, we didn't know she was related to Jack Taylor. To add more drama, we also learned that relations between Taylor and his sister were strained and tense—just one more twist in an ever-changing panorama of events. As for the purpose of this gathering, it was an intimate opportunity to acquaint these men with each other and with my family. In pursuit of that goal, the dinner and the discussions over the weekend with Wyman and Loeb went well. They seemed to warm to each other, and I think they came away with mutual respect. Nothing definitive on a national scale was laid out, but they encouraged my plans for re-election and beyond.

The first domino that really led to my legal troubles fell in the later part of 1973, when I received a telephone call from Sunny Jenkins, asking me to meet him at small airfield in Tulsa. On the way to an engagement in northeastern Oklahoma, I left Oklahoma City and flew there to see him. This meeting took place prior to Jenkins's indictment by the Oklahoma County grand jury; it was our first face-to-face encounter in over six weeks. I landed at the Ross Aviation airport on the west side of the Arkansas River southwest of Tulsa. I exited the plane, walked into the small terminal, and was ushered by Jenkins into a private room. We took our seats across a desk from each other.

Jenkins then proceeded to ask me what he should do about the bank account that "we" had opened in Mexico City. For the first time, I was directly confronted with evidence that Jenkins was trying to embroil me in a scam of his own making. I looked across the desk at that slightly built, casually dressed, supposed friend, whose brownish hair looked uncombed, and whose face and eyes seemed to reflect a smirk. Once seated, his apparent nervousness in finding a place to put his hands raised my antenna. I thought, *Watch your step. Something's wrong here.* The rage inside me at this revelation came barreling up, and I reached across the desk, grabbed the lapels of his coat, dragged all 150 of him across the desk, looked him in the eye, and said, "You son of a bitch! If you have done anything illegal, you're going to jail!"

Holding him tight, I said, "I'm not now and never have been involved in any bank account with you in Oklahoma or Mexico or anywhere else—and for you to attempt to involve me in your illegal transactions is the last straw." I shoved him back across the desk and stormed out of the office.

As I boarded the plane, I surmised that he had been equipped with some kind of a recording device in an effort to prove to the federal government that he had been acting on my behalf rather than on his own separate illegal scheme. Later, as I talked with Frank McDivitt in his Oklahoma City office, he was surprised that after two years of investigations, this heavy-handed attempt by the US attorney to gather evidence of some illegal activity on my part had narrowed down to this aborted effort to use Jenkins as his pawn. Frank asked me, "Governor, has Sunny ever said anything like this to you before?"

"No way," I responded. "I had heard rumors that Sunny was raising money that I never knew about, but this is the first concrete inkling I had that he had gone rogue. I am satisfied he was wired, the way he twitched and couldn't get his hands comfortable. I thought of all the lying witnesses I had ever cross-examined who had the same body language."

"Well, Governor," Frank said, "the die is cast, and now you know what to expect from that corner. When someone like Sunny is caught, the first thing he does is point his finger."

After the encounter with Sunny, I was surprised and troubled. What was next? Where else had Sunny crossed the line? There is nothing worse in a friendship than when a trusted pal betrays his principles and tries to cover it up. Even though I had previously fired Sunny as campaign finance chairman, now my worst fears were confirmed.

I would never see or talk to him again.

I knew from that meeting that the US attorney was desperate, and that his investigation was in trouble. The money he had squandered on interviews, and the use, as I later learned, of some 90 IRS and FBI agents without results, was beginning to damage his credibility with his superiors. Time was running out for Burkett to pursue his vendetta, and the authority for the second grand jury would be expiring in the next year.

Breathing something of a sigh of relief, I was able to focus more energy on the upcoming re-election campaign. In the overall strategy for the continuation of my administration in Oklahoma, and the ultimate goal of running for national office, the plan still revolved around a successful re-election and then a move to be at the 1976 Democratic Convention to burst onto the national scene.

Optimistic though we were, my team and I recognized that the biased stories and bad publicity of the first three years of the administration were taking a heavy toll, and that propaganda had encouraged two strong candidates to consider the race for governor on the Democratic ticket in 1974. Those two candidates were Clem McSpadden and David Boren. My inability to secure the post of vice president at the University of Oklahoma for Boren now weighed heavily on my mind, as I saw him as a very viable rival in the race to come.

Ruell Little, the American Party candidate for governor in my 1970 victory—and the father-in-law of David Boren —had received more than 3,000 votes. During my first year in office, Little wrote me a letter stating that the votes he had taken from Bartlett and the Republicans had been my winning margin, and he had a favor to ask regarding David Boren. Little requested in that letter that I appoint David Boren to a VP post at the University of Oklahoma. I talked with David, and he said that such an appointment was a life's dream of his. I wanted to help him not because he was a potential candidate, which he was not at that time, but in reward for his staunch support of my programs while he was serving on the appropriations committee in the State Legislature. David, a Rhodes Scholar, was an ideal candidate for the university position.

I arranged a dinner at the university with the provost, Pete Kyle McCarter, and presented my request to him. McCarter said it would take approval by the university board of regents. At the time I had appointed only two of the seven regents, and the other five members were beholden to former Governor Bartlett. McCarter tried his best, but the board said no. I lost that one. But when David later decided to become a candidate against me, I truly believe it was because of all the bad press and my poor showing in the polls that gave him the incentive to run, rather that trying to get back at me for not being able to secure the appointment for him.

Meanwhile, McSpadden, who was a very popular rodeo announcer, former state senator, and relative of Will Rogers, was set to make a spirited and very difficult campaign opponent. However, McSpadden was from the "Old Guard" era of Oklahoma politics, and I felt that the real challenge for the 1974 campaign was going to be Boren because of his clean record and the integrity that he had shown over the years in his work in the Oklahoma Legislature.

In the fall of 1973, an ironic twist raised its head on the national scene. John Loeb, Sr., father of John Loeb, Jr., my friend and point man on the East Coast, was convicted of giving an illegal campaign contribution to the Nixon re-election campaign. Loeb immediately called me on the phone. "David," he said, "I wanted to tell you personally about my father's problem. It may put me in a dicey position to help you secure funding on the national level."

"John, thanks for telling me about it," I responded, as I thought to myself what a class act he was. I listened as he explained his father's role, and after his summary I thought that his dad was more of a victim than anything else. "Let's see how this all plays out before making any decisions." I continued. "Please tell your father how sorry I am that he got caught up in Nixon's troubles."

All the while, talk was swirling in certain Democratic circles about a possible Scoop Jackson -David Hall ticket in 1976. This was given impetus by the appearance of Senator Jackson at my 1973 birthday celebration in Oklahoma City. A major event in our preparation for the 1974 Oklahoma campaign, it was held at the Myriad Convention Center in Oklahoma City on the weekend of October 20. Senator Jackson was the main speaker, and Glen Campbell, the country-music star, was the headliner of the entertainment for the gala event. Five thousand people gathered that evening, and we felt that some of the bad press we had been receiving was being overcome by the loyalty of these people.

All during that festive evening, I marveled at the pillar of grace that Jo displayed under the bombardment of the political potshots that seemed to be increasing. Her beauty on the podium was enhanced by the positive body language she displayed throughout the evening. Our children, Nancy, Doug, and Julie, dressed to the nines, seemed to be enjoying the evening. Later, at the mansion, at the supper for the celebrities, our children where perfect hosts, making Glen Campbell, his wife, and their nine-year-old son feel at home. My chest swelled with pride at those three and their upbeat, head-high approach to the event. Those kids of ours took the negativity in stride, and were able to celebrate my 43rd year and my accomplishments—a really happy birthday!

In another twist of fate, that same night as we celebrated my birthday, President Nixon was executing his Saturday Night Massacre by firing special Watergate prosecutor Archibald Cox. The protective cocoon that Nixon had around him was crumbling like an old earthen dam, with fissures spouting water like the headlines across the nation, screaming the American people's anger.

A bright spot in an otherwise difficult year for me was the work of my campaign finance chairman, J. Don "Donnie" Harris, a popular Oklahoma City dentist who had helped erase the stigma of Jenkins's fundraising activities. Donnie Harris was to serve the rest of that year as the campaign finance chairman, helping us to assemble the necessary war chest for the 1974 campaign.

The year 1973 ended with the goals that I had set out in the first two years being met by the Legislature and my administration. The fruits of that legislation were now ripening for Oklahoma by providing the educational needs and the business development that had been so badly neglected in the previous administrations. By the end of 1973, it was a certainty that we would surpass the three previous governors in the attraction of new industry to the state of Oklahoma. This was due to the unparalleled efforts of the industrial-development team, and other state agencies whose excitement and enthusiasm about Oklahoma had generated these new jobs and these new industries.

Other bright spots in 1973 were the kudos that I received from National Education Association (NEA), the Oklahoma Teacher's Association, and numerous educational groups across the nation. That year I was runner-up for the NEA's award to the most outstanding governor dedicated to improving education. I felt very honored, and wore that mantle proudly, along with my chairmanship of the Education Commission of the States. In a lighter vein Oklahoma University football had a banner year, beating Texas in the annual Red River Shoot Out at the Cotton Bowl in Dallas.

Governor Hall and Texas Governor Dolph Briscoe, meeting before the annual Texas University-Oklahoma University football game to view the trophy, Texas State Fairgrounds, Dallas, Texas, October 13, 1973 (OU won 52-13)

Presentation to First Lady Jo Hall of the American Airlines medallion from the cabin of the aircraft on which she had made her final flight as an American Airlines stewardess, summer 1973

Nonetheless, I have to admit that the clouded local political situation, and the investigations of me and my administration, put a damper on much of the excitement that had been generated toward the election campaign in Oklahoma, and the ultimate focus on the national level. True, I was still aided tremendously by the power and authority of Carl Albert as Speaker of the House; access to many power corridors of business and politics in those parts of the nation would be difficult had it not been for his influence. What's more, I had made relationships with folks across the country who were counting on me to bring to the nation the reform agenda that we had successfully enacted in Oklahoma in order to bring our state into the twentieth century.

But it not long after my birthday celebration started to fade from recent memory, I began to realize the level of corruption of which Bill Burkett was capable. His federal grand jury slogged on with unnecessary interruptions in the lives of friends and supporters of mine across Oklahoma. Whenever I allowed myself to soul-search and again ask why, I couldn't find an answer. Was I worried? Only a fool wouldn't have been worried at this point, with a rabid dog like Burkett on the loose. And yet I was infinitely encouraged and grateful for those around me—and I would not be intimidated by the tactics of Burkett.

Burkett Disbarred

Revelations of the Watergate scandal were raising the anger of the American people to a fever pitch. Historians and talking heads were speculating on the future: Would Nixon be impeached? Would the House and Senate hearings uncover more sinister issues? Confidence in the federal government was at an all-time low, and cynicism prevailed across the nation.

It would be a year before syndicated columnist Jack Anderson would expose the investigations that had been ongoing since the early 1970s against a number of this country's Democratic governors. These were all conducted by US attorneys appointed by the Nixon administration in a concerted effort to undo the careers and lives of duly-elected officials.

In December 1973, a cascade of articles in *The Daily Oklahoman* was designed to prejudice my attempts to combat the leaks from Burkett's grand jury. Symptomatic of these was a December 5, 1974, front-page headline speculating that I would be denied chairmanship of the Interstate Oil Compact Commission because of the federal grand jury investigations and the investigations of the Tulsa County and Oklahoma County juries. Yet the truth was that my election to that post was a foregone conclusion, and despite this front-page, banner headline article, I was subsequently elected to the post.

As January 1974 dawned, I was as optimistic as ever about the future. I had to contend daily with the malicious articles and a newspaper cartoon of me smiling while my enemies skewered me with numerous voodoo pins. The tension was palpable even among some of our strongest loyalists, as the federal investigation was ratcheted up on many fronts. Somehow I managed not to become overwhelmed, partly because I now had years of experience balancing many personal and political balls in the air at the same time. It was also becoming evident that crosscurrents much more powerful than just personal political anger boiling over were at work.

But I hadn't yet figured out that the actions of US Attorney Burkett were proof that I was marked to become one of the first innocent victims of the poisonous national mood created by President Nixon and his lackeys.

Against this backdrop, on a dreary cold mid-January morning, Jo and I were having breakfast alone in the mansion dining room in a rare chance to be alone before each of us started our very busy day. Lenora, our cook, had prepared scrambled eggs just the way we like them, dry and fluffy. Good-smelling bacon, buttered wheat toast, and coffee were placed before us.

"You look a little worried," Jo observed when we were alone.

"Tough day yesterday, with appointment issues for judges and an upcoming spot on the Oklahoma University Board of Regents," I answered. "That's not the real problem, though. We're getting ready for a battle with Burkett about finding Dorothy Pike."

Jo looked at me and put her hand on mine. "You and Frank [McDivitt] will figure it out. You always have—and I know you can handle this. Eat your eggs and enjoy the breakfast."

Feeling her loving touch, I smiled. Jo was right; nothing had changed to alter my ability to be as optimistic as ever, to laugh at the cartoons and let the barbs roll off my back. As always, I knew it was going to be great day. "You know, Jo," I said, "I am not going to be bullied, get angry, or retreat. Instead, I am going to smile even bigger—and beat these SOBs in the end."

Jo laughed and flashed her dazzling smile. Then she got up, put her arms around me, and hugged me tightly before straightening my tie.

With Jo in my corner, I headed back into the ring, and soon scored what I hoped was a knockout. To combat the scurrilous leaks from the US Attorney's Office about the ongoing federal grand-jury investigation, I employed a few different private investigators to look into the illegal activities of the IRS. The culmination of one of these investigations was the filing of a federal lawsuit against the Internal Revenue Service to force them to produce the "kidnapped" witness, Dorothy Pike, for our examination; as it turned out, she was a "guest" of the federal government in a safe house in Virginia under a false name, being kept there so that she was not available for subpoena by any of my attorneys.

As a result of the filing, we were granted a hearing on January 14, 1974, in which my attorneys sought information on the whereabouts of the witness. Judge Chandler put it directly to Burkett, asking if he or his office knew Mrs. Pike's current location. Burkett denied any knowledge of her whereabouts.

You could almost see the steam coming out of Judge Chandler's ears as he heard those lying words trip from the prosecutor's lips; a hush fell over the courtroom, as it was apparent that the authority of Judge Chandler had been challenged by an arrogant prevaricator. Judge Chandler's stern reaction to that affront to his judicial power brought a dramatic decision: On the spot, he disbarred US Attorney Burkett and five of his assistant US attorneys! The disbarment, of course, would exclude them from practice in the federal courts in that district.

The fact of the matter is that we may never know whether Burkett knew the exact physical location of Dorothy Pike, but he did know she was in the "custody" of the IRS. It seemed incredible to Judge Chandler that, after nearly three years of a federal grand-jury investigation, Burkett, working all that time with IRS and FBI agents and being privy to countless briefings, would disclaim such knowledge.

After all, Burkett knew that Dorothy Pike's sister talked with her almost every day, and Burkett had direct access to the sister just by picking up the telephone. This was Burkett's legal means to say that, as an officer of the court, he did not know her whereabouts; to the layman, this might be splitting hairs, but on its face, it was an out-and-out lie to Judge Chandler. In law school, we are taught that as an attorney, you have a duty as an officer of the court to assist the court in the pursuit of justice. This was one more example of Burkett running wild and loose with the apparent blessing of his superiors at the Justice Department—and a textbook example of "credible deniability."

Burkett was nonplused. It was the first time in his misguided and abusive pursuit of me that he had been punished. He immediately gave notice that he would appeal to the Tenth Circuit Court of Appeals for relief. But the same day that Burkett was disbarred, he was a dealt a body blow by Oklahoma County District Attorney Curtis Harris, who issued a statement at the conclusion of his Oklahoma County grand jury; he said that the jury's finding should halt any rumors that I was involved in any alleged illegal practices, because "there was no evidence to connect the governor to any wrongdoing."

At this point, my legal team and I met to determine the strategy to pursue during the interim period while Burkett was appealing his disbarment. Based on the information produced in the hearing, and Burkett's playing fast and loose with the truth, I should have marched out the courtroom door at the end of that hearing, walked four blocks to the county courthouse, and filed a perjury charge against him—along with a grand larceny charge against Dorothy Pike for stealing my records. And if the local DA refused to file, then I should have called for a county grand jury to investigate the issues and determine whether, in fact, Burkett had committed perjury.

My defense team and I missed a golden opportunity; sworn testimony before a grand jury might have stopped the abuses. In my years of law practice and public service in the courts, I had never witnessed such disregard for the truth, for the attorneys' oath, and for the Constitution of the United States that William Burkett committed that day.

Even if the local district attorney had refused to file the charges, I would have had the option of petitioning for a local county grand jury to investigate the allegations and decide on an indictment of Burkett and Pike. However, neither of these choices was made, and while we awaited the decision of the Tenth Circuit on Burkett's disbarment, my investigators continued amassing evidence of FBI and IRS abuses.

But Monday-morning quarterbacking doesn't win ball games. This was the first of three major mistakes I made over the course of the next two years that could have changed the ultimate outcome—and possibly kept my public life intact.

For three weeks, Burkett's appeal to a friendly Tenth Circuit panel of judges would work its way through the judicial process. Even though officially disbarred from the federal courts, Burkett was not disciplined, nor was he asked to step aside during this period by Attorney General John Mitchell. It was now finally apparent to my team that Mitchell was determined to carry out the plan to destroy me that he had put in motion in April 1971.

The Daily Oklahoman tried to play down the fact that their "white knight" prosecutor was now defrocked. With their grip on state media through their circulation and financial heft, they were able to create a muddled understanding of how serious this disbarment was for Burkett. A background factor, lying in wait at the Tenth Circuit, was the little-disguised rumor that the Republican judges on that bench were thought by many court observers to have a bias against Judge Chandler. The rumor was that Judge Chandler was a maverick, and the Tenth Circuit had picked him apart in prior cases. So it was no surprise that the Tenth Circuit court reversed Judge Chandler and reinstated Burkett and his assistants.

This action stunned my legal counsel and Judge Chandler, but the politics of the situation played an important part. The three judges who made the decision to reinstate Burkett had been long-term critics of US District Judge Stephen Chandler, and apparently decided to use this event in an attempt to discredit him and, in effect, label him a "maverick" judge.

I was upstairs at the mansion, getting ready for dinner, when Frank McDivitt, my attorney, called to tell me of the decision. The guard on duty rang me. "Governor," Frank said, "I have some bad news. The Tenth Circuit just overruled Chandler and reinstated Burkett and his staff."

"Well, I'll be damned," I replied. "We knew they had their stingers out for Chandler, so we shouldn't be surprised. But why the devil did they have to choose me as their whipping boy?" With that, I thanked Frank and hung up the phone. How was I going to explain this decision to Jo, and what was it going to mean in the future?

Now I was faced with an unscrupulous, disbarred-and-reinstated US attorney hell-bent on doing me in by whatever means it took—legal or not. Having now been tacitly given the green light to continue his abusive practices, Burkett appeared on TV, preened before the camera, and trumpeted his claim that he would call as many grand juries as possible and would have me in court crying on my knees one day.

A braggart with government resources at his command can be a daunting force.

Attorney Frank McDivitt had represented me against all the IRS allegations. He continued his brilliant work and fashioned a strategy that gave me a fighting chance against the federal forces. We also enlisted the services of Sheldon Cohen, the former IRS commissioner then practicing law in Washington, DC. Mr. Cohen and Mr. McDivitt together were formidable adversaries against forces amassing on different playing fields—and in some instances, the government flinched.

As all this was unfolding into a full-scale battle, I still awoke every morning to tell Jo that it was going to be a great day. But more and more, I felt like Jean Valjean in the superb Victor Hugo novel *Les Miserables*. I felt that at every turn, around every corner, in every dark hall in every building, and every time I picked up a telephone, there was a federal agent waiting to pounce—just as Valjean is haunted by Inspector Javert as he valiantly tries to escape.

The Justice Department had a powerful cattle prod at their disposal to ensure Burkett could continue unabated in his unscrupulous conduct. That prod was newly elected US Senator Dewey Bartlett. Still anxious to take revenge for his defeat, he had the power now. Of course, as reprehensible as Burkett and his lackeys were, they had strong competition in the form of an angry Republican US senator.

Now in Washington as a legislative spokesman for the oil industry, Bartlett continued his vendetta against me. An early rumor reported to me and my legal team alleged that a commitment had been made to US Attorney William Burkett that if he was successful in obtaining indictments and conviction of State Treasurer Leo Winters and Governor David Hall, he well might be in line for an appointment to a federal district judgeship in the future. Everything that Burkett thought had gone out the window with my victory was back in play, provided he delivered on my destruction. Or so that rumor suggested—and it persisted throughout 1973 and 1974.

From the point of his reinstatement, the leaks from Burkett's federal grand jury were more like broken water mains.

The continual themes from the slanted stories of the metropolitan press got a jolt in the summer of 1973, however. The allegation that I had failed to pay federal income tax on certain monies was dealt a body blow: In the middle of all these allegations, and during the time that Burkett's grand jury was in session, the Internal Revenue Service refunded $8,500 to me for overpayment of taxes during the three previous years!

Although this gained little attention in the four major metropolitan newspapers, it made a front-page story for *The Oklahoma Journal*, which was the one big-city newspaper that supported me. Publisher Bill Atkinson even ran a full-size picture of a photostatic copy of the refund check on the front page of *The Oklahoma Journal*, and it was a bombshell to those people in Oklahoma who had been led to believe that I was violating the law. The difficulty was that the limited circulation of the *Journal* and the radio and TV reporting of that event could not match the vilification going on in the other four newspapers. It did help in our fight, but it never had the impact I would have liked.

Jo and I knew it was critical to be upbeat on a daily basis. That wasn't so tough in public, but in private, we could feel the stress. We were intent on protecting the kids, and focused our efforts in that direction. I don't know why we worried so much, because Nancy, Doug, and Julie had lived through similar travails and accusations during my days as a prosecutor, and they were steel-plated in bouncing off any criticisms that reached their ears. In years to come, each of them would recount how their friends had rallied to their side and supported them when the slanted stories were making the news.

In private, Jo and I practiced our childhood mantra: *Sticks and stones can break your bones, but words can never harm you.* It works, believe me. Our faith in my vision for Oklahoma and its future never wavered; I knew there would be political fallout, but as long as I kept doing great work for the people of Oklahoma, I could overcome the onslaught. With the reelection battle coming in the next year, I had a wariness, a watchful attitude, and a pragmatic approach to our prospects. Hard work could win the day if I had a rhino hide and the ability to come up off the floor each time I got knocked down.

I had chosen to be a progressive warrior in the political kitchen, and I could stand the heat.

The drumbeat of slanted stories from *The Daily Oklahoman* continued unabated, with reporter Jack Taylor writing in a front-page headlined story in January 1974 regarding the plans of Attorney General Derryberry to probe my administration; the story claimed that "it was believed that the investigation will be aimed at the awarding of state contracts. There is little doubt that the investigation will involve Governor Hall as well as past and present associates"—rumor without attribution or substantiation.

Two days later, another front-page story by reporter Taylor speculated, "[C]apitol sources say the attorney general's investigations will delve into kickbacks ranging from road contracts to the liquor industry." Same old tripe! But only in hindsight is it possible to observe how the context of the times was about to figure into my fate.

It was a very troubled time nationally. Nixon's overwhelming victory in the 1972 election had erased the stigma of his disastrous defeat for governor in his home state of California. The hubris following his reelection seemed to give a paranoid, power-hungry President and his underlings *carte blanche* to rule the country; they appeared to think it was now a monarchy. However, in 1973, the startling revelations of criminal acts, corruption, abuses of presidential powers, convictions of Nixon cohorts, and resignations of senior White House staffers came cascading across the nation. These events spanned a broad spectrum of the federal government, causing a depressed feeling in the nation and leaving a cynical taste in voters' mouths.

Looking back, the undercurrents might be compared to the Tea Party energy that impacted the Congressional national elections of 2010, when the anger of that group developed into a virtual tsunami effect that swept the Democrats out of control of the US House of Representatives, and also gave the GOP an additional nineteen state governors. The focus of the anger of the Tea Party in 2010 was to "throw the bums out," while the focus of the anger of the American people in 1974 was to convict any abusive office-holder, regardless of party—and regardless of evidence. Again, I did not know at the time that I would be one of the first victims of that tidal wave of hate and cynicism.

That said, by early 1974 I did recognize that after the millions already spent on Burkett's fishing expedition, with him coming up with absolutely nothing except for one small, stinking fish in the form of the illegal doings of Sunny Jenkins, any event could be blown so far and wide out of proportion that I had to be prepared to combat it. On the local scene in Oklahoma, the county grand juries in Tulsa and Oklahoma City were still in session. The Oklahoma County grand jury proceeded to indict Sunny Jenkins and several others on schemes regarding State of Oklahoma construction projects.

During the proceedings involving the disbarment of US Attorney Burkett, and the action against the IRS to produce Dorothy Pike, we were furnished with information that may have given us part of the answer as to why the federal government was so intent on blocking any subpoena and testimony under oath by Mrs. Pike. That information appeared to substantiate the rumors that Dorothy Pike's mental condition may have been questionable during the time that she had been assisting the federal government. In addition, there were certain exculpatory statements and information given by her that would have been embarrassing to the federal investigation if they ever came to light. But as we were unable to subpoena and quiz Dorothy Pike under oath, we had no possibility of verifying this information—and we were unable to find a way in the legal system to overcome the power of the government to secrete this witness.

The early months of 1974 were a challenge to focus on the reelection campaign coming up that summer, as well as to concentrate on trying to complete the remaining issues of my administration's program—to continue to bring more new industry to the state, and to streamline government—all the while battling the IRS probe and the spurious, political grand jury investigations. Continuing to aid Burkett and paint him as the good guy in the federal grand-jury activities, *The Oklahoma City Times* on February 26, 1974, in a five-inch-high front-page headline, trumpeted his denial that federal agents were tapping my telephones. This was an orchestrated follow up to an editorial in the same paper the night before, defending Burkett's actions in denying knowledge of Dorothy Pike's whereabouts.

After arguing for Burkett for three paragraphs, the editorial concluded, in reference to Judge Chandler and his disbarment order, that "meanwhile, there is such a thing as judicial temperament. In this episode, one wonders whether it was temperament or just plain temper." Harsh comments about a federal judge trying to rein in a federal prosecutor who was not adhering to his oath of office!

I was determined to expose the illegal activities of the Internal Revenue Service and what I believed to be those same activities by certain FBI agents. But the cost of fighting the federal government was staggering; up to this point in my efforts to defend myself and my administration, we had spent nearly a million dollars with funds that were forthcoming from every source imaginable. The bulk of this money, however, did not come from contributions to help us in the fight; it came from my retirement funds, from the properties that my father and I had pieced together over the years for real-estate activity upon my retirement from government, and from the few investments that Jo and I had made. By the beginning of 1974, I was approaching the point where I was nearly stripped bare of any future monies for retirement—or even for my family's immediate needs—because of the cost of defending these allegations.

The costs piled up even though I had never been indicted for any of the alleged improprieties of which I was accused. It appeared to my legal team that the weapons most effective for the federal government were their selective interviews, in which they only wanted statements that would bear on the alleged illegal activities; they did not wish to take any statements—or write down any notes—of exculpatory material that were presented to them by witnesses. I got my first proof of this when Rowdy Sanger, an insurance executive in Tulsa and one of my lifelong friends and fraternity brothers, called me in early February 1974. The feds had questioned Rowdy about any knowledge that he might have that I had diverted campaign funds for personal use. Gerry Strain, my administrative assistant, put Rowdy's call through to me. "David," he began, "thanks for taking the call."

"You bet, Rowdy. How may I help you?" I asked with both familiarity and formality.

"I called to help you."

'What do you mean?"

"Well, to put it bluntly, the feds are trying to screw you."

I laughed and said, "So what's new?"

Then, deadly serious and determined, Rowdy said that an agent had interviewed him, asking about his fundraising and what he did with the funds. He insisted that he didn't know of anything wrong, and tried to tell them that; Rowdy tried to explain that I had directed him to give the money to my finance chairman. "But they didn't want to hear that," he said. "They only wanted information of corruption, or even just rumors of wrongdoing. They wouldn't even take notes on anything good I said."

As I listened to Rowdy, any doubt I had about the methods in use was erased; I now had confirmation of what I had suspected. I thanked him for telling me, and asked him if he would talk to my lawyers and sign an affidavit.

Rowdy paused, and I could hear his intake of breath. "David, I can't do that," he said in a low tone. "If I put my name out there, they will audit and harass me, and I won't be able to take care of my family."

With that, I thanked him again and ended the call. I would later learn of many, many interviews that were conducted the same way.

The conversation with Rowdy revealed a major weapon in the federal government's quiver of arrows: the terrible threat that if any witness came forward to support me openly and positively, they could be subject to an IRS or FBI investigation themselves. This strategy was made all the more clear a year, in the summer of 1975, when one of my best friends, Joe Bob Harrison, called me at home. He was almost in tears; he said he had to talk with me because something had been weighing on his conscience for more than a year. I could feel how much he was hurting, and I urged him to go ahead. "You know I never came forward last year to try and help you, and I must tell you why," he said, his voice wavering but steady. "I was interviewed twice by federal agents regarding my financial support of your campaign in 1970. I was asked all kinds of questions about any business dealings you may have had with my dad or me while you have been governor."

"Go ahead," I said.

"Well, I could handle that part, but in that first interview, I got what I thought was a veiled threat that if I didn't cooperate, then Dad and I would both be audited, and I could expect a full investigation of our affairs."

"Did you talk to your lawyers?" I asked.

"Hell, no, I was scared shitless! I didn't talk to anybody. I didn't call you or do anything to help you, because I thought they would know and come after me. I know I should have let you know, and I'm sorry. But every day I read in the paper about what they were doing to you and others."

My heart went out to Joe Bob. True, I was disappointed in what he said, but I understood. I struggled to comprehend how close we had been in the past and how intense his fear must have been for him to act this way. When I put down the phone, I gritted my teeth and became more determined than ever to keep my spirits high, my chin up, and to live every day to its fullest, with the hope and optimism that had carried me this far in life. With this thought paramount in my mind, I felt better; I put on my sneakers to went out to the driveway and shot some baskets to get rid of my frustration.

This distancing by friends became more evident in the spring of 1974, as many of the long-term friends and supporters who had come to my aid over the past two to three years began to be less enthusiastic about helping to halt this federal action. The drumbeat of continued leaks, innuendos, and allegations—coupled with the articles in *The Daily Oklahoman* made it extremely difficult to combat the twisted perceptions of me and my administration.

With all the external pressure, which was mostly not of my own making, I recall this period as one in which the internal pressure finally got to me. Since early childhood, I had mastered the ability to compartmentalize my feelings; rather than give in to blame or vengeance, I tried to follow the teachings of Jesus—yes, to turn the other cheek, and to forgive others for their transgressions as I would seek to be forgiven. That said, I know that by ignoring feelings, they don't necessarily go away.

On the contrary, sometimes they take root and spread like weeds in our soul. For me, compartmentalization meant that not a day went by that I didn't mourn for the loss of my brother or wonder if my mother was receiving kindness from her caretakers—but those thoughts had to be set aside to meet the challenges of the day. It also meant that the complicated relationship with my father remained one of those weeds that caused me the most pain during times of stress. The idea that I had disappointed my father, especially in regard to the loss of money, was inwardly crushing—even more than the loss of reputation.

I am sure my stepmother and my sisters were also put to the test, as their friends and acquaintances would question them about what was being written about me. Dad had enjoyed unrestrained access to me during my years as governor, coming often to the office, and I am sure he shared his experience with his friends. As the heat from the federal government intensified, Dad must have suffered in trying to be positive in his own life, as I was at the ramparts fighting the battle for my survival. He had the added burden of being an object of cartoons by *The Daily Oklahoman* because of his frequent visits to my office. One in particular I found very funny, but it embarrassed him to no end: It showed me sitting in the governor's chair hard at work, and Dad approaching my desk, dressed like a hippie with his hand out. The caption read, "Can I use the car tonight?"

Now, I found that hilarious, and I tried to console Dad. It didn't work. He commented on that cartoon many times in later years.

Earlier in my struggles with all the federal investigations, much of their actions were in secret and unknown to me. But by the spring of 1974, I knew that I had enemies in many places. I was not paranoid, but I was every vigilant and on guard. Meanwhile, an expanded offensive by Burkett came at me from every direction, and he succeeded in getting the grand juries in Tulsa and Oklahoma counties to continue investigating the phony allegations against friends and supporters of mine to try to frighten them into testifying against me. An example of these misguided attempts was the calling of two of my oldest friends, Pat and Gayle Oller, Oklahoma City, to testify—even though the investigators knew of before issuing the subpoenas that there was not one scintilla of evidence that they or their contracting company had any involvement in anything illegal. This type of action was repeated time after time in those grand-jury proceedings.

This tactic also served Burkett's purposes as a process for weeding out exculpatory evidence that had been included in the documents stolen from me by Dorothy Pike. Any statements favorable to me were deleted, or were buried in the county grand juries' secret files. What Burkett wanted was to be able to leak his version of my financial affairs, without the danger of truthful retribution being brought against him—a sweet deal for a prosecutor given free rein by his superiors, and then protected from public scrutiny.

Adding insult to injury, Burkett was being protected all along by *The Daily Oklahoman* in covering his leaks involving intimate details of my tax returns; the paper somehow failed to question or investigate Burkett for those leaks. As for the illegal grand-jury leaks by Burkett and his assistants, apparently they justified their actions as payback for their embarrassing disbarment.

To add insult to injury, my financial and IRS records were shared with The Daily Oklahoman's investigative reporter, Jack Taylor. There was never any smoking-gun proof as to how Taylor gained access to these records—but he didn't get them from me!

Reflecting on the matter in later years, I would pose this hypothetical scenario: The Leo Winters prosecution in 1974 by US Attorney Burkett ended in acquittal; it was a disaster for the US attorney. But during that trial, Burkett had developed a pawn in the person of Oklahoma Attorney General Larry Derryberry. For whatever reason, Derryberry was beholden to Burkett, and this would play out in my hypothetical theory with the same plot twists as the movie *Absence Of Malice* with Paul Newman and Sally Field. In the movie, the US attorney leaves his confidential file with damaging information on a potential witness on his desk, then leaves the room while a reporter is left sitting alone with that file. The prosecutor is absent from his office just long enough for the reporter to read the derogatory file, which is then written as a story for the paper.

My hypothetical would have Derryberry receiving my personal IRS files from Burkett, then leaving them on his desk for Jack Taylor to see. That way, Derryberry and Burkett could deny ever furnishing those files to anyone. A counter-argument might be made that without proof, this hypothetical would forever remain only speculative. True—but as we say in Oklahoma and in other tell-it-like-it-is parts of the country, when it walks like a duck, it's a duck. And we also knew that the Burkett -Derryberry -Jack Taylor cabal was where the quacking took place.

Another issue playing out that spring was Attorney General Larry Derryberry's attempt to bring impeachment proceedings against me for various "alleged activities." These activities were unproven allegations and innuendos that had been presented to him by the US Attorney's Office. The apparent motive for Attorney General Derryberry to impeach me was his desire to run for governor; he had already made known his intentions to the media. Now he analyzed the past year and the terrible publicity I had been given by the actions of various grand juries and the US attorney; his daily pronouncements on the progress of the impeachment investigation were meat and potatoes for his political ambitions.

In an effort to mount a public relations response to Derryberry's ploy, I sought answers from Norman Ozzner, a professor of journalism at the University of Oregon who had been an important advisor in my winning campaign in 1970. After I left a message, he returned it within the afternoon, immediately asking, "Governor Hall, what can I do to help?"

"Professor, I need your assistance in finding a proper word to describe a political turncoat."

"Right up my alley," he replied. "Do you want a swear word, or one that can be used in mixed company and the media?"

"I need one I can broadcast to the state by every means," I answered enthusiastically. Then I explained that I had an opportunistic Democratic attorney general, who had been my political friend in fair weather, but was now more like an avenging Republican hellbent on destroying me by impeachment. I told the professor I was determined to take the fight to Derryberry with all the forces I could amass. I further described Derryberry's personality, his waffling loyalty, and his penchant for deserting causes when trouble arose.

The professor got the picture. "Give me until morning, and I will find the correct word," he responded. True his word, the next morning Ozzner called back with a word that was perfect to describe Larry Derryberry: quisling.

For those not familiar with the history of World War II, Vidkun Quisling was the Nazi puppet president, enemy collaborator, and the Benedict Arnold of Norwegian history. This label had a devastating effect upon Derryberry's bid for the Democratic nomination for governor; coupled with the legislature's refusal to bring impeachment charges against me, it finalized the decision to withdraw his candidacy. With his tail between his legs, he slunk off to his race for re-election as attorney general, and his withdrawal gave credibility to the whispered rumors about his reputation: "Larry Derryberry had a limp handshake—and integrity to match."

The political ground had shifted during those impeachment debates. Of course, Republican State Senator Frank Keating and his cohorts in the Oklahoma House of Representatives were being egged on with *The Daily Oklahoman*'s slanted news stories and vitriolic editorials. But on the side of the Democrats, cooler heads prevailed, and thanks to the leadership in the Oklahoma Legislature of House Speaker Bill Willis and Senate President Pro Tempore Jim Hamilton, the attempt to bring articles of impeachment was soundly defeated in the House. The House leadership found the allegations unfounded.

Hall Administration 1, Derryberry 0.

It was a tremendous boost for my preparation for the 1974 campaign to have the Legislative Committee refuse to bring impeachment charges, and that result gave my team the impetus to portray all of the other investigations as specious and illegal. Ever optimistic, I forged on, still certain that the people of Oklahoma would not be hoodwinked by false allegations.

Unfortunately I had underestimated the magnitude of the nearly three-and-a-half years of continual bombardment of my reputation; even though polls were showing the effects of the negative difficulties that I had faced, I felt that with a vigorous campaign, I could overturn public opinion. There were a few sound heads among my advisers, though, who counseled me at length about withdrawing from this race with all of the problems hanging over my head. Chief among these—one of the most valued political minds in Oklahoma—was former State Senator Ray Fine. Senator Fine, in his forty years of service, had seen these types of issues come and go; he told me that he had never seen such a heavy barrage of accusations. His advice was that the war chest that we had amassed for the governor's campaign, thanks to the efforts of Donnie Harris in 1973and William R. Nash as the finance chairman in 1974, should be kept intact for a future race, while I used this year to prove my innocence.

In my mind, I debated at length—and then I consulted with Jo. Sitting in the upstairs den next to our bedroom at the mansion, we caught up with the late news on TV after my appearance earlier before a local schoolteachers' group. "What do you think I should do about running for re-election with all this bad publicity?" I asked her.

"I believe you should do what you heart and your political brain can agree on," she replied. "I've told you many times over that I am with you whatever comes. This is a tough time, and you have to see clearly a victory in the end. You need the same courage you had in 1970."

Then, to break the tension, she laughed and added, "You'll remember that when we got married, I always thought you would be a corporate lawyer."

Jo's advice echoed when impeachment charges were officially dropped on March 16, 1974. That night I went to bed confident of the future. The next morning I told Jo I had made my decision: I would run for re-election.

To my surprise she didn't argue, but said emphatically, "Let's go for it." What a wife!

In the summer of 1974, US Attorney Burkett was thwarted in his efforts to convict Oklahoma State Treasurer Leo Winters. Earlier, Burkett had secured an indictment against Winters for, among other things, using his position to extort campaign money from banks. In a sensational trial, Winters was found innocent of four counts of the indictment, and others were later dropped.

An anomaly was exposed in that trial, and later admitted in sworn testimony by Oklahoma Attorney General Larry Derryberry in a proceeding against me: Testimony in the Winters trial showed that Burkett had influenced the federal grand jury that indicted Winters, convincing them not to indict Derryberry—a witness for Burkett in the Winters trial— even though evidence showed that Attorney General Derryberry had accepted campaign donations from banks in the form of a free car and a free apartment to use during his campaign.

Within a few weeks after his acquittal, Leo Winters was re-elected State Treasurer—and served a total of five terms in the post.

As time would tell, there was a second reason for Attorney General Derryberry's continued pursuit of me: the relationship with Burkett he had formed during the Leo Winters trial. I would later discover the details of this bond during the sworn testimony of Derryberry in a proceeding against me in February of 1975. Derryberry became the malleable toady for Burkett, used to pursue his all-out efforts to indict me. This would explain Derryberry's later eagerness to embrace and conspire with John Rogers to try to bring me down. For Derryberry to have taken on the baggage of John Rogers, there had to be a powerful incentive on his part; a quisling would be just the one to make such a compact with the devil.

There was little attention given to the primary race for the Democratic candidate for governor. US Congressman Clem McSpadden, State Representative David Boren, and I made up the field. McSpadden was the Old Guard, and spent most of his TV commercials slinging mud at me. Boren stayed positive in his reform campaign, and energized the young people and independents. The primary was held in August 1974, and I was soundly defeated; I ran a poor third in the three-man race, garnering only 27% of the vote. Boren and McSpadden were pitted in a run-off primary three weeks later; Boren emerged victorious.

With a historical perspective, however, I know that my staying in the race had been a tremendous boon for David Boren's political ambitions. Clem McSpadden, a household name and a relative of Will Rogers, represented the establishment and the traditional type of candidate in Oklahoma, and, although he advocated some reforms, he was not characterized as much for fresh ideas as was Boren. Had I stayed out of the primary, McSpadden would have had a much greater chance to beat Boren in a two-man primary. As it turned out, Boren had the advantage of the sniping that went on between McSpadden's campaign and my own. The back-and-forth of our campaigns left Boren as a kind of white knight of that primary campaign.

Boren's ability to stay above the fray in the gutter politics practiced by the McSpadden campaign was a great, calculated strategy. Added to that, most of my supporters and all progressive voters liked the message of reform that Boren brought, while at the same time he vowed to keep in place the progressive reforms that I had put into place. Chief among those that Boren did not want to repeal was the increase in the wellhead tax that was now enriching the coffers of our state, with oil over ten dollars a barrel at the time of the election and the looming specter of an oil embargo by the Arab countries. Boren had also been a loyal supporter of my program while serving on the House of Representatives Appropriations Committee, and I never took a political shot at him during the campaign. Boren's tacit assurance that the advances I had achieved would not be lost was a powerful force.

In the runoff primary, because McSpadden had run so many negative ads against me, voters were sick of him, and moved solidly toward Boren. If it had been a runoff between me and McSpadden, the political winds wouldn't have favored me in the same way; Boren fashioned an outstanding victory in that runoff primary, and went on to soundly defeat the Republican nominee in November. With the dark side of politics playing out in the Nixon administration, a reform agenda like Boren's was a welcome change.

These are the broad strokes of the political events of 1974 known to most Oklahoma historians. Of course, behind the scenes, there were other events unfolding of grave magnitude—not only in my life and career, but to all Oklahomans.

Political Showdown

April 1974: The Watergate investigation ramps up as the House Judiciary Committee demands the Nixon tapes—and not just the edited transcripts furnished by the White House. On July 24, 1974, the US Supreme Court rules that Nixon must turn over the tapes and rejects claims of Executive Privilege. Three days later, the House Judiciary Committee passes the first of three articles of impeachment, charging obstruction of justice.

On August 8, 1974, Richard Nixon becomes the first US President to resign from office. Vice President Gerald Ford is now President.

The bias of the part of Judge Fred Daugherty toward me suddenly came home with certainty when I opened up the newspaper on May 23, 1974. I had suspected his feelings in earlier hearings, where I felt he was giving Burkett and his team more latitude than an impartial judge would do. Daugherty denied my request for transcripts of the federal grand-jury investigation, which was now more than three years old. He had laid a precedent on March 25 by granting Burkett's request to release the transcripts to the IRS and Attorney General Derryberry. My legal team objected vehemently, stating that Burkett had breached the secrecy of the grand-jury proceedings by his request. Daugherty flatly stated, without any justification, that such an action "did not breach the secrecy of the grand jury."

He went on to say that he denied them to my team because I had not been indicted, and I had provided no compelling reason that I should have the transcripts. C'mon, Judge, don't you read *The Daily Oklahoman?*

Of even greater interest were the statements made in *The Daily Oklahoman* that greeted me on the morning of May 23. Reporter Mike Hammer wrote that the IRS had received information on my personal finances, and that Derryberry had received information on state building contracts. What sources could have given this information to reporter Hammer? Burkett—a nd it was all happening with the full knowledge of Judge Daugherty.

The summer of 1974 ended in a disaster for my political ambitions. The fact that I ran a distant third in the primary was undeniably bruising; coupled with a vendetta that had taken on a life of its own—and showed no sign of abating—the incessant hammering served to crush any optimism for future political forays. During the runoff primary period, the federal grand jury that had been in session throughout the campaign and in prior years now turned its direct attention to calling me as a witness to testify. Upon receiving this notice, my legal team gathered around, and we discussed the ramifications of my making such an appearance.

Ironically, as Tulsa County attorney, I had conducted nine grand juries, and issued the same notices. So I knew well the awesome power of the prosecutor responsible for weaving the story intended for grand jury members to accept, without the outside world knowing what had been said. No evidence can ever come before the grand jury unless the US attorney presents it; the prosecutor's power gives him an almost free rein in the secret recesses of that room—and Burkett used it with abandon. *The Daily Oklahoman* loved the grand-jury approach to investigation because it sold more newspapers. A perfect storm of the two, Burkett and the paper, could blacken the name of any innocent target.

I was now being subpoenaed to appear before that body at the height of the anger and frustration of Burkett, the IRS, and the FBI. After more than two years, no indictment had been returned, and no credible evidence had been presented to the grand jury on which they could take action. Burkett had carefully scripted the timing of this subpoena for me to appear after the Democratic primary had been completed. Extra gravitas was added by President Nixon's historic resignation just days before my appearance. I expected the grand jurors to be mad as hell over the national news; I would be "fresh meat" for them to devour and vent their rage.

At the same time, I knew that no exculpatory evidence had been presented to the grand jury, and I knew that since would be in charge of the questioning and the presentation, there would be no opportunity for me to present my side of the case in a manner that would be effective with this body. From my own experience, I knew that these men and women had already been brainwashed and biased against me.

So on that fateful morning, a sunshiny September day, I dressed with care and attention to make my appearance as authoritative as I knew Burkett would make his: dark suit, white shirt, conservative tie, and shoes shined to a high gloss. As I drove to the courthouse, I imagined myself standing before the grand jury straight, tall, and self-assured, because I knew of my own innocence, and wished it to be reflected in my demeanor.

The federal courthouse stood on Fourth Street just east of North Harvey Avenue in downtown Oklahoma City, just a few short yards away from the future site of the single most devastating act of domestic terrorism in American history, the April 19, 1995, bombing of the Alfred P. Murrah Federal Building by the cowardly Timothy McVeigh; the ominous feeling that shrouded me that morning on my arrival at the courthouse might have been the demonic presence of that future evil taking stock of its target. In any case, I couldn't shake it, even as I walked briskly into the federal courthouse, took the elevator to the proper floor, and approached the entrance to the grand-jury chamber.

I had always felt a lift in my step and an eager anticipation in all my years as a prosecutor and attorney whenever I entered the halls of justice. But today was different: The stage was lonely and bleak.

I would be one against nearly thirty assembled in that inquisitorial chamber, eager to rip my spiritual flesh. Like the moments before an Oklahoma tornado twists its funnel across defenseless towns and rips their homes of wood to shreds, I felt I was stripped of all defenses, but standing tall, with my chin up, I made my way to the entrance of the grand-jury room.

Grand juries have tremendous power. Burkett's dashed hopes of an indictment, and his furious tirades, had been conveyed to me through various channels. On a major television broadcast just days before my appearance, in an interview, Burkett had vowed, "I will call as many grand juries as it takes until they return an indictment against David Hall." With that knowledge in mind, my legal team and I had devised the strategy that I would use in my appearance.

As I walked through the dark, wood-paneled doors and into the grand jury room, I saw the members of the grand jury sitting in tiered seats with an empty chair at a plain table at the foot of this group. I knew how Don Quixote felt at his inquisition—like a descent into hell. To the right was a lectern with numerous yellow legal pads that appeared to already hold a great number of written notes.

Standing at the lectern was my nemesis, US Attorney Burkett, former chairman of the Republican party, previously disbarred attorney, and the architect of the campaign in which I defeated his darling candidate, Dewey Bartlett. When I had entered the grand-jury room, the animosity was thick enough to cut with a knife. The jurors' collective desire, real or imagined, was like a flashing neon sign that read: "Nixon resigned, and we're gonna get you." What an opportunity for Burkett !

The initial quiet when I entered the room was interrupted when the US attorney asked me to state my name. I did so. Then I added in a firm, deep voice that I had a short statement to read. After I briefly looked up at the rows of the grand jury glaring at me, I said in a clear, distinct voice, "I invoke my Constitutional rights under the Fifth Amendment of the US Constitution and decline to answer any further questions."

After my statement, there was an audible intake of breath, and several minutes of silence as the US attorney glared at me. At that point I stood up, looked down at him, and waited for him to make the next statement. With a glare of contempt, Burkett said, "That will be all."

My heart cried out for me to make a passionate defense for myself, but I fought back the urge. My discipline, self-control, and the wise advice from my legal team carried me through the day, as any statement that I made could be twisted by the US attorney in an attempt to make me appear culpable. I turned on my heel and left the grand-jury room.

In the hallway, I was mobbed by the press trying to quiz me on whether or not I had exercised my Constitutional rights. Several times I repeated the words, "No comment." And then I pressed through the crowd.

Although I made no statement to the press, within minutes, broadcasts on radio and television reported that I had taken the Fifth Amendment. It was obvious to me and my supporters that a prearranged leak had occurred from the grand-jury chambers, and that it had been confirmed by some coded message. This was just one more instance of the insidious nature of Burkett's slanderous attacks. He displayed a kind of maniacal desire to see that some sort of federal indictment was returned against me. This was so far past political payback; it was personal. If he could have found a way to legally kill me, he would have done so without a second's thought.

The confirmation of the leak of my exercising my rights under the Fifth Amendment to the US Constitution came in the unequivocal headline in *The Oklahoma City Times* that same afternoon, September 6, 1974: "Hall Takes Fifth Amendment." Reporter Judy Fossett obviously acted on inside information, and a companion story on the same page by reporter Jack Taylor featured questions that would have been asked by Burkett. Those stories were followed the next morning by an editorial in *The Daily Oklahoman* on September 7, 1974, entitled, "Hiding Behind The Fifth Amendment" with an accompanying degrading cartoon. Those news stories, choreographed with a subsequent editorial, were in the yellow-journalism style that had been used against me for the past three years.

Later that day, my legal team gathered, and we again brain-stormed all of the avenues to expose the political conspiracy and seek redress for the illegal investigations, grand-jury leaks, and other acts of apparent illegality of the past three-and-a-half years. On the political side, my team and I saw the sunset of any plans for the 1976 presidential election, or even a possible senatorial run in Oklahoma. Hopes in those areas had evaporated; many of my lead supporters for the quest for national office were no longer in the picture. John Loeb, Jr., in New York, and others had already begun withdraw-ing their involvement due to the IRS investigations, and apparent threats of investigations to some of their friends.

Out in California and elsewhere on the West Coast, I had lost my champion, Gene Wyman, when he left us too early following a heart attack in 1973. His untimely death left a devastated wife and family, and a void in my heart for a lost friend.

Meanwhile, the very real danger of being targets of IRS or Justice Department inquiries had dampened the spirits not just of my sup-porters inside Oklahoma, but also across the nation. In September 1974, in an attempt to expose what had been done, I made a very important trip to Washington to visit with Senator John McClellan, chairman of the Permanent Investigating Committee of the United States Senate. Senator McClellan, a Democrat from Arkansas, and I had only met once before, but the rapport I had with him seemed to be instantaneous.

The first time we had met was that joyous occasion at the dedi-cation of the Arkansas River Project at the Port of Catoosa, which had brought that modern marvel of transportation and commerce development to Arkansas and Oklahoma. At our second meeting, we discussed the irony of the presence at the dedication of some of the principal Watergate figures on the podium that afternoon. In the two hours we spent together one-on-one, Senator McClellan con-fided in me that he had once been the target of an IRS investigation during the first two years of his service in the US Senate. He, too, had suffered from unfounded allegations, and was particularly sensitive about the manipulation of the justice system to gain political ends. But the net result of our conference was not hopeful; without hard credible evidence on my part, it would be very difficult to call for an investigation by his committee.

His words still ring in my ears today: "Good luck in your efforts. I wish you Godspeed and success."

All sorts of information and rumors were coming to my team about the activities of the US attorney in his attempts to gain an indictment. In late September, one of the rumors presented to me would later prove to be the most significant: Secretary of State John Rogers was under investigation by the federal government, but Attorney General Larry Derryberry, acting as a surrogate for the US attorney, had offered a deal to Rogers. If he were to provide evidence against me of some indictable offense, then Rogers and his father, the inspector and examiner of the state of Oklahoma, would both be given a pass on the federal investigations. Our legal and investigative team worked hard to try to substantiate this rumor, because it would have given us the credence that we needed for me to return to Senator McClellan and begin a federal investigation.

My mind was filled with a steely determination to seek redress for wrongs already committed against me, mainly political destruction and the political lynching that had robbed me of a political career—and of my family savings. I knew that if I could substantiate the rumor of the Rogers deal, it would be a smoking gun, and proof of a conspiracy. I now felt positive about this possibility, because I believed it would prove my side of things; I shared my feelings with Jo, and I believe it helped her spirits to rise.

Jo had always been the repository of my secret strength, and she continued to be. Our children were bolstered by their friends both at school and in church, who did so much to keep outlook positive and let them know they were loved and admired. A source of support were their friends in the Temple Baptist Church who did so much to help them.

After the August primary, my September appearance before the federal grand jury and my late-September trip to Washington were playing out against the day-to-day workload that I still had in my remaining four months as governor of Oklahoma. My plate was full in attempting to complete all of the commitments that I had made to the people of my state.

But certain facts were being twisted in the nightmare of the ongoing investigations. Kevin Mooney had been a law-school class-mate, a trusted friend, and very nearly a law associate after I completed my term as county attorney. Mooney had fashioned a success-ful career with Unit Rig, an oil-field-supply company in Fort Worth, Texas, but was anxious to move into a business of his own. He had met and become friends with W.W. Taylor, a respected investment banker in Fort Worth. So I was happy to accommodate my old friend Mooney when he asked me to meet with Taylor regarding a proposed plan they had for Oklahoma that could be beneficial to taxpayers. After all, I had great confidence in Mooney, and had never known him to be involved in anything that was not straight-forward and aboveboard.

The meeting was arranged, and Mooney and Mr. Taylor pre-sented a plan for investment of the Oklahoma Teacher's Retirement Fund that would give the fund a far greater return on its money than was presently earned by the management of these funds by First National Bank of Oklahoma City, which had long been the investment authority for the Teachers Retirement Fund. Taylor's plan would invest the monies through the Small Business Adminis-tration and receive a guaranteed return to the state several percent-age points higher than First National; it carried a full-faith-and-credit guarantee of the funds by the US government, which greatly outweighed the protection afforded by the First National Bank of Oklahoma City.

However, unbeknownst to me, Mooney had made overtures to Secretary of State John Rogers regarding this investment plan, because Rogers was chairman of the board that was the overseer of the investment funds. That board consisted of seven people, six of whom I had personally appointed and who served at my pleasure. Rogers set the agendas, and was a major force on the board's decisions as to the investment of those funds.

When I was listening to these details, I ought to have recalled the old adage that when a deal sounds too good to be true, there's something more that you don't know. In this case, Mooney had decided to hedge his bets with a kickback scheme, and Rogers took the bait. Mooney betrayed my trust by secretly offering a bribe to Rogers in return for Rogers ' vote on the investment plan; Mooney stood to profit greatly if this plan succeeded, and hoped to become a partner in Taylor's investment firm. Shades of *Wall Street* and Gordon Gekko's unparalleled greed and lack of morals! Mooney's kickback scheme with Rogers was a classic example of that greed.

First National Bank, on learning of the inquiries to change the investment control of the fund, became enraged, and began a concerted effort not only to shoot down this plan, but to do everything in their power to eliminate this competition. First National Bank had even more incentive because of two previous situations: The first was that the State of Oklahoma's funds, which were part of the authority of State Treasurer Leo Winters, had been taken away from their control and one other Oklahoma City bank, with the funds then spread equally to more than five hundred banks across the state according to each bank's capitalization. This ended the control that those two Oklahoma City banks had over the bulk of deposited funds of the state of Oklahoma.

A second banking plum that First National had lost with my election was their position as the repository of all turnpike receipts for the entire state. Under Leo Winters's direction, and with my full support, every bank across Oklahoma shared in those deposits.

As the weeks rolled by, it became evident to me that First National was determined to do anything, fair or foul, to kill the transfer of the Teacher's Retirement Fund. I had several meetings with Taylor and members of his team, and consulted with other members of my administration. I informed the members of the Teacher's Retirement Fund, who had been my appointees, of the advantages of the plan. Having done that, I left it in their hands to make the decision of what should be done.

The ominous winds of fate were again at work behind my back. By this time, Rogers had been cornered by investigators—but with Attorney General Larry Derryberry's serving as a conduit to Burkett, he found his way out. Derryberry arranged a meeting between Rogers and Burkett.

It was in the late fall of 1974 when Rogers hatched the Big Lie—one that he hoped would save his hide. In the meeting arranged by Derryberry, Rogers told Burkett something to the effect of "Governor Hall offered me a bribe," and referenced the investment of the Teacher's Retirement Fund. In fact, I had never offered a bribe to Rogers ; it was a complete fabrication. It was true, however, that he had taken a bribe from Kevin Mooney.

It was like manna from heaven for the anxious and distraught Burkett. Time was running out for his grand jury to take some action; after three-and-a-half years of investigations and the calling of several grand juries, he had yet to come forth with an indictment. The cachet of sweet success in leaks, innuendos, and alleged illegalities that Burkett had enjoyed for the last three years was about to end.

Desperate as he was to bring some kind of charge against me, Burkett embraced Rogers ' accusations with enthusiasm. Burkett was not naive about Rogers ' checkered past; he knew his reputation for distorting the truth, an he was not unaware many people's opinion that Rogers was a psychopath. But it was now Burkett's job to coach Rogers to secretly gather evidence against me.

Burkett's dilemma was that Rogers ' story might be a lie. To protect himself, Burkett chose to have Rogers wear a wire and record conversations with me, rather than authorize the government to bug our telephones. Burkett cleverly designed a plan in which Rogers would be given a recording device so that he could get as many taped conversations between Rogers and me as possible. This would give Burkett creditable deniability if it were later proved that Rogers had manufactured the story.

But to save his floundering reputation, Burkett was willing to push the envelope in nearly violating his own oath of office by vouching for a witness, John Rogers, who he must have known was committing perjury. Burkett's reputation was floundering not only for his failure to indict me, but the disaster of losing his case against Leo Winters in the summer of 1974. It had given the public a very sour taste in their mouths regarding his ability as a US attorney.

At this stage of my life, there is nothing I would put past Burkett;, but as the years have passed, I still don't know why it was worth his oath of office to vouch for John Rogers. After all, Burkett could simply have claimed victory, having destroyed my political career, packed up, and gone home. But no; he wanted blood—and John Rogers needed to avoid a federal sentence. The die was thus cast.

For more than two months, Rogers attempted to have individual conversations with me for the purpose of taping me in hopes of fabricating some credible evidence that would indicate my participation in the Mooney -Rogers bribe scheme. These tapings continued through November and December of 1974 and into the early part of January 1975, prior to the inauguration of David Boren as Oklahoma's 21st governor.

None of this, I should add, was happening completely in a vacuum; the activities of US Attorney Burkett became so egregious that in the first week of December 1974 that Federal Judge Luther Eubanks called me at the governor's mansion on a Tuesday night to personally express his concern. He wanted to tell me that the activities of the US attorney were perverting the administration of justice, and that I should gather my legal team to prepare for the worst kind of manipulated prosecution that I had ever seen.

That conversation was the only one that I have ever had with Federal Judge Eubanks. He was so incensed about the seeming illegalities of Burkett's actions that he had taken it upon himself to call me personally to advise me about what was going on. The troubled conscience of that sitting federal judge did more to sustain my spirits through this time than I could have imagined; Judge Eubanks's call was an unparalleled act of courage, a quest for justice seldom matched by those in positions of power during my tribulations.

The last months of my administration, November and December of 1974, ended with a frustrating and bewildering cloud over my life. I knew that there was going to be some sort of federal charge brought against me; I wasn't sure what it would be, or when it would come. Most disturbing was that there was no letup on the onslaught of derogatory press, leaks from the grand jury, and insinuations of all kinds of nefarious acts on my part.

Jo and I spent many anguishing hours making plans for what we considered "the afterlife" that we would be going through, leading to a possible trial—and then what we would do with our lives after the trial was over. The entire family all seemed to be holding its collective breath as we waited to see what January 1975 would bring.

We had purchased a beautiful home on North Barnes near Penn Square in Oklahoma City. Some two weeks prior to the actual end of my term, all of our possessions had been moved from governor's mansion to our new home, and becoming acclimated to that was the first priority. With the ending of the administration, our new life focused on our children's school activities, caring for our pets, and generally preparing for an entirely new lifestyle after four years in the governor's mansion.

However, there were issues to be decided during those dark days: Issues of finances, preparation for college expenses, and what each child would be able to expect in the coming months weighed heavily on our minds. My biggest obstacle was deciding the steps that I would take to earn a living to take care of my family, and to have the funds to defend myself against what I knew were the coming charges.

Ironically, our personal lives were playing out against the background of some of the fortuitous things that had happened for the state of Oklahoma during my administration.

Many of the new industries that had come to the state were beginning to bear fruit, and the unemployment rate was at a point appreciably lower than it had been when I took office. The oil embargo of the Saudi government in the summer and fall of 1974 had created an enormous stream of revenue flowing into Oklahoma because of the increase in the price of oil per barrel; this created a $200,000,000 surplus by the end of my term. The effect of that increase in oil revenue was that the Teacher's Retirement Fund was fully funded, and given security for years to come. It also enabled education to be funded at an all-time high level, including budgets for special education and kindergarten, two of my top priorities. This was a major change for Oklahoma education, and a giant step forward.

One of the greatest sources of pride for me was the opening of the first new rural school district after almost twenty years of collapsing rural schools. That school district was in southeastern Oklahoma, and was probably the greatest single local triumph that occurred during my administration, as far as elementary and high school education were concerned.

In November of 1974, I traveled to Japan to seek new industry for Oklahoma. Although no major agreements were signed, it laid the foundation for what was later to become an influx of commerce from Japan. I learned how meaningful it was to be the first Oklahoma governor to come to that country to personally ask for the hand of the Japanese in a commercial adventure. The previous major Japanese industrial venture in Oklahoma had been the purchasing of high-sulfur coal that was transported by ship to Japan to be used in their steel mills.

Christmas 1974 brought our family closer together than perhaps any other time. It seemed that the Holy Spirit surrounded us and gave meaning to our determination to persevere as a family through all that might lie ahead in the months to come. I don't think I was ever more proud of our children at any phase in their lives than I was during these months of their stoic determination to show me their best sides, to create as few problems at home for their mother and me, and to always be supportive in helping to do their chores, staying positive, and praying for us in defeating the forces of evil that had brought us to this point in our lives.

After living in the mansion for four years, Jo and I wanted to show our affection for our staff. In choosing the most meaningful gifts for our cooks, we decided to give them custody of two of the most beloved members of our household pets. Willie May had been a special friend of one of our dogs, a Heinz spaniel named Fiji. Fiji had black and white markings, was of modest size with a lovely personality, and had centered his attention on Willie May for most of our time at the mansion. This small, black dog had given so much joy to our family and to the staff that we were thrilled that she would take him into her home. This same euphoria was repeated when Lenore accepted our gift of our full-grown black lab, Noah. Noah had developed a special affection for Lenore, so it was appropriate that she should have him. Our last look at Lenore and Noah was when they drove out the mansion gate with Noah's head nestled against her shoulder.

It had been a hard decision to decide to give Noah and Fiji away, but our new home would only accommodate two of our dogs, our St. Bernard, Hilda, and the miniature poodle, Paul, who was the joy of Jo's life. Our cats and rabbits, who had lived with us for four years in the mansion, had also found new homes during the months after our loss of the election in August 1974. One of the treasured mementos that we took with us was a small, exquisite, silver-engraved candy dish given to us by the Highway Patrol Cadets, who had served as guards for those years in the mansion. We treasured the silver candy dish, and it has graced our dining-room sideboards through-out these 36 years since leaving the mansion.

Of course, we took much more away from our experiences, both amazing and daunting, that occurred during our stay in the man-sion, moments that would live prominently in our memories forever. Especially vivid were those last days before we walked out of the mansion for good.

With January 14, 1975, as the official ending of my term, our focus had been on that date and on the preparation for Governor-elect Boren and his family's move to the mansion. Toward that end, a week earlier Jo had invited the next first lady, Jana Boren, to come for lunch, tour the mansion, and become acquainted with their new home. It was a both a sad and a sweet experience, as Jo and Jana were friends and had much in common.

What a strange set of dueling emotions that day set off, as we counted down the days to the final passing of the torch! I had spent so much of my life accepting the proverbial slings and arrows that are unavoidable, no matter what path we all walk. Likewise, I had learned early in childhood to compartmentalize and even ignore the pain that challenges bring, while focusing on the Good Lord's merciful deeds, His wonders to behold. My faith had taught me to look back and see how God was with me in the journey to the top, and to rest in the knowledge that He would be with me and my family in the days ahead, no matter how uncertain.

But I would be inhuman to say that I wasn't bewildered by the antagonistic forces that had amassed against me, or that I wasn't deeply, profoundly full of regrets that the journey would not continue with a second term—or with a shot at national office. At the same time, I wanted only the best of our experiences for the Borens—not only for their sakes, but for the good of Oklahoma. The morning of January 14, 1975, Jo and I greeted Governor-elect and Mrs. Boren at the mansion entrance. This was the first of our two last official acts; the second would be appearing on the inaugural platform at the swearing-in ceremonies.

Willie May Grey had prepared cakes and coffee for this event. Carefully she placed the tray on the side table in front of the large fireplace that graced the south wall of the library on the first floor of the mansion. Seated comfortably with our coffee cups in hand, we played our roles as custom dictated. We were friends, and first names were used on this traditional occasion. Jo and Jana discussed the idiosyncrasies of the mansion, such as security measures and the like. David and I discussed how proud his father would have been to have lived to see this day, and how fortunate I was that my dad was still living.

This interlude ended after fifteen minutes due to the press of the day's agenda. During our visit, the "seven-hundred-pound gorilla in the room" was never mentioned. That was the impending action by the federal grand jury. I later learned that Governor-elect Boren had been sworn to secrecy; he knew that I would soon be indicted.

Handshakes were in order and completed as the Borens left to be taken to the capitol. Jo and I then turned to complete our own farewell departure. Before the Borens had arrived, we had completed all but one of our good-byes to the staff. Now I helped Jo put on her lovely tan coat, adorned as it was with her favorite long-tailed mouse broach, and cast an admiring, fond glance at her tailored look. I pulled on my black cashmere overcoat over my dark-blue suit, complete with white shirt and striped silk tie. At the mansion's north entrance stood John Coldiron, who had served as the greeter to all visitors, as well as an adjunct to our security team. He had become Jo's close friend, and we respected him for his care and affection for our family during those years. We said good-bye and warmly thanked John for his service.

As Jo and I walked to the car under the north portico of the governor's mansion, we looked at each other, kissed, and embraced with an intensity that matched our determination to weather the storm that lay ahead. We walked a few steps to the waiting official limo. Jo got in first, and I followed. I shut the door, and we were driven to the state capitol for the inaugural ceremony and my last official act as Oklahoma's twentieth governor.

The Trial

In January 1975, John Ehrlichman, Robert Haldeman, John Mitchell, and Robert Marian were convicted of Watergate crimes. On January 8, 1975, US District Judge John Sirica ordered the release from prison of Watergate figures Herbert W. Kalmbach, Jeb Stuart Magruder, and John W. Dean, III. Since Nixon's resignation, President Gerald Ford had valiantly tried to heal the wounds of Watergate. But the cancer that had been eating away at democracy in the Nixon circle had not been done in entirely with his resignation.

Injustices still abounded, and no investigative body at the federal level had ever exposed the Mitchell, Bartlett, Kleindienst conspiratorial meeting of May 13, 1971. My counsel, Frank McDivitt, had received the office-log page for US Attorney General John Mitchell for that day. The office log page read as follows:

9:35 a.m. Attorney General John Mitchell personally conferred with former Oklahoma governor Dewey Bartlett and Deputy Attorney General Richard Kleindienst.

10:10 a.m. John Mitchell personally conferred alone with Richard Kleindienst.

10:21 a.m. John Mitchell made a telephone call to Assistant Attorney Robert Mardian [the publicized liaison for "dirty tricks" through the Internal Revenue Service].

12:35 p.m. John Mitchell personally conferred with Robert Mardian.

Two weeks later, the investigation was launched by the Internal Revenue Service against Governor David Hall. It was further revealed that James Inhofe, the Republican candidate for lieutenant-governor on the ticket with defeated Governor Dewey Bartlett, made oral allegations against Governor Hall in a meeting with two Internal Revenue Agents between the date of May 13, 1971, the Mitchell, Kleindienst /Bartlett meeting, and the commencement of the four year IRS investigation.

In December 1975, in his syndicated column "The Washington Merry-Go-Round," Jack Anderson confirmed that in the early 1970s, US attorneys appointed by President Nixon began investigating sitting governors across the country who were also Democrats. This column, appearing in The Washington Post, *detailed the fact that certain chief executives in several states, all Democrats, found themselves under searching federal scrutiny. These included Kentucky's Wendell Ford, Louisiana's Edwin Edwards, Maryland's Marvin Mandell, Pennsylvania's Milton Shapp —and Oklahoma's David Hall. Anderson noted in his column that transcripts of tapes used by the FBI in the Hall investigation had been altered.*

My worst fears were realized on January 17, 1975, just two days after the new governor, David Boren, had been inaugurated. That morning the indictment was returned, filed with the US District Court for the Western District of Oklahoma, and arrest warrants were issued for W.W. Taylor, Kevin Mooney, and David Hall as co-conspirators in the attempt to bribe Secretary of State John Rogers. How they must have been celebrating in the US District Attorney's office and in the boardroom of *The Daily Oklahoman!* John Rogers had saved them from the ignominious fate that befalls those who abuse the American judicial process.

We later learned that there had been a major discussion within the Justice Department among the staff, now that Edward H. Levi had been named attorney general by President Gerald Ford to replace John Mitchell. The troublesome issue for them was whether to return the indictment prior to the inauguration, and attempt to arrest me during the inaugural events. First, we learned, Attorney General Levi thought it would be overtly political for it to be staged in that manner, even though there was much support from Burkett, as well as from his staff and many of the FBI agents. The other issue was one that was more practical: whether an attempt to arrest me with my security staff guarding me would cause an exchange of gunfire.

It was decided in the halls of the Justice Department that the public announcement of the indictment would be carried out after the inauguration. Cool heads prevailed, and the "cowboy mentality" of Burkett was overruled—at least in this instance.

Jo and I had known the indictment was probably coming, so now our efforts were directed at explaining to our children what the immediate future would hold. That first night, long after the children were in bed, we sat in our living room before the large fireplace, where a glowing flame gave a look of peace and harmony to the room that belied the serious discussion we were having. That night is blurred in my memory, but I do remember Jo's loving arms around me as we prayed for the strength to get through what lay ahead.

Over three decades later, I asked Nancy, Doug, and Julie what they remembered about this time, and their answers were almost identical. Each of them said that in the flurry of activity as we moved from the governor's mansion to our new home on North Barnes Avenue, the inauguration of Governor Boren, and the Christmas holidays, they could not remember their feelings at the time. Julie was the only one who voiced an explanation: "Dad, I really think all three of us buried that pain, and we don't ever want to bring it up again. That was the beginning of a tragic and difficult time in our lives, as well as the burdens you and Mom were having."

I didn't press her further.

Life gives each of us different ways of coping with the destructive forces that come our way, and I was not surprised at Julie's answer to my question. In many ways, her answer reflected my apprehension about even bringing up the subject.

My attorney, Frank McDivitt, was contacted by the US attorney's office, and I was allowed to present myself to court for arraignment; no formal arrest at my home or in the streets of Oklahoma City was made. Mooney turned himself in to the federal authorities. Unknown to my legal team, Mooney had been quietly cooperating with the federal government and the US attorney during the period prior to the indictment. W.W. Taylor was another matter.

In an effort to intimidate Taylor and to try to make him become a witness for the government, the FBI had planned a scenario in which he would be arrested on the downtown street of a city in south Florida. The particular location that they chose was approximately six blocks from the federal courthouse. A number of agents surrounded Taylor, presented him with the warrant, and handcuffed him, adding chains to his body—and then, instead of driving him to the federal courthouse, they marched him through the crowded streets, handcuffs secure and chains rattling. The intent was to humiliate and frighten Taylor so much that he would flip and become a witness for the prosecution.

But Taylor surprised the federal agents and the Justice Department with his determination to prove his innocence. He never wavered under the pressure, and he frustrated every attempt by Burkett and his forces to coerce him. The crude attempt to break him down by publicly shackling him in chains had just the opposite effect; it steeled his resolve to fight the case to the bitter end. It appeared to all concerned that he became stronger as a result of this attempt, and this played out not only in the trial, but over the years until his death.

It did, however, give us a preview of what was to come, and indicated the lengths to which Burkett and federal forces would go to ensure that their evil, misguided prosecution moved ahead. I can only speculate what Taylor's feelings were when he recognized the abuse for what it was.

In my subconscious was the nagging thought that perhaps Mooney, in his original conversations on the Taylor plan, wasn't giving me the whole picture. The analytical part of my brain had been reviewing Mooney's prior actions in his association with Ken W. Davis, Sr., his employer at Unit Rig in Fort Worth. Davis had treated Mooney like one of his sons, and allowed him to buy a very valuable lake property next to the Davis family property near Fort Worth, with the understanding that Mooney would not sell it, but use it as a retreat so their families would be near each other. A short time after Davis's death in 1968, Mooney broke his promise and sold the lot when offered a lucrative price for the land. That was one previous incident that should have been a warning to me of his character, or lack thereof. But I had trusted him, and my normal instinct of skepticism had not kicked in.

Another incident regarding Mooney in my first two years as governor seemed odd to me, and that was his insistence that I use a suite at the Waldorf Astoria Hotel in New York City that Unit Rig kept as a perk for their executives, customers, and people they wished to influence. I was wary of any such offers as county attorney, and I felt the same way as governor. Mooney must have tried four or five times to have me use the suite, and I turned him down every time. In my career in politics, I had seen so many bright men lured by a fringe benefit like that, and then pressure was later applied by the benefactor. Still, my warning system regarding Mooney hadn't made it to my conscious mind.

At the arraignment, Taylor, Mooney, and I came before Judge Fred Daugherty to enter our pleas to the indictment. Judge Daugherty was as handsome as a matinee idol—dark hair with silver streaks on each side and dark eyes that could give gravitas to his words from the bench. He had distinguished himself as a general commanding the Oklahoma 45th Division, and was in his tenth year as judge in the Western District. He had been a fervent supporter of Democratic causes during my rise in politics, and we had become friends over that period of time.

But Daugherty had already exhibited bias in earlier hearings. Still, I never would have guessed at this time that less than three weeks later, his prejudice would be unveiled with the fiery force of a military flame thrower—with me as the target.

As I stood before Judge Daugherty, alongside Mooney and Taylor, I reflected on the thousands of criminals who had come through my office when I was county attorney. Now I was standing before the bar about to enter a plea of my own. Judge Daugherty broke my train of thought when he asked us, one by one, "How do you plead?"

Standing as tall and straight as I could, I answered in a strong, clear voice, "Not guilty." Taylor followed suit with his firm statement of innocence. Then it was Mooney's turn, and, with shoulders drooping, he answered in a hushed tone, "Not guilty."

The die was cast, and the participants for this historic show trial were in place.

In later years, I would think about how innocent victims of conspiracy and a prosecutor's ambitions must have felt at their arraignments, and the blessed relief that those innocent people must have felt when the scientific breakthrough of DNA exonerations set them free. Alas, in the case of political smears, innuendos, and falsehoods that ruin the lives of good men and women, there is no political DNA exoneration.

There was a part of me that felt like so many accused and innocent defendants—that justice would prevail because God and the truth were on my side—while another part of me realized that dark forces wouldn't rest until my destruction was made public. This led me to think, Comes now the crucifixion.

My first order of legal business after the arraignment was to secure an experienced trial lawyer. Frank McDivitt had been an excellent strategist up to this point, but our team needed an experienced criminal lawyer familiar with the federal court system. Because of the tremendous financial drain that had occurred in the last three years in attempting to battle the Justice Department and the IRS, and the cost of investigative services, I had depleted all of my resources; I was now faced with trying to find legal counsel that I thought could do the job—and that I could afford.

McDivitt, who had been the guiding light for the three-and-a-half years that we had resisted the federal government, recommended that I meet and interview a very bright contemporary of his, Attorney D.C. Thomas. He had an outstanding record in the federal court of defending various criminal cases, and had been one of the most successful in the western district of the federal court. However, D.C. had one blind spot: his lack of political acumen in understanding the nature of a "show trial," and what had transpired during the years prior to this indictment. However, I felt that D.C. was a person of integrity who would do the best possible job; perhaps, with the assistance of McDivitt and others, his lack of dealing in the political arena could be overcome. Again, I thought long and hard about the option of defending myself—but eventually concluded that between Frank and D.C., I would be in good hands.

This was the point at which Taylor hired James Linn as his defense counsel. He was one of Oklahoma's premier criminal-defense attorneys at that time; his excellent reputation came from defending himself in the Four Seasons real-estate-fraud trial, in which he was found innocent. Kevin Mooney chose two attorneys: First was Judge Rooney McInerney, a former Supreme Court justice who had been appointed to that position by Governor Dewey Bartlett. The second, and most interesting, was Frank Keating, a Tulsa attorney, former FBI agent, an Oklahoma state senator, and son of a Tulsa county commissioner with whom I had served in the county government during my term as county prosecutor.

Fate plays some interesting tricks. One of them was that Keating would later become governor of Oklahoma, accept a payment of $250,000 from a man doing business with the state in connection with a Department of Corrections' program, and be accused of the same type of crime for which I was indicted—but he would not be prosecuted by the Justice Department. He even admitted receiving the payment, despite telling conflicting stories of the incident. He would never suffer the degradation and humiliation of a grand-jury investigation, or have any state or federal charges brought against him. But history has a way of revealing the truth in one way or another; in fact, that incident would later deny Keating the position of United States Attorney General under the administration of the second President Bush— and would completely ruin his opportunities for higher political office.

In later years, that anomaly of selective prosecution drove home to me even more the sinister deceit that was practiced during the run-up to my indictment, my trial, and the proceedings thereafter.

With trial counsel now in place, I turned to the burning issue of how to make a living while preparing for the trial and the burdens of daily living. Just before the indictment, I had been approached by Clint Murchison regarding a legal assignment for one of his highway-construction companies. Two years before, his company had contracted to build several roads within the kingdom of Saudi Arabia. The work was completed, but now there was a dispute over the payment due him. At this time I still had my license to practice law, so he employed me to go to Saudi Arabia to attempt to collect what was owed his company. It was a good fee for me, and I eagerly accepted the engagement.

But several roadblocks stood in my way. Judge Daugherty had taken my passport after the arraignment, and I was released with no bond. However, I could not leave the jurisdiction without the court's permission. McDivitt and I made the application for permission to leave the country on business. My request was granted, my passport returned, and I quickly arranged my flight to Riyadh. After the January 17 indictment, the pace of events accelerated; within ten days, I had purchased my ticket to the Middle East, begun arrangements for my entry permit through the Saudi Arabian Paris Embassy, and been briefed in Dallas by Clint Murchison's aides on my legal mission. On January 25, I left on an American Airlines flight on the first leg of my journey.

While those particulars were falling into place, I sought the counsel of my dearest friend on the national scene, Louis Nizer. He was not only was an outstanding author of many books relating to legal issues in the country, but was also a student of government and a student of politics, and he understood the atmosphere that pervaded the nation better than anyone I knew. After analyzing our situation, it was Nizer's opinion that we should attempt to delay the trial for at least six months. He indicated—from what source I'll never know—that there could be events shaping up on the national scene that would directly affect any prosecution against me by the US Justice Department or by the Federal Bureau of Investigation. He said that any investigations of governors or politicians in positions similar to mine were going to change in a drastic manner.

This advice was tempered by my belief that my innocence would prevail before any jury of my peers—because of the manner in which I conducted myself, my reputation, and the fact that no credible evidence could be presented to show that I was a part of any scheme to defraud the state of Oklahoma or to bribe any public official.

That decision was a huge mistake of judgment on my part; I should have followed Nizer's advice. His prediction was to come true in less than 180 days after the conclusion of my trial, when heinous abuses by the FBI and the US Justice Department in a myriad of cases across the nation were uncovered. Those abuses became headline news, and the focus of investigation after investigation by congressional committees. Had this evidence of the unethical tactics by the FBI been available to us prior to the time that we went to trial, I believe that the perjured evidence presented at my trial—and the illegal actions taken against me by a US attorney operating outside the normal Justice Department rules—could have been offset if the extent of corruption within those agencies had been presented to a jury. Corrupt evidence, when coupled with a federal scandal within the FBI of such a magnitude, would have shaken the core beliefs of even the tainted jury pool that was used in my case.

Now, looking through the historical rearview mirror and seeing my impetuous insistence on proceeding without delay, against Nizer's advice, I see that I should have known better. But rushing headlong into the fray, believing my innocence would prevail, I was poised for the start of the most outrageous political show trial in the history of the state of Oklahoma.

After another chapter of my professional life began in Saudi Arabia, I returned from the region just two days before a hearing was held before Judge Daugherty on a motion by my attorney, D. C. Thomas, joined by the attorney James Linn on behalf of Mr. Taylor, to attempt to force *The Daily Oklahoman* reporters Jack Taylor, Judy

Fossett, and Mike Hammer to disclose the sources of leaks of information from the federal grand jury that had appeared in their news reports. A second issue to be explored was whether or not pressure had been brought to bear on John Rogers by US Attorney William Burkett to secure his cooperation. Third, this hearing would also determine whether the prejudicial pretrial publicity was sufficient to order a change of venue for the trial.

It was now February 7, 1975, just seventeen days before my trial was set to start. D.C. Thomas had subpoenaed the three reporters as witnesses, and they were standing by. Judge Daugherty laid out his ground rules on the testimony that might be given in this hearing. He started with these words: "I don't believe that the court would be interested in the source of alleged prejudicial publicity. So I would decline to hear this testimony."

I was shocked and dumbfounded. What he was saying was that he had no interest in hearing testimony of a federal crime—leaking secret federal grand jury testimony. Further, he apparently felt there was no connection between those leaks and the prejudicial publicity that was produced in the articles in The Daily Oklahoman. I knew then that this hearing was a self-serving way for Daugherty to eliminate an issue that could be used in an appeal. With a cavalier tone in his voice, and body language indicating indifference, Judge Daugherty added, "Since I don't think the testimony [of the reporters] that counsel indicates they would supply the court is relevant or material to this hearing, they may be excused."

There it was, as bold as brass: There was no way Daugherty was going to let this case get transferred to another venue and cause him to lose his best chance to try a case that might lead to a federal circuit-court judgeship. In the emotional ballgame of that hearing, Umpire Daugherty called Strike One on the efforts of my team.

The second issue was whether John Rogers had agreed to have his telephones tape-recorded and wore a wire as the result of pressure and coercion by the federal government. This was a humdinger! Rogers was called as a witness by D.C. Thomas and James Linn to secure testimony to show that he had been pressured. In the course of the questioning, Rogers disclosed that he and his father had been under federal investigation by the Internal Revenue Service for alleged criminal charges; Rogers further stated that he had invoked the Fifth Amendment by refusing to testify when Burkett called him before the federal grand jury in 1973 to answer questions regarding allegations by the Internal Revenue Service of criminal conduct. No indictment was returned by that grand jury against Rogers.

Rogers then testified that he had an alleged conversation with me on December 4, 1974. Further, he stated that he told Attorney General Larry Derryberry that I had allegedly offered him a bribe. Rogers then testified that Derryberry urged him to report this to US Attorney Burkett.

Rogers, accompanied by Derryberry, did go to the federal agents. Rogers testified that this occurred in early December. Rogers was asked to appear and testify to this allegation before Burkett's federal grand jury, which was trying to indict me. Rogers testified in the hearing—and later at the trial—that he wanted a written "no prosecution" letter from US Attorney Burkett, granting him immunity, before his appearance; Rogers was in fear of an indictment against him until he received that letter. It took Burkett nineteen days to produce the letter of no prosecution for Rogers. With letter in hand, Rogers could now go to the federal grand jury and repeat the big lie he had told the authorities.

The obvious reason that it took so long for Burkett to produce the letter was that he had to cover his tracks, so that if Rogers was later proved to be a liar, it could not be blamed on the US attorney. The scheme for Rogers to make the tape recordings of my conversations, instead of using federal-government wiretap evidence, was the buffer, or safety valve, in case Rogers was lying. Remember that Burkett had been trying for more than three years to get a federal grand-jury indictment against me; now, with his last-ditch effort to save his reputation, preserve his legacy as US attorney, and try to keep the door open for a possible federal judgeship, he had good reason to protect his rear end from Rogers.

The sinister part of Burkett's action was that he must have already been told by Derryberry that Rogers was the subject of an impeachment investigation for criminal charges by the Oklahoma House of Representatives Committee. In my opinion, this was the black cloud lurking over Burkett's head as he took those nineteen days to determine whether he would roll the dice and use John Rogers in his efforts to indict me. Burkett must have had a tight sphincter and some sleepless nights deciding that one.

Judge Daugherty then struck down the efforts of D.C. Thomas and James Linn to show pressure and coercion by the federal government for John Rogers' cooperation and testimony. Daugherty ruled that, in his opinion, there was no pressure. Strike Two for my team.

But there was one more legal dart that Daugherty would use to burst the balloon of our attempts to have the federal agents search other federal investigative agencies for wiretaps or tapes. A brilliant young attorney from Washington, DC, David Austern, who had joined my team to help in our efforts to thwart the tricks of the IRS and the FBI, posed the question near the conclusion of the hearing. Austern said, "Very candidly, Your Honor, the reason I asked that question was that, in every other case that I've ever seen in which the government has made a response to a motion to disclose electronic surveillance, the government has reflected in the response that they didn't know of any either illegal or legal electronic surveillance, but they will search their files and search state files and search intelligence files of domestic intelligence agencies for the purpose of ascertaining whether such surveillance was made. Certainly Mr. Burkett, and nobody else, for that matter, can possibly know at any given point whether somebody for whom he is not responsible has made surveillance, and that is not contained in the government's answer."

In a gruff tone, Daugherty summarily dismissed that contention.

Everyone in that courtroom had been reading for months about the abuses of the Nixon administration in manipulating the Justice Department and the IRS, and their use of wiretaps in an effort to bring down their enemies. It now seems almost ludicrous to believe that Daugherty was not aware that justice cried out for a search of the other federal agencies that might have such electronic surveillance evidence. But Umpire Daugherty had just called Strike Three, and the Hall team was out.

Never mind waiting for Daugherty's written opinion, which would not come until the next week; it did not take a crystal ball to know we had lost this round.

The trial opened February 24 on a cold, blustery day with overcast skies and the wind blowing a chill through all of us as we walked to the federal courthouse, where we took the elevator to the second floor. There, Judge Daugherty had reserved the largest courtroom due to the interest in the trial; there would be news coverage, not only by the local media, but reporters from *The New York Times* and other publications. And then there were those who just wanted to be spectators at this singular event in the state's history.

The courtroom was very wide, sixty feet across with a center aisle through many rows of highly polished dark wood benches, and the ceiling was extremely high as well. The judge's imposing bench was in the center at the highest elevation in the courtroom, with a giant seal of the United States emblazoned on the paneled wall behind him. The jury box and the counsel tables were also made of polished, fine dark wood. The grandeur and size created the intended atmosphere of reverence, a most intimidating setting even for those with courtroom experience.

The *voir dire* or jury selection was the first order of business, and began in an orderly and tightly managed manner by Judge Daugherty. *Voir dire* is the questioning of the prospective jurors to determine whether they can serve as fair and impartial deciders of the facts of the case, and render a decision of guilt or innocence based on those facts. Federal jury selection is much different than it is in the state courts; very little latitude is given to the defense to question jurors, because the judge carries out those duties; in fact, he does his best to move the trial along in an effort to "aid justice by speed." This turned out to be a decided detriment to my defense, because there was no opportunity to explore the political nature of this trial and its influence on the selection of the jurors.

Another impropriety was the fact that Judge Daugherty failed to review any of the evidence of the tainted jury pool, including the shouts and harangues by prospective jurors who said they wanted "to get on the jury and convict the SOB." These improprieties in the jury-pool room were reported to my team by a respected journalist, Jim Nance, the editor of one of our small-town newspapers. These statements were repeated numerous times in the jury waiting room by jurors who had never heard any of the evidence except the pap spewed by *The Daily Oklahoman* and their reporter, Jack Taylor. So in jury selection, my defense team was placed on an uneven playing field, tilted in favor of the prosecution.

Judge Daugherty's continued bias and disdain for a search for the truth was illustrated in the following excerpts from the *voir dire* transcript. An argument by defense counsel that two jurors who stated they had an opinion should be *voir dired* individually to see what that opinion was, and not summarily dismissed. My counsel addressed the judge:

Mr. Thomas : "Well, Your Honor, the last time we discussed it, I advised that the same opinion I am voicing now, that I think out of the presence of the other jurors, these two jurors should possibly be questioned. But the mere fact that they held an opinion at this time, I would suggest to the court that they must hold an opinion of a presumption of innocence—that must be their opinion. I would respectfully move the court to, outside the presence of the other jurors, that the individual jurors, separate from each other, be questioned as to what opinion they have."

Court: "At my discretion, I do not propose to do any *voir dire* of the jury except as a body, do not intend to, nor desire to question them privately or individually."

In an exchange that followed shortly thereafter, Thomas again addressed a question to the court:

Mr. Thomas : "Comes now defendant Hall and moves the court to inquire of the panel concerning how many persons on the panel, to raise their hands, who received a newspaper at their homes published by the Oklahoma Publishing Company *[The Daily Oklahoman]* and how many have received copies of *The Oklahoma Journal* at their homes."

Court: "All right, Mr. Thomas, I decline to put your question to the jury. I think it's been covered by my questioning of anything they have ever read. They have not formed an opinion and would ask them to put aside anything that they have read."

D.C. was doing his best to show the almost suffocating coverage that *The Daily Oklahoman* possessed over the jury as compared to the sparsely read *Oklahoma Journal,* which produced unbiased reporting. D.C. was doing his best to pick a fair and impartial jury, but Daugherty was refusing any attempt to get at what the jurors had read in *The Daily Oklahoman* for the three years proceeding this trial. Daugherty ruled against any inquiry of the individual jurors, never offering any explanation other than it was "within his discretion."

Court: "With reference to your request that the court conduct an individual *voir dire* of the jurors, as set out in Section Two of defendant Hall's requested procedure and question and selection of jurors, I decline, in my discretion, to proceed in this fashion, as I do not believe it's necessary in view of the answers that the jurors have given me and their response to my questions."

I am now certain another factor brought pressure to bear on Daugherty, his rulings, and his cursory voir dire: When the trial ended, *The Daily Oklahoman* would still be printing each day. Daugherty could well become a target if the result of my trial ended in acquittal. He had seen what that paper had done to me over the past three years, and I believe that was a powerful force in his decision to refuse to question the individual jurors. Had the judge in my case been Stephen Chandler or Luther Ewbanks, it would have been a different story. These judges in that same jurisdictions had the courage, the regard for justice, and the legal backbone to search for the truth.

The jury selection had several other obvious disadvantages for the defense. One was that the FBI had done extensive background checks on each of these potential jurors. None of the defense attorneys were ever given any original copies of FBI reports, the agents' notes, or any of their recordings of these investigations. Nor were my counsel permitted to question all of the agents who had done the inquiries. We learned later that the agents investigating the potential jurors assiduously avoided any possibility of adverse comments being made that might have been discovered by the defense. Apparently this was done on orders from Burkett.

So the jury selection proceeded, with Judge Daugherty's heavy-handed rulings blocking any attempt to explore the political backgrounds of the jurors, or to have them questioned individually outside the hearing of the other jurors, nor did Daugherty ever ask the question, "Did any juror while waiting in the jury-pool main room hear a prospective juror loudly proclaim that they wanted to be on the jury to convict Governor Hall?" Instead, Daugherty slammed that door shut, and the jury was chosen.

The evidentiary part of the trial in the presentation of the prosecution's case proceeded, but it was soon obvious that the crux of the trial was going to be the tapes that had been made by John Rogers, and Rogers' testimony. To prepare for introducing the tapes, Burkett called FBI agent Paul Baresel, who had instructed Rogers on how to use the tape recorder. For the first time in the case, the jury learned that Rogers could erase, rewind, and otherwise alter the tapes.

D.C. went right for the jugular and cross-examined the agent.

Question: "Let me ask you this, Mr. Baresel: under that arrangement you had on John Rogers' telephone, could this—he could do this, could he, the telephone rings, he pushed the button, record it, then, not like the recording, rewind it, tape back over it?"

Baresel: "Erase and re-tape. Yes, sir."

Question: "Mr. Rogers could erase and re-tape, couldn't he?"

Baresel: "Yes, sir."

Question: "Have you ever asked him if he erased or re-taped anything?"

Baresel: "I did not ask him in that specific way."

There you had it: Burkett was about to put Rogers on the stand as the government's chief witness, knowing that Rogers was about to be impeached by the legislature, that he could erase or alter the tapes, that he was testifying only because he could not be prosecuted for other charges, and that the Rogers' story might be proved to be one big lie.

But Burkett's gamble didn't end with Rogers ; he had also used secretaries and stenographers from Larry Derryberry's office and others outside the federal government to transcribe the tapes. Burkett knew of Derryberry's prejudice against me in the failed impeachment attempt in 1974, yet Burkett let him control the typing of many of the transcripts of the Rogers tapes. Burkett was pressed for time and threw caution to the wind. Result: The first transcript my team saw that was typed by the Derryberry crew had 136 errors. It was obvious to observers of the case, including some of the news reporters who shared their thoughts with me, that Burkett was relying on the years of bad publicity against me by *The Daily Oklahoman* to overcome any doubts that the jury might have about Rogers telling the truth.

In his column, "The Washington Merry-Go-Round," in The *Washington Post*, Jack Anderson later confirmed that the FBI transcripts used in my trial had been altered—a stunning revelation that was never reported by *The Daily Oklahoman.*

Burkett was very clever in presenting John Rogers as a witness before he called Oklahoma Attorney General Larry Derryberry to testify. I believe it was Derryberry's job to confirm Rogers' story, and explain to the jury how the "evidence" came to Burkett. Burkett knew that Rogers's and Derryberry's stories had to match, and he wanted to be sure Derryberry filled in blanks or explained any errors that Rogers might make. But Burkett's careful orchestration was almost derailed by the adept cross-examination by D.C. Thomas. D.C. had done his homework on the Leo Winters case, and he knew that Burkett had influenced the federal grand jury not to indict Derryberry at the same time.

D.C. used cross-examination to expose Derryberry's motivation for bolstering Rogers by helping type the transcripts of the tapes— his need to repay Burkett. The following questions refer to the federal grand jury that indicted State Treasurer Leo Winters in 1973 for extorting campaign contributions from banks where there were state funds deposited.

Mr. Thomas : "Well, let me inquire. In an indictment that was handed down, there was an unnamed candidate who had taken political contributions, had used an apartment and a car, isn't that correct?"

Derryberry : "Yes, sir"

Mr. Thomas : "And that unnamed mystery candidate was you, was it not?"

Derryberry : "Yes, sir."

Mr. Thomas : "Had to do with a bank here in town, which paid an agency five hundred dollars for a car for you to drive around during your 1970 campaign, is that right?"

Derryberry : "Yes, sir."

After the indictment of Leo Winters and the unnamed "mystery candidate" appearing therein, Burkett had issued a favorable press release clearing Derryberry. This was an unprecedented action for a US attorney; again, this act harkens to the movie script of *Absence Of Malice*, in which a fictional federal prosecutor does the same. With this information before the court, D.C. put the clincher to Derryberry.

Mr. Thomas : "Well, it went even stronger than that, Mr. Derryberry. Did Mr. Burkett say, quote, speaking of you, 'he had no way of knowing where they came from,' meaning the car and the apartment. Didn't—let me ask you before I proceed, did it ever occur to you, Mr. Derryberry, to ask somebody who was paying for the car that you were driving?"

Before Derryberry could answer, Burkett jumped to his feet to object to the question, red-faced and angry. Somehow he had to stop Derryberry from answering. A major argument developed between Burkett and Thomas that resulted in a long delay while

Judge Daugherty called them to the bench for a side-bar admonition to act as officers of the court and stop bickering. The crux of the nearly half-hour argument resulted in D.C. restating the question.

Mr. Thomas : "Mr. Derryberry, back in June when Mr. Burkett said, did he not, speaking of you, and the apartment and the car, 'He had no way of knowing where they came from, he neither knew or could've known, that's why he wasn't named in the report.' Did he say that?"

Derryberry : "I believe that's a correct account of what I read in the newspaper."

Now the cat was out of the bag in D.C.'s efforts to show Derryberry's motivation for assisting Rogers in the scheme against me. But with the tainted jury pool, the bias of Judge Daugherty, and the lies of Rogers, D.C. had a tough assignment to overcome that prejudice.

The sessions that Rogers and Burkett must have had in this preparation were never made a part of the case that was brought against me. No written memos or notes were ever kept by Burkett and his minions that could be subject to my team's subpoena. Of course, in all the hours of Rogers ' taping, there was never a smoking-gun statement made by me that would provide the evidence that the US attorney was hoping for.

No one on my defense team was given the opportunity to examine the original tapes; only later were we given copies. We had no way of proving whether or not the original tapes had been altered. Nor were any government back-up wiretaps on Rogers ' telephones ever made available to the defense.

But then a possible ray of hope entered the proceedings. After bad news upon bad news, D. C. scored a small victory when he persuaded Judge Daugherty to exclude the transcripts of the tapes from being given to the jury. Clearly Daugherty couldn't dismiss the argument that jurors ought not to be given erroneous and altered transcriptions. It was clear to us now that, in the absence of a smoking-gun tape, Burkett's strategy was to attempt to prove guilt by using tapes of questionable accuracy. If today's communication and

24-hour news cycle had existed, the public outcry over some garbled and possibly altered tapes would have been deafening—and another aberration of this trial was the decision by Judge Daugherty that the jurors would use listening devices to hear the tapes instead of playing them in open court!

After the trial proceeded through the prosecution's preliminary witnesses, Rogers was called to identify the tapes to set the stage for his testimony. During this testimony, the one taped conversation that might have helped me the most was referenced—and then Rogers, smiling apologetically, carefully testified that it had somehow been erased. Rogers offered an implausible explanation: His young son had tipped over the tape recorder attached to his home phone and erased the evidence. It was similar to the pathetic sight of Rose Mary Woods, Nixon's loyal secretary, trying to show how she might have accidentally erased 18 ½ minutes of the White House tapes. Still, the members of the jury nodded as though they themselves had experienced such mishaps, apparently believing what ought to have been laughable.

Those erased minutes might well have at least proved that there was reasonable doubt. Shades of Watergate—with a 180-degree difference. The admission into evidence of those statements might well have saved me from this courtroom masquerade, while President Nixon's erased tape prevented him from ever seeing the inside of a courthouse or a prison.

What actually caused the alteration of the Rogers tape—and what was said on it—will never be known. That issue was never allowed to be developed, it was never explored, and to this day it remains one of the great mysteries of the trial.

Of course, if the three-and-a-half minutes of this tape had been made available to the jury, I might well have later won a malicious prosecution judgment against Burkett and the federal government.

Another impediment to our seeking character witnesses was the fear felt by those men and women; if they testified on my behalf, they might be subject to baseless investigation and harassment. This fear was real, because of what was playing out nationally in the exposure of the Nixon administration's enemies list, with individuals being subject to investigation by the Internal Revenue Service or the Justice Department whether they had committed any illegal act or not. The threat of being dragged through the investigative mud was a powerful deterrent, experienced by those who would have otherwise spoken out for me.

This stifling effect even translated into my attempts to bring character witnesses that I thought could most represent my integrity and my reputation to the jury, offsetting the lies and innuendos that had been presented against me. For example, let me contrast two of my friends: The first was James Fellers, the former president of the American Bar Association. He had been a friend who had come to me at the capitol, entered my office, and on bended knee begged me for assistance in helping to have his son treated fairly in McAlester State Prison, where the boy was an inmate for a minor marijuana violation. In helping his son, David, I did nothing untoward; but I did make sure that his son was treated fairly, and that the regulations affecting him were enforced correctly. His son and his wife thanked me profusely after that. His son wrote me a powerful letter—which I still retain—about how those changes had helped him survive, and made his prison time bearable.

Now fast-forward to my trial, when I approached Jim Fellers about being a character witness for me and was flatly turned down. Stunned, Jo and I were never to understand his reluctance to stand up for me. I now think it was his fear of possible harassment by the federal government and pressure from *The Daily Oklahoman* that caused him to stonewall my request.

Some three weeks after the trial, Jo boarded an aircraft headed to California, and as she walked up the aisle past the first-class seats, she saw Mr. and Mrs. Fellers seated there. As Jo approached their row, they averted their eyes and stared into the side of the plane. They would not meet her gaze. Jo walked on by, went to her seat, sat down, and wondered how those two could live with their consciences. We later learned from mutual friends that Mrs. Fellers had been adamant that her husband should appear and testify for me, and that a major family rift was caused by his refusal.

Long ago I forgave Jim Fellers and lifted that burden from my own shoulders, but I recount it here to alert others like me who may be falsely accused and have some of their friends fall by the wayside. I want you to know that you can survive such indignities and breaches of friendship. And you will find staunch, loyal supporters in your truest friends.

It takes uncommon courage to be that small, truthful voice in the face of dark, powerful forces. Contrast the human frailty of a Jim Fellers with the best of human nature and formidable courage exhibited by Oklahoma Supreme Court Justice Robert D. Simms, my longtime friend and legal mentor. When I asked Judge Simms, bless his heart, to be a character witness, he agreed enthusiastically, although he knew that in a few months he himself would be before the electorate. He stood up like a man and testified for his friend—and he was handily re-elected, proving the power of integrity.

After the trial's evidence was concluded by both sides, the issues drawn, the closing arguments and closing statements made, and the judge's instructions given to the jury, my fate was in their hands. Deliberations continued for two days—*two days!* On the morning of the third day, we met in the courtroom with D.C. Thomas and Frank McDivitt. Frank described to the full team a turn of events we had learned of earlier——one that made me believe a reprieve was about to be delivered. "A juror, Dell Meyer, was taken ill, hospitalized overnight, and released this morning," said Frank. "Judge Daugherty wants the parties and counsel in his chambers. He has ordered Mrs. Meyer and her two doctors to report to the court at 1:30."

Upon entering Judge Daugherty's palatial chambers, I was reminded that there was certainly no lack of space in it. With classic appointments of wood paneling, a heavy, ornately carved desk, and dark leather upholstery on chairs and sofas, the office was the size of a small ballroom, at the end of which Judge Daugherty sat with all counsel before him.

Given the news that we had a juror, Mrs. Meyer, in a medical emergency, I had expected to see on the judge's face at least a semblance of concern. Alternates having been dismissed, this hearing, in my view, was a slam-dunk to move forward with a mistrial. And as I surveyed the faces in the room—my attorneys, D.C. Thomas and Frank McDivitt ; co-defendant W.W. Taylor, and his lawyer—not present was Kevin Mooney, who had turned state's evidence in return for a reduced sentence, and was not tried—it looked like everyone assumed there was no alternative but to bring the charade to an end. Even the usually sneering face of the prosecutor, US Attorney William Burkett, appeared to be doubtful and defeated, as did his assistants'.

But Judge Daugherty did not look one bit concerned—as he summarily denied the motion for a mistrial by saying that Mrs. Meyer was well enough to return to deliberate! It was obvious that he had no interest in her health and what the ordeal was doing to her, but the extent of his misrepresentation of the true situation wouldn't come out until much later. As we would discover, Mrs. Meyer had a history of both angina and anxiety, and had been admitted to the emergency room with complaints of chest pains, nervousness, and constipation, after Dramamine and Valium failed to give her relief. Elevated cardiac enzymes were not conclusive of a heart attack, but her chest pains were enough of a factor that they caused her regular heart doctor and the ER doctor to recommend that she stay in the hospital for observation for the next 24 to 48 hours. On the morning in question, she had been given Demerol for relatively acute pain, which was accompanied by nausea.

When Judge Daugherty cited his conversation with Dr. Shafeek Sanbar and stated that the doctor gave his assurance that Mrs. Meyer was well enough to return to deliberate at 1:30 p.m., something immediately didn't smell right. So it was not surprising when we later found out that Dr. Sanbar had expressed the belief that she should be hospitalized!

But that was only the half of it. Even more outrageous was Judge Daugherty's following up his ruling with a question that we couldn't believe he had the audacity to ask. He wanted to know if, in the event Mrs. Meyer returned but could not complete deliberations, would we accept eleven jurors and proceed with the case?

D.C. Thomas's hackles were up, for good reason. He conferred quickly with me and then answered, "No, sir, we will not proceed with eleven."

Judge Daugherty looked at D.C., then at Frank McDivitt, and finally at me, asking again—through my attorneys—if I wouldn't agree to proceed with eleven. Again, D.C., as directed by me, answered, "No, sir."

Not giving up, Judge Daugherty, with apparent irritation, asked the question a total of four times. Each time our answer was the same: a resounding no. The law was that twelve jurors should determine innocence or guilt, and I wasn't about to agree to a lesser number.

So Judge Daugherty ordered Mrs. Meyer back on the jury.

D.C. again vehemently renewed his request for a mistrial, asked for an immediate hearing, and requested that Mrs. Meyer's two doctors be subpoenaed to testify at 1:30 as to her fitness to deliberate. Judge Daugherty's acid response: "Do whatever you want to do, Mr. Thomas."

D.C. flinched. I quietly controlled my growing anger. From his pattern of rulings, we already knew the judge had a bias against me. But why? There was that question again. Was it because I knew too much about his personal life? That's putting a congenial Southern spin on it, I should add. Information is a dangerous thing; ironically, he had confided in me as one of the few people he trusted to watch his back. Was the possibility that I might use it against him enough to make me a threat? On the one hand, I regretted that I hadn't used my knowledge; on the other, I had more faith in the system than to stoop to that level.

Coolly, as if to show he wasn't daunted by me or my counsel, the judge issued the subpoenas. Then he said to D.C., this time with an incongruous mix of joking and irritation, "I would suggest to you now that if you want to assist the administration of justice that you just drop this juror and proceed with eleven."

Again, on my instruction, D.C. for the fourth time said no.

Judge Daugherty shrugged. "You want to have your cake and to eat it, too. I'm simply speaking as a neutral person trying to administer justice. I don't look with much favor on one who has a right [to drop a juror] and will not utilize it and just wants to make a technical record. And I want the Circuit Court of Appeals to know this is how I feel about this."

This was what even a high-school psychology student would identify as an acute case of projection. You'd have to be crazy to think anyone present wouldn't see through it. Not only was I asserting my right to a fair trial with twelve jurors, not eleven, but the procedural effort to fairly claim a mistrial—what he called a "technical record"—was to prove my innocence. To him it was a nuisance and waste of time that might make him late to dinner at the country club, where he wouldn't be able to brag to his circle of friends about how he tidily got rid of another messy case on his docket. Why would he want to report it to the Circuit Court of Appeals?

Maybe as a preemptive move to get there before we did.

Little had been heard during this time from attorney James Linn, nor from his client, W.W. "Doc" Taylor. Though he was a co-defendant facing similar allegations, the focus on him was different from the forces coalescing against me—once again because of the personal politics at work. The first time Taylor and Mooney brought the investment plan to me, I'd paid too much attention to how this could benefit teachers in my state—and, yep, how it could reinforce my legacy as a governor who left office still fighting for the public good. If I had been guilty of anything, it was that I had been too trusting.

With my former classmate Kevin Mooney —the oil company executive who first brought me the investment idea and proposed all the ways that it would benefit public employees—being too trusting could have been forgiven. There was no reason not to trust him. But Doc Taylor was another story. As writer Paul Erdman observed in *The Billion Dollar Sure Thing*, one ought never trust a moneyman who goes by the name of Doc.

Doc Taylor was a beefy, fleshy guy with big eyes, a ruddy complexion, and a hurry-up attitude. Of average height, he wore his hair wetted and combed straight back; he reminded me of so many of the men I'd heard pitch their emerging companies over the years. Up to a point, he was engaging. He was an expert in his field, not to mention that he came with high credentials and was much revered by one of the bigwigs in the Small Business Administration, all of which held weight with me. But, looking back, I did recall that he was so pumped up on his project that it was almost overkill.

I would never know whether, or to what degree, Taylor and Mooney originally planned to profit from our acceptance of the fund plan, nor was I certain how far they would have been willing to go once a bribe was solicited by Secretary of State John Rogers. What I did know, by these closing hours of the trial, was that the strategy— a full-court press carried out by Nixon's cronies in Washington, and those of US Attorney Bill Burkett here in Oklahoma—had been to get Rogers, Mooney, and Taylor all to plead guilty and testify against me. It had worked with Rogers and Mooney, but Doc Taylor proved to be less malleable.

I should interject that the black community had been solidly behind me at every step of the trial. However, with the exception of a handful of friends and a prominent African-American state Senator, E. Melvin Porter who testified as one of my character witnesses, the jury and the courtroom were packed with Oklahoma City's white, upper-crust, Republicans. Of course, community support inside or out of the courtroom was not supposed to matter; what mattered above all was the reaction and ultimate decisions reached by the jury.

During our trial, jurors had responded well to Linn's personality. I, too, had been impressed by Linn's incisive wit and his pragmatic approach to surprises and unforeseen tactics. But if Linn had any strategy up his sleeve when the judge refused our motion for a mistrial, he wasn't sharing it with us.

Later, I would have occasion to wonder whether Linn's friendship with Bill Burkett —the two would become law partners a few months after the trial—had influenced his performance in these last days of deliberation. But I do recall that when we all exited the judge's chambers and huddled in our respective camps before going upstairs for the hearing with Mrs. Meyer and her doctors, James Linn appeared to be as shocked as we were by the hearing that had just concluded.

How surprised the two doctors must have been at the nearly empty courtroom when they arrived at 1:30. Their footsteps echoed loudly as they entered with only a handful of us there—the prosecutor's table to the left of the aisle as they walked down it, and the defense table to the right. Judge Daugherty had excluded the public and press from the courtroom for this hearing. As both doctors stated that they needed a release from Mrs. Meyer before they could testify about her condition, Judge Daugherty called Mrs. Meyer before him to make sure she was agreeable to sign such a release.

With my background as a prosecutor, a job that helped me hone my ability to read the body language of jurors and witnesses, I had been concerned about the majority of the jury members in my own trial. In both rows of six jurors, I saw the telltale signs early on—folded arms, pursed lips, diverted eyes—that they had already made up their minds, never good for any defendant. But no such signals came from Mrs. Dell Meyer, a grandmotherly woman in her mid-sixties, with short, whitish-gray hair and light-blue eyes under rimless glasses. In her seat, third from the left in the front row, she appeared at all times to be listening intently. Her kindness and soft-spoken sincerity had impressed me during the *voir dire*, and I felt certain she understood the import of her position and her duty.

Now, without her fellow jurors, the urgency with which she had been asked to return to the courthouse to appear with her doctors had to be nerve-wracking. It was obvious to my team that she was moving and speaking with difficulty. Did she sign the release because Judge Daugherty ordered her to? Or was it because she wanted her doctors to testify and put her back in the hospital? Whatever the reason, she signed the release, and then said to Judge Daugherty, "Are there any of my medicines that you would like to see?"

Judge Daugherty declined. Again, that information alone—that is, the name and the amount of medication she might have taken, which we would never know—should have been crucial in deciding her ability to deliberate. The judge not only declined to hear what medications she had been taking, but before he even heard from the doctors, he ordered Mrs. Meyer back into the jury room, telling her not to discuss any of the medical problems and release matters with the other jurors. Instead, he said, "You may tell them to begin deliberations immediately."

Next, just to be sure no time was wasted in the event of her collapse or worse, Judge Daugherty directed the bailiff to make sure the deliberations were indeed proceeding.

We were all astonished. A pall settled over the defense side of the courtroom. Over at the prosecutor's table, US Attorney Burkett and team barely veiled their smiles. For Judge Daugherty to order Mrs. Meyer and the other jurors to resume deliberations before the sworn testimony of the doctors was heard was not only a violation of the rights of the defense, but it was endangering a juror's health. But he did just that.

Judge Daugherty became more and more edgy as the questions and comments by the doctors continued. At approximately 3:30 p.m., my heart raced with the appearance of the bailiff, who informed the judge that the jury had reached a verdict. I turned and looked over my left shoulder into the empty gallery, as if by an involuntary action, to the empty seat in the front row where Jo usually sat during the trial. To our further shock, Judge Daugherty didn't respond at all to the bailiff, but instead continued the hearing on our motion for mistrial!

By this point it was readily apparent that Judge Daugherty was now engaged in an all-out effort to justify his ruling by bearing down on Dr. Sanbar to elicit some form a statement that he had told Mrs. Meyer she was okay to go back to deliberations. Yet Dr. Sanbar, hard as Judge Daugherty pressed him, refused to be badgered, and continued to reiterate his position that she should be observed for one to two full days before going back to deliberations. In the end,

Dr. Sanbar still maintained that he could not express an opinion about her ability to deliberate without an additional exam.

Dying inside, I watched helplessly. At this point, the only right thing would have been for Judge Daugherty to suspend the deliberations and at least have Mrs. Meyer examined by Dr. Sanbar for a determination of her condition by a professional, and not by a lawyer-politician-turned-judge. I am certain that Dr. Sanbar would have accepted Mrs. Meyer's offer to show the medicines she had, and what she had been taking that morning, an offer that Judge Daugherty had refused. But this was not done.

My greatest fear was that if Dell Meyer had been a holdout for innocence, and she had spent the last two hours deliberating, the pressure of the others might have been too much for her physically and psychologically.

Judge Daugherty finally forced Dr. Sanbar to accept the judge's own representation that Mrs. Meyers appeared okay when she signed the consent form for Dr. Sanbar to testify. But it was only on being forced to accept this assumption that Dr. Sanbar said that she may have been able to deliberate. With these words, Judge Daugherty now felt he was safe. With alacrity, he formally overruled the motion for mistrial, dismissed the doctors, and again assumed a more confident air.

Before anyone could object or ask for any kind of a delay, with the news that a verdict had been reached, the courtroom doors opened, and the agitated crowd came flooding into the gallery.

All of these particulars pulsed in my awareness as the moment of truth approached. There I stood, waiting to hear the verdict, after the roller-coaster ride that had begun that morning when I so confidently believed a mistrial would be called with the hospitalization of juror Dell Meyer. Anguished, I recalled Judge Daugherty's anger and his outrageous comment, "You are just trying to have your cake and eat it, too"—a flippant statement for a federal judge to make to a defendant whose fate was in the hands of that juror, and who was entitled to twelve men and women to decide his case. The great pillars of justice were crumbling, and my legal heroes, Justices Holmes and Brandies, were rolling over in their graves.

And there I was, in those irrevocable moments after Judge Daugherty opened the verdict and looked at the result, when time stood still and my whole life seemed to pass at warp speed and then into slow motion. In the blink of an eye, I relived the trial and the anguish caused to Jo and my family. In that darkness, I sought the light, praying that God would deliver me from the political, personal persecution brought about by malevolent forces. That reverie was broken when Judge Daugherty handed the verdict back to the bailiff for return to the foreman. After hearing the Judge's direction to me and Mr. Taylor to stand with our counsels, I listened as only one word shattered the deathly silence in the courtroom: Guilty.

My world came crashing down. I had earlier braced myself for such an outcome, but the brute force of its impact shook me to the core. How could a judicial system to which I had dedicated my life be twisted to return such a verdict against me? I turned and looked at Jo in the front row of the courtroom, and our eyes and hearts locked. Our worst fears were now realized; life as we knew it would never be the same.

After the verdict was read, the jurors were polled at our request, and each of them stated that it was his or her verdict, including a very distraught Mrs. Meyer. Then the jury was excused. Judge Daugherty asked the defendants to stand, and he proceeded to set the date of March 14 for sentencing and ordered a pre-sentence investigation to be done on each of us. Taylor and I were released on our own recognizance. I was asked to turn in my passport, and the judge brought down his gavel, ending the court session.

I would later learn that Mrs. Meyers had eventually confided to a friend that when she had been forced to return to deliberate, her will to live and to escape the pressure from the other jurors caused her to cave in to their demands and return a verdict of guilty. She said she had no choice because her life was in danger.

In a fog-like state, I went to Jo's side. We walked the long aisle out of the courtroom. Then, with no comments, we moved past the reporters and cameramen into the elevator, taking it down in order to accompany McDivitt and Thomas to his law office. That walk from the courthouse to Thomas's office was a heart-wrenching, unforgettable experience. The gray, somber skies echoed our mood, and none of us spoke.

Inside the office, Jo slumped into a chair, buried her head in her arms, and uttered a long, crying wail that reminded me of that horrible night when my mother had collapsed and was taken from me. I'll never forget Jo's expression of anguish; it ripped into my soul, and I pray continually that no one else will ever have to suffer what Jo had been through at that trial.

My heart nearly burst, and my spirit cried out for the Lord to ease Jo's pain. I knew she saw our hopes and dreams destroyed by the twisted justice of that perverted trial. Fate dealt that crushing blow to the person who had sacrificed everything for the greater good and the person I cherished most—my beloved Jo.

Those first minutes in D.C.'s office would be a horror that I would relive in my dreams for months to come. Words failed us all.

Practicality then reared its head, as McDivitt and D.C. starting to discuss the motions that would be filed, the appeals that would be taken, and what we would do to try to reverse what all of my counselors considered a miscarriage of justice. Jo and I left that office with heavy hearts. We knew within the hour we would be with our children and must be prepared to try and ease their fears. As distasteful as it was, we discussed how to tell the children when we arrived home. "David, I don't know what to say to the kids."

I reminded Jo how brave she had been throughout the nightmare. I said that, if she wanted, I could suggest how we might brave the next few hours together. "Tell me," she said.

My suggestion was that we ought to be seated, making sure there would be no interruptions, with all five of us sitting close to each other. "I'll start with my thoughts on the trial and the verdict," I offered. "Then you tell them that we will do everything in our power to appeal and try for a new trial. While we're waiting, we'll close ranks as a family—and do whatever it takes."

Jo agreed, adding only that we needed to be sure to give them a chance to express their feelings. So our decision was made, and we drove in silence.

Arriving at home, we parked in the driveway. We could see the lights inside, and we knew the children would be waiting. With our hands clasped tightly, we resolved to be brave as we opened the front door.

In the early-morning hours the day after the verdict, two life-changing incidents occurred at our home. The first event, before dawn, is best described in Jo's own words:

"The morning after verdict, I was unable to sleep. I finally went downstairs to have a cup of tea—anything to avoid thinking of facing the bottom of the barrel of reality. During the trial, our house had suffered our absence; the stove was so dirty when the kettle was positioned on the burner it set off the smoke alarm. At about 4:00 a.m., the doorbell rang. Ordinarily, this would have caused concern, but I felt I could face anything after hearing the verdict from that kangaroo court. I opened the door with only the lights from our paintings showing the way. A man stood in the doorway, a complete stranger. He said, 'I saw your lights and could not pass by without telling you and your family how sorry I am for what they have done to you.' We embraced in a big hug, and without further conversation, he turned and disappeared into the darkness. Seems every time it got almost too unbearable, there would be some sweet kindness to get you to the next stop."

My own experience occurred less than two hours later. In my case, I was up at six in a daze. I could hardly eat breakfast, and I have no memory of what Jo fixed. I wandered through the house, dressed in comfortable slacks and a white button-down dress shirt, trying to create a normal routine for the day. While pulling on my socks and loafers, I was trying to visualize the coming day; I walked back downstairs and stood in front of our fireplace, looking at the cold ashes. The doorbell rang, and I called to Jo that I would get it. With some apprehension, I opened the door and saw two old friends from Tulsa standing before me, Jim Head and Paul Johnson. They had driven from Tulsa that morning. I could not imagine why they were here. We shook hands. Both were dressed in suit and tie. Again I wondered why they were here.

Jim said, "May I come in? We need to talk with you." I ushered them into the living room. They sat on the couch, and I pulled a chair close so we were facing each other. Then Jim said, "David, I have come to ask you to pray with me and for you to forgive those who have persecuted you." He mentioned the chief witness John Rogers by name.

My mind was a blur, and I had a very hard time assimilating my thoughts. The next thing I knew we were both on our knees, facing each other with Jim's right hand on my left shoulder. Paul was looking on. Jim spoke a prayer of forgiveness and asked me to do the same. Time stood still. All the hurt, anguish, unfairness, and terrible injustice pressed on my mind.

Then I could hear myself speaking a prayer of forgiveness for all who had wronged me. I know I was sincere and believed what I said. Afterward, I would revisit that moment many times during the nightmarish period still to come. I did not know it then, but that act of Christian kindness by Jim and Paul was the beginning of a reaffirmation of my own faith.

The next few weeks were consumed with preparations of motions to reconsider, and other motions—all of which were summarily dismissed by the judge—and the stage was set for our appeal to the Tenth Circuit Court. Again, the Number One challenge for the appeal was not the lack of legal precedent for the appeal, or the lack of legal research that could be done, but the lack of finances to carry on the detailed and laborious task that lay ahead. I was extremely fortunate in obtaining the services of attorney Mack Oyler, who prepared the appellate application asking the court to reverse the action of the jury and to grant a new trial.

In preparing for this, I knew, as did my counsel, that the chances of obtaining any kind of relief at the appellate level were very slim. Less than 15% of all the appeals taken from a criminal-case decision at the US District Court level ever result in a retrial or a dismissal of the lawsuit; 85% of those appeals are held in favor of the prosecution. Even with this knowledge, we persevered, and Oyler began his research and his preparation of the appellate brief.

Another factor that we were facing, another practicality, was that the same appellate court that had reinstated the disbarred Burkett would likely be hearing our appeal for what we considered egregious errors on the part of the trial judge in a number of areas, most prominent of which were the forcing of the sick juror to return to deliberations, the allowance of the questionable tapes of John Rogers to be used, the exclusion of the public from the hearing on Dell Meyers's medical condition, the altered transcripts, and Judge Daugherty's refusal to review or even consider the tainted jury pool prior to the trial. So began what would be an eighteen-month journey through the appeals court—and, ultimately, to the United States Supreme Court

Meanwhile, as soon as Judge Daugherty had set the date of sentencing, I immediately reviewed my options for my work and for taking care of my family during the time that the case would be on appeal. At this point, I still had my legal license and could practice law. Because of my trip to Saudi Arabia, I made the decision that I could probably make more money developing business opportunities than in practicing law. However, until the sentencing was carried out, I would be unable to travel, and my passport was still in the custody of the federal court.

On the day of sentencing, Judge Daugherty first reviewed the pre-sentencing reports and advised Mr. Taylor and me that he would not allow either of us to receive probation, despite the Federal Probation Department's report that showed a clean record for each of us prior to the accusations made by John Rogers. This was no surprise, as the judge had all but signaled that decision during the trial. Judge Daugherty reviewed the federal sentencing guidelines; he then pronounced a three-year sentence for each of us, with the counts all running concurrently. Our counselors immediately made the court aware of our intention to appeal, and noted that the proper papers would be filed at the appropriate time, perfecting the appeal to the Tenth Circuit Court of Appeals.

Taylor and I were again released on our own recognizance. As if to underline his earlier remarks, Judge Daugherty let us know in no uncertain terms that if the appeals failed, we would go straight to jail.

My life began to move at a furious pace again. The appeal to the Tenth Circuit Court was being prepared, and would be filed in April 1975. During the interim, I was able to secure the court's permission to have my passport returned and was allowed to travel overseas to carry on the business interests that I had started earlier that year.

Against this background was the certainty that my legal license would be removed, and I would be unable to practice law because of this conviction. However, I felt that there were some extenuating circumstances in this trial, and that if the appeal was upheld, then perhaps I could not only stay the disbarment proceedings that were about to take place, but I could save my license if we were able to secure a retrial of the case. Therefore, I asked the Oklahoma Supreme Court to take the disbarment case under advisement while the appeal was going on.

This proved to be an exercise in futility. Although my counsel, William Berry, did a masterful job in presenting my side of the case, we were unable to convince the Oklahoma Supreme Court to stay my disbarment. The hardest thing for me to understand was why: With the appeal pending and the case not yet resolved or concluded, how could these justices strip my means of providing for my family? Until the appeal had run its course, the court had no way of knowing if the case would be reversed or not. Did the poison of the press impact their decision to refuse a stay of the disbarment?

With no answers to those questions, decisions weighed even more heavily. Never before had I stood at such a crossroads. The choice was clear: On the one hand, I could accept my fate, give up, and be left as a has-been, somebody who once climbed the ladder but who had been knocked down, unfairly or not. On the other hand, I could continue to fight, both to clear my name and to regain a sense of purpose necessary for me to live and to provide for my family.

The choice wasn't difficult to make.

Yes, for the present, I was disbarred, my legal license cancelled, and another avenue of supporting my family was closed. But even as dejected, frustrated, and angry as I was over the conviction, it was my determination to rekindle the optimism that had carried me all my life—and to go out and make a success of my business ventures while pursuing the goal of retrying the case and winning my acquittal.

Part Three:

Dismantling of Career, Reinventing a Dream

1975 to 1999

Shedding Skin

In mid-1975, the convictions of H. R. Haldeman, John Mitchell, and John Ehrlichman were wending their ways through the appeals courts. It would be 1976 before these conspirators would actually begin serving their sentences after the convictions had been affirmed.

Cases involving lesser Watergate figures such as Charles Colson were front-page news. Senate investigating committees were still probing the manipulation of national intelligence agencies for political gain. These hearings continued during 1975.

At this point in my life, I had to dig down to the deepest part of my being to again resurrect the optimism that had always been uppermost in keeping my spirit indomitable, and to keep hope for the future alive. The verdict, and the pronouncement of the sentence which I faced if an appeal was unsuccessful, lit a fire in my heart that burned fiercely; my first priority was to take care of my family.

Two possibilities had to be explored: First, the success of our appeal and a later retrial; second, the chance that I would be going to prison. In that event, I would be unable to care for my family for those three years.

I remained in Oklahoma City from the end of the trial to the filing of the appeal to the Tenth Circuit Court. Running parallel with our efforts to appeal the conviction was the ongoing battle I was having with the Internal Revenue Service over allegations of unpaid taxes on campaign contributions that were allegedly used for personal expenses. I continued to fight this allegation, and to wrestle with the IRS in every possible way to get out from under the tremendous stress that this was creating. They claimed that I owed something between $300,000 and $400,000 in back taxes; this was untrue.

An odd fact was that the IRS had advised me during my first year in the Governor's office that I had been randomly selected for an audit of my tax returns for the years 1969 through 1971—the two years before I became governor and my first year as governor. Then, despite unbelievable odds, the IRS notified me that I had also been randomly selected for the years 1969 through 1982. If I could have been that successful with the lottery, I would have been a wealthy man.

With all this in mind, in the interim between the announcement of the verdict and the filing of the appeal in late April, I had made an important business trip to Palm Beach, Florida. Also, I had developed two business ideas for Saudi Arabia. In addition to motorhome venture, I had a plan to build a climate-controlled greenhouse, producing plants to rent to businesses and government offices.

The purpose of that trip to Palm Beach was to confer with one of my mentors, John MacArthur, the founder of one of the greatest life-insurance empires in the history of the country—and one of America's wealthiest entrepreneurs. At this time MacArthur was 77 years old, a clear-thinking, practical man who had become my friend over the years.

We had met when he called me while he was researching a defunct Oklahoma insurance company as a possible acquisition. I was in my second year as Governor; we developed that friendship through his inquiries, although he never bought the insurance company or attempted to resurrect it. In our many conversations, he impressed me with his sharp mind and business know-how. A year later, I was invited to his 77th birthday party in Chicago, with Paul Harvey as the host. Three other billionaires were honored at the same event. The phenomenal success of Mr. MacArthur's business ventures and his building of Banker's Life into one of the major insurance companies in America was a story told and retold across the country.

Another part of this story was the fact that he made Paul Harvey the voice of the Banker's Life, and Harvey had developed into a major force in American thinking with his radio programs and that marvelous, distinctive voice. Of course, I had a special affinity for Harvey because of his Oklahoma roots. I had first met him through Ross Porter, the outstanding editor of the *Shawnee News Star* newspaper, and one of Oklahoma's premier journalists.

Harvey was visiting him, and Ross arranged an hour-long meeting at the Shawnee airport. I enjoyed that visit immensely, and though I already listened to his broadcasts, I became an even more devoted fan. I trusted the way in which he presented the news and the accuracy of his reporting. My favorite segment was his famous, "The Rest Of The Story." A year later, he had invited me to MacArthur's birthday celebration.

Jo accompanied me on the trip to Florida. It was late in the evening as we arrived at the hotel. MacArthur had arranged for us to stay the night as his guests and meet with him the next morning. Rising early, Jo and I ate breakfast in our room and prepared for the meeting. The desk clerk had told me the night before that our meeting would be in the restaurant area of the hotel. At the appointed time, Jo and I checked in with the restaurant maître d'.

Previously, by telephone, I had briefly told MacArthur of my plans in Saudi Arabia, and he had been keenly interested. This meeting with him was not only significant in helping to forward my goal of providing for my family, but it was one of the most interesting encounters that I've ever had in all of my legal, business, and political life. Our meeting was set in the dining room in an open elevated area around a large circular table that would seat about six people. The restaurant was busy, people were coming and going. As we were ushered to the table, we saw MacArthur already seated. His eyes were alert, and his slight build belied the stature of the man. He smiled warmly and greeted us. Next to him sat a ruggedly handsome, no-nonsense type of man in his fifties who appeared athletically fit. MacArthur introduced him as his bodyguard.

Jo and I sat opposite them, and MacArthur spoke first. "David, I am so glad you and Mrs. Hall could come to Florida to see me," he said. "I appreciated you coming to my birthday party and helping make it a success."

"We had a wonderful time at the party, and were honored to be included."

"I am keen to hear the details of your plans in Saudi Arabia. How can I help?"

"In my research," I began, "I see two excellent business opportunities, one in the sales of motorhomes, and the other in a climate-controlled greenhouse."

"Go on," he responded. "Please tell me how this will impact your family life and how you will handle that."

Then I carefully outlined the plans that I had for the two ventures and for the family.

The cast of characters at the conference table were so interesting because Jo and I had never had the opportunity to sit down face to face and have as frank a discussion about own lives, our own hopes, and our own dreams with such a successful man. We learned that MacArthur's bodyguard was a former colonel in the Cuban army during the reign of dictator Fulgencio Batista ; he had been Batista's personal bodyguard until the takeover by Fidel Castro. This man said nothing during the discussions, but was acutely attentive to everything that was said, and continually swept the room with his eyes during the time that MacArthur, Jo, and I conversed.

The meeting lasted nearly two hours, during which time we explored the Winnebago business plans, the greenhouse venture, our family situation, where we expected to be in the future, and most importantly, how we might conduct business together. As the meeting started to wind down, MacArthur said, "I have decided to back your ventures. You need to contact my associate, Norbett Genus, and he will work out the details. Here are the numbers for him." He slid a paper with the information across the table to me.

"Thanks for believing in me," I said. "It's going to be an exciting association, and Jo and I are so grateful for your help."

In addition to the normal business practices on which we both agreed, MacArthur asked for a detailed report of my activities to be sent to him every week—not only when I was in Saudi Arabia, but also when I was back in the United States. He wanted these to be in the form of a written document that he could read, and on which he could make comments that might be beneficial to further the ventures. Our meeting ended on a high note. MacArthur and I shook hands, and our eyes met in a look that seemed to say, "We are a team, and we will be successful."

But I am getting ahead of the story. I've already explained that I had gone to Saudi in January 1975, after my indictment and arraignment in Federal Court. That work was on assignment from Clint Murchison's construction company; I spent nearly ten days in Saudi Arabia, wrestling with government bureaucracy in an attempt to recover money owed the company. But the Saudis would not budge; they never paid Murchison.

However, during the trip I was amazed at the construction, the energy, and the optimistic attitude of the businessmen and merchants in this desert kingdom of some 4,000,000 inhabitants. Since the oil embargo and price increases of 1974, the kingdom was awash in money; it was like the California Gold Rush of 1849—or the Oklahoma oil boom of the 1920s. Just as Murchison's construction interests had lured him to Saudi Arabia, so had every major construction firm in Europe and the U.S. set their sights on the immense building programs in the kingdom. America's giants, Bechtel and the Ralph Parson Company, were prominent.

I knew that if I were convicted and lost my license to practice law, perhaps the best avenue for my business future might well be in Saudi Arabia. With this in mind, I took the time to research two possibilities that I believed had merit. During that trip I had counseled with members of the American Embassy staff in Jeddah, and with various business people that I had met in an effort to learn the best way to proceed in operating a business there. I was advised that first it was imperative that I have an agent in Saudi Arabia who would help me secure a Saudi Arabian partner, because I faced the possibility that if anything went wrong, my chances of prevailing in the civil or religious courts without such a partner would be nil.

Through the associations that I made in Saudi, I was introduced to the Triad Holding Company, which at that time was the largest trading company in Saudi Arabia—and best connected with the Saudi government. Triad had been founded by Adnan Khashoggi and his two brothers. During this period, Khashoggi was considered the richest man in the world, although his life turned somewhat unsavory later.

Triad was the premier trading company of the kingdom, and the story of Adnan Khashoggi and his use of bravado and aggressiveness to obtain a contract with Lockheed Aviation was a legend in Saudi Arabia. It was all accomplished with adroit opportunism and contacts with the Saudi military. He was able to pyramid that contract into the multibillion-dollar company that became Triad. Khashoggi prospered during the late '70s, but his reputation as an arms dealer and his involvement as a middleman in the Iran Contra arms-for-hostages affair led to financial difficulties in the 1980s. He was later charged in the U.S. on federal charges and brought to trial, but was acquitted.

But that all came later. In 1975 and for years to come, Triad would seek out partners within the kingdom for entrepreneurs who wished to do business there, and charge an override for all business done within the kingdom. The Saudi partner would make certain the business complied with all laws, civil and religious. Triad assigned John Finney, a retired military officer from Great Britain, to be my agent. Mr. Finney was a man of integrity and proved to be very able at his job. He developed into a good friend over the years that I spent there.

Finney, had searched out Sheik Abdul Rahman Almutref as a potential partner, and arranged a meeting for us in May of 1975. We had an instant chemistry; we liked each other immediately, and had many common interests, and although Sheik Almutref spoke rudimentary English, he had excellent comprehension of my words. We had his younger brother to translate for us when the details of the business were discussed, but our communications in private were easily understood. My ability to use the Arabic language was almost nonexistent, but I rapidly picked up words and phrases that helped.

Sheik Almutref was a world traveler and a very sophisticated businessman. He was intelligent, wrote poetry, and had a stable of Arabian horses. I was very fortunate to have a man of his caliber for my partner. He was 46 years old, a handsome man of medium build, just under six feet tall; he could have doubled for Omar Sharif.

His main business was the Almutref Stores in Jeddah, Riyadh, and Dhahran, which imported furniture from all over the world, especially very-high-end modern Italian furniture. His customers included members of the royal family and up-and-coming successful and wealthy Saudis throughout the kingdom. One of his closest friends and advisors was Princess Madawi, one of the daughters of King Abdul-Aziz, who had united the kingdom and brought the tribes together to form modern Saudi Arabia. She was married at the early age of fourteen or fifteen, and had eight children before she and her husband separated. At the time that I was introduced to Sheik Almutref and Princess Madawi, her eight children were all living in Riyadh. She lived in a palace in a twenty-acre compound surrounded by high walls, and was a most interesting lady.

Sheik Almutref and I sensed that our association could be profitable, and our friendship seemed to move quickly. I felt I could trust him, and he appeared to feel the same. I had briefed him at the very start about my troubles with the government in the U.S., and told him about my conviction. I told him what the future might entail, and answered all his questions with truthfulness and candor. He was very sympathetic to the injustices that I had suffered.

The two ideas that had been maturing in my mind I now discussed at length with Sheik Almutref. First was the idea of bringing a recreational-vehicle franchise to the kingdom and selling the units. I outlined my rationale from the research I had done on the almost universal desire of Saudi citizens to use the desert on weekends,and emulate the culture of their nomadic ancestors. I had seen only one or two RVs, and they were General Motors products. I decided to do a survey to see what brands were known.

One brand was identified by more than 70% of the people I interviewed: Winnebago. I learned that the reason was that a Walt Disney film that was very popular in Saudi Arabia had a dramatic scene in which a Winnebago flew through the air and over a mountain. Nearly every child in the kingdom had seen *Escape To Witch Mountain* and knew the Winnebago name.

My goal was clear, and Almutref and I agreed that I would try to acquire the franchise.

My second research project concerned operating a greenhouse with the objective of growing ornamental plants in a climate-controlled hydroponics structure, then rent live plants to various businesses and governmental agencies for their buildings. Almutref endorsed this as our second venture, and asked me to pursue the expertise in the U.S. that could make it happen.

Agreement on these projects resulted in Almutref and me signing a partnership agreement. This completed, I immediately returned to the United States in a very upbeat mood. I could now see the avenue that would take me to the necessary financial goals that would pay off the debts and perfect the appeal of my case. I returned home after a two-week stay in the kingdom. From then on, I developed a pattern of going back to the U.S. for a two-week stay, then returning to the kingdom for two weeks.

When I arrived back in late May in Oklahoma City, the filing of the appeal to the Circuit Court had been completed. We could now only hope that we would gain a chance to make oral arguments and impress the court with our reasoning to win a retrial sometime in the future. At the same time I was locked in a fierce battle with the Oklahoma Supreme Court in an effort to keep my license to practice law until my appeal was decided; Attorney Bill Berry did a valiant job of defending me.

I badly needed to keep my license to help provide for my family, but it was not to be. In a unanimous decision, the Oklahoma Supreme Court disbarred me and removed me from the rolls of attorneys permitted to practice in the State of Oklahoma—another door slammed shut on what would have been a major source income for the family.

Faced with the reality of losing my license, and the mounting debts from the appeal of my conviction, the battle with the IRS, and getting ready for the college terms that would soon have two of our three children enrolled, gave Jo and me a myriad of problems to solve. However, with the excitement of the beginning of our venture in Saudi Arabia, and the euphoria that enveloped us for finding Sheik Almutref for a partner, Jo and I looked to the future with optimism.

These days were clouded by another factor that had hit our family just three weeks after the trial. I was on a trip to Washington, DC, to confer with our tax counsel regarding the IRS investigation, when in the near-dawn hours, I developed a constrictive chest pain and thought I was having a heart attack in the motel. It was 6:30 a.m. I had experienced such symptoms before, and felt they would go away, but after some two hours, the pain was still present. I managed to get a cab to take me to a doctor recommended by the motel. The doctor checked me, then with a face as grave as I have ever seen, told me that I must hospitalize myself immediately; he even went further to say that he didn't know how I had made it to his office. He told me the hospital was just blocks away, but he warned me that I might have a heart attack on the way.

Since the cab was waiting for me, I decided not to call an ambulance. Instead, I rushed out of his office, jumped in the cab, and was whisked to the hospital emergency entrance. I was immediately admitted. I called Jo as soon as I could.

It was now nearly 9:30 a.m., and the constriction of my chest was still hurting. Since the pain first started, it had been hard to breathe at times. Jo was very frightened, of course, because I had a history of fainting spells over my lifetime. This condition was not publicly known, and had been previously diagnosed as a stress-induced vega-nerve reaction, which had the effect of closing the carotid arteries to the brain and causing me to black out.

Jo had no way of knowing if this was a continuation of that condition or whether I truly had suffered a heart attack. I was put into intensive care, and remained there for the next three days. Jo caught a plane late that evening to Washington, checked into a hotel just a block from the hospital, and prepared to stay until my diagnosis was complete.

Since 1956, I had experienced stress-induced blackouts. The remedy that I found later was just to elevate my feet, and within a few seconds to a minute I would return to normal. The first time it happened was when I was home visiting my father in Oklahoma City for the weekend while I was a law student in Tulsa University. Jo and I had just started dating, and we had arranged for her to come by Dad's home to be with us for the evening. I had been working in his yard removing a stump. Extremely tired, I went into the bathroom, and then collapsed. Jo found me unconscious on the floor, and it scared the living daylights out of her. However, I regained consciousness and felt fine within a few minutes. I thought nothing of it, other than perhaps I had heat exhaustion from overwork.

Thirteen years later, I had the second of these attacks during the 1970 campaign, and I was hospitalized for about six hours at the Oklahoma Osteopathic Hospital in Tulsa after I fainted at home. I had never had one of these attacks outside my home until the Washington incident—and it was the most severe.

After three days in intensive care, and three more days in the hospital, I was released with a clean bill of health, and Jo and I returned to Oklahoma City. The doctors, in the interest of safety, required me to convalesce for about two weeks before my return trip to Saudi Arabia to begin the business activities. That convalescent period was one of the most enjoyable times that Jo and I had shared since the rigors of the trial, the frustration of the conviction, and the beginning of our future business ventures in Saudi Arabia. We had two weeks of uninterrupted time—an exceptional opportunity to make plans for the future and have a chance to be with the children.

During the last few days of my stay at home, Jo and I were having coffee next to our kitchen in the brightly lit, glass-enclosed room that served as den and family room. It was a sunny May morning, and our spirits were high due to my speedy recovery. "This would be a good time to work out plans if the U. S. Supreme Court accepts our appeal," I said, "or in the alternative, if they decline."

"Let's start with the bright side first," she said. "I would like to stay here with the children while you rebuild our finances in Saudi. I know it's tough on you going back and forth, but we're okay here, if you can stand the pace."

Laughing, I said, "Compared to those days at the capitol, this work is much easier—and I really enjoy the traveling."

We agreed on plan A. "Now," I continued, "what if the court turns us down?"

"I am ready to do whatever it takes," Jo said.

"My thought is to make sure I make enough money in Saudi to carry you and the children for the time I'd be in prison."

"We can do it together—whatever it takes," she responded.

At the end of those two weeks, I prepared for my return to Saudi Arabia. Upon arriving in the kingdom for my fourth trip, I was extremely impressed by the progress that had been made in modernizing the Riyadh Airport. On my first trip in January of 1975, I had been processed through a Quonset hut. It was vintage World War II—and was the main terminal.

Fast-forward to May 1975: On the day I arrived, the number of corporate and business jets that lined that airport tarmac numbered seventeen. This was at the height of the rush for business in the kingdom, and plans were being implemented to make a world-class airport to replace the make-shift facility.

You were likely to see someone in that Quonset hut of the stature of George Shultz, president of the Bechtel Corporation, and Caspar Weinberger, Bechtel's general counsel, or any of those men who later became so prominent in the Ford and Reagan administrations. So many of these men were in Saudi Arabia in the middle '70s helping to further advance their companies' causes. The Parsons Corporation, Bechtel, Halliburton, and many other giants of American construction congregated in Riyadh, and you would see many people who later became famous in business and politics at the capital's only four-star hotel, the Intercontinental.

At that time, communication in the kingdom was very difficult; most of the telephone lines were laid without any diagrams of their location, so, with all the construction, many times the lines were cut, and you might be out of communication for a number of days until the line could be repaired. International communications through long-distance lines was the main means other than Teletype. Long-distance calls were very, very expensive—and very difficult. There was always a waiting period for an international call, and there being no fax communications available at that time—and of course no Internet—communication ran at a snail's pace back and forth to your home office in Europe or in the United States.

On this trip, I outlined my plan to obtain the Winnebago franchise. In a nutshell, I was to return to the Winnebago Company and ask for the franchise, knowing that they probably would want a significant amount of money for it. I had been informed earlier that this might range from $50,000 to $100,000. So that we would not be required to put up that kind of money, the plan that we fashioned was to pre-sell ten Winnebagos to contacts that Almutref and I had in the kingdom, and take those with me to the Winnebago home office.

With those ten sales in my hip pocket, I returned to the U.S. and went directly to Forest City, Iowa, headquarters of Winnebago. I was ushered into the office of the vice-president of sales for my first meeting. They were very eager, of course, to gain any new business they could, with their stock now selling at around two or four dollars a share—after having been at $94 just a few months before. After a conference of an hour or so, they outlined what they considered the requirements for obtaining a franchise for Saudi Arabia. The terms included a $50,000 deposit, a three-year contract, and certain other limitations that I felt were onerous.

As a counteroffer, I said, "If I bring you ten orders for Winnebagos, and prepay 50% of those orders, would you give me the franchise without the deposit—and without some of these other limitations?" We conferred for about another thirty minutes to an hour, and they agreed that they would.

I left Forest City, flew back to Oklahoma, waited five days, and then called the vice-president of sales and told him that I now had ten contracts for him. I said that I would like to bring them to Forest City and obtain the franchise, not just for Saudi Arabia, but for the entire Middle East. I had investigated the fact that no one had the Winnebago franchise for anywhere in the Middle East, or for Iran or Egypt. I returned to Forest City, we negotiated again, and at the end of that meeting, I was granted the franchise for Winnebago for all of the Middle East, Iran, and Egypt.

The buyers of the ten Winnebagos had come primarily from Sheik Almutref's contacts with Princess Madawi, who bought eight of the Winnebagos, one for each of her seven children and one for herself. The other two came from business contacts that I had made with an engineering company out of Houston, who would be the very first business client to use the RVs.

I returned to Oklahoma City for a brief overnight stay. Jo and I celebrated our good fortune with dinner alone. The next morning I started arrangements to ship those ten vehicles, and then I flew off to Saudi Arabia. The Winnebago company would deliver the ten vehicles within the next 45 days to the port of embarkation, and the units were scheduled to be delivered in Saudi Arabia four to six weeks later.

So began the Winnebago business, which thrived; there was only one really bad bump in the road with Winnebago after we started. That occurred when, without asking the permission of the parent company, I adopted the name Arabian Winnebago. However, since we were selling vehicles at a brisk pace, they decided not to make an issue of it, and our company operated the entire time in Saudi Arabia, the Middle East, Egypt, and Iran with that name. Our sales force consisted mainly of Sheik Almutref and me; I imported a mechanic from Great Britain who specialized in the kind of engines that the Winnebagos were using at that time. He was one of the best investments that we ever made; when a Winnebago was sold, he would go to the purchaser's location, work with their mechanics, and teach them how to maintain the RV. Maintenance was a problem, as there were no organized repair facilities available.

At that same time that Arabian Winnebago was beginning to prosper, we were completing our research using information gained from the University of Arizona from their work in Abu Dhabi, where they had been experimenting with just the sort of climate-controlled greenhouse that we wished to build in Saudi Arabia. The knowledge from the University of Arizona was invaluable.

In the three months of partnership with Sheik Almutref, I became more and more aware of the need to follow the Saudi style of negotiations, respect the hours of our workday, and to be certain that I never violated any of the customary practices of their country or of their culture. My adaptation to working within their system included following Sheik Almutref's advice that I dress appropriately in the *thawb*, or white robe that Saudi men wore. He also requested that I orient my schedule to work in the evenings and late nights rather than just during the daytime. This nighttime schedule was the pattern of most of our contacts in the wealthier class. The governmental agencies and most foreign nationals doing business in the kingdom conformed more to normal Western daytime business hours.

One of the most frustrating things in working with members of the royal family or other wealthy Saudis was the invariable wait times. Actual meeting times seldom coincided with appointment times; I would usually wait anywhere from one to four hours in a reception room before meetings. During these waits, I made many friends and contacts, because the other people, regardless of their station in their companies, were relegated to the same waiting procedure. The only exceptions were officials of the American government, or someone with a particular networking contact that allowed them to move ahead of the line.

A most interesting person I met during one of these four-hour wait sessions was Allan Paulson. I had an appointment to see a prince of the royal family to present a landscape-and-gardening concept for his palace. Paulson, an American entrepreneur, was there trying to sell the prince a used Boeing 707. We talked at length during our four-hour wait; Paulson went on to build corporate jets in his Gulfstream Aerospace Corporation, and later owned and ran the famous racehorse Cigar.

The climate-controlled greenhouse operation proceeded slowly because of the difficulty of controlling the temperature inside the structure, as there were frequent power outages on the electrical grid in the Riyadh area. The issue of training personnel who could maintain the greenhouse operation was another problem. To oversee and manage the company, I secured the services of Ron Manley of Oklahoma, who had been the horticulturist and landscape developer for the mansion and surrounding area during my term as governor.

Manley and his wife came to live in Saudi Arabia and were instrumental in establishing the company, International Greenhouses. While we put together the greenhouse, we forged ahead with developing a landscaping-and-foliage business that was greatly aided by contract work with the Landscape Architecture Department at Oklahoma State University.

One of the major projects that we presented to the prince, with whose waiting room I was now quite familiar, was a $14,000 scale model that we had made in the Landscape Architecture Department of OSU. I transported it by a first-class seat from Oklahoma to Saudi Arabia to present to the prince. It was all for naught, as the prince did not like the plan and turned us down—this in spite of the outstanding job Manley did in preparing this project.

As it turned out, the timeframe ran so long that our budget for International Greenhouse was depleted. It was a tough decision, but Sheik Almutref and I cut our losses and ended the greenhouse venture in the summer of 1976.

But at about the same time that we were organizing International Greenhouses, an opportunity arose for a third venture in Saudi Arabia. It was an unusual academic pursuit that was novel, to say the least. The idea came from an issue faced by Saudi Arabian students studying in colleges and universities around the world; there were no major reference books written in Arabic that these students could use in their studies. The Saudi government had invested millions in sending students to colleges around the world, paying their tuition and expenses in an effort to create a greater intellectual pool to help build the kingdom.

A friend of Sheik Almutref's asked that we consider translating the Encyclopaedia Britannica into Arabic, and contract with the Saudi government to install a set of these in the libraries in major universities around the world where Saudi students were enrolled. The Saudi Education Ministry agreed that this was a viable project, and encouraged us in our preparation of a business plan. I made contact with Encyclopaedia Britannica, presented the idea to them, had many conferences, and after we made a $100,000 deposit of good-faith money, they agreed that they would consider allowing us to do the translation.

We began to plan how we would actually accomplish the translation. They assigned their executive vice-president, Charles Van Doren, to oversee the project, and to help me personally. Van Doren was one of America's most famous—some would say infamous—intellectuals, whose life was portrayed in the movie *Quiz Show*. He was one of the most articulate, bright men with whom I had ever worked. He also was a tremendous mentor, and a source of information not only of the publishing world, but also in the concepts and political issues that were to develop in attempting to carry out this project.

One of the most humorous incidents in this whole eight-month period was Charles Van Doren's first trip to Saudi Arabia. Mr. Van Doren, after our acquaintance had developed, felt that he should learn the ropes just as I did as we went to call on the various ministries and to work with the Saudi Education group, which would finance the project. So, prior to his arrival in Saudi Arabia, I had made copious notes and prepared a very detailed itinerary of the three days that we would spend with the various appointments.

I gave the notes and the itinerary to Van Doren the night before our appointments. The next morning he asked me if I could meet him about thirty minutes early, so my driver took me to pick him up so we could have a cup of coffee and discuss the itinerary and the notes. He handed me a copy of what I had given him the night before, complete with red checkmarks on issues of punctuation, grammar, and correct English usage. It was absolutely hilarious; my new partner had a doctorate in English, and he had gone over my notes and found that I had failed to follow all the proper rules! Although there were no spelling problems, there were grammatical errors, and he had revised the whole schedule to meet his very rigid standards. We both had a good laugh about it, and it helped to make us much more comfortable in our appointments and in our activities.

We had arranged that the translation would be done at Oxford University in England, but we planned to have the Arabic Britannica printed in Poland because of a tremendous price break. All of the research, the business plan, and our hopes and dreams were put together in a report—and we were ready to meet the first and most deadly hurdle that we would face.

That was the issue of how we would portray the history of Israel.

Britannica insisted that the history of this country be portrayed accurately, but the Saudi Ministry did not even want to include the history of Israel in the translation. We proposed a compromise by which the history as Britannica saw it would be put into the book; a second history, put together by the Ministry of Education in Saudi, would be included in the translation; and a third, written by independent scholars, would provide their interpretation of the history of Israel, giving the student three options to read.

However, after weeks of negotiation, no compromise could be reached; as a result, the project died—after nearly eight months of preparatory work. In looking back, I realize now that if the project had been successful, it would have become obsolete in ten years or so anyway, because of the development of computerized translation and the development of the Internet.

During my work in Saudi Arabia, I had arranged a schedule of time in Saudi and time in the United States that ran on about a fourteen-day cycle; I'd fly to Saudi Arabia, take care of my business for two weeks, and then return to the United States to carry out the coordination necessary to arrange for transportation of vehicles and other business activities to augment what we were selling. In an effort to broaden my education, I made those trips going one way around the world to get to Saudi Arabia, and coming back by a different route. Normally I would fly to Great Britain, then onto Paris, where it was much easier to get a visa for Saudi—much quicker than trying to get it through the Saudi Embassy in London. From Paris I would fly to Riyadh, where I worked out of Almutref's office.

On my return flight, I would fly from Riyadh to Bahrain, from Bahrain to Bangkok, Bangkok to Hong Kong, Hong Kong to Hawaii, and from Hawaii to California, and finally to Oklahoma. Those were interesting and exciting times, because so much of the Far East's commerce was developing; the Japanese, in particular, were heavily invested in Saudi Arabian development.

During these trips around the world, my back-and-forth travels to Saudi, my time away from home was very difficult for Jo and the children. Jo was only able to come to Saudi Arabia twice with me, but those were two of the most meaningful trips in the 54-year history of our marriage. On the first trip, Jo came alone, and she was treated royally by Sheik Almutref and his family during her stay. Princess Madawi developed a special friendship with Jo, and after the first few days of her stay, we were invited to an outing in the desert at Princess Malawi's remote campsite. Jo and I had no idea of what this outing would entail. As it turned out, we were driven from Riyadh to a remote area some 150 miles into the desert.

Once there, we encountered an amazing, luxurious tent compound. It was composed of twenty tents: individual tents for sleeping, tents for eating, tents for the foodstuffs and furniture that was brought to the desert. The quarters were opulent, with Persian rugs on the floors, very elaborate bathroom facilities, and a main tent for evening entertainment and feasting that would rival anything we had ever seen in the movies.

We spent three days in the desert on that trip, and had one of the most enchanting experiences we could imagine with Sheik Almutref and Princess Madawi. These included nighttime dinners, late-night entertainment, and very interesting nature walks to see the flora and fauna of the desert in the morning hours after a good night's sleep. Sheik Almutref was particularly well versed in desert flowers, and as the time in which we made this trip was about thirty days after the rainy season, the desert was in full bloom.

Jo's second trip to Saudi Arabia included all three of our children. We had made extensive preparations for this trip, and it was a revelation to them—and a source of great pride for me. Nancy was nineteen, Doug, eighteen, and Julie was fifteen; Nancy and Doug were better prepared for the adventure than Julie. She was going through that interim teenage period when it is very difficult to agree to do much of anything with one's family; Julie would rather have been back home in Oklahoma with her friends.

The five of us flew to Saudi Arabia for a visit to see the kingdom and become acquainted with Sheik Almutref and Princess Madawi. It was a week full of culture up close, including trips to Madawi's palace in the evenings, the shopping *souks* of Riyadh, the prolific construction, the camels, the street vendors, and time spent in our villa learning the customs and history of this desert country.

One of the cultural traits that I found unique in Sheik Almutref's makeup was that if you admired any of his possessions, you were very likely to be given that thing as a present at some point. So I cautioned the children to be very careful about their praise of particular items. However, before this admonition had been given, we had enjoyed several dinners at Princess Madawi's palace compound. Jo and the children commented on the beautiful formal gowns of the Princess, the rose water that was served at meals, and the tastefully prepared rice that was served with each meal.

The week flew by, and it was time to leave Saudi Arabia. Jo and the children had planned to go ahead of me to Rome, and then travel by car to Geneva; they were to stay in a house there which we had rented for six weeks in the mountains just outside of town. I had to remain for about two weeks, and then would fly on to meet them.

The morning that Jo and the children were to leave, our driver came to take us to the airport very early, because, he said, Sheik

Almutref wished to see the family before they left. The driver took us to Almutref's office, and we were ushered into his private retreat, where he announced that he would like to give each of us a gift. He opened his safe and brought out a dazzling display of diamond-encrusted watches that would rival any Tiffany's showroom, and asked each of us to select something from the offering.

When it was Nancy's turn, Almutref requested that she remain in his office, as he wished to talk personally with her. He had never met an American nineteen-year-old who could drive a car as well as any man, and who was bright and articulate, and who had the kind of exuberance that very few teenagers in Saudi had displayed in his lifetime. He was quite taken with her, and felt that she should have a special gift to remember him.

Jo and I were somewhat concerned about this private meeting, but I did not wish to offend Sheik Almutref, and they were only alone for five minutes. Nancy was given the most beautiful watch we had ever seen; it was truly a keepsake of great importance to her, and she has cherished it ever since.

Finally we said our goodbyes and gave many thanks to Sheik Almutref, and I went with the family to put them on the plane to Rome. However, a bigger surprise was awaiting us when we arrived at the airport and the SUV that we were riding in was opened: From the back of that vehicle came three large trunks. These were to be included in the baggage to Rome.

Princess Madawi had sent these three trunks full of presents for the family to take to Rome, Switzerland, and then on to Oklahoma. Of course, we had no knowledge of what was in the trunks at the time, so we had them put with our baggage and sent them on to Rome. The extra baggage charge was very close to the cost of one of the tickets for the trip!

The family left that morning; it would be two weeks before I saw them, but three days later, I finally got a call through to Jo.

What transpired in the three days after they arrived in Rome and continued their trip to Geneva would have made a Keystone Kops story back in the days of silent movies. As it turned out, they did not know the contents of the trunks until they arrived at the Excelsior Hotel in Rome, where they were spending the first night in preparation for their drive to Geneva. The children and Jo were very excited as the bags were delivered to their room at the hotel, and they all began opening the trunks. The first trunk contained three beaded formal dresses, so heavy that you almost needed two attendants to put one of the dresses on. These dresses were extremely beautiful, but so heavily beaded and ornate that the girls and Jo wondered where it would be appropriate to wear them.

Now, with wonder at treasures to come, all four began to anticipate what might be in the second trunk. Doug opened that one; to the surprise of all, it was completely filled with the rice that had been the subject of our praise during the meals at Princess Madawi's palace! This trunk was approximately four feet by two, completely filled with rice!

Now the family came to the third trunk. By this time they had no idea what they might find in this one. Nancy opened the third trunk, and found it filled completely with the bottled rose water that had been so prominent at all the meals we had enjoyed at the palace—enough rose water to last us for an infinite period of time.

Now the issue was what to do with these three trunks of presents from the Princess. First, Jo and the children carefully wrote thank-you notes to Princess Madawi, which were mailed to Saudi Arabia post-haste. After a family conference, it was decided that the trunk of dresses would be shipped on to Switzerland, and then home to Oklahoma. However, it was determined that only a very small portion of the rose water and the rice would make the trip back home.

Thus began their odyssey of giving gifts of rose water and rice, all the way from Rome to Geneva. The hotel staff at Excelsior in Rome was very appreciative of the rose water and rice gifts that we left for those who cleaned the rooms, and those who assisted them at the hotel. Then, at various stops along the way to Geneva, gifts of rice and rose water were presented to somewhat astonished service people, who were not used to this type of gratuity.

The family arrived three days later in Geneva. Oddly enough, an Oklahoma State University graduate owned the house that I had rented for them; I did not know this when I had selected the rental, but the attorney in Geneva who had handled the transaction for me later informed me of this coincidence. It was an unusual house, about three stories high, all plain, very narrow, with no more than two rooms on each floor, and the bath facilities had stand-up tubs which none of us had ever experienced before. When I joined the family two weeks later, we laughed hilariously when they described their experiences of giving the rice and rose water away on their travels.

The time I spent with my family, and the moments of laughter we shared, were priceless to me while I worked on the appeal of my conviction, and while I was away from home for many months involved in my business activities. Then, in the fall of 1975, Jo and I received the discouraging news that the Tenth Circuit Court had affirmed the conviction.

Unless we decided to appeal to the US Supreme Court, we were now faced with a prison sentence of three years.

Again we circled the wagons, conferred with our trial counsel, then with Attorney Mack Oyler, who had prepared the appeal to the Tenth Circuit Court, and finally, with McDivitt and Louis Nizer regarding the prospects in the U. S. Supreme Court. Nizer and his firm in New York agreed to represent me in that appeal, so the decision was made that I would attempt to obtain the court's acceptance to grant a writ of certiorari. That's a discretionary writ, or order, by the Supreme Court to review the decision of a lower court—in this case, the Tenth Circuit Court. If the Supreme Court did accept our case, they would determine whether the law had been applied correctly or not. That long process began in the fall of 1975; more than a year would pass before the result would be known.

Meanwhile, in Saudi Arabia, the work continued, but Jo and I had to be pragmatic, so we began to make arrangements in our lives regarding the status of my legal problems. One possible scenario was that the Supreme Court would reverse the case, and we would be granted a new trial. But there was another possibility: If the Supreme Court refused to grant a writ of certiorari, then I would be required to serve the three-year sentence.

Another drama in my life had been coming to a head in 1975. My mother, who was still institutionalized in the Texas mental health system, had been ill with continuing heart trouble. The last week in October, just before I made my monthly trip to Saudi Arabia, I visited her at a nursing home in Whitewright, Texas. We had a warm and lengthy visit. She was convalescing and was bedridden. She still found it difficult to relate to me as an adult; in her mind, I was frozen in time as a six- or ten-year-old boy, rather than a man who had served as a governor and who was now involved in international business.

I will treasure forever those hours I spent with my mother, as they were some of the most meaningful we had shared since my childhood. The unspoken questions that she must have had about my brother, Wendell, were never voiced. I would later think on this and decide that somehow she must have known that he was dead, but I cannot believe she knew the cause of his death.

The room where she lay in the nursing-home bed was well-lighted and airy. Fall was ending and winter approaching, but there was no chill in the air, and she seemed comfortable with the bed elevated to a sitting position, the sheets neatly arranged over her lap. She wore a soft, pastel-colored bedcoat around her shoulders over a simple white nightgown with small flowers on it. I ached as I thought how alone and vulnerable she was, and how brave she had been in never showing those feelings to me. "Mother," I said as I leaned close to her, "I'm going to be overseas for several weeks, and then I will be back to see you."

"I will be praying for your safe return," she said softly.

"It looks like I'll return home near the first of December."

She brightened. "Seeing you will be a good Christmas present."

Later, as I prepared to leave, I kissed her, gently smoothed her snow-white hair, and said goodbye. As she gazed at me, I looked deeply into her lovely hazel eyes and held back my tears. We were acutely aware that it might be our last time together on this earth. I can still feel that last touch of her hands on mine as we parted.

I moved toward the door, and looked back as she waved and smiled at me. I would hold that last look in my heart forever. My mother passed away at the nursing home on November 2.

Jo received the news from my Aunt Essie, but she decided, because of the effect that stress had upon me, that she would not to tell me of my mother's death, for fear it would trigger an attack. Another consideration was that, since I was in Tehran, I might be unable to book a flight back in time for the funeral. The burial plans were to place Mother next to her mother and father in a family cemetery plot in Sherman, Texas. The funeral was held without me, but Jo and the French family were in attendance.

Mother's death left a cloud over the end of 1975. I shared my pain with Jo, but I didn't let our children see how much I was affected. Still, there were bright signs as the year ended. Our Winnebago business was doing well in Saudi, the family was all together for the Christmas season, our appeal was now in the Supreme Court, and, as the New Year dawned, Jo and I thanked the Lord for the blessings of the past year.

In 1976 my business activities took me to London, Paris, Saudi Arabia, Osaka, and Hong Kong, as well as Southern California and Oklahoma City. My trips in Europe were necessary because so many of my prospective clients among the wealthiest Saudis maintained residences in Paris and London as well as Saudi Arabia. My trips to the Far East were centered on my representation of a Japanese manufacturer of desert housing.

In October 1976, Jo met me in Paris on my 46th birthday. We were the guests of a business associate, Claude Green, who hosted us at a very posh restaurant in the downtown district of the city. Green was a dead ringer for Charles de Gaulle; tall, with ramrod posture, he moved with the same aristocratic gait. Claude was invaluable in helping me to conduct my business in Paris. He arranged transportation, worked out appointments, and allowed me the use of his office; we enjoyed a close relationship.

This short visit ended sadly for me when Jo flew back to Oklahoma. We had no way of knowing that in less than two short months, fate would force two emotionally shattering events into our lives.

In 1975 and 1976, while in London, my base of operations was the Carlton Tower Hotel, as it was a favorite of Saudi businessmen who shuttled between London and Riyadh. Between my first and second visits there was a terrorist shooting at the hotel; automatic-weapons fire destroyed the windows of the second-story restaurant. The Carlton Tower was also a favorite of my California friends who came to visit London; I had met many of them through Gene Wyman in our activities for a possible national political run. One of those acquaintances was the famous "Let's Make A Deal" game-show host, Monty Hall.

It was an eye-opener to see the changes that had occurred since my first trip to London in 1968, while representing a client during my law-practice days in Tulsa. I was astonished at the tight security at all the hotels and airports because of the IRA bombings. I could never have imagined that in just 24 short years, the United States would be securing its own airports, public buildings, and other targets of terrorism in the wake of 2001's September 11 attack on New York's World Trade Center and the Pentagon, resulting in the horrific loss of thousands of lives.

At times, I seemed to think and move in slow motion in 1976, as the appeal process inched forward on its way to the U. S. Supreme Court. On the flip side, I would reflect how quickly business activities were moving; the trips to Saudi Arabia seemed to go at warp speed compared to my time in Oklahoma. These trips to and from the kingdom, and the trips to the other cities where I carried out my work, provided me with enough travel that in my later years I had no desire—nor did Jo—to travel overseas, as so many of our friends in their 60s, 70s, and 80s would be doing. In fact, in the years after I returned to the United States for good, we became more homebodies than we had ever been before.

Throughout the fall of 1975 and into 1976, Nizer's predictions were coming true. The dirty tricks of the FBI and the IRS, and the abuses of the Nixon administration, were laid out in lurid detail in daily newspapers and on the nightly television news. These included FBI harassment of political figures, secret files on people involved with politics, and the collection of evidence using illegal methods. The sequence of events that started with the Saturday Night Massacre in the fall of 1973 and culminated in President Nixon's resignation on August 9, 1974, had included the Nixon's administration's intent to end my career in politics and send me to jail. The continued disclosure of Nixon's misdeeds provided fresh "red meat" for the press, and widened the division between Democrats and Republicans.

President Ford managed to keep the country on an even course after he became president, despite the criticism that he received for pardoning Richard Nixon. Initially, I felt that the pardon was premature; upon reflection over the years, however, and as I matured into my 70s—and now my 80s—I realized that Ford made not only the best decision for the country, but the best decision for humanity. Had the United States been put through the kind of turmoil that a public trial of President Nixon would have generated, there is no telling what kind of split would have occurred in this country. There is even the possibility that a crisis nearly rivaling the Civil War might have ensued if all of the abuses of those years had been played out in trials over a period of years. It may have caused the government to come to a complete standstill—and the rest of the world would have lost its greatest champion.

It is my hope that historians will reward President Ford, for what I now consider a most courageous act—and it is typical of how the Lord provides the right man at the right time to keep this country whole.

November 1976 came rushing at me; the time for the Supreme Court's decision on a writ of certiorari was at hand. We had monthly reports from Louis Nizer and his firm about the progress toward a decision. At the same time, the family issues of college, schoolwork, and our children's future weighed heavily upon the hearts of our entire family.

I was proud that our three children were able to cope in the manner that they did, and accomplish so much in their studies and their religious and social activities. Nancy was elected president of her senior class at Northwest Classen High School. Doug was one of the outstanding academic students, and was also given the Athlete Of The Year award when he graduated from high school. Along with these achievements, they were also active in their church groups, and held their heads high during this time when much of Oklahoma was split politically as to whether I was actually guilty of the charges that had been brought against me.

I returned to Saudi Arabia in late October, and then continued a planned business trip to Cairo and to Tehran, Iran, knowing that I might have to wind up my business if the Supreme Court did not grant my appeal. In early November, Jo received a call from Frank McDivitt. The U.S. Supreme Court had denied writ of certiorari, and with that our last hope vanished. McDivitt asked Jo to call me and tell me to return home as quickly as possible.

Over the preceding months, I had prepared Sheik Almutref for the possibility that I would have to serve my prison sentence, and that our business relationship would end. After hearing that abysmal news, I met with him, and we discussed at length our business activities and how they would be concluded. Our partnership ended satisfactorily—and our friendship remained harmonious and as warm as ever. Those years with Sheik Almutref had given me many great opportunities, and I will always be indebted to him.

Before leaving the kingdom, there was one last madcap scene that resulted from the archaic ways in which many official activities were carried out in those times. Since my business in the kingdom had ended, I was required to have a copy of my original entrance visa with my passport when I left the country. But I did not have that copy, because the Saudi immigration officials had retained it at their office in Jeddah. I quickly got a flight that afternoon to Jeddah, and with their permission and aid from the staff, spent the night at the immigration office perusing 60,000 immigration visas that were randomly filed, with no categorizing and without any sorting system. It took all night and into the next morning to find the document.

The one blessing was that it was November, so the normal blazing heat of the Saudi summers was absent. By noon the next day, I had found the copy of my original entrance visa, and, with visa in hand, I flew back to Riyadh. The next day I was to fly back to the United States, but first I had to secure my passport. Part of my requirement as a partner with a Saudi businessman was that I had to deliver my passport to him to keep while I was in the kingdom, then he would return it to me and I could exit the country. Almutref graciously gave me my passport. It was a sad goodbye, as he knew that I was headed for prison. His driver loaded my bags, and Almutref directed him to take me to the airport. Sheik Almutref and I shook hands firmly and hugged each other. He then wished me well, with the traditional "Insha Allâh" (God willing).

As we drove away, I looked back and saw Sheik Almutref, looking for all the world like a desert chieftain, standing in his flowing white robes, waving farewell to me.

Many years later I learned that in the months after President Jimmy Carter's inauguration in January 1977, Sheik Almutref was in a quandary. He could not understand why President Carter, as my friend and fellow Democrat, had not pardoned me and ended the injustice against me. I was never able to satisfactorily explain it to him, either.

As I flew away from Saudi Arabia, I had a wish for the future: I felt that with what I had learned in the kingdom, and what I already knew about Israel, perhaps someday I might be able to help alleviate some of the Israeli-Arab conflicts. This was especially true in light of even more contentious issues in years to come. Since those days, I have followed closely every one of the peace initiatives on both sides, and I have been amazed at the patience and resilience of our negotiators. The work in President Carter's time, and in the closing weeks of President Clinton's administration, was most noteworthy. Indeed, I think the adroit statesmanship of these two presidents avoided much greater potential disasters.

I've never considered myself an expert on the Middle East, but I do feel, just as I did on the trip that I took with the governors to Russia, that the individual people whom I met gave me an entirely different and deeper insight than the officials. I found this to be true in the various countries where I worked and traveled; the confluences of ideals, family values, and feelings that run concurrently in all nations are so evident when you get down to a certain level of communication that it is almost incomprehensible that we have not been able to work out more harmonious relationships in the Arab-Israeli conflict.

I don't have an easy answer—there is no easy answer. As a work in progress, it's something that I hope that the younger generations—my grandchildren and the grandchildren of so many others—will address in the future. So many young people are now world travelers, conscious of all cultures, and have the means to communicate instantaneously around the world; I believe they will strive not only for better living conditions around the globe, along with better health and improved commerce, but will also channel their energies into solutions short of armed conflict. As for the Israeli-Arab issue, I believe that the nearest we have come to a resolution is the two-state proposal. The right of Israel to exist as a nation must be recognized and protected. Palestine deserves a homeland as well. May God show our world leaders the way before it's too late.

Serving Time

In the fall of 1976 and early 1977, Watergate was slowly being relegated to page three and page four of the national press, and it was no longer the lead story on nightly television across the nation. The spirited presidential campaign between Jimmy Carter and Gerald Ford had grabbed the headlines. Carter's victory in November 1976 was considered to be the dawn of a fresh new era in national politics.

It was the hope of most Americans that the tarnished image of the American presidency could be cleansed by the new administration. Perhaps the innocence that had been stripped from the national psyche by Richard Nixon and his henchmen in the Watergate scandals could be re-established. But only time would tell; no one on the national political scene had any inkling that these events would be the harbinger of the divisiveness and lack of traditional compromise at all levels of government that would become the norm in the 1990s and beyond.

The flight back to Oklahoma from Riyadh in November 1976 was one of the most discouraging times in my life. Now I knew that I would be headed to prison to serve three years. The struggles that were ahead for my family almost broke my heart as I contemplated their burdens; they would have to maintain themselves, to keep their faith, and have the optimism and determination to thrive in the sunshine of future possibilities.

As for me, I had several attributes that would prove to be of extraordinary significance. The first was the devotion of my wife, Jo, who had already formulated plans about how she and the children would be able to cope during my absence. In her undying optimism, she felt that someday—perhaps on his deathbed—John Rogers would recant his fabricated accusations, and we would be spared the historical taint of this conviction. We both felt that the Lord, in His infinite wisdom, would provide us with a positive future—one that would not contain the terrible pitfalls that we had experienced in our life in politics.

When I arrived in Oklahoma City, we gathered the family together and talked for hours about the future. I first explained the end of our business in Saudi Arabia, and outlined the plans that Jo and I had put together now that we knew prison was certain. I told them what I anticipated and expected of each of the children in the years to come.

What astounded me was the resilient attitude and the continued optimism of our children. Their eyes reflected an almost fanatical desire to do their part in making life pleasant and less challenging for Jo and me. I stored their thoughts in my heart, because I knew I would need that reservoir of strength in the months to come.

One of the terrible side effects of all of these past events was that the real estate we had purchased for our retirement had to be sold to pay the legal bills. We were also forced to sell the sanctuary of our cabin at Lake Fort Gibson, and many of the dear possessions we had collected in these last twenty-plus years of our marriage. And the fight was not over; I felt like a piñata as the incessant barrage of accusations from the IRS continued.

And finally the day came for me to report to the prison camp where I would serve my sentence.

Prior to my arrival back in the United States, Jo and I had learned that the destination would be the Swift Trails Prison Camp, maintained by the Federal Prison System in the remote southeastern corner of Arizona near the town of Safford. It was a small town nestled in the high mesa area, hot in summer and cold in the winter. The dry terrain was flat, but sloped upward to the Pinale'o Mountains in the Coronado National Forest a few miles away. Trees dotted the landscape to the west, but the camp proper was somewhat barren. The historical background of the 8,000-plus residents started with three settlers, driven from the Phoenix area by floods, who established the town; with farming the predominant vocation, the place had a pastoral feel.

The time left for me to put my affairs in order was short, but I had saved $26,000 to bank for Jo; she would have to live on that during the first year-and-a-half that I would be in Arizona. It was my hope that I would considered for parole sometime in the second year; this had been the pattern in many cases I had researched. I made the deposit in our account at the Fourth National Bank in Tulsa. Nadine Ralls, who had been our bookkeeper and faithful friend for all the years of my administration, through the trauma of the trial, and during my overseas work, was the custodian of this account; she had been managing our business and bill-paying affairs for almost seven years. She was an outstanding woman, an unbelievably good accountant, and the best catfish cook in all of northeastern Oklahoma. Her catfish and hush-puppies were second to none.

Her husband, Carroll, and I first met as employees of Shell Oil Company in their Tulsa office when I was a lease-acquisition analyst and land man for Shell Oil during law school. Nadine and Carroll became our lifelong friends.

One of the few bright spots in the reporting to the prison camp was that Dr. Paul Plowman, a prominent Oklahoma City dentist, had volunteered to fly Jo and me to the location rather than us having to drive the sixteen hours from Oklahoma City. This was a godsend, as it gave me more time with the family. The night before we were to fly to Safford, the family came together after dinner before a flickering fire in the large, round brick fireplace that formed one wall of our circular living room. Our grandfather clock, a gift from the grateful educators of Oklahoma, showed 7:00 p.m. as its Winchester chimes echoed through the house.

We sat on the same couches where eighteen months before, Jim Head from Tulsa had asked me to forgive those who had wronged me. As we talked, I looked into the children's faces and stored in my mind their words of encouragement. Nancy and Julie expressed their abiding faith in me, which Jo and Doug echoed. We talked intensely about their lives. Jo and I encouraged them to be as diligent in their studies as possible, along with their part-time work, and in their social and church friendships. I admonished them not to feel guilty about Jo traveling to Arizona without them. We talked until nearly ten o'clock, then Doug leaned forward and said, "Dad, I am so sorry I can't fly with you tomorrow."

"Just do your best to help Mom, and I will be proud of you."

He looked me straight in the eye and said, "Depend on it, Dad. And what's more, I'll be at the camp gate to meet you when you get out."

We stood and hugged in a circle, each uttering a silent prayer; and although we were determined to hold back our tears, many were shed that night. Those moments ended as, almost in chorus, we said, "Amen" and went to our rooms.

The next morning we drove to the airport to meet Dr. Plowman's plane. It was a single-engine aircraft, comfortable and speedy. By mid-morning we were sailing into the clear blue skies for a rendez-vous with a destiny that I had never envisioned.

The flight to Safford was uneventful, as Dr. Plowman's expertise in handling the aircraft made it shorter than I wished. Jo and I had little to say as we contemplated what lay ahead. We landed in the afternoon on the narrow blacktop runway of the small, undeveloped Safford airstrip. Paul parked his plane near the modest one-room airport office and we stepped out. I thanked Dr. Plowman and told him how much we appreciated his generosity in flying us. As Jo was to fly back with him after she had delivered me to the prison, he remained at the plane and we went into the office. We asked the one man we found there about transportation to town. He looked up from his desk and said, "There isn't any, but I could drive you in my truck."

"We'd sure be grateful if you would," I said. While he and Jo walked the few steps to his truck, I told Paul about our good fortune and said that Jo would be back soon.

The truck was parked to the rear of the office. It was a vintage flatbed that had seen some hard years of wear and weather, but we were thankful for the ride. I walked to the truck as if in slow motion, dreading the ride to the prison camp. "Climb in," said the driver. With Jo in the middle, I got in and closed the door with a bang that jolted me back into the reality of that depressing day.

Jo and I held hands tightly, sending waves of strength to each other as the truck bounced and rattled down the gravel road to the highway into town. I had told the driver where we were going, and he was very sympathetic about what lay ahead for me. Fifteen minutes later, we entered the parking lot of the Swift Trails Federal Prison camp, which would be my home for the next three years. I asked the driver, "How much do I owe you for the trip?"

With a knowing smile, he said, "No charge, I was glad to do it. Good luck." I thanked him and reached across Jo to shake his hand.

Jo and I stepped out of the truck and stood for a few moments looking at the buildings spread out before us. I had arrived about 45 minutes ahead of my reporting time, but we knew Paul was waiting to fly home, so we agreed that I should go on in. It was November 22, 1976, at 5:15 p.m.—a date and time I will never forget. The darkness was gathering, as the last light of day had already disappeared behind the mountains to the west.

The layout ahead reminded me of all the Army basic-training camps I had seen in my life. There was a large rectangular reception building, perhaps 150 feet in length and 40 feet wide, that stretched out in front of us. A concrete walk led to the main entrance. It was a one-story wood building, painted white, with an asphalt-shingle roof with TV antennas on top. There were no guard towers, fences, walls, or other security devices surrounding the camp; this was a minimum-security prison, and every man there knew that if he tried to escape and was caught, he would be sent to a maximum-security prison such as Leavenworth, Kansas, or Atlanta, Georgia.

Jo and I paused before taking that final walk to the front door. "Are you okay?" she asked.

I had steeled myself for this last parting, and I answered, "Yes, I am—thanks to your coming with me and believing in me all these years. I know I can make it, if I have you to come home to." We both were fighting back the tears, but we had determined that no one would ever see us cry.

Jo brushed back her hair; then, with her arm in mine, we walked toward the building. I stopped just short of the entrance, turned, and hugged Jo with all my might. I wanted this embrace to carry us until her first visit, and to sustain me through those first lonely nights and days. We kissed, and I said goodbye.

Jo last words were simple. "I love you," she said. "Be brave—and I'll see you next weekend."

As I turned and entered the building, it seemed that a glaze came over my eyes. Jo would tell me later that the same glaze never left them during the whole time I was at Safford. It was almost as though a trance-like state had begun to exist, perhaps as a way in that my body was coping with what my mind was still trying to comprehend. I took one last backward glance to see Jo retreating and entering the truck for her ride back to the airport.

Two guards met me at the door. I was surprised to see that one was a female officer, a lieutenant about 35, wearing a white uniform shirt and black trousers. The male officers were dressed the same. I entered the wide main hallway of the administrative building. To the right were the prison offices, and to the left I could see the reception area, where visitations were to take place on the weekends. As a part of the reception area, there was a lounge with a single television that prisoners could watch at certain times of the day.

The guards directed me to the intake office. As I walked to that office, I could see out the rear of the building, where there was an open courtyard with two barrack-type buildings on each side facing the yard. I was surprised to see the sidewalks around the courtyard lined with lighted luminaries made of paper bags filled with sand. In the background, I could see a large building, which I later learned was the mess hall. Behind the mess hall was an even larger building, the glove factory where the illegal immigrants were employed.

In preparing for entering prison, I had received all kinds of advice from attorneys, from people whose friends had experienced prison life, from my own experience with prisons as a prosecutor, and from the many reference books that I read about how one copes with such a sentence—especially when maintaining, as I did for the whole time and still do today, my innocence of the charges for which I was accused.

All of these thoughts raced through my mind as I walked down the corridor to the intake portion of the prison camp. The protocol for becoming an inmate was routine, nothing out of the ordinary—until it came time for the cavity search. This was a very detailed probing search of all the body's orifices for drugs that some inmates might try to bring in at the time of processing. This was one of the most degrading things that occurred during my imprisonment; it was a ritual performed every time we left the compound for any reason, and it was randomly done after visitations on the weekends for the whole time I was there. I gritted my teeth, and soon it was over.

A second and even more degrading portion of the intake process was not required of me. That was a delousing operation, which was mainly reserved for the illegal aliens who made up 450 members of the 500-member contingent of the prison camp. The delousing procedure was accomplished by a guard taking the nude prisoner into a confined area of a tile enclosure, similar to a bathroom shower, and systemically covering every part of his body with a substance spewed from a blower very similar to a vacuum cleaner. It was guaranteed to kill all of the lice or other bodily insects that the inmate might be bringing into the prison. I learned that very few of our incoming U.S. nationals had been subjected to this same type of humiliation.

During the intake process, my billfold, pocket change, and civilian clothing were taken, bagged, and tagged with my prisoner number. I was issued prison garb: standard khaki castoffs from the military, which of course were apparently the most ill-fitting garments available. It took some two or three weeks of exchanging and trading prison uniforms with the supply officer to be able to get something that fit.

The intake process took approximately two hours, and by the time it was over, the prison camp was very dark. As the guards took me from the intake processing area into the main courtyard, I again saw the luminaries, which I learned were part of the Thanksgiving celebration that would go on during the coming weekend. To the left as I came into the main yard were three telephone booths that could be used for outgoing calls, if the person at the other end would accept a collect call. There were loudspeakers throughout this common area for announcements, and for music playing during certain hours of the day.

My first night I was assigned to a barracks that included 40 Mexican illegal immigrants and four U.S. nationals, all of whom were federal prisoners. I was assigned a steel cot in the open barracks area, with 22 cots on one side and 22 on the other side. The four U.S. nationals were in cots near the entrance.

I took the few personal possessions that we were allowed to have, such as toothpaste and medicine that had been approved by the intake officer. I sat on the side of my bunk, and the enormity of these last few hours came crashing down on me. I sat with my head between my hands and tried to analyze how I would cope these next three years. A hand touched my shoulder, and I was astounded as I turned to see John Ehrlichman standing next to my bunk. "May I sit down?" he asked.

I motioned to him, with the thought racing through my mind that this man was one of the main architects of the disaster that had befallen me. "I've been here 30 days," he continued, "and I know how you feel."

Bewildered, I said, "How did you stand it?"

John told me of his first few nights at the camp, and of his difficulty in sleeping. "The trick is to obey all the rules, keep to yourself, and remember that you are just another inmate during this time," he said. "Be open to conversation with the others, because they all know that you and I are attorneys, and they'll be asking for advice."

I listened intently, surprised at his apparent sincerity. "Are you hungry?" he asked.

"No, but thanks anyway."

Ehrlichman proceeded in a quiet, calm, sympathetic voice to try to explain to me what the first 30 days of my imprisonment would be like. In the next hour he talked and I listened. I learned that there would be a two-week period of no definite work assignment, but I would be part of the clean-up crew for the common areas and be assigned certain other janitorial duties before I received my first prison job.

My anger, just below the surface, was difficult to control while he was talking. However, I determined—as I had in so many stressful situations—that I would learn all I could from him before making a final judgment about how our relationship would progress during the months to come. In reflection, I look back at our test conversation and feel that Ehrlichman did me a great service by easing some of the tension that gripped me those few hours, and also by being very frank about what I could expect and not expect in the next thirty days.

Ehrlichman had completed the introductory period, which included such things as body-cavity searches, random inspections, urine-testing at sporadic intervals, learning the do's and don'ts, the issues that arise with other prisoners, and trying to get a feel for what kind of routine would make it possible to do the time. As I absorbed all of his reflections of those first 30 days, the anger subsided, and I decided I would be more like a student listening to a lecture than an antagonist. That mode was so valuable to me in those first few hours, and on through the first two-week period.

John's comments ended when he stood up and said, "Lights-out will be at ten, just a few minutes away."

"Thanks for the advice."

"I'll see you at breakfast at 6:30."

"Good night," I responded.

John turned and walked out the door, headed for his barracks on the opposite side of the compound.

It seemed like only an instant before lights-out occurred; a small dim light at the end of the barracks near the toilets was the only illumination. I pulled off my shoes and clothes, prepared to sleep in my underwear. I pushed between the sheets, pulled up the thin army blanket on my steel cot, and tried to clear my mind to go to sleep. But sleep was not easy that night; it must have been near 2:00 a.m. when I dozed off.

The next thing I knew, a flashlight flickered in my face, awakening me. It was the 4:00 a.m. bed check—and I was into the routine of prison life.

The next morning I awoke to a bustling barracks, as all of the Mexican men were busy cleaning and preparing to go to the mess hall, which was at the east end of the compound. As I walked into the latrine area, I got one of the first shocks of my experience at Safford. In the corner next to the toilets, there was a two-foot pile of used toilet paper that had been discarded by the incoming aliens who had arrived at the camp the day before.

I soon learned the reason for the pile of used toilet tissue. Most of these men had come from remote Mexican villages where there were no toilet facilities; they had never learned that once they had used the toilet tissue, it should be put into the toilet and flushed away. Instead, they threw it in a pile in the corner next to the toilets, where it remained until the next morning.

Those first fourteen days in the camp were almost a blur. My anger at being there, the unfairness of the trial, and the lack of control over my life was more oppressive than I had ever dreamed. I later learned that during this time I wrote many angry, privileged letters to my attorney, Frank McDivitt, which he thankfully destroyed and never showed to anyone—especially not to Jo.

Discharging my anger in this way may have been part of the mental process that enabled me to create a structure that would allow me to complete the coming ordeal. In those first fourteen days, I decided that, if I were to be effective as a human being, and carry on my life as best I could, I had to separate the David Hall I knew I was from the David Hall who was serving time at a federal prison camp. It was as if my normal persona, my David Hall spirit, was able to stand off to the side as if I were an interested observer watching someone else do the prison time. I promised myself that I would obey all the rules, be very careful in the associations that I made, and make certain that I met every situation that arose with careful consideration and as much accommodation to my fellow inmates as was reasonable.

Immediately after making this decision, I began to feel that not only could I do the time, but I could be effective in using my spirit to accomplish something good during this period.

The most important events in the first and second weekends were Jo's drives of sixteen hours from Oklahoma City to Safford. The sacrifice she made enabled me to serve my sentence just five days at a time. Thanks to her courage and fortitude, I never went more than five days and five nights without the loving attention of the most important person in my world. Her appearance at the visitors area each Saturday morning made it seem like each week was a new beginning; I had only to endure another five days before I would be in her arms again. The eight hours Saturday and eight hours Sunday that we spent together would sustain my spirit and feed my soul with thoughts of family, home, and a future together. With Jo's love and attention, I did not have to look forward to serving three years; thanks to her, it would only be five days at a time. I could do that.

In my third week, as I lay on my steel cot trying to keep the troubled memories of these first few weeks from blocking my sleep, I suddenly sat bolt upright. I put my feet on the floor, sat there with my head in my hands, and realized that when I had assumed the "spirit mode" and stood to the side as an observer, I had also affirmed in my heart and mind the forgiveness that Jim Head had asked me to pledge so many months before, while kneeling in my living room as dawn broke the morning after my darkest day. In that shadowed barracks, with sounds of men sleeping, the wind whistling outside in the high desert, and the bright compound lights filtering in the windows, I knew that I would be true to the promise I'd made to Jim. My affirmation that night eased the burden I was carrying, and the clouded thoughts were now swept away as if an angel had brushed by me and energized my soul to carry on.

On the practical side of life at Swift Trails Federal Prison Camp, after the first two weeks I was assigned as a clerk to the mess-hall steward, and served in that capacity at the pay scale of 25¢ an hour for the next eight months. During that time, I tried to make myself as useful to the mess steward as possible, and to do my job in a manner that would bring credit to the efforts of those working with me. I meant it to be a reflection on my service as a prisoner.

There were many poignant times during those workdays, but the most memorable of the entire incarceration was the inauguration of Jimmy Carter as the 39th President of the United States. It had been one of my continuing dreams since my twelfth birthday that during my 46th year, the most momentous event of my life would occur. All the positive energy that I possessed between twelve and 46 had as its theme, and ultimate goal, that this dream would in fact become a reality. One step toward that dream was winning the governor's seat in a race that nobody thought I could win in 1970; the next step in that dream was the rudimentary actions taken to develop a national strategy for a possible run for national office in 1976.

The bi-coastal contacts and friendships that were made with the Loeb family in the East, and Gene Wyman and his great influence in the West, had accomplished what I considered the second rung in approaching that 1976 goal. But reality clipped my wings—and pierced my heart and mind—as I sat in the mess hall after the morning breakfast was finished, and I watched my contemporary take the oath of office as President of the United States. I was not jealous of Carter's success—just the opposite. As I listened to him repeat the oath of office, tears came to my eyes; I was so proud that a member of that dramatic class of governors elected in 1970 had reached the pinnacle of our political climb!

Regardless of my own destiny, I still believed that I had been a part of a transition across the nation, in which the more traditional experience of executive work at the governor's level was translated into a belief by the majority of the citizens in this country that such background and expertise could better manage the country than the legislative backgrounds of such presidents as Richard Nixon and Gerald Ford.

That moment passed, of course, and the dream ended with the force of a violent thunderclap. I knew that my life was now moving in another direction. In the hours after witnessing the inauguration, my spirit mode took over, and I became more determined than ever to raise my level of optimism while incarcerated, and to accomplish something of merit.

This determination translated into three projects that began in the spring of 1977. The first was to outline an autobiography and a memoir of the years that I had worked and aspired to become governor, including the show trial in Oklahoma that resulted in my political conviction, the ensuing years; I was determined to record how Jo, the family, and I were able to cope with the disastrous results of that conviction.

The second was an exercise in escapism: writing a spy novel, which had long been another ambition of mine. I wrote the novel first, but it took me four-and-a-half months to put it down on paper. I developed a rhythm during those months that made Jo's visits and her critique of my work each week most enjoyable, and gave us many hours of thoughtful discussion.

The third project was to try and develop some sort of an activity that would help me to take myself less seriously, and to look on the humorous side of prison life. That morphed into a 100-page treatment of all of the humorous, incongruous, and outlandish things that occurred during my incarceration, to me and to the prisoners around me. I wrote this without Jo's input, and when I delivered the finished product to her, her reaction stunned me. Jo said that I must never publish that work during her lifetime, because she had never—I repeat, never—experienced any such language or humor. I have honored her request, and no one except Jo and me has ever read those pages.

The outline for the autobiography and memoir progressed on a week-by-week basis until I had more than 50 pages outlining all the facets that would later make up this book. The rhythm that had developed in writing the novel was a very smooth operation; I wrote in longhand on yellow legal pads, two to three hours a night after the evening meal. Each weekend, Jo would critique those pages and forward them to Pam Prescott Paterson, a young friend of ours in Carlsbad, California. Early on, Pam had volunteered to type whatever written material I might send her, and process it back to me for editing and the ultimate creation of a manuscript. Jo's editing and critiques, and Pam's typing, and their devotion to the novel made it possible in those first four or five months to complete that work.

During that time, an attorney friend of mine in San Francisco, Bruce Flanagan, had introduced me to a best-selling author named Paul Erdman. Paul and Bruce had met as joint commuters on the ferry between Sausalito and San Francisco over the years, and had become friends. Paul agreed to mentor me in some ways in the development of the novel. He was most helpful with dialogue, developing suspenseful patterns and pace. I valued Paul's advice very much, and it was my great joy over the years to read all of his bestsellers, including *The Crash Of '79* and *The Billion Dollar Sure Thing*. We have gone on to be friends for many years since those days.

Erdman had experienced his own unfair encounters with the justice system, and had been able to fashion a successful and productive life in later years. During the 1980s and 1990s, he would become one of the leading voices of economic analysis, and was frequently quoted in the media across the United States.

In finishing the novel, I was fortunate enough to receive an introduction to Michael Korda of Simon and Schuster; John Ehrlichman introduced us by way of telephone, and submitted my manuscript to Korda for his consideration as the publisher. To Korda's credit, he took the time to read a first novel from an inexperienced writer, and to report to me in writing what his thoughts were. He was practical, incisive, and very blunt: He said the novel was like three or four cats in a bag; it was very difficult to follow the storyline. Further, it was too long, and it needed a more definitive plot line. But, he continued, if a hundred pages were cut off, and it was reoriented, it had possibilities.

Of course, I was crestfallen. At the same time, I felt that I had the advice of an expert, so I decided to put the novel away for a few months, and later revisit it to see if it could be resurrected.

That third project, the humorous treatment of my incarceration, still lies in a safety-deposit box, as I had promised Jo that it would. During those eighteen months in the high mesa near that remote Arizona town, I tried to hone my writing skills, but at the same time I tried to return to the regimentation of physical fitness that I enjoyed in my civilian life. I had entered Stafford weighing about 230 pounds, suffering from what had been diagnosed as a spastic esophagus due to nerves and stress—which may have been the potential for a heart attack. With a daily exercise regimen, in the first twelve months I went from 230 to 175 pounds, and was running four miles a day. This routine not only enabled me to tone my body and return to peak physical fitness, but it also provided an outlet for any suppressed anger or other psychological issues that I could remove from my mind during those sessions.

The day's routine during the five days between Jo's visits was almost always the same: breakfast at 6:30 a.m., work at 7:30. Normally, the day ended at 3:30 in the afternoon. The evening meal was served at around 4:00 or 4:30, with free time from the end of the evening meal until lights-out at ten o'clock. My exercise routine was usually accomplished early in the morning before breakfast so that I could have the maximum oxygenation for the work of the day and for my writing in the evening.

The camp administration was very conscious of problems that might arise because of the large volume of mail that Ehrlichman and I received each week. Within two weeks of my arrival, he and I were given our mail at a separate time from mail call, so there was never an open delivery of the enormous volumes of mail that we got in front of the other prisoners. Ehrlichman received probably double the number of letters that I did in the first twelve months of our time in Stafford; he would sometimes average as many as 300 or 400 communications a week, and I would average maybe 100 to 200. These letters, cards, and subscriptions that were sent to us began to drop off after the first year, but there was never a mail call that went by in those eighteen months when we did not receive a number of letters.

The mail sent to me could be divided into three categories, with each category accounting for about a third of the total. The first—and most important—category came from the genuine friends and supporters who wanted to help bolster me during those months, and give me hope and optimism for the future. I treasure those letters, and I have saved them all. The second group of people wrote me out of guilt because they had not done anything to help, nor had they stepped forward at a time that they might have been of assistance, such as volunteering as character witnesses, telling me about tricks of the FBI and IRS of which they had knowledge, and certain other things that could have helped me. I was amazed at the deluge of letters I received in the second category.

The third category—one of the oddities of my prison life—were what I named "punch the whale" letters. That term comes from the practice of sea-coast inhabitants who would go to the shore when a whale beached itself; as the whale lay there, they would take sticks and canes and punch the whale to see if it was still alive. It was their way of expressing their curiosity about a denizen of the deep. Some people who sent me this type of letter received replies, and some didn't.

I tried to answer letters in the first two categories quickly. However, I was somewhat restricted in being able to turn these letters out as fast as I would have liked. The first time I tried to create a label for my letters, rather than hand-addressing each one, I was called down by the administration and told that it was against the rules to do that.

All of the mail that came into the camp had been censored in some way or another, although I sometimes thought that Ehrlichman's mail and mine were done on a spot-check basis. One of the guards had a particular bias against me, for reasons that I never did understand; every time I got a letter addressed to "The Honorable David Hall," he would use a marker to strike through the word "Honorable." I saved these letters because it is interesting to me that he felt that part of his duty was to make sure that this term was no longer applied to me. I think there must be a special place reserved in the afterlife for those people who feel that it is their job to inflict additional punishment over and above the normal sentence.

The rigors that Jo faced in making the sixteen-hour trip to Stafford from Oklahoma City each weekend—and then sixteen hours back after the weekend visitation—were completely unimaginable to me. She was very fortunate to have friends who accompanied her on some of these trips, but for the great majority—I would say 80% of the trips—she made the drive alone. In the glove compartment of her 1974 Volkswagen convertible, she kept a .38 caliber revolver. Her only regular companion was Paul, her wonderful toy poodle, and that was it.

The two of them would make their way, starting before dawn each Friday and getting into Safford late Friday night, and then starting back home early Monday morning, or sometimes driving overnight Sunday. How Jo maintained her health and her positive attitude during these times is more than I can understand; it was such a boon to me to have her beautiful face each weekend for those sixteen hours of visitation that I sometimes forgot about the heroic effort that it took.

Jo had one particular friend, Diane Hickman, who made the trip many times. Diane was a culinary artist in preparing food that all of us would enjoy, as visitors were allowed in those days to bring food into the visiting area to share with the inmates and other visitors. This was very common among the Hispanic families, who brought enormous amounts of food to share with all the relatives and friends who were there.

The visiting hours started 8:00 a.m. and ended at 4:00 p.m. These hours were spent reviewing the events of the past week, playing the card game "hearts", reading to Jo the passages of my novel I had written that week and speculating on the future. Jo always brought gua-camole and chips (my favorite) along with delicious meals she had prepared. These Saturdays and Sundays took us "to another place in our minds" far away from the tedium of prison life. I was so blessed to have only one weekend in those 18 months without a visitor.

Jo was treated well by the townspeople of Safford, particularly the owners of the motel where she stayed, a very religious Mormon family who took her under their wing and treated her like a favorite aunt. They helped her in any way that they could; they monitored her safety while she was in town, and were always there to wish her well both on her arrival and departure. Jo has told me many times how much it meant to her to have that kind of friendship and kind-ness from strangers who had never known her before.

Another spiritual support that was manifested in those months was the number of Oklahoma friends who knew about our financial situation, and helped by contributing to enable Jo to make these trips, and to maintain our home in Oklahoma City during the first year of my incarceration—people such as Lena Kelley of Heavner, Okla-homa, the Democratic Chairman of Le Flore County. She was one of our dearest friends, and she helped immensely in making certain that Jo had enough money for gasoline and the expenses of many of the trips back and forth. Also, the County Commissioner's Organization of Oklahoma, over a period of time, had gathered funds together that they presented to her specifically for making these trips.

Other issues that I faced during those eighteen months were various lawsuits that were filed against me by business interests that felt that they had me at a disadvantage. This was true of some of the people with whom I had attempted to do business in preparing the climate-controlled greenhouse operation. One person in that cat-egory felt that I had not completed my part of our contract, and filed a federal lawsuit against me. I defended myself in that lawsuit, and it was ultimately dismissed as baseless—but this sort of thing was a source of continued stress. Add to that the IRS's unrelenting pres-sure on the results of the many audits that they had done over the period from 1969 forward; these issues were to plague me until the early 1980s, when those matters were finally resolved.

Jo continued driving every weekend from Oklahoma through the summer of 1977. However, it became apparent in the spring and summer that the cost of maintaining the home in Oklahoma City was going to prove impossible, so Jo and I decided that we would sell the Oklahoma City house. Jo and Julie, the only remaining child at home, would move to our condominium in Carlsbad, California. This condominium had been rented all during the time that we were in office through the trials, up until the summer of 1977. We were very fortunate that Nadine Ralls, our friend and bookkeeper, had monitored this property; she not only kept the books, but kept contact with the doctor who was renting our condominium, making certain that this property interest was protected.

Once we decided that we would sell the house, Jo put it on the market, sold it as quickly as possible, and used the proceeds to pay off debts and to bank enough money for Doug and Nancy to finish their college days and get their degrees. Jo and Julie closed the house and held a massive garage sale that netted them enough money to make the trip to California from the memorabilia, extra furniture, and other items that they were able to sell.

The trip west was difficult on all concerned: Jo, because of giving up a home that she had so lovingly cared for since the days after I had left office; and Julie, who was changing her whole life, giving up school, her church, and the social relationships that she enjoyed with so many of her friends in Oklahoma City, to enter a brand new environment at Carlsbad High School in California.

After the move, Julie came many times to Safford with Jo. Money was tight, but they both did their best to shield me from the difficult times they were having. With money short, Jo took odd jobs during the week that would allow her the freedom to leave each weekend and visit me; these included a stint as a flower packer in the greenhouse of a San Diego County orchid grower. Jo loved working with flowers and became an authority on orchids.

The days in prison turned into weeks, and the weeks into months. Two events occurred during those eighteen months that would not have been possible in a higher-security prison in the federal system. By following the rules and exhibiting good behavior, inmates at the prison camp could be granted family furloughs of three or four days perhaps once a year. This made it possible for me to participate in our older daughter Nancy's wedding in Oklahoma. I will be forever grateful to the powers-that-be and to the Lord for giving me the opportunity to attend the wedding. It was a beautiful event for our whole family, and a chance for me to thank so many of the people who had been so supportive to us during this terrible ordeal.

I was so proud of Nancy and honored to give her away! She was a vision of loveliness as she held my arm and we walked down the aisle that wedding day. She was so beautiful it nearly took my breath away. As we walked, I thought of her first baby steps, her love of people, always championing the underdog, and her witness in carrying on the Lord's work. Nancy had persevered so well in her college work and done everything in her power to help Jo.

The wedding was held at the First Presbyterian Church in Oklahoma City. Dr. Dale Milligan, the church pastor had been chosen by Nancy to perform the ceremony. Dr. Milligan was a man of exceptional faith, and a wise counselor; Nancy had chosen well. I got to know him over that weekend, and he was one of many who gave me not only spiritual inspiration, but anecdotal evidence of how in his own life he had overcome challenges just as threatening to the spirit as mine. He echoed the sentiments of Jim Head and Paul Johnson, who had counseled me the day after my conviction to forgive those who had wronged me.

As time rolled on, I approached the fourteenth month of my sentence—and the issue of parole at the end of eighteen months was paramount in my mind. I had the advantage of watching Ehrlichman's progress, as he was in the same situation and would be considered for parole a month before I was. During the months preceding that deadline, I had the benefit of two outstanding lawyers to advise me and prepare for the hearing before the federal commission that would sit in Safford, interview each of us, and decide on the parole. Those lawyers were John West, the former Governor of South Carolina, and his son John West, Jr. These men had done so much in the years I was confined to make my legal position as strong as possible; John, Jr., made the trip to Safford to sit with me in the days prior to the parole hearing, and to prepare me. As it turned out, his counsel was invaluable, and when I was ushered into the presence of the commissioners who would decide my fate, I felt very well prepared.

West was not permitted to enter the hearing room, but remained in the hallway until the session ended, and then counseled me about my having patience until the decision was made. Before I found out the results of my parole hearing, I was very encouraged by the decision of the commission that Ehrlichman would be released at the end of eighteen months.

In the time that Ehrlichman and I had served together, we had become "close acquaintances." I would equate the situation in some ways with Patty Hearst's experience: being close to someone who was sharing a common experience, even though that person had been among my most strident antagonists. I even went to the extent of writing a letter on his behalf to the head of the Department of Interior, a dear friend of mine named Cecil Andrus, who had been appointed to that position by President Carter. Cecil's reaction to my letter was strong and to the point; he wrote back to me saying that not only would he not honor my request, but he thought that I had made a big mistake in trying to help one of the men who had helped put me in my unfortunate position—and he would have no part of it.

I still have that letter from Andrus, because it jolted me back into the real world: Although Ehrlichman and I had accommodated each other during these months in prison, there was no forgiveness in the hearts of my friends for what Ehrlichman and his crowd had done to devastate my life. This was a very good lesson in understanding how insidious the proximity of a shared stressful experience can deaden the hurt caused by another person. That letter from Andrus made me face up to the fact that I may have assisted Ehrlichman more than he ever deserved.

Other governor friends of mine, such as Edwin Edwards of, Louisiana, felt the same way, and thought that I was being entirely too nice to "that SOB"—and they didn't hesitate in our conversations to berate me about letting this prison experience ease my anger.

It was more than three or four weeks after the hearing that I learned that I would be granted a parole in May 1978. I would be allowed to go to California to live with Jo for the remaining eighteen months of my sentence, and I would report to a parole officer at the Federal Courthouse in San Diego during this time.

So the final week of my incarceration at Safford approached, with the target date for my release in May 1978. Jo had made preparations to come with me as I walked out the door, and our son, Doug, would accompany her. Nancy was working at this time, and could not make the trip, as she was helping her husband to complete his education at Oklahoma State University. Julie was in California in school, and could not make the trip, either. But I talked with both girls during that last week, and their spiritual uplift gave me hope and determination to make a success of my life once I was out.

The last week at the prison camp was dedicated to thanking those among the staff who had treated me so well during this time, including the medical people who had helped monitor my heart condition, the dentist who had saved some of my teeth, and the warden, who had treated me very well—although he required me to rigorously follow the rules. Indeed, the warden, John Hadden, had accommodated my family and some of my visitors in ways that I sincerely appreciated.

I donned my civilian clothes the morning of my release and made ready to move out into a normal life, reflecting on how the Lord had brought me through this trying passage. Dressed, with my few personal possessions in hand, I headed for the outside world. As I crossed the compound for the last time, the morning sun was shining, and a moderate breeze, so characteristic of the high mesa, played across the camp.

I passed a number of guards in the reception hall who wanted to shake my hand and say goodbye; I appreciated them very much.

Waiting just inside the front door was the female lieutenant who had joked with me many times during my incarceration, when we were required to give urine samples for drug testing. Just before I crossed the threshold, she handed me a memento to take home: It was a small vial of the type that we had used for our urine samples, with a note inside wishing me good luck. We both had a good laugh and shook hands. Then I stepped out the front door—and I was free.

I walked the six or seven steps to where Jo stood waiting, threw my arms around her and Doug, and the three of us walked arm-in-arm, slowly down the sidewalk to our waiting car.

I met briefly with the press who were there from Oklahoma. I reiterated again that I maintained my innocence, and would continue to do so until the Lord took me. I also said that I felt that sometime during my lifetime, before I went on to meet my Maker, some form of vindication would occur. That's been nearly 35 years—and it's still in the hands of the Lord.

Rebuilding a Life

Jo had done much to prepare for my release from prison by moving to our condo, north of San Diego, in Carlsbad. She and Julie had now been there for over a year, and it was an exciting homecoming for me. When I stepped in the front door, the familiar furniture, collectibles, paintings, and photographs that had graced our Oklahoma City home were beautifully displayed in the tri-level condo in Carlsbad. The vibrant green pine trees, the bird-of-paradise flowers, the bright red bougainvillea and the greenery surrounding the condo were a powerful stimulant to my spirit. Just steps away was a manicured golf course where I might walk in the early mornings, and that was food for my soul.

I spent those first few weeks home trying to reclaim my life that had been regimented to the Nth degree for eighteen months. Now Jo and I were faced with creating a plan for rebuilding and revitalizing our lives together. Our children had become exceptionally well-adjusted, despite the difficulties of my incarceration; Doug had completed his studies at Oklahoma State University, and was beginning to execute his life plans. After his graduation in June, he came to spend the summer with us, and worked as a waiter at the La Costa Resort and Spa nearby. Nancy was completing her first year of marriage, working and helping her husband earn his degree in accountancy. That sacrifice on Nancy's part was typical of what the children had gone through to make sure that their lives, and the lives of those close to them, were successful and productive. Julie had finished her junior year at Carlsbad High School, and was already making plans to attend Palomar Junior College in nearby San Marcos.

Julie's academics during junior high and the beginning of high school in Oklahoma City were average; she had no particular enthusiasm for good grades. But a dramatic transformation occurred in her senior year at Carlsbad High; she began to develop disciplined study habits, with a great curiosity for learning—the kind of preparation that would earn her extremely good marks in her university career.

She created a discipline in athletics and became a first-class runner. Doug, Nancy's husband Mike, my father, and I all considered ourselves good runners, but as we came to learn in Julie's senior year at family gatherings, she could smoke any of us in a 5K race. Julie continued to develop as a runner after her marriage and the birth of her three children; in 2005 she ran in the San Diego Rock 'n' Roll Marathon, competing with 8,000 other women, and placed 181st. She is the only one in our family who has run a marathon.

The spiritual part of our lives was never stronger. We had persevered through the years of my incarceration, difficult financial times, and the slings and arrows that resulted from my conviction by those who delighted in the "I-told-you-so's" of politics. But that was all behind me now, and the plans for the future were more of a challenge than a chore.

After two weeks of acclimation, Jo and I had made the plan for our first business activity. One of my friends in Carlsbad was a realtor and builder. He had found a 52-acre tract on a lakeshore in Northern California that was ideal for a planned-unit housing development. He needed a partner with a legal background, someone who was used to working out strategies. This was a perfect opportunity for me; the next eighteen months, which coincided exactly with my probation, were jam-packed. We arranged the zoning for the property, secured commitments on financing, and prepared the plans.

Then, before a shovel of dirt was turned, we had a very attractive offer to buy us out. It was a proposition we could not resist, so we sold at an excellent profit. The chance to do real work again—and then have it pay off so handsomely—was precisely what I needed to regain my confidence. I now saw the prison days at Safford receding in the rear-view mirror of my life.

My parole officer, Stephen Blake, was fair and dedicated. I had rigorously followed all the rules and his directions. When I completed my parole, we parted as friends, and I appreciated that such a man had been assigned to my case. Now I was completely free, and I wore my survival as a badge of courage. I felt no shame for what I had endured, for I was innocent of the charges against me; but I felt that in the past three years I had paid for all of my sins, real and imagined.

My antagonists had yet to atone for theirs.

In conversations with Louis Nizer after my release, I was buoyed by his anecdotes of famous men who had suffered as I had, and gone on to lead productive and successful lives. Nizer's encouragement and guidance gave me such a boost that I will always be grateful to him. He reminded me about the life of John Bunyan, who in 1660 was imprisoned in Bedfordshire, England, for preaching without a license. While in prison, he wrote *The Pilgrim's Progress,* one of the most influential works in Christian literature. He overcame the stigma of prison and retired as chaplain to the Lord Mayor of London. His contributions have endured and impacted millions of lives, and his writings are still in print today.

A more recent example of overcoming adversity was Nelson Mandela, who was a political prisoner for 27 years, then emerged to lead the reconciliation movement. He was elected president of South Africa, and won the Nobel Peace Prize in 1993.

Pretty good examples to follow!

Beautiful and resilient, dedicated and resourceful, Jo was ever the optimist, and my chief cheerleader; she challenged me to compete in tennis again. I returned to the game with the same drive and focus that I brought to my business endeavors. Jo joined the ladies' tennis group at the La Costa Resort, and I served for two years as the chairman of the members' tennis activities in 1979 and 1980. Playing with my partner, retired Marine Colonel Bob Prescott, we won the men's doubles in 1979 — a amazing achievement just a year after Safford.

During the next four years, many of our Oklahoma friends visited and renewed our bonds, including Governor George Nigh ;

Tom Brett ; Chris and Judy Rhodes, of Tulsa; my former press secretary, Joe Carter; Jim Hartz, my favorite NBC host; and many others. Our children also had friends who made the long trip to California to visit us. Life was good; I welcomed each sunrise. The out-of-body experience of prison was a thing of the past. Jo said the most significant change was the disappearance of the glaze that seemed to cover my eyes. She often remarked how the piercing blue and bright sparkle of my eyes had returned.

I had rediscovered and reclaimed the essence of my soul.

Having gained such confidence, and feeling comfortable in the business world again, I worked harder than ever. From my 50th birthday in 1980 until 1987, I was in involved with partners in the oil business, in gas pipeline construction, and manufactured housing. I also worked on a project to find a solution to the acid-rain problem.

Jo was an inspiration during these seven years. She worked in a succession of jobs to supplement our income and repay the many debts we had incurred in the humiliating years of my imprisonment. Jo worked as a florist, a bank employee, and a bookstore manager, all of which helped to rebuild our lives.

Our children were making tremendous strides in their lives, too. After the summer with us in Carlsbad, Doug began his first professional job, which launched him on a successful career. His initial position was with Arthur Anderson, which at the time was the nation's premier accounting firm. He was a part of their emerging consulting business. Nancy presented us with our first grandchild the following year.

There was never any bitterness or rancor among the family members about the sacrifices that we had made in the crisis years. In fact, we took great pride in starting from scratch after the terrible ordeal that had stripped my legal license, leading to my disbarment and the resulting enforced career changes. These challenges of finding employment where we could, and meeting the needs of our daily lives, gave us confidence and an affirmation that our Christian beliefs would sustain us through difficult times.

My life's normal high-energy level was still burning intensely at age 57, and I needed something to offset the tensions of my new business life. Tennis provided some of that release, but my participation in basketball for the first time in twenty years was like adrenaline to my spirit. I rediscovered my passion for the game by competing as a senior athlete in the 1988 and 1989 San Diego Senior Olympics. I was so enthusiastic and passionate about these games and their positive effects on seniors' health that I decided to become involved in the organization.

At that time, San Diego had more than 360,000 men and women over 50 who could benefit from these games. All of my life has been dedicated to good causes and helping others—and this was just such an opportunity!

Sam Cohen at the Jewish Center in East San Diego started the San Diego Senior Olympics. In the first two years, more than 250 people over the age of 50 took part in the games. I helped raise money and assisted in planning the games; I became a board member, then the director of the games, and finally, the chairman of the governing board. From 1990 to 1995, I worked with Senior Olympics in San Diego, helping to give it the strategy and guidance to take it from a small local endeavor to a statewide and national competitor in senior sports. Paramount in my mind was the goal of changing the lives of seniors for the better. Hundreds of men and women volunteered their free time to make the events possible.

Many dedicated board members—Ash Hayes, Armando Rodriguez, Roger Martin, David Pain, Luther Henderson, Ben Weir, Al Isenberg, Dale Pursel, Sam Cohen, Mario Cefalu, Walter Turner, and many others over those years—gave extraordinary time and effort to help achieve our goals. Ash Hayes had been a member of President Reagan's National Council on Physical Fitness, and I tried very hard to get him to be the chairman. Ash and I joked continually about who should volunteer for that post. "David," he said, "you have had more committee experience than I."

"But Ash, you're a Republican—you can raise twice the money I can!"

"You've run a state, and handled all those problems!"

"Yes, and I used to dream that I would never have to go to another committee meeting!"

"Besides, David, you're younger and more energetic."

"But with your connections in Washington and your knowledge of San Diego, you'd be great!"

So it went, back forth over a period of time, until finally, with the existing board's encouragement and Ash's promises to help, I took on the task.

Those years of directing Senior Olympics I worked with many outstanding people in the city of San Diego. One powerful supporter of our program was Herb Klein, editor-in-chief of *The San Diego Union-Tribune*. I met him through Bob Witty, a classmate of mine in high school and the University of Oklahoma, who was an executive with the *Tribune*. Klein was the primary "mover and shaker" for most of the important sports activities in this area. I proposed that his newspaper become a sponsor—and he decided that the paper would be the Number One major sponsor of Senior Olympics in San Diego. The newspaper's endorsement was the springboard for our fledgling organization to present the most outstanding senior sports event in the city and throughout the state of California.

One of the paper's first articles was on women's basketball on the section page, with an adjacent two-column picture of a senior woman athlete, Jackie Ives, lofting a free throw. That one picture and the accompanying story generated 80 inquiries by senior women who wanted to play! From that seed, the senior women's basketball organization grew in the next twenty years to be one of the best in the nation. Gen Kessler and Audrey Pasture guided those first efforts, as our women won an abundance of gold medals and inspired other senior women. I was proud to have had a part in making that dream come true. I recruited the first women's team for the San Diego Senior Olympics and they went on to win gold medals and honor for their efforts. The women named that first team "David's Dream Team".

San Diego Senior Olympics first women's basketball team—"David's
Dream Team." From left: Jackie Ives, Meg Skinner, Dot Wissell, Gen
Kessler, Jean Munson, Willene Merriman; kneeling, David Hall

In the summer of 1993, a silent killer developed inside Jo. She was
having unexplained fatigue and a lack of energy, but she thought
that more rest would soon alleviate it. Unknown to either of us, a
congestive heart condition was threatening her life.

At the same time, in order to handle my job as San Diego chairman and to compete in basketball, I was scheduled to attend the
National Senior Olympic games in Baton Rouge, Louisiana. The
afternoon I was to depart, I was late arriving at the airport and
missed the flight; I could not get another flight until the next day.

God, in His infinite wisdom, had kept me in San Diego for a
purpose that night. Late in the evening, Jo started having crushing
chest pains, shortness of breath, and an overall weakness; it was serious and I rushed her to Scripps Memorial Hospital, where she was

admitted and immediately placed in the intensive-care unit. She was in the throes of congestive heart failure. A friend of mine, Dr. John Trombold, recommended a heart specialist, Dr. Peder Shea.

Dr. Shea treated Jo and administered the care that saved her life. She remained in intensive care for several days before she could be declared out of danger. With Dr. Shea's medical wisdom and guidance, she recovered, and still follows the medical regimen designed by him that has enabled her to remain healthy ever since.

Over the years, Jo and I have thanked the Lord for intervening on that horrible day. Had I made the flight, she would have been alone that evening—and we can only speculate on what might have happened.

In the years I worked in Senior Olympics, so many civic and business leaders volunteered time and money to help make the program grow. These included Leon Parma, Arjun Waney —chairman of Beeba Corporation—Gene Luth, Ray Blair, Malin Burnham, Alan Greenway, Admiral Lou Williams, Dr. Bill McCall, attorney James Marino, John Carlson, Ron Blair, and scores of others throughout the county. San Diego State University, the University of California San Diego, and Point Loma Nazarene College worked with my committees to provide facilities and volunteers to help stage our sports events. Our two State Championships at the UCSD campus drew then-Governor Pete Wilson and such local political figures as State Senator Lucy Killea to appear at the games.

I was chairman of the first California State Championships for Senior Olympics, and held that position through the two State Championships. The participation increased tenfold over that period of time, and the last year that I served as chairman, there were 2,300 participants in twenty different sports, making it one of the most successful senior-sports ventures ever seen in San Diego County. My tenure with Senior Olympics ended in 1995, when I resigned to move back into the legal field. Although I had enjoyed the work and had been successful, it was time to move on—and I was excited about returning to the law.

As an octogenarian, my father continued an exercise routine of running around the three-acre tract where he lived in Oklahoma

City. However, in 1991, at the age of 90, he suffered a serious bout of depression, which lasted for several months. In an attempt to bring him out of that depression, my stepmother and I made a plan: We convinced Dad to compete in the Senior Olympics, first in Oklahoma, and then later across the nation.

The transformation was spectacular. Ninety days after his first two races, he began to lose all symptoms of the depression that had plagued him. By age 92, he had embarked upon a mission to become the best Senior Olympic runner in his age group in the nation. From 1991 through 1996 he competed in every National Senior Olympic championship game, as well as the Oklahoma and California State Championships. His greatest achievement was setting the national Senior Olympic record in the 1500 meters for 92-year-olds. He did that in San Diego at the UCSD track in front of several of his grandchildren. A year later in Baton Rogue, Louisiana, he placed second in the National Senior Olympic meet in the 100-meter dash and won the Silver Medal in the 1500 meters.

One of the most memorable pictures that I have ever seen of my father was his finish after sprinting the last 60 meters of the 1500-meter race in Baton Rouge. The photo-finish camera caught him with both feet in the air as he crossed the finish line. The officials at the Senior Olympic Games said that it was the most extraordinary finish-line picture ever taken of an athlete his age.

Dad continued to compete until the latter part of 1996, when he developed a foot problem which ended his running career. In the next year, his health began to fail, and he died just after his 97th birthday. Four months later, my stepmother passed away. I've always thought that if there had been some way to repair his damaged left foot, he would easily have still been running at 100.

In introducing Dad to Senior Olympic running, I felt in my heart that I was repaying some of the many sacrifices he had made for me—the security of his home in my youth, his encouragement to fulfill my dreams, and most of all, his inspiration to achieve in education. In 1995, at the National Championship games, seated beside me while he waited for his turn to run against four other 94-year-olds, he said, "You know what I love most about competing?"

"No, Dad, what is it?"

"It's the fact that I am living today, and I am not just remembering past races. Every time I run, I feel younger and more alive. It gives me a future goal to strive for each day. I have a future—and not just a past."

I leaned into him, hugged his shoulders, and almost wept with joy. I knew then that I had succeeded in helping him.

My dad, William A. "Red" Hall, age 94, walks off the track with me after he won the gold medal in the 1500 meters at the Senior Olympic National Championship in the 90+ age division at Trinity University, San Antonio, Texas, summer 1995.

During the time that I had been involved in Senior Olympics, Jo had been working with Robert Geile, an attorney who was an associate with one of the most outstanding trial lawyers in the nation, Milton J. Silverman. His practice was housed in a historical landmark structure, the 100-year-old QuarterMass House, a three-story City Historical Landmark. It was one of the classic houses of the successful and wealthy from the 19th Century. Perched on a high bluff just east of downtown San Diego, it overlooks the harbor, with Coronado and Point Loma in the background. The grand entrance was paneled with dark mahogany, which gave prospective clients a feeling of professionalism and confidence.

I took a position with Silverman's firm. Even though I could not practice as a lawyer, I could work as a legal assistant. I was impatient to return to the law, and this was a wonderful opportunity to participate with such an outstanding firm. It developed into one of the most enjoyable times of my legal career.

I worked as the intake person for new business, prioritizing the prospects for Silverman and Geile to make decisions about which cases to take. During the three years that I did this, I must have interviewed more than 400 prospective clients, of whom the firm accepted less than twenty. By the late 1990s, the firm was so successful that Silverman decided to cut back on his workload.

I left at the same time and joined another law firm headed by attorney Dan White, an outstanding trial lawyer. He was famous for his defense of attorneys charged with malpractice, and had become a legend in that field. He was counselor for the Boy Scouts of America in San Diego, and for numerous insurance companies. It was a different kind of practice, with new opportunities for me; most of my work as a legal assistant centered on case preparation, interviewing witnesses, conducting research on fact situations, and presenting those results to the firm. This was extremely gratifying, and I enjoyed my three-year association with White's office.

During my third year, one of the friends that I had made during my work with Senior Olympics, Alan Greenway, approached me about joining forces to tackle a number of his business problems. So just as the new millennium was opening, I joined Greenway, one of Australia's most successful entrepreneurs, who now made his home in San Diego. The founder of Travel Lodge worldwide, he was an outstanding hotelier and had received worldwide recognition in the years prior to my joining him.

Alan turned out to be one of my best friends. For the next seven years, I worked closely with him as business partner and advisor, handling all sorts of problems and interfacing with law firms that were involved in his various activities across the nation. The most remarkable law firm that I was privileged to work with through the years on behalf of Alan Greenway was the Diepenbrock Harrison firm of Sacramento; it is known as one of California's premier business-transaction firms, with an impeccable reputation. Partner Karen Diepenbrock was a mentor as well as a friend, and reminded me so much of my favorite Harvard Law School contracts professor, Lon Fuller.

It was the most stimulating business activity since my years in Saudi Arabia because of the breadth of Alan's interests. These years gave me an opportunity to work one-to-one with a man of such outstanding ability on a daily basis. Alas, this association ended with his death in December 2008. It was a very sad time for me, as he had been a dear friend and mentor.

After my work with Alan Greenway, I determined that it was time to finish the book that you are now reading. Thank God I have this forum to tell my life story—and set the record straight as to the political and legal injustices that I endured. I want to give advice to those men and women who have been unjustly treated, to mentor them on how they may overcome problems and return to a positive, productive, and optimistic life. Most importantly of all, I want to urge them to forgive those who have wronged them, and lift that burden of demanding revenge from their shoulders.

Since my political show trial in 1975, I had never made a public appearance in Oklahoma. I had often wondered how I would be received. I got my answer on a cold wintry night in February 2007.

The occasion was the very successful "Inspired To Lead" exhibit and celebration presented by the Oklahoma History Center under the leadership of Dr. Robert Blackburn. The exhibit, and the program at the center, focused on the lives of each of the governors who had served Oklahoma. All six of the living former governors, as well as the sitting governor, Brad Henry, attended. The former chief executives included Henry Bellmon, George Nigh, David Walters, Frank Keating, David Boren, and me.

"Inspired To Lead" event, Oklahoma History Center, February 2007, hosted by Dr. Robert Blackburn, director of the Oklahoma Historical Society, with all the living former governors and current governor: from left: Governor George Nigh, Governor David Hall, Governor David Walters, sitting Governor Brad Henry, Governor Frank Keating, Governor David Boren, and Governor Henry Bellmon

I was thrilled to be part of this event, and to see so many of my friends and supporters who attended. That night my heart was lifted; the warmth and sincerity of those attending sent my spirits soaring. I had been very apprehensive about appearing, but those thoughts were quickly erased. I truly felt reconnected with my Oklahoma roots. As the crowd at the celebration treated me like a rock star, the outpouring of their love humbled me. Young members of the state legislatures who had never met me asked for my autograph; old friends hugged me; strangers eagerly shook my hand; and radio reporters asked me what this was all about.

I had no ready answer—except that I felt at home.

The newspapers of Oklahoma covering this event gave me favorable stories, and I sincerely appreciated every word that was written. The upbeat column by Ken Neal in the *Tulsa World* led off four or five days of the kind of coverage that made my homecoming a wonderful occasion. I am most appreciative of John Greiner of *The Daily*

Oklahoman for his excellent article covering my press conference the morning after the celebration, and to the other newspaper, radio, and television correspondents who rose early on that cold February morning to give such favorable coverage to the event.

I truly felt a new day had dawned in my relationship with the metropolitan press in Oklahoma.

Since finishing my work in 2009, my writing and charitable activities have consumed most of my time, with the exception of my weekly routine of tennis and basketball. I am proud to be a member of a Senior Olympic basketball team, made up of 80-year-olds, who competed in our age group for the National Championship this past June in Houston, Texas. We won the bronze medal.

San Diego Golden Aztecs, winner of the Bronze medal in basketball for age 80+ division at the National Senior Games Association Championship (Senior Olympics), Houston, Texas, June 2011

Jo and I have been blessed during this time with good health and an opportunity to be of service to others.

Part Four:

2011 AND BEYOND: A NEW HOPE FOR AMERICA

The United States Can Be Greater Than Ever

In the eighteen months that I spent in that remote prison camp in Arizona, I had the time to consider the issues facing the nation, ponder how to solve the problems of filling the basic needs of my country, and determine how to help it reach its promising future. In my mind, I have continually reviewed solutions that might help solve the problems and meet the challenges, rather than add to them. I wanted to focus on developing an even brighter future than the times we had enjoyed up through the late 1970s.

After my release, I engaged in various activities that gave me insight into what I thought was needed as we progressed into the 21st century. As so many others have observed, I was dismayed by the sharp divisions throughout the United States that were perpetuated by both political parties. Most egregious were the "wedge issues" touted by the very extreme conservatives in their attempt to manipulate the electorate.

The development of the wedge-issue political strategy with matters such as women's reproductive rights, equal rights for gay and lesbian citizens, and other social issues gave the far-right fringe a more powerful voice in the media than their numbers would reflect at the polls. This is best illustrated by the willingness of the extremist to financially support divisive talk-radio and television commentators. That funding far out weighs the number of actual citizens who share those fanatical beliefs.

As we rounded the turn into the new century and the political fiasco of the Clinton impeachment began to recede into history, I felt more than ever that the country needed to find ways to agree on the major challenges. It is my firm belief that there are three absolutely necessary changes that this country needs to make to develop the patriotic fervor that we have had in our previous military encounters, especially during World War II, and to avert any future financial crises that have resulted in so much suffering.

The long military conflicts in Afghanistan and Iraq have created a patriotic vacuum that I feel is moving this country into a very vulnerable position. That situation was best expressed in a roundtable discussion that I heard on national television as the returns came in on the congressional elections of 2010. The most erudite analysis came when former NBC anchorman Tom Brokaw shared his views. To paraphrase Brokaw, the tragedy of these drawn-out conflicts was that 1% of the country was actively engaged in the military actions, while 99% of the country went about its daily business, unconcerned in many ways.

That one statement brought home to me the first of three needs that I see for the United States in the next ten to twenty years. The first of these initiatives would be the passage of a strict universal-service act requiring all eighteen-year-old citizens, male and female, to give two years of either military or civilian service to the United States of America.

Politicians have been reluctant to take the bull by the horns and pass this bill. Instead, they have pointed to volunteer groups such as Peace Corps, Vista, and AmeriCorps. These organizations have done excellent work, but the number of young men and women who are involved is minuscule compared to the millions who have no inclination to participate.

Think about the enormous impact that a mandatory service act would have in supplying the civilian personnel to work in the inner cities and in the poverty-stricken areas of Appalachia, to provide basic health care assistance in remote areas, and to help remedy the educational disadvantages of states with low per-capita expenditures on their students! Visualize the pride of accomplishment that these young people would have after completing two years of service that would change so many lives for the better!

I would counsel with those who draft this legislation that they make it mandatory, with very few exceptions or deferments possible. I'm convinced that the two years that these young men and women would spend giving service to our country would have several advantages: It would inculcate a distinctive patriotism for all the good things of the United States. It would instill discipline and direction for many young men and women, particularly high-school drop-outs; this service would give them training, education, and something important to do with their lives. It would help eradicate "gangs" as it would substitute a camaraderie in the service to fill that need. If properly drawn, it should provide for at least two years of future college education. It would increase the health awareness of that age group, and possibly lay a foundation for good health practices in years to come.

The choice of military service, in these troubled times of terrorism in the world, would provide this country with a reservoir of patriotic, well-trained young men and women who could respond to any emergency. Our current military is stretched too thin, and it's unfair that so many must participate in multiple tours of duty. It's high time that the criticism of ROTC programs in our universities be tempered with the practical need for citizen-soldier officers, and not just professionals who see continued conflicts as their only way of advancement.

There is a side effect that would be important to those of us who are opposed to preemptive wars. Having more young people serve in the military would almost guarantee that no engagement such as the Iraq war would ever happen again in the future. The families of the young men and women who have given their two years of military service would demand that there be no question about the need for any military mission before we commit their children to unprovoked wars, or use such a tremendous amount of our financial resources on such a conflict.

The second major initiative that has enabled states such as Oklahoma, and numerous others, to maintain their solvency is a balanced fiscal policy. I believe that we should pass a Constitutional amendment for a balanced budget. This amendment could give us back the economic health that the Chinese and our other creditors are draining from this country.

However, a federal balanced budget should be accomplished not in a draconian manner, but over a ten- to twenty-year period of planned budget reductions, frugal entitlements, greater individual responsibility, and—most importantly—the removal of the influence of lobbyists in the legislation of this country. Historically, during the 1930s, the 1940s, and into the early 1950s, government agencies such as commerce, housing, health, agriculture, veterans' affairs, and others have carried on the bulk of helping Congress develop legislation. Currently, lobbyists have too great an influence in shaping the legislative agendas of the House and the Senate.

In the 1950s, 1960s, and beyond, a shift in Congress to greater personnel expansion and empire-building among congressional staffs has added to budget-busting excesses. With that expansion, the traditional role of the agencies of government began to shift to the individual congressman. This fueled the desire for greater power by those elected officials; in the case of the late US Senator Ted Stevens, for example, this hubris led to his endorsement of a "bridge to nowhere" in Alaska. Nowadays many professional office-holders at the national level are far more concerned with re-election than they are in meeting today's budget challenges; the philosophy of "kick the can down the road" to the next Congress became a fact of life, whether it was the issue of a balanced budget or many others that were considered to be "third-rail" issues that could be disastrous in an election.

That selfish practice must end if we are ever to bring this country back to the kind of comprises that were fashioned by Republican Senator Everett Dirksen of Illinois in his many years of service—and which enabled so much to be accomplished. His support of President Lyndon Johnson's legislative program in many areas is legendary. This was the hallmark of majority leader, then Senator Lyndon Johnson in his early years; it's the magic of our system of government that diverse opinions are recognized and protected, but the shared goals provide the cement of compromise that has made us the world's most powerful nation.

A third major initiative that needs to be undertaken by those who have no fear about re-election is the passage of immigration legislation that stops the problem dead in its tracks. This political pill is not an easy one to swallow; still, there are many facets of legislation that could aid brave and statesmanlike congressional members. The first, and perhaps one of the most controversial, would be to do what many states such as Oklahoma and Texas have already done: Make English the only language in their schools and government. But this is no anti-immigrant position; I simply favor the most immediate immersion and assimilation into the language and culture of the new nation. The greatness of the immigrant populations throughout the history of this country has come about because of their assimilation into the American way of life, not into separate divisions of Hispanic-Americans, Asian-Americans, Irish-Americans, Italian-Americans, or any other immigrant groups. Fulfilling the American Dream happens when people embrace our unique American democracy and culture.

What makes this issue most difficult is the question of what to do with the 12,000,000 to 15,000,000 illegal immigrants who have been good *de facto* citizens during their residency in this country. I say they should be given the opportunity to become legal citizens; they have demonstrated, in most cases, through their work ethic, their family lives, and their payment of taxes that they deserve to achieve this goal. It would be impossible to deport 12,000,000 people; it would decimate many of our workforce activities. It's also illogical to punish a group who has only sought the same things that we all seek: a better life and a chance to participate in the American Dream.

In the present mood of this country, I think that all of us might be surprised about how quickly an amendment to rectify this issue could be passed. What makes the problem even more complex is the possibility of the deportation of undocumented parents who might be forced to leave behind their children who are citizens; this is the gnarly issue of what anti-immigrant pundits call "anchor babies." One solution that I feel might work, if the Constitutional amendment to close this loophole is passed, would be to legislate a very restricted form of amnesty for those parents. Forget the wedge-issue extremists who use amnesty as a buzzword for fund-raising—all of us need to use a little common sense!

These three initiatives I present as distinct possibilities for joint efforts by Republicans, Democrats, and minority parties to form a coalition that could agree on a plan to move this country forward, to continue our leadership in world economics and military power, and—most importantly—to guarantee a prosperous future to our children and grandchildren, one that will match the abundance and good works that the men and women of my generation and generations before me have enjoyed all these years. Let's forget trying to reconcile the wedge issues until after we have completed the big-picture problems that have to be remedied if we're to maintain our leadership in the world.

It is important not only to us as citizens of the United States, but to humanity on this planet, that the kind of leadership we have displayed in the 223 years of our nation's existence is perpetuated as a beacon for those who have yet to experience the blessings that we have enjoyed. Without our example, without our military protection around the world, and without our innate sense of fairness and the worth of the individual, the world would be ill-served with our decline.

Epilogue

My thanks to all the readers who have joined me on this journey through a life of success and failure, hills and valleys, and the highs and lows that those of us who have lived to four score and more have experienced. I have never felt stronger about the power of positive thinking than I do today. I have never felt more thankful to have experienced good health, family love, and the blessings that I've had to be a citizen of the United States, the state of Oklahoma, and the state of California.

In all my travails with the federal government, through the trial, imprisonment, and beyond, I have never questioned our judicial system. Our judiciary is unique in the history of mankind. It is not the law that becomes perverted, but it is the attempt of individuals to manipulate the law to their advantage. That is how injustices can occur. The incredible and revolutionary development of DNA testing is making it less likely in the future that innocent people will be convicted of crimes. The Internet, the twenty-four-hour news cycle, the educational advancements, and the innate curiosity of our younger generation are going to make it less possible for political injustices to be committed. That is my great hope.

As so many survivors of political injustices have found, and it as it was well expressed by President Ronald Reagan in his analogy to that shining city on the hill, "the best days of the United States are still ahead." In all of these years, I've never regretted the decision that I made to forgive all of those who I felt had wronged me, ended my career, and imprisoned

me. I've had to reaffirm that decision many times, but every time I have done that, I have become stronger and more resolute in my faith. My legacy, I believe, will be to pass on to my friends and associates, and most importantly to my children—Nancy, Doug and Julie —and my grand-children—JoBeth, Elizabeth, Katherine, Tommy, Jessie and Jenny —my belief that no matter how difficult times may seem, the Lord will never give us more burden than we can bear.

The normal human reaction for revenge when one has been wronged haunts all of us. But once you have forgiven your enemies, your chances of a happy life are increased a hundredfold. Those people who wronged me are either dead or have unrealized dreams of their own; the Lord has wreaked punishments upon them that I could never have accomplished on my own. God moves in mysterious ways His wonders to perform, and His judgment is better than any of ours on this earth. One of my dear friends, John Brett, gave me a bound copy of the Book of Proverbs, without know-ing that this portion of the Holy Bible had already given me solace in my darkest hours.

From my childhood I have favored the King James version, and in progression into manhood I had tried to live by the advice of Proverbs 3:5—"Trust in the Lord with all thine heart and lean not unto thy own understanding"—and Proverbs 3:6: "In all ways acknowledge Him and He shall direct thy paths." Long ago I had accepted those wise words as my credo, my confession of faith. In coupling those words with my belief in the Holy Trinity, I found that the anxiety, the sleepless nights, and the inde-cision that I may have experienced in stressful times would melt away.

Now my life is filled with thoughts of good works, positive initiatives, and most importantly of all, sharing the love of my family in the years to come. The wise counsel and support that I've had from so many of my friends, some for sixty years or more, have meant so much to me—as they do to all of us—but I've found time and again that to have good friends, you must be a good friend. This truth and my other life experiences have led me to a series of beliefs about how to conduct myself that I still practice every day.

I make it an important part of each of my days to try to make at least one new friend. This is a sincere effort to create a ripple effect of fellow-

ship, extending my beliefs. *My father gave me some wonderful advice as he turned 90 years of age. He said, "It's important with the genes that you have that you make as many younger friends as you can, because you will most likely outlive your contemporaries." He also said that when I turned 60 that I should find a doctor at least fifteen to twenty years younger than I am so that he would not pass on before I do. Good advice, and it's given me a chuckle many times over the years.*

Another part of my daily routine is to try to dispose of the most difficult challenge I have as early in the day as possible, so it does not dwell on my mind for the rest of the day. This isn't always possible, but nine out of ten times it is. In my own psyche, I find that decisions made between 7:00 a.m. and noon turn out much better. These may seem like simple solutions to the stress of daily life, but they have come to be powerful tactics for me in my everyday living.

It's now late at night, the house is quiet, Jo has already gone to sleep, and so I'm ready to close this book and enjoy a good night's rest. It's my plan for tomorrow morning, just as I've done for almost every day of my life, to wake up, put my feet solidly on the floor, stand up, and say to myself, "It's going to be a good day."

—David Hall, 2011

Index

About the Author

At 81, David Hall has been married for 55 years to Jo Hall; they have three children and six grandchildren. Hall has led an exciting life as an outstanding student, U.S. Air Force officer, county prosecutor, Governor of Oklahoma, unjustly convicted victim of Watergate conspirators, global businessman, and finally a Senior Olympics athlete competing in basketball and tennis. Throughout his ordeals and triumphs, David Hall remains a man of supreme optimism, firm in his belief in the great future of the United States of America.

Recount Volunteer Lawyers 1970

Attorneys and others who represented David Hall in the recount of the ballots for the November 1970 general election for Governor of Oklahoma, listed by county. These are the men and women who preserved the victory.—D. Hall

Adair
> Lloyd F. Cole, Jr.
> Jack E. Rider

Alfalfa
> Vernon Collins
> H.W. Wright

Atoka
> Representative Gary Payne

Beaver
> Dick Trippett

Beckham
> Holland Meacham

Blaine
> Tom Stephenso
> Fred Shirley

Bryan
> Farrell M. Hatch
> Paul Dean Spears

Caddo
> Haskell Pugh
> Virgil Upchurch
> Leslie Pain

Canadian
> James E. Bass
> John V. Whelan

Carter
  Jack Smith
  Ernest Tate
  Wilson Wallace

Cherokee
  Jack Durrett II
  Bruce Green
  Bill Bliss

Choctaw
  Vester Songer
  James Bounds

Cimmaron

Cleveland
  Senator Phil Smalley
  G. Dan Rambo
  Richard Bell
  John H. Patton

Coal
  James L. Clark

Comanche
  Sam H. Johnson
  Sam Joyner

Cotton

Craig
  Lacey L. Mckenzie
  Jack McLean

Creek
  Harry M. McMillan
  Thomas D. Lucas
  Bill Wilson

Custer
  J.Z. Barker
  C.B. Graft

Denver C. Meacham II
  Sid Arney
  John Donley
  E.J. Meacham

Delaware
  Representative Jody Mountford
  Gene Davis
  Keith Smith
  Jack Durrett II

Dewey
  Tom Hieronymus

Ellis
  Samuel K. Barton

Garfield
  Bob Gregory
  James R. Cox

Garvin
  Walter D. Hart

Grady
  Walt Allen
  Mr. & Mrs. John Nelson

Grant
  J.C. Drennan

Greer
  Jim Garrett
  Paul Stumbaugh

Harmon
  H.K. Myers
  Bill Fancher

Harper
  Dick Pickens
  Bryan L. Wright

Haskell
John F. Hudson

Hughes
George Oliphant
James W. Rodgers, Jr.
John R. Turner

Jackson
Bob Scarbrough

Jefferson

Johnston
Tom Shaw

Kay
David R. Garrison
Senator Fred L. Boettcher
Charles Johnson
Charles L. Drake

Kingfisher
Tom L. Baker
Ancell Simpson

Kiowa

Latimer
Wayne Russell
Bill Jones

LeFlore
Senator James E. Hamilton

Lincoln
Mrs. Paul (Jan) Vassar
J.T. Criswell
Terry West

Logan
Thomas R. Williams

Love
Kenneth D. Bacon

Major
Edward C. Montgomery

Marshall
Floyd Miller

Mayes
Ernest R. Brown
William M. (Bill) Thomas, Jr.

McClain
Representative Charles Elder
Jim Nance
Smith Hester

McCurtain
Donald M. Stevenson

Murray
Fred Gibbard
Paul Reed

Muskogee
Bruce Green
Don Pearson
Mike Norman
Bill Settle

Noble
David Matthews
Robert L. Kasper

Nowata
Jack C. Brown

Okfuskee
Coleman Nolen

Okmulgee
Edgar R. Boatman

Osage
Cecil Drummond
Bill Heskett
Kelly Young
Matthew J. Kane

Ottawa
Representative Jody
Mountford

Pawnee
Robert J. Scott

Pittsburgh
Senator Gene Stipe
Willard M. Gotcher

Ponotoc
Frank H. Jacques

Pottawatomie
Terry West
Representative   Charles   T.
Henry
Jim C. Winterringer
Lindsay Peters

Pushmataha
Joe Stamper

Roger Mills
Kenneth C. Perryman

Rogers
James W. Summerlin
Gary Waide Sibley

Seminole
Richard A. Bell, Sr.

Sequoyah
Fred Green
Bruce Green
Lloyd E. Cole
Jack Durrett II
Paul V. Carlisle

Stephens
Richard (Rick) Rodgers
O.L. Peck, Jr.

Texas
Mike Balenger
Larry Field

Tillman
Howard McBee
Loyd L. Benson

Wagnor
Earl Youree

Washington
Bill Heskett
Jack Heskett

Washita
Ron Wesner

Woods
Don Benson

Woodward
C. Jack Annis
Tom Hieronymus

Governor David Hall

Governor's Staff 1971-1975

Mary Lee Anderson

Mona Barnes Gordon

Gene Blackburn

Larry Brawner

Joyce Brown Sanders

Merrilee Bost

Bill Buxton

Joe Carter (Press Secretary)

Beverly Cheadle

John Coldiron

Jerry Cook (Security)

Bill Crain

Edna Durrett

Elizabeth Eidson

G.M. Fuller

Lynn Goff

Willie Mae Grey

Jim Hart (Chief of Staff)

Pam Henthorne

Linda Howard Fishel

Pat Kight

Spike Kelly

Eddie Ladd

Norda Lyles

Ruth Trammell Malaske

Steve Moody

Peggy Mose Cole

Evelyn Moreland

C. J. Murphy

Dan Newman (Security)

G. Dan Rambo (Legal Counsel)

Sandy Rea

Bob Scully
Marilyn Storm
Gerry Strain (Administrative Assistant)
Cheri Snipes
Charles Swinton
Becky Trent
Linda Walters Richardson
Betty Ward
Frances Ward
Gladys Warren
J.T. Weedman
Robert White
Richard Wilkinson
Mike Williams
Richard Wiseman (Chief of Security)

LIST OF THE COUNTY COORDINATORS IN THE 1970 ELECTION

The county coordinatiors were the 1970 campaign's front line troops. Here is a county by county listing of those valiant men and women who overcame tremendous odds to produce our victory.

Adair
    Lloyd F. Cole, Jr.
    Jack E.Rider
Alfalfa
    Ron Ford
Atoka
    Harold Thomas
Beaver
    Dick Trippet
Beckham
    Dr. Carl Ward
Blaine
    Tom Stephenso
Bryan
    Leon Sherrer

Caddo
    Robert J. Stephens
Canadian
    James Ross
Carter
    Darryl Burton
Cherokee
    Jack Durrett II
Choctaw
    Bob Massengale
Cimmaron
    Bill Gowdy
Cleveland
    Dick Rodgers
    G. Dan Rambo

Coal
    Frankie Kuhn
Comanche
    Jack Carter
Cotton
    Ray Brannan
Craig
    Lacey L. Mckenzie
Creek
    Harry M. McMillan
Custer
    J. C. Meek
Delaware
    Dick Lock
Dewey
    Robert M. Berryi
Ellis
    Paul Huffman
Garfield
    Dr. Hope Ross
    Dr. George Ross
Garvin
    R. E. Carlton
Grady
    Ray Giles
Grant
    George Shultz
Greer
    Paul Stumbaugh
Harmon
    Genevieve Charlton
Harper
    R. A. Lotspeich
Haskell
    Henry Roye

Hughes
    George Oliphant
Jackson
    Dale Dowdy
Jefferson
    Dale Allen
Johnston
    Mr & Mrs. Fredo
    Hamilton
Kay
    Claude Braudrick
Kingfisher
    Charlie Kale
Kiowa
    Boone Hazlette
Latimer
    John Sokolosky
LeFlore
    Bob Plummer
Lincoln
    Mrs. Paul (Jan) Vassar
Logan
    Lorray Dyson
Love
    Charles Lain
Major
    Cam Steele
Marshall
    Marvin Wheeler
Mayes
    Jim Henry
McClain
    Ralph Wall
McCurtain
    Bob Passmore

McIntosh
    Dr. F. D. Parman
Murray
    Hayden Thompson
Muskogee
    John T. Hanna
    Bill Settle
Noble
    Walt Kehres
Nowata
    Owen Taylor
Okfuskee
    Mac Curry
Okmulgee
    Raymond Sewell
Osage
    Cecil Drummond
Ottawa
    Paul Sanders
Pawnee
    Pauline Sharpnack
Payne
    Dr. John Goodwin
Pittsburgh
    Mrs. Ethalee Hale
Ponotoc
    Jean Servais
Pottawatomie
    J. T. Weedman
Pushmataha
    Joe Stamper
Roger Mills
    G.F. Butch McGuire
Rogers
    Don Wilson

Seminole
    Ruby Lovelady
Sequoyah
    Gilbert Green
Stephens
    Ric Rodgers
Texas
    Mike Balenger
Tillman
    Howard McBee
Wagnor
    Dr. John Wright
Washington
    Merrill Schnitzer
Washita
    Roma McKee
Woods
    Gene Filson
Woodward
    Dr. Knight Braly